PRAISE FOR *THE FIRM OF THE FUTURE*

"This is an absolute must-read for any business (and that includes accounting practices) that wants to be in business in the future. Written in a highly readable style and laced with hundreds of practical 'how-to' notes and comments, this book is a prerequisite business manual for any practitioner of any professional service organization. This really is a stunning book. I've thoroughly enjoyed the philosophy as well as the practical how-to and why, and the book will further refine our approach to the business. Loved the style and class of the book."

—Peter Byers, Chartered Accountant, New Zealand

" 'Excited' is probably the most appropriate word for how I felt as I read the book. Excited at the learnings, excited at the possibilities that opened before me, excited at what it would be like to work in a practice with no timesheets, value pricing, passionate team members, and clients more than delighted with the "concierge service" provided by every team member. Ron Baker and Paul Dunn have clearly described what the firm of the future MUST look like. They clearly debunk all the old theories and practices of managing and operating an accounting firm and clearly explain the methods and FEELINGS that must exist in *The Firm of the Future*."

—Harry Rosenberg, BKR Rosenberg + Partners, Melbourne, Australia

"For many years now, I have utilized and professed within my firm my working theory, 'Our next new client has to have a thirst for our knowledge and the willingness and ability to pay for it.' *The Firm of the Future* embraces this theory and provides readers with the sound fundamentals to capitalize on their intellectual, social, and human capital."

—Robert A. Gaida, Vice Chairman, BDO Seidman, LLP

"Without doubt the single most important book ever written for professionals. It will force the entire profession to question, rethink, and rework everything it does. It's a book that will change your practice and your life—for the better, forever. Thanks to this book the professions will never be the same again."

—Steve Pipe, Founder and Chairman, The Added Value Network (U.K.)

"Like all brilliant business findings *The Firm of the Future* is simple, it is available to all, and it is practical. It requires only a willingness to accept, to change and to grow."

—Dr. Chris White, Doctor of Business Administration,
PhD, MBA, B.Bus, ALGA, CA, FCPA, CFP JP, Partner KPMG, Cairns

"For many years Ron Baker and Paul Dunn have been wonderful drivers for change in how professional service firms can become more successful. As a result of their collective wisdom, they have now co-authored a powerful and insightful book that should require many firms to reconsider their strategy. The true benefit of adhering to their New Practice Equation will not only be a more profitable firm, but one that will also have a distinct competitive advantage in the marketplace. An absolute required reading for business leaders and managers of professional firms."

—Robert J. Gallagher, CPA, President—R. J. Gallagher and Associates, Inc.

"Like everything that challenges conventional thinking, this book takes time to absorb. There were many parts that I just had to 'read over' so that I could filter through the brilliant combination of evidentiary and emotional interplay that Paul and Ron do so well, and reveal the truth for myself. The book reads like the early conversations I was privileged to be privy to, and it will be touted through the ages as a seminal work on the new evolution of the professions."

—Jason Johnson, CEO, Kipara Consulting

"*The Firm of the Future* imparts the accumulated wisdom of two key people who are helping to shape the profession, in a readable and memorable manner. And Paul and Ron have wisdom-a-plenty to impart. The profession has a vital role to play if our capitalist system is to continue its enormous record of success and prove to the doubters that it is universally the best system man has invented for improving the well-being of all people on earth, not just those in the wealthy developed nations. Paul and Ron chart the course by which the profession can regain its significance and, more importantly, help achieve the bigger goals, both for the benefit of its own members and the wider world . . . I heartily recommend *The Firm of the Future* as a 'must-have' guide for anyone in practice."

—David Hartley, Director, ElanElan Ltd.

"Between the covers of this book are more good ideas than you typically find in a dozen business books. Take notes. You'll want to remember these ideas for a long time."

—David Maister, author and consultant

"Paul and Ron have brought together their business philosophies under one cover of a book that should be the practice manual in every professional office. It truly is the answer of having the business do the things the professional used to do in a more effective and profitable manner. Who wouldn't want to work in the firm of the future described here?"

—Nicholas Newton CA, CMA, Creative Director, Frouin Group

"Ron Baker and Paul Dunn have put together the modern almanac of best business practices. Their firm of the future focuses on its intellectual, networking, cultural, and customer-focused capital to build wealth. They demonstrate over and over how making meaning, not just money, is the key to a leader's success. The book is an excellent read for those who want to learn the best-of-the-best business practices proven in the past decade."

—Sheila Kessler, Ph.D., President of Competitive Edge and author,
Measuring and Managing Customer Satisfaction

"*The Firm of the Future* brings a huge number of great ideas together in one place to provide a road map of what a professional service firm must do to position itself for the future. The book provides key success factors any firm can follow in creating a customer-driven firm."

—William Cobb, Cobb Consulting, Houston, Texas

"Finally! A book that catapults professional firms to a more sophisticated, more effective approach to management, leadership, and providing value. Any firm that follows the theory and practical advice advocated by Ron and Paul can retain happy and qualified team members, assure growing and loyal clients, reduce the stress of public practice, and reap the benefits of significant profitability."

—*Martha Sawyer, president of Hudson Sawyer,*
publisher of Bowman's Accounting Report

"It's refreshing to see a book that focuses the accounting practice on who we truly are—and more importantly, who we should be. We didn't learn this trade to have our services discounted and be held to a minute-by-minute gauge of value. Ron and Paul keep your focus on the ball rather than the scoreboard and clearly define our role as 'Intellectual Capitalists,' not bean counters!"

—*Mark J. Koziel, CPA, Director, Dopkins & Company, LLP*

"When I first received my copy of *The Firm of the Future* I was intimidated by its size and began reviewing the table of contents for the sections that seemed most interesting to me. But, as I am prone to do, I began at the first page. I soon found myself pouring through the book, chapter by chapter. Paul Dunn and Ron Baker have compiled a work that has incredible depth, wisdom, and insight. What I enjoyed most, however, was the conversational tone that makes this book hard to put down. I feel like I have had a personal conversation with wise counselors who understand my business."

—*Michael C. Knowles, Partner, Frank, Rimerman & Co., LLP,*
Menlo Park, California

"Sometimes, this book takes your breath away with its ambition. Not content with burying a fundamental paradigm of the professions, it offers a new one that challenges all who think about and care about, their profession to reevaluate what they do—and why they do it. Brimming with ideas, Baker and Dunn constantly challenge accepted wisdom, but thankfully provide cogent alternatives for your choice. Quotes, illustrations, and examples from all sorts of sources drive home points to ensure the book is a fantastic read and will have profound effects on your business—and the rest of your life. The future of the firm you inhabit will undoubtedly be shaped by *The Firm of the Future*. Ambition fulfilled."

—*Paul O'Byrne, Partner, O'Byrne and Kennedy,*
Chartered Accountants, United Kingdom

"Ron Baker and Paul Dunn are two of the deepest thinkers in the professional services business. This book is a thought-provoking look at our future. If you are leading a firm or planning to lead in the future, you must study this book carefully."

—*Troy Waugh, President, The Rainmaker Academy, Brentwood, TN*

"Ron Baker and Paul Dunn are truly guiding lights for our profession. Their insight into the future of professional service firms is visionary, especially during a time when the accounting profession is struggling with its future identity. Ron and Paul's passion for what the professions are able to accomplish is encouragement to us all."

—Daryl B. Golemb, CPA, San Diego, California

"Any accountant who is fighting with stagnant profitability in his firm needs to read this book. It will make you reassess why you are in business, how you conduct your business, and what you want from your business.

The reader is challenged to think about professional services within the framework of a new paradigm. The question you are left with after reading it is "Have I got the guts and the gumption to change the way I work at the moment?," because you are totally convinced by the simple logic of the paradigm.

The combination of Paul's laconic style with Ron's more academic and philosophical terminology makes this book compellingly readable. Peppered with quotes and examples to illustrate the theory, this is a business manual that reads like a novel.

If you find yourself short of time to think about how your business is working, this is the one book that will repay the time invested in reading it. It may just change your thought process to such an extent that time will never seem to be in such short supply again."

—Mark Spofforth, FCA; Senior Partner,
Spofforths Chartered Accountants and
Chairman Education and Training Board,
Institute of Chartered Accountants of
England and Wales

THE FIRM OF THE FUTURE

A GUIDE FOR ACCOUNTANTS, LAWYERS, AND OTHER PROFESSIONAL SERVICES

PAUL DUNN

RONALD J. BAKER

WILEY

JOHN WILEY & SONS, INC.

Copyright © 2003 by Paul Dunn and Ron Baker. All rights reserved.

Published by John Wiley & Sons, Inc., Hoboken, New Jersey
Published simultaneously in Canada

For general information on our other products and services, or technical support, please contact our Customer
Care Department within the United States at 800-762-2974, outside the United States at 317-572-3993 or
fax 317-572-4002.

Wiley also publishes its books in a variety of electronic formats. Some content that appears in print may not be
available in electronic books.

For more information about Wiley products, visit our web site at www.wiley.com.

Library of Congress Cataloging-in-Publication Data

Dunn, Paul.
   The firm of the future : a guide for accountants, lawyers, and other
professional services / Paul Dunn, Ron Baker.
      p. cm.
Includes index.
   ISBN 0-471-26424-5 (alk. paper)
  1. Business—Handbooks, manuals, etc.   2. Professional
employees—Handbooks, manuals, etc.   3. Human capital—Handbooks,
manuals, etc.   4. Customer relations—Handbook, manuals, etc.   I.
Baker, Ron.   II. Title.
   HF1010 .D86 2003
     658—dc21

                                                     2002153131

Printed in the United States of America

10 9 8 7

PAUL To Chelsea, Jamie, Jacob, Tyliesha, Jade, Ben, Arki, and Milla. I enjoy watching you grow so much.

RON To Angelina Maria Zimmerman, rest in peace. Not a day goes by in which you are not in my memories.

You have set sail on another ocean
without star or compass
going where the argument leads
shattering the certainties of centuries.
                    —Janet Kalven, "Respectable Outlaw"

CONTENTS

FOREWORD

You, like me, may not agree with every idea you read about in this book.

You might consider the previous statement to be a curious way to start a Foreword. But for me, that's what makes this book such an important work. I have always believed it is a waste of time reading any book that confirms what you think you already know. The purpose of a book such as this is not to confirm but to challenge. This unique work does that and more.

The accounting and legal professions are at a watershed. The collapse of Enron, WorldCom, and more recently Adelphia Communications, means that, for accountants at least, their reputation is tarnished and their future is uncertain. The challenges the professions now face are the inevitable consequence of a malaise that emerges from complacency and a failure to respond to the forces of change that are inexorably impacting the environment in which they operate. To put that another way, the paradigm that has served the professions well for the past 100+ years is now largely irrelevant.

This book challenges that paradigm in very significant ways. That alone makes it a timely addition to the literature and a MUST-READ for any professional who has any interest at all in the future of his or her firm and the profession.

For more than 30 years now I've been working in and studying the professions and how they operate. In 1992, I took that study to new levels when Paul Dunn and I started working with the accounting profession. Back then we had no idea where that journey would take us. We started Results Accountants' Systems with the idea of helping the profession move from a compliance focus to a focus on adding value in other ways (e.g., business consulting). This was a time when many members of the profession were starting to question the significance of their contribution and, more importantly, the level of personal satisfaction they were getting from their work.

For the vast majority of people who elected to participate in the Accountants' Boot Camp, the song we sang was music to their ears. What Paul and I talked about made sense and was what they wanted to hear. Many of them went back to their firms and did extraordinary things. The stories of some of these amazing people are recounted in this book. However, we quickly realized that we were in the business of effecting change, and this required a lot more than simply conveying a coherent and compelling argument for doing something different and providing tools and resources to help them do that. Most importantly, it called for a change in mindset and in particular one's fundamental reason for being in business as a practicing accountant. *The Firm of the Future* addresses these critical issues.

Ron Baker's first book, *Professional's Guide to Value Pricing* (first published in 1998), challenged, and profoundly changed, the way I and many other people view the operation of, and critical issues in, professional service (or what he might call knowledge) firms. Many people tell me that book changed their life. I can guarantee the book you are about to read has the potential to do the same. Ron's ability to express complex ideas in a simple, compelling, and entertaining way is a rare talent. I, for one, love his writing style if not all of his conclusions.

This book is a logical extension of his previous work and has benefited greatly from Paul Dunn's insights and the experience he has gained from working with thousands of accounting firms around the world. In the ten years that I had the pleasure of working with Paul I was constantly amazed at his ability to zero in on the essence of an issue. That ability shows through in this book. In our partnership I was the guy who would say, "Why?," and Paul was the guy who would say, "Why not?" At the end of the day it is that willingness to challenge the status quo that leads to better things most times and to a more interesting life all the time. I have learned many things from Paul, but the most important lesson was never to confuse "what is" with "what could be."

When I first read the manuscript for this book and reflected on what I had read it was "Why not?" that occupied my mind. If you do the same (and I think you will) then Baker and Dunn will have achieved their objective, which is to encourage you to change the way you think about your firm and your profession. If enough people do the same thing there is an exciting future for the professions. This book helps you prepare for your part in it.

Ric Payne
Chairman and CEO
Principa

PREFACE

I like the dreams of the future better than the history of the past.

—Thomas Jefferson

PAUL I'd like a plaque on my grave that says, "He made a difference to the profession."

That was my response in 1992 to a friend who wondered out loud, "So why are you doing all of this?" "All of this" was working 18-hour-plus days to establish Results Accountants' Systems (RAS). RAS marked the first time that someone outside the accounting profession (me) had staked everything he had on building a company and a process (the Accountants' Boot Camp) that would forever change the profession.

People said it could not be done. People said that accountants would not travel to one central place in Australia and spend (at that time) $4,000 (Australian) and four days learning how to deal quite differently with their clients. "Accountants," they said, "are strange creatures. They have strange value systems. They'll be sitting there all day counting up the hours they're in the Accountants' Boot Camp "classroom" and multiplying it by their hourly rate and calculating how much money they're losing. Not only that, there's no way you'll keep them interested from 8:30 in the morning until 10:30 at night."

Well, those people were wrong. At the first Accountants' Boot Camp, 170 people crammed into the room. And they loved it!

We told them to halt immediately the concentration on compliance and really get out and *do* things with their clients. We told them not to position themselves as historians but to establish a position of helping their selected clients *create* history. And they invested in specially created systems to help them do just that.

The basis for the firm of the future had been well and truly laid.

From there, the RAS and Accountants' Boot Camp phenomenon (for that is surely what it was) spread rapidly—first to North America, with the help of John Dunleavy and the California CPA Education Foundation, and then to the United Kingdom, through the Institute of Chartered Accountants of England and Wales (ICAEW). Later on it would spread even further, to Germany, Austria, and Hong Kong.

By the end of 1999, RAS had a staggering 3,500 firms onboard just in Australia, New Zealand, North America, and England, and had most of those firms connected in an international network called the Results Accountants' Network.

The 18-hour-plus days may not have been lengthening but they were certainly getting more complicated. From 4 people in one small room in 1992, we were now 75 people spread across multiple time zones. From running the business on my own, I'd taken on a partner. And my life was airplane after airplane, hotel room after hotel room, seminar after seminar. Yes, I was contributing—I'd probably get that plaque on the gravestone. The problem was I'd be in the grave long before I wanted to be!

So on April 20, 2000, I sold my interest in RAS and moved to France. Naturally, I was severely tied up by legal restraints that prevented me writing to or otherwise dealing with accounting firms. Yet the passion was still there. This book with Ron Baker reflects part of that passion.

But let's just go back a little in time. All of us have cathartic moments in our lives, moments that we look back upon later and recognize that they were a step-function, a break with how we'd thought or acted before that moment had occurred. One such moment had occurred in April 1996, though I didn't know it at the time. I'd been presenting a seminar in San Francisco for the California CPA Education Foundation. At the end, an affable man came up and told me how wonderful he thought the program had been. "Right now I'm presenting programs for the Education Foundation and it's clear to me that we're on the same wavelength. I hope we can find a way to work together," he said.

I thanked him profusely and said something about having to catch another plane. Ron Baker shook my hand again and left.

Two-and-half years later in London, in 1998, I received an e-mail from a client in the United States. "I've just read the most fantastic book on the profession. Drop everything and go get a copy."

The e-mail was from what you might call a respected source so I did as instructed: I bought the book on Amazon. Upon learning it would take a week to arrive, I remember thinking, "for $99 plus freight, this better be a darn good book."

Not only was it darn good, it was (and still is) a book that is an absolute landmark. I could not put it down; and I highlighted more stuff in yellow in this book than in any other book I'd read. I e-mailed the author to tell him how impressed I was and that I would love to do a taped phone interview with him from London in a few days.

Three days later, Ron Baker and I were on the phone together discussing his book. The *Professional's Guide to Value Pricing* is, I said, "by far the best book I've ever read on the professions. When the history of the profession comes to be written, people will look back and say that this book forever changed the way accounting is done."

And then Ron reminded me of our meeting two and a half years earlier in San Francisco.

Since that phone interview in 1998, Ron and I have become the firmest of friends. We've spent days together on stage at seminars. We've written many thousands of words to each other in e-mails. One such e-mail came in from Ron on April 21, 2000: "We absolutely must do a book together; we have so much to say," he wrote.

So began a long and synergistic process.

Often synergy is defined as "one plus one equals 3," a process whereby two people work together but get much more done. Yet Stephen Covey in his book, *The 7 Habits of Highly Effective People,* points out a very important thing about synergy. He explains how when you get two people *who are alike* coming together, you do not get synergy; you often get one plus one equals one. "True synergy occurs," says Covey, "when two or more *different* people get together."

Ron and I are different. Ron has a real analytical streak in him (thank God!), whereas I tend to function more from a "gut" instinct (women often rather kindly say I have a feminine sense of intuition). Being different means that Ron and I can dispute points. It means we can argue. But most of all it means we can blend our unique experiences into a new whole.

For example, we argued about the title of this book but never about the direction. And, sometimes, both of us had difficulty *seeing* the layout of the book, though we both knew we wanted to indicate our individual voices so the reader would always know which one of us was talking.

Then in March 2002, Ron's analytical streak came to the forefront. He made a significant modification to an equation originally developed by Ric Payne at Results Accountants' Systems. It's an equation that we'd been working with for a long time. We called it the *Practice Equation* since it defined the relationship between revenue in a professional firm and several key variables. Soon you'll read about the modification that Ron suggested. For now, suffice it to say that my "gut" got it immediately. It was a modification that led us to open our minds even more and to more effectively solidify what we were trying to say.

Let me get back to our title for a moment: I'd always worried about a title that implied to some that we could predict the future, especially since the firm of the future is here right now, in any event. It's just that for you, our reader, some of the things we suggest you need to do may not yet be things that you've embraced wholeheartedly.

Moreover, the firm of the future is not something that begins at some future point in time. It's something that, for me at least, began in 1992. The firm of the future is not a Presto!-once-in-a-lifetime event; it's something that you know first emotionally is right. It simply *feels* right. Then you'll use some logic to justify how you feel. Next you'll implement systems to make it a reality for you. It's a process not an event, like a living organism. Most firms, as we now know them, will either evolve and adapt or they will die.

And that's where the future of the firm comes in. Be under no illusions, Ron and I cannot predict the future of the firm—particularly the future of your firm. After all, your future is mostly influenced by you, the way you think, the way you act and, yes, even the way you dress. Not only that, some external events can influence it too: the most obvious one is the Enron scandal and the effective demise of a major accounting firm (Arthur Andersen) in early 2002. Before Enron, few people thought there was even the slightest chance of firms (particularly big ones) going under. What the Enron scandal does is illustrate that there may not actually be a future for some professional firms.

But there are other reasons why there may not be a future for some firms too. Consider this simple phrase delivered to me forcibly by a fellow Australian: "The profession is stuffed," he said. "Stuffed" needs an explanation like many words that Australians use. Perhaps the polite way of translating it is to say it means "broken" or "does not work any more."

Well, in one sense my colleague was wrong—the profession clearly is not broken and it clearly does still work. But in another sense my colleague was right on—it's hobbling along and it does not work anywhere well enough. It is its own worst enemy.

If that sounds extreme, go up to anyone and ask if he or she were able to change his or her profession for the most exciting, stimulating, challenging, and rewarding profession on the planet, which profession would he or she choose? That person could give you a variety of answers, of course. But we're certain there's one you would not hear. That person would not say "accounting" with a pump of his or her fist.

Little wonder is it? Here is this wonderful profession—the only one that's been given a built-in mandate to work with businesses—absolutely blowing it. Want some evidence for that? Regrettably very, very few accountants I know get up in the morning looking forward to their day. Most get religion twice a week: first on Friday ("Thank God it's Friday") and second on Monday ("Oh Lord it's Monday and I've got to do all this again this week").

It doesn't have to be that way.

Our work on the new Practice Equation shows where the old equation led to the problems we see in the profession today. Put that another way: adopt the new Practice Equation you'll read about here and it's certain your firm and the way you practice accounting will be exciting, stimulating, challenging, and rewarding.

Our contention is simple and upbeat. Follow the thought patterns and ideas here. Embrace them, make them yours. Do that and your firm will automatically become a firm of the future. More important, perhaps, you'll have a stunningly bright future to look forward to as well.

RON Someone once asked the physicist Albert Michelson why he worked so hard on measuring the speed of light; he replied he did it because it was such great fun.

Ever since I made it publicly known that my one mission in life was to bury the billable hour in the accounting and legal professions, I have frequently been asked how I came to seek this rather strange quest. The short answer is because, like Michelson, it is great fun to challenge the conventional wisdom of your colleagues and try to persuade them there is a better way.

The long answer is that I am passionate about wanting to improve the quality of life in the professions. For me, the book you are now holding began in 1989, when I started to seriously discover the philosophies of Total Quality Service and apply them to my accounting practice. Out of that research grew my experimenting with fixed-price agreements and then change orders. Then I began the privilege of teaching my colleagues.

I have always wanted to teach and to write a book. I was given my first opportunity to do the former in 1995 by the California CPA Education Foundation, teaching a course entitled, "How to Build a Successful Practice with Total Quality Service." I had one very short section in the course about the shift from hourly billing to value pricing, which generated enormous discussion and debate. Being more of an economist than a CPA, I began to study what the economics profession had to say about price and value; and, to say the least, it is overwhelming. There is truly no better profession to look to for these topics, since economists have been studying them for centuries.

I read the best minds in economics, from Milton Friedman and his son David to Steven Landsburg, Mark Skousen, Thomas Sowell, and many, many others. But it was from the Austrian school of economists that I learned the labor theory of value and—

more important—what replaced it. Richard Burton described in *The Anatomy of Melancholy* (second edition, 1624): "Pigmies placed on the shoulders of giants see more than the giants themselves." This is exactly how I felt. With further study, I learned price discrimination and how ubiquitous it is in the marketplace. I also learned price psychology and the importance it has in setting a price, especially for professionals. From this research I developed my second course for the California CPA Education Foundation: "The Shift from Hourly Billing to Value Pricing." This course caused quite a controversy wherever I taught it, because it strongly advocated that CPAs offer fixed-price agreements, change orders, a service guarantee, and fixed payment terms, all agreed to up front with their customers for every service they provide. Not only that, I was even advocating the elimination of timesheets, which back in 1996 was unheard of, even though I had eliminated them in my firm in 1991.

Along with teaching I began to write more, and as any knowledge worker knows, both are acts of discovering what you think. Mark Twain said at one point, "I don't write a book now unless it can write itself." That was my experience with my first book, *Professional's Guide to Value Pricing* (now in its fourth edition). The book, in many ways, did write itself since I had been teaching it for several years before actually gathering my thoughts in book form. The first edition was published in July 1998, and sold more copies than we expected in the first year, and every year thereafter.

I continued to teach and write, and I updated the book each year, adding knowledge I had learned from teaching my colleagues around the world. Paul describes our first meeting in 1996, and I certainly knew who he was by reputation, since I had talked to so many CPAs who had gone through the Accountants' Boot Camp process. It is hard to describe the passion Paul has for the profession—you have to *experience* it. I recall being in his 1996 San Francisco seminar thinking "this guy is *outside* the profession, and yet he is revolutionizing it and making it better."

When he contacted me in 1998 after reading my book, we began a dialogue that has continued ever since. But let me share with you some elements from that dialogue that Paul didn't. I did my first program with Paul in September 1999 in San Diego. By some cruel twist of fate, the organizer of the event scheduled my talk *after* Paul's. A mediocre speaker should *never* follow an excellent one, and while I rarely get nervous before talking, I did this time, with Paul sitting in the back of the room.

That night, Paul and I had dinner and talked for so long we closed the restaurant and bar. It is rare to meet someone who is truly passionate about what he or she does, and so committed to bettering his or her chosen profession. You cannot help but ask, "Why do you do this?" Paul supplies the answers with his actions—he truly enjoys it, and it shows.

C.G. Jung defines synchronicity as "a meaningful coincidence of two or more events, where something other than the probability of chance is involved." This describes the relationship Paul and I have. It certainly seems as if fate brought us together. From that first meeting in 1996, little did I know four years later I would be sitting at the top of a Ritz-Carlton hotel overlooking picturesque Sydney, Australia, having cocktails, and going over a PowerPoint presentation with Paul, which we would do together in 10 cities in Australia and New Zealand and countless others across the United States. From a professional perspective, it was the apogee of my new career as an author and public speaker, setting off shock waves that are still reverberating through my life.

When our tour was over, and Paul sold his interest in RAS, I knew we had to write a book together—we both have so much to say, and felt passionately the professions could be better than they are.

We experienced a wide range of emotions writing this book—from optimism and pessimism to incomprehensible and unknowable thoughts and plenty of cognitive dissonance in between—and no doubt you will do the same as you read it. We do not consider this a disadvantage or a sign of unclear expression on our part. On the contrary, it is the indisputable consequence of dealing with the most significant aspects of the professions—you simply must struggle with them if you are to seek the truth. We engage in this strife daily, and as I continue to educate around the world I am constantly taking one step closer to the truth. I know I will never arrive.

Most of all, what you are about to read is a shot across the bow of the present orthodoxies of the professions, because we have discovered most of what passes for conventional wisdom is more conventional than wisdom. Consider the 1989 edition of the *Statistical Abstract of the United States*, a Bureau of the Census publication, which draws from data provided by a wide range of government agencies including the Central Intelligence Agency. One of the published estimates was the size of the economies of the Federal Republic of Germany and the German Democratic Republic, or West Germany and East Germany as they were then known. Per capita output in 1985 in both countries was shown to be *equal*, with the Gross Domestic Product of East Germany slightly higher.

But as any Berlin taxi driver crossing through Checkpoint Charlie after the fall of the Wall could have told you, the economy of East Germany was manifestly inferior to that of West Germany, yet somehow—probably due to the *trained incapacity* of the experts—those in the know got it terribly wrong. Think of Paul and me as your taxi drivers, as we wind down the wonderful road that are the professions. We are not sure where we will end up, but we will make many pertinent observations along the way. We sincerely hope you enjoy the journey.

Paul Dunn
Provence, France

Ronald J. Baker
Petaluma, California

October 16, 2002

ACKNOWLEDGMENTS

PAUL Every major work you undertake is rarely, if ever, the result solely of your own efforts. This book is no exception.

In one sense, this book began as a sentence in an email. But in a much deeper sense it began in 1981. To every single customer since 1981 when the concepts started to form, thank you. Thank you for having the faith. And thank you for sharing with me all the ideas you've implemented so that I can share them with others.

I think particularly of people like Ken Bowen of Bowen Petroleum; Chris Downs of Clark Australia; the late Wally Hawryluk; and Geoff Smith of The Bavarian Restaurant.

In more recent years, the people who come to mind include Bruce Allen, Fiona Anson, Maria Berntson, Pat Brown, Peter Byers, Peter Cowley, Stephen Dawes, Ken Dewitt, John Dunleavy, David Hartley, Greg Hayes, Brad Jones, Charlie Jones, Jack Kreischer, Barry Melancon, Shirley Nakawatase, Steve Pipe, Col Purkis, Randy Reimer, Julian Roylance, Steve Stravolo, Katrina Street, Mark Sullivan, Chris Tolevsky, Geoff Vines, Tom Weddell, Peter Zwaggerman, and countless others who played significant parts in the learning environment for me.

Others played a huge part, too. Some (like Tom Peters, Stephen Covey) wrote books that inspired. Others (like Michael Gerber and Jay Abraham) inspired with books and much more. Then came Andrew Geddes and his work with the Financial Management Research Centre: thank you Andrew for the material, the fun, and the wine!

Between 1992 and 2000, I shared my journey with Ric Payne. Ric's thought processes and ability to translate them into software, into writing, and into systems is extraordinary. The fact that he can share that with his customers is a special gift.

Then to my old team at Results Accountants' Systems around the world, people who "did their thing" so well yet still found time to innovate and to develop systems, ideas, and concepts that take us into new and unchartered territory. I'm indebted particularly to people who have now moved on to do their own great things, among them Shannon Vincent, Jason Johnson, and Robert Nixon. Thank you team: "Together everyone really does achieve more."

And in the middle of all of that, along came Ron Baker. You'll read more about this extraordinary contributor as you read the book. Suffice it to say here that without his amazing talent and gifts, this book would still be just a sentence in an email. Ron knows how to use the English language better than most people I know so he'll understand that the words "thank you" are inadequate to describe his contribution here.

Then there's my new business family at Solutions Press, wonderfully led by Fletcher Potanin. Fletcher and I go back 12 years. And every year, he keeps surpassing his own extraordinarily high standards. And, of course, Paddi Lund, whom I've also known now for 12 years. When I say that Paddi is the world's most amazing dentist, believe me, because he is surely that. But he is also one of the most gifted geniuses of business because he can bring to the world the magical power of thinking about business in a new way—thinking first and foremost about being happiness-centered.

Finally, to Desley, who did more than anyone else to keep me on track, focused, and motivated (as well as fed and watered).

My good fortune has been to be a part of the learning and to be able to present it to others, to make their businesses more fun and valuable. That remains, above all, a special privilege and pleasure.

RON A book is purely the product of intellectual capital, and is represented in the tangible form we call structural capital. What the reader does not see is the human and social capital without which this book would not exist. I have leveraged the intellectual capital of some true giants, and though it would be impossible to thank them all, the prominent ones deserve special mention.

So many of my views of the way the world works have been influenced by economists that I feel I owe them a special debt of gratitude. Milton and Rose Friedman gave me my first introduction to serious economic ideas and I would like to thank them for making complex issues understandable to the masses. It is a very good thing the actuarial exams are so difficult and that Milton Friedman chose his next-best alternative and became an economist instead. Their son, David Friedman, an outstanding economist in his own right, taught me much through his textbooks and general economics books, not to mention through the lectures I have been privileged to attend. Like his mother and father, he provides incredible insight into human behavior.

Another economist who has taught me more than I could ever repay is Steven Landsburg, through his text and general books and his "Everyday Economics" articles in *Slate* (www.slate.com). Landsburg is an incredibly brilliant and innovative thinker; and in unison with a gifted and engaging writing style, he makes one *want* to study the dismal science in greater depth. I had the great good fortune of meeting him at the October 2000, Cato University in Montreal, Canada, where he added even more to my intellectual capital.

I owe a truly special debt to George Gilder, who gave me my first serious introduction to supply-side economics and the primary importance of the role of the entrepreneur in creating growth, dynamism, and wealth in an economy. It is nearly impossible to classify Gilder since he writes and speaks on a wide range of topics, from sociology and poverty, to feminism and the Telecosm. He is truly an eclectic thinker, and is one of the best writers of his time. He taught me the moral case for capitalism, and I believe he will go down as the Adam Smith of the twentieth and twenty-first centuries.

Michael Novak, who presently holds the Jewett Chair in Religion and Public Policy at the American Enterprise Institute, along with Gilder, makes the moral case for business and capitalism from a religious perspective; he introduced me to the encyclicals of the Pope, which also affirms the morality of capitalism while at the same time recognizing any system devised by Man is destined to fall short of the Kingdom of God.

Many other economists have shaped my thinking on human behavior and, especially, the theories of value and price: Charles Adams, Martin Anderson, Bruce Bartlett, Robert Bartley, Warren Brookes, Ronald H. Coase, Hernando DeSoto, Nicholas Eberstadt, Robert H. Frank, Friedrich A. Hayek, Arthur Laffer, Deirdre N. McCloskey, Ludwig von Mises, Charles Murray, James Payne, Virginia Postrel, Paul Craig Roberts, Julian Simon, Mark Skousen, Thomas Sowell, George J. Stigler, Jude Wanniski, Jonathan B. Wight, Walter Williams, among innumerable others, all of whom have served as absent teachers through their works.

Peter Drucker is one of the only true management consultants who has consistently contributed real insight and wisdom to a profession constantly enamored with the latest fad of the month. In one way or another, everyone who writes on business issues stands on his shoulders. Not only has he originated most of the management theories other so-called gurus now take credit for—and coined terms such as *knowledge worker, privatization*, and others—he did it long before most of them were born. His legacy is large, and will endure for the ages. I believe he deserves a Nobel prize.

Thomas T. Nagle and Reed Holden are two heroic individuals. As the authors of *The Strategy and Tactics of Pricing: A Guide to Profitable Decision Making* (now in its third edition), they have put pricing on the map—and the organizational charts—in companies around the world. I owe them full credit for the arrow diagram we use in Chapter 9 that proves price determines costs, not the other way around. Also I owe them for the five Cs of value, and many other lessons I have learned from their books, public speeches, and their course at the University of Chicago Graduate School of Business, "Pricing: Strategy and Tactics," which I attended in April 2001. They both are my mentors and I only hope to have a fraction of the impact on the accounting and legal professions they have had on companies of all sizes in all industries around the world.

Thank you Eric Mitchell, president of the Professional Pricing Society, for giving me the opportunities to speak at your excellent conferences, and for creating a forum where people responsible for pricing in their organizations can exchange intellectual capital.

Thanks to Richard Reed, editor and author of three seminal works on alternatives to hourly billing, published by the American Bar Association, between 1989 and 1996. Though I have never met Mr. Reed—whom I understand is now retired—he has blazed the trail in the legal profession I am now on in the accounting profession.

Special mention must be made of the American Bar Association, and its president, Robert E. Hirshon, who formed the ABA Commission on Billable Hours, which issued its report in August 2002. This is an excellent start in reevaluating the existing pricing orthodoxies that are inflicting so much damage on the professions.

The Talmud says, "I have learned much from my teachers, more from my colleagues, and most of all from my students." It is my good fortune that my students are also my colleagues; and indeed they have taught me more than I could ever requite. The word "colleague" comes from the Latin *colligare*, "to bind together," and that certainly describes the relationships I have developed throughout the years with many professionals. Thank you to the tens of thousands of professionals around the world who have listened to me rant and rave about the deleterious effects of hourly billing, but more importantly, for implementing the ideas I have proffered. I have learned from your failures and even more from your successes, and there is no greater pleasure than watching your colleagues do better for their customers—and, in turn, themselves—than even they thought was possible.

Special thanks to Patti Carpenter—and the entire gang at Bradley, Allen & Associates, LLP—Diane Green, Leslie Chapman, and Gus Stearns, for allowing me to reprint your correspondence in these pages. Your continued successes inspire me. Also, to Mark Koziel, a young talent who I know is destined to make an enormous contribution to the CPA profession, for providing the information on Dopkins University we include in Chapter 7 on social capital. I know more firms will follow your innovative idea, thereby leveraging their own social capital to improve the lives of their customers and businesspeople in their communities.

Thank you William Cobb, consultant to the professions, for innovating the beloved Value Curve, and providing us permission to use it in our work. It is truly the best graphical representation of the professions, and is imbued with many lessons.

August Aquila, one of the foremost consultants to the profession, has taught me much over the years. Thank you, August, for continuing your thought-provoking newsletter, "Partner-to-Partner," and giving me a forum to present my ideas.

Allan Boress was the first to publish my articles in his newsletter and introduced me to the publishing world, not to mention giving me a much-needed push to overcome my fears, stand up, and speak out. Thank you, Allan.

Troy Waugh is another excellent consultant to the CPA profession I deeply admire and respect; he has impacted my thinking on the profession.

An enormous debt is owed to John Dunleavy, Kurtis Docken, and the rest of the team at the California CPA Education Foundation. They continuously take risks by letting me teach new and unproven courses in my home state, and have gone above and beyond expectations in support of my work. They gave me my first chance at teaching to colleagues in 1995, and I will continue my pledge to provide them with the best educational offerings I am capable of.

Sheila Kessler continues to provide me with wisdom, insight, inspiration, and knowledge I could not live long enough to learn on my own. I have said it many times and in many places, Sheila is a remarkable woman, whom I deeply respect and admire for her accomplishments. I am proud to call her a colleague.

To Daryl Golemb, Michael McCulloch, Arthur Jacob, Shirley Nakawatase, Ron Crone, Ed Miller, and Larry Lucas, colleagues who engage me professionally and whose friendship I am grateful for.

Newspaper columnist Calvin Trillin remarked, "I believe in open immigration. It improves the diversity of the restaurants. I'd let anybody in except the English." I would gladly make an exception in the case of my British trusted advisor, chartered accountant, quasi-Marxist, and—perhaps most noteworthy—creator and Webmaster of www.ronbakersucks.com, Paul O'Byrne. Your Monty Python sense of humor and wit is outrageous; your guidance and advice invaluable, and your friendship priceless—even *subjectively*. Thanks for who you are and all you do.

Ric Payne, founder and chairman of Principa, is my mentor; he has taught me an inordinate amount of knowledge in our relatively short time of acquaintance, and was kind enough to write the Foreword to this work. Ric may think some of the theories in this book are not just nonsense, but nonsense on stilts—especially the advocacy of no timesheets; and though we may be engaged in a friendly debate over this topic for the rest of our natural lives, there is one salutary effect. If it were not for this disagreement, I would agree with Ric on everything else relating to the profession, therefore rendering one of us superfluous—me, I'm afraid. Thanks, Thugger. I cherish our friendship.

To my friend, colleague, partner, and cofounder of VeraSage Institute, for over 15 years, Justin Barnett. He has lived through the early stages of many of these ideas and has always kept an open mind, not to mention a willingness to experiment. His ability to take the theories and apply them to the software VeraSage Institute has developed will have a beneficial effect on the diffusion of our ideas.

Dan Morris, the other cofounder of VeraSage Institute, and fellow Cognitor, has been a constant source of inspiration. Conversing with Dan is like stepping into a batting cage of ideas, and the result is frequently an even better idea—usually from him. I admire his passion, skill, talent, and commitment to bettering our chosen profession. Most of all, I am grateful for our friendship.

To our editors at John Wiley & Sons, Inc., John DeRemigis, Judy Howarth, and Kerstin Nasdeo, thank you for taking the ultimate risk by publishing this book, improving every page with your adept editing, and for being patient with the late manuscript by understanding the first thing every writer needs is another source of income. Writer Alice Hoffman says, "It is the deepest desire of every writer, the one we never admit or even dare to speak of: to write a book we can leave as a legacy. If you do it right, and if they publish it, you may actually leave something behind that can last forever." After all, *Littera scripta manet*: It is the page that endures.

What can I say to Paul Dunn that I have not already tried to express in these pages? He means so much more to me than merely a coauthor; he has been a mentor, teacher, advisor, counselor, forensics coach, inspiration, motivator, sounding board for impulsive ideas, editor, and most importantly, a dear friend. I am proud to have developed this legacy with him, and if I know Paul, the next book will be even better. Thank you, my friend.

Another forensics coach, indefatigable supporter, and companion—who also happens to be my brother—Ken Baker, deserves special thanks. He always says he cannot possibly live through another one of my books, but he came through again. I'm sure he is tempted to say what Groucho Marx did upon publication, "From the moment I picked this book up until the moment I put it down, I could not stop laughing. Some day I hope to read it."

To my mother, Florence Baker, who taught me patience, understanding and tolerance; and my father, Sam Baker, who taught me the spirit of service from the inside of a barber's chair, and was my first introduction to an entrepreneur, though I didn't know it at the time.

To my late grandmother, Angelina Maria Zimmerman, to whom this book is dedicated. Thank you, Granny, for always believing in me, being the center of the family, and always showing your pride in your grandson. I only hope I continue to earn it.

ABOUT THE AUTHORS

Paul Dunn is an engineer by training, but he soon discovered people were more interesting than things. After graduating in London, England, he began his career in Australia at Hewlett Packard, where he was one of just 10 people in the Australian start-up of the company.

In 1974, Paul did early creative work on some innovative software that became the basis for one of Australia's early technological successes—Hartley Computer. Hartley sold its systems only to accountants in public practice. Until 1980, Paul was the marketing genius behind the company, growing globally to a $23-million enterprise.

In late 1980, Paul decided that his real love was marketing and speaking, so he formed The Results Corporation (TRC). Paul was in high demand for his marketing and speaking skills, working with major corporations like QANTAS, ICI, Sun, and others, and presenting more than 200 conferences each year. But the real soul of TRC was the Small and Medium Enterprises (SME) marketplace. By 1992, his company had grown to a $20-million enterprise, serving 23,000 businesses worldwide.

Paul developed innovative video-based training programs—his program Towards Awesome Service is still the largest ever video-based program sold in Australia. All told, Paul's audio and video programs are now in use by more than 26,000 businesses around the world.

In 1992, Paul left TRC to form Results Accountants' Systems (RAS) to focus again on accountants in public practice. RAS grew quickly under Paul's guidance and vision, with what is now known as the Accountants' Boot Camp process. By 1994, the company had offices in Australia, Europe, and, most significantly, the United States. By 1999, RAS was serving more than 3,000 practices and their clients worldwide. Among many other innovations, Paul developed the Results Accountants' Network, then the largest network of leading-edge accountants in the world.

In 2000, Paul sold his interest in RAS to (a) smell some roses at his home in France, (b) continue writing books, and (c) take a continued interest in leading-edge marketing and service companies and associations.

To contact Paul Dunn:

Mas Camphoux
Chemin des Ballardes
Lagnes, 84800, France
Phone +(33) 490 385516
Fax : +(1) 630 2147561
E-mail: pauldunn1@mindspring.com

Ronald J. Baker started his accounting career in 1984 with KPMG (Peat Marwick's) Private Business Advisory Services in San Francisco. He is the founder of VeraSage Institute, a think tank dedicated to teaching value pricing to professionals around the world.

As a frequent speaker at CPA events and conferences, and a consultant to CPA firms on implementing Total Quality Service and Value Pricing, his work takes him around the world. He has been an instructor with the California CPA Education Foundation since 1995 and has authored seven courses for them: "How to Build a Successful Practice with Total Quality Service," "The Shift from Hourly Billing to Value Pricing," "Value Pricing Graduate Seminar," "You Are What You Charge For: Success in Today's Emerging Experience Economy" (with Daniel Morris), "Alternatives to the Federal Income Tax," "Trashing the Timesheet: A Declaration of Independence" (with Daniel D. Morris and Justin H. Barnett of VeraSage Institute)," and "Everyday Economics."

Ron is the author of the best-selling marketing book ever written specifically for the CPA profession, *Professional's Guide to Value Pricing*, *Fourth Edition* (2003), published by Aspen Law & Business, a division of Aspen Publishers, Inc. The book has been ranked number 1 on amazon.com in Australia and New Zealand. He is also the author of *Burying the Billable Hour* (2001), and *Trashing the Timesheet* (2003), published by The Association of Chartered Certified Accountants.

Ron has shared his value pricing vision to more than 50,000 professionals around the world. He was appointed for two consecutive years to the AICPA's Group of One Hundred, a think tank of leaders to address the future issues confronting the profession, and named on *Accounting Today*'s 2001 and 2002 Top 100 Most Influential People in the profession.

Ron graduated in 1984 from San Francisco State University with a Bachelor of Science in accounting and a minor in economics. He is a graduate of Disney University and the University of Chicago Graduate School of Business course, "Pricing: Strategy and Tactics." He is a member of the Professional Pricing Society and presently resides in Petaluma, California.

For more information on the California CPA Education Foundation Courses offered by VeraSage Institute, contact the California CPA Education Foundation at: (800) 922-5272 or visit its Web site at www.educationfoundation.org.

For more information on the dates and locations of the events, conferences and Continuing Professional Education (CPE) seminars presented by VeraSage Institute, please visit our Web site at www.verasage.com.

To contact Ron Baker:

VeraSage Institute
Toll Free: (800) 757-0222
Fax: (707) 781-3069
Home Office: (707) 769-0965
E-mail: Ron@verasage.com
Web site: www.verasage.com

How to Read This Book

RON As Paul mentioned in the Preface, we are different. Yogi Berra said about George Steinbrenner, "We agree different," and that is an apt description of Paul and me. Because of this, we have decided to write in our own voices, and identify for the reader who is speaking at all times. This is unusual for a business book, but not without precedent.

One of Paul's favorite books, *The Art of Possibility,* written by Benjamin Zander and his wife, Rosamund Stone Zander, identifies each voice throughout the book. For me, the inspiration came from Milton and Rose Friedman's autobiography, *Two Lucky People*, which I read in 1998, and thought the voice distinction was an enhancement to the book. We hope you agree with our approach.

We need to mention one other point, about the words we use in this book. Words have meaning, and we use them to label and help us comprehend the world around us. Yet many of them are distorting lenses that can make us misperceive and misjudge what we are observing. The great nineteenth-century English jurist Sir James Fitzjames Stephen, put it aptly, "Men have an all but incurable propensity to prejudge all the great questions which interest them by stamping their prejudices upon their language."

Throughout this book, for example, we use the words *customer, price, invoice*, and *team member* in lieu of, respectively, *client, fee, bill*, and *staff* (except when we are quoting from other sources). We do this because we believe these words convey better images of what they are attempting to describe. The welfare state has *clients*, while businesses have *customers*. A *fee* is negatively associated with a tax or some other charge, while *price* is a benign term most customers easily comprehend, conjuring up no positive or negative images.

It is not our objective to change your vocabulary, we simply are far more comfortable using words we believe elicit superior images in others' minds.

1

INTRODUCTION

Everything has been thought before, but the problem is to think of it again.

—Johann Wolfgang von Goethe

In the comedy *Raising Arizona,* Holly Hunter and Nicholas Cage play a couple that cannot conceive a child and so decide to steal one. They read in the newspaper of a woman who has just given birth to quintuplets, so they drive to their house, where Cage's character climbs a ladder to the second-story bedroom window and takes one of the babies. On his way out, he spots a copy of Dr. Spock's best-selling book on child-rearing and places it in his back pocket. As he hands over the baby to his wife, Holly Hunter, who is waiting behind the wheel of the getaway car, he remembers he has the book and gives that to her, too, saying, "Oh, yeah, here are the instructions."

RON We can no more provide you with the "instructions" for the firm of the future than Dr. Spock could provide one for the raising of a child. Both are perilous—and wondrous—adventures, fraught with risk and uncertainty, and subject to the roll of the genetic dice. Instead, we have decided to provide a *qualitative*, as opposed to a *quantitative*, book. The former deals with *what* to do and *what* to think about, while the latter covers *how* to do. We want to have you think *with* us, not *like* us, regarding the future of your profession. We have no solutions; rather, we offer values that hopefully will lead to solutions. We will attempt to mark the difference between what is and what could be.

The thirteenth-century Spanish king, Alfonso X, said with no apparent modesty: "Had I been present at the creation, I would have given some useful hints for the better ordering of the universe." Likewise, Paul and I were not present at the creation of the professions. I entered the CPA profession in 1984 as a young, eager, and determined "staff" person in the ranks of one of the then Big Eight, and believed my destiny was to become partner. I was taught from day one what approximately two generations of accountants had been taught before me: "You sell your time." I had no reason to believe this conventional wisdom was not true. After all, I now had an hourly rate, which defined my status and rank in the pecking order of the firm. I completed a time-sheet every two weeks, in increments of a quarter-hour, or my paycheck was dutifully withheld. It seemed quite logical and rational that all I had to provide the customers of the firm was my time.

When I launched my own firm, I was the epitome of what statisticians call *path-dependent*—that is, the older I became, the greater the chance that what I would be in the future would be influenced by what I was in the past. It was not until I had been out on my own for a few years that I started to wrestle seriously against the conventional wisdom of my chosen profession.

As they say, the results of a life are uncalculable and unpredictable, as we make our journey toward the future. The years teach so much of what the days never knew. If I had known then what I know now, like Alfonso X, I certainly would have offered a better ordering of the professional service firm and a deeper understanding of the value that knowledge workers provide to their customers. This book is a result of the education of those intervening years.

In the 1960s, Princeton economist Fritz Machlup and management consultant Peter Drucker simultaneously and independently coined the terms *knowledge society* and *knowledge worker*, the latter in his book, *The Age of Discontinuity*. When I entered the profession, I never thought of myself as a knowledge worker—one who works with his head and not his hands; instead, I thought of myself as a *service worker*, a term coined around 1920. But this is far too simplistic a term to describe a knowledge worker's functions; and, today, approximately 40 percent of the workforce labor in knowledge industries. It is also the fastest-growing segment of the labor force. In the past, corporate executives and leaders were chosen because they were doers, not thinkers. They did not spend their time working on theories, but rather on the practical challenges of, say, building a Pepsi plant in Leningrad or an auto factory in Brazil. Ideology and abstract theories were reserved for political elections, not the day-to-day operations of a business.

Today, lawyers and accountants are among the ultimate knowledge workers, creating wealth for the customers they are privileged to serve from the ideas and *intellectual capital* they generate. Yet, too many of us still believe we are service workers, not knowledge workers, and there is an enormous difference. We are operating under a theory of the firm that is increasingly irrelevant to the critical success factors that determine our—and our customer's—destiny. We are still mired in the notion that the way to create wealth in the firm is to leverage people and hours. This is somewhat understandable. After all, this thinking created success in the past, building the large firms of yesteryear and providing professionals from all sectors with a decent standard of living.

But all things human, given enough time, go badly. Nothing fails like success, and it always creates new realities and challenges. Knowledge work is a practice in search of an accurate theory, and what is wrong with the old practice is not theory per se, but *bad* theory. All theories are subject to falsification, and we will do our best to falsify the old theory of the firm once and for all. We then will attempt the more difficult task of proffering a new theory of the firm; and here we are on more perilous ground. Nevertheless, a new theory is needed, and we will offer ours in the spirit and hope that somewhere, sometime, someone will falsify it and offer and even better one. This is how knowledge progresses, in a never-ending iterative process best characterized as *knowledge creep.*

This is a rather interesting phenomenon, because it implies that most new theories—and especially management fads of the month—have to be wrong or irrelevant, or else knowledge would proceed at lightening speed and advance by Newtonian or Einsteinian leaps every day. It doesn't. This makes it difficult for editors and publishers of business journals and books, since if they are honest with themselves they have to admit most of what they publish is trivial, or just plain incorrect. The French have a wonderful saying for this: *Tout nouveau, tout beau*—which freely translated means, "Fools see beauty only in new things." We suffer the same risks—and perhaps the same fate—with this book. The difference is, we understand the phenomenon and do not assume we will have the last word on the firm of the future. We have not set out to reinvent the wheel. On the contrary, we are attempting to repair the old one.

That being said, we still find it necessary to challenge the conventional wisdom and dominant theory among the professions. *The Firm of the Future* is not about predicting the future; it is about helping to shape and create the future. No one can predict the future, and only a fool tries. But we can influence the future based upon the decisions and choices we make. The world is not controlled by the ever-swinging pendulum of history or some outside fate. We create the future by the actions we take today. The Berlin Wall did not fall because of inclement weather—it was *pushed.* Ultimately, all history is biography.

Over its 30-year history, it was not until the year 2000 that pricing became a Top Five Management of Accounting (MAP) issue, largely as a result of my first book, *Professional's Guide to Value Pricing.* This book was nothing more than applying the knowledge creep in the area of value and pricing—predominantly from economists of centuries past—to accountants and lawyers. Individuals can indeed shape the future.

Trying to shape the future is a risky business, fraught with peril, derision, ridicule, violent opposition, and periods of profound pessimism. As the great auto inventor Charles Kettering said, "If I want to stop a research program, I can always do it by getting a few experts to sit in on the subject, because they know right away that it was a fool thing to try in the first place." Still, it is even more risky *not* to attempt to alter the future, and instead merely rely on what was successful in the past. Not only that, but in some respects, "The future has already happened, it's just unequally distributed," as William Gibson remarked (quoted in Hamel, 2000: 128).

Nowhere is this truer than in knowledge industries, where the critical success factors are understood and leveraged appropriately. From Microsoft and Oracle to McKinsey and Accenture, more and more companies are realizing that it is knowledge and ideas that create wealth, not tangible things like real estate and oil. We live in a world dominated by *mind*, not *matter*. Most of these knowledge companies now have a chief knowledge officer whose job is to make sure the company knows what it knows—that is, can access the deep reservoirs of knowledge that exist within the firm in order to leverage it to create even more wealth for their customers. There is a wealth of intellectual capital waiting to be tapped into from these companies by the willing student.

Education is not simply a matter of someone pouring knowledge into another's head. The root of educate, *educere*, means to "draw out," not to stuff in, and the ultimate responsibility rests with the willing student, not the educator. While books may be absent educators, you, the reader, will have the last word. We have followed the Law of the Lesson: *The truth to be taught must be learned through truth already known*. By studying the best minds we could find in the area of intellectual capital and business philosophy, we hope to change the way you think about the future of your firm and profession.

THE BELOVED VALUE CURVE

One of our favorite theories of the firm was posited in the 1980s by William Cobb, a consultant to the legal and accounting professions. The Cobb Value Curve posits what we believe is the best graphical representation of the professions we have ever seen, it being rooted deeply in economic theory. Cobb was kind enough to let us reproduce what we have come to call, affectionately, the "beloved Value Curve" (see Exhibit 1.1).

EXHIBIT 1.1   The Cobb Value Curve

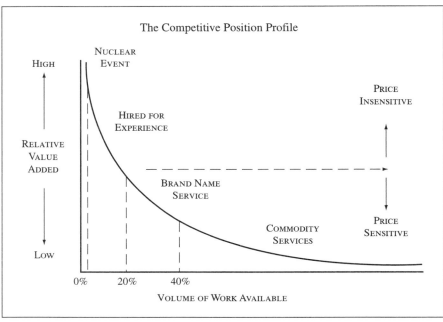

The curve shows the relative value added by the professional has an inverse relationship to the price sensitivity of the customer; and while we do not prefer the term *commodity* in any way—as we point out in Chapter 9—the lessons embedded in this curve are many. For now, it is important to understand your firm is all over this curve for any one given customer, at any one point in time. The major mistake professionals make is in treating all customers equally by pricing their services with one hourly rate method, no matter where they are on the curve. The old practice theory has no mechanism for capturing—with innovative pricing policies—varying levels of value provided by the firm.

One of the main objectives of this book is to help you understand where, exactly, you are on this curve, and attempt to propel you to the top. But that is not enough. The most fertile minds in business—Thomas Edison, Henry Ford, J.W. Marriott, Stanley Marcus, Ray Kroc, Thomas Watson, Bill Hewlett, Dave Packard, Bill Gates, Fred Smith, Larry Ellison, Richard Branson, among others—did not just climb the curve. They left it. To the extent we can stimulate that type of behavior and have the professions constantly strive to raise the bar by offering new and innovative services to their customers—thereby creating more wealth for each of them in the process—this book will exceed even our modest expectations.

In order to achieve behavioral change in the future, we must affect your present thinking. This book will cover a lot of territory, often in very great depth, and no doubt it will challenge the conventional wisdom of the ages. But we have always tried to keep Milton Friedman's most terrifying seminar questions in the back of our mind as we make our various positions and beliefs known: "How do you know?" and "So what?" All research and new knowledge needs to constantly answer those questions, and I am sure we, despite our best efforts to do so, will fail at times in your mind. To the extent you may disagree with us—and we hope you will—we challenge you to ask those two questions of your beliefs and opinions as well.

Traveling around the world and meeting with professionals is an exhilarating educational opportunity. We always learn more knowledge than we ever impart. By doing so, we have learned that professionals in all countries—despite the varied cultural and nuanced deviation in their skills and practices—have more in common with one another than differences. One of those commonalties is a steady erosion in the morale of the professions. When the majority of professionals say they would *not* enter the profession if they had to do it all over again, something is wrong.

The professions are a noble calling, providing the opportunity to serve and contribute to others and make a difference in the world beyond one life. Despite this, the passion and morale in the profession—a leading indicator of the health and vitality of any calling—has been in decline for decades. We believe this in part is caused by the component in the old theory that says the road to success is paved with ever-higher billable hours. No one enters the profession in order to bill the most hours. This theory—which is at the very core of the thinking of most professionals—is slowly eating away at the very sustenance of our calling. It is time to supplant it; and we suggest this not so you can make more money, but so that you can make more of a difference in the lives of those important to you. This book sounds a tocsin to our colleagues around the world in the hope you will join with us to restore the quality of life in the professions.

PAUL When people came to the Accountant's Boot Camp that I started running in 1992, they came with great expectations and with enormous skepticism too. Here was someone from 'outside' the profession saying that there were far better ways to do things. Here was someone giving them new sets of skills—skills I knew their clients wanted them to acquire. Here was someone giving them a new zest for the profession—it need not be dull and boring any more. We worked them hard for four very long days (from eight in the morning through ten at night), giving them new concepts and skills to deal with their clients and their teams. As they left the Accountant's Boot Camp, it was quite normal for them to say, "This experience has changed my life." In a very deep way, we want this book to do that, too.

Both of us have seen what one friend of mine describes as "the good, the bad, and the ugly" of the profession. We know it can do so much good. We know there is so much that is ugly about it, too. We want to tip the balance greatly toward the side of good. And we know that can be done.

An accountant (John George) in Brisbane gave me a major insight into that. I visited John's office and saw all the wonderful things he was doing. He showed me proudly through his reception area (which looked for all the world like a reception area you'll read about in the book). He even insisted I go to the washroom to see the range of perfumes on display there!

Then we sat down in his office and talked about the staggering growth he'd achieved. He'd added over $1 million in one year to revenue. He showed me the letters he had received from his clients praising how he had helped them turn their businesses around. He told me about the amazing new spirit in his team and how they were doing more than he ever believed possible. He told me about how he had completely repriced his services and turned them effectively into products with fixed prices rather than pricing by the hour.

And then he returned to the extra million dollars. "You know Paul," he said, "you always said it's never about the money. And you're right. It isn't."

"So what is it about for you John?" I asked. He paused, not because he didn't know how to answer but because the answer was going to take him to places we had not spoken about before. He spoke about how he now had so much more time to spend with his wife, and how much he enjoyed taking time to play with and educate his young son. I thought that's where he would stop. After all, those are laudable achievements worth aiming for and getting. But he didn't stop there.

"All my life, since I was a young boy, I've wanted a telescope to look up at the stars. They fascinate me. So not long ago, I bought the very best telescope money can buy—quite a huge thing. And just last night I was able to sit on my balcony and point that telescope up to the sky. You know, Paul, it's beautiful up there."

I love that story. Not just because it is indeed "beautiful up there," but because it gets to the point about there being more to life than grinding out accounts.

My own realization of that came when I bought the house in which I now live for part of the year in Provence, France. There's real learning in looking in wonderment at the change of the seasons here. And the most important part of the learning is this: There is a much bigger picture than most of us see in our normal workaday lives. For example, on the Monday morning that I write this, I've been spending time in the garden wondering at the marvel of spring. How do those buds blossom? I never thought it was possible to look at buds and ponder questions like that.

For example, just outside our door is an ancient (and big) grapevine. Right now in late March it looks just like a craggy old stick. A typical Australian reaction would be to rip it out. But that would be a mistake, because in just a few months it will be replete with more grapes than I can imagine. And my newly planted plane trees are shooting buds everywhere. It truly is wonderful to look at and staggering to contemplate.

All too often we miss that wonder. We work away at whatever it is we do, absolutely oblivious to what's going on around us. It's my hope that reading this book will make you stop and take a look at things in a very, very different way. It's my hope, too, that it will, if nothing else, force you to step back and question. Indeed, you may not find answers, as such, but I'm certain you'll ask better questions as a result of your reading.

And it's precisely those questions and the answers you get that will lead to a rebirth of the professions. Not only is that desperately needed, but it's wonderful to contemplate as well.

2

A FLAWED THEORY

There is nothing so practical as a good theory.

—Ikujiro Nonaka and Hirotaka Takeuchi,
*The Knowledge-Creating Company:
How Japanese Companies Create
the Dynamics of Innovation*

One day, a man walking along a road in the countryside comes across a shepherd and a huge flock of sheep. He says to the shepherd, "I bet you $100 against one of your sheep that I can tell you the exact number in this flock." The shepherd thinks it over; then, because it's a big flock, he takes the bet. The man says, "973." The shepherd is astonished, because that is exactly right. So he says, "Okay, I'm a man of my word, take an animal." The stranger picks one up and begins to walk away.

"Wait," cries the shepherd, "Let me have a chance to get even. Double or nothing that I can guess your occupation." The man says, "Sure," thinking the poor shepherd could never guess correctly. "You are an economist for a government think tank," says the shepherd. "Amazing!" responds the man. "You are exactly right! But tell me, how did you deduce that?"

"Well," says the shepherd, "put down my dog and I will tell you." (Boulding, *April 16, 2001*: 2).

RON Theories are powerful because they seek to do one of three things: explain, predict, or prescribe. Yet, when one reads a typical business book today, the author will usually begin by saying something to the effect that, "This book is not based on some 'ivory tower,' theoretical model, but on practical, real-world experience and examples." Beware when you read such a qualifier, because as Dr. W. Edwards Demming used to say, "No theory, no learning." If a nonfiction book has no theory, it is nothing but a collection of common sense or prosaic platitudes. Especially in a business environment, whether we know it or not, we are guided to a large degree by theoretical constructs that have been developed in order to simplify—and thus explain, predict, or control—our various behaviors. As Immanuel Kant said, "Concepts without perceptions are empty; perceptions without concepts are blind." Theories build buildings, bridges, fly airplanes, and put men on the moon. As John E. Flaherty points out in his biography of Peter Drucker, *Shaping the Managerial Mind: How the World's Foremost Management Thinker Crafted the Essentials of Business Success:*

> Drucker's explanation for the astonishing output of innovation during this period [the Industrial Revolution] was based on his insight that historically the introduction of a tool preceded its theoretical verification. For example, the lever was used for centuries before Archimedes developed a scientific formula to explain its operation. Eyeglasses were in existence in medieval times, but it was not until the eighteenth century that Sir Isaac Newton and Gottfried Wilhelm Leibniz gave us the theory of optics. It took about seventy-five years before William Thomson, first Baron Kelvin, provided a theoretical explanation of thermodynamics for James Watt's steam engine. And it took several decades before a theory of aerodynamics could satisfactorily explain why the Wright brothers' flying machine actually flew.
>
> Drucker argued that throughout the era of Western civilization, technology and science had been uncoupled. Because technology (the art of doing) focused on utility, and science (the art of thinking) concentrated on metaphysical abstractions, they had only the most coincidental and distant contact with each other. It was not until the last half of the nineteenth century that the technological and scientific streams interconnected, resulting in an explosion of new knowledge (Flaherty, 1999: 230).

The purpose here is not to debate the chicken and egg question of which comes first, theory or practice. It is self-evident that both are important. Certainly there is enough practice based on the theory of the professional service firm to examine the validity of its theoretical constructs. Indeed, the purpose of this chapter is to examine the flaws in the old theory in order to construct a better theory. After all, the theory that originally explained the Wright brothers' flying machine has been significantly enhanced by Boeing in order to keep its 777 in the air. This is how theories progress—and they can have an enormous impact on our behavior. So even though discussing theory may be much maligned in today's business environment, I believe all learning starts with theory, and thus we will start by critically examining the predominant theory of the professional service firm.

"ANALYZING" THE PREDOMINANT PRACTICE EQUATION

In Greek language, *analyze* means "cut to pieces," which we will proceed to do with this theory before positing what we believe to be a better theory in the next chapter. When you think about the traditional theory of a professional service firm, you will no doubt construct a model such as:

$$\text{Revenue} = \text{People Power} \times \text{Efficiency} \times \text{Hourly Rate}$$

One could make a very convincing argument that this paradigm has ruled the thinking—and thus the behavior—of professional service firms since the dawn of their existence.

PAUL Perhaps just as importantly, it was a model we both spoke about in many a seminar until 2001. Actually, it was more than just speak about: We used the model as the opening construct, the opening line almost, of nearly every program we did.

And from the stage, we got to see what some call the "nod factor." This, as you might expect, is people nodding their heads in agreement as if to say, "Yes I'm on your side." We got a *lot* of head nods. We knew we were on firm ground from that point on. Yet, internally in our postseminar chats, we also knew that something was not gelling. The model had something fundamentally wrong with it. Why? Simply because it did not fit what we were coming to believe (although we were skilled enough to make it sound very believable on stage); and it certainly did not fit what we were finding in the firms of the future with which we were sharing new ideas. The point is that the model has dominated the thinking of firm leaders almost without question, and we think it's high time some big questions were raised.

RON Since this model has dominated the thinking of firm leaders, it is worth explaining the model in greater detail in order to understand both its strength and—as will be increasingly detailed—its fundamental weaknesses.

The archetypal pyramid firm model rested on the foundation of leveraging people power. The theory is this: Since the two main drivers of profitability are leverage (number of team members per owner) and the hourly rate realization, if each partner could oversee a group of professionals, this would provide the firm with additional capacity to generate top-line revenue, and thus add to the profitability and size of the firm. If a firm wanted to add to its revenue base, it had two primary choices: work its people more hours or hire more people. It is no secret which choice the average firm tends to choose, much to the chagrin of its already overworked team members. There was a time, perhaps in the halcyon days—mostly in the 1930s to the 1950s, and again in the 1970s through the mid-1980s—when the labor force for accountants in the United States was burgeoning, when firms may have added people at a faster rate than they added work. However, in most firms, the partners wait till demand is bursting at the seams before they add any more professionals.

If this part of the theory makes sense, pause for a moment and consider this axiom. Compared to other industries, this process of adding capacity *after* revenue is backward. If you think of any other industry or company—from Intel to General Electric, from FedEx to Microsoft—capacity is almost always added *before* revenue. Consider specifically FedEx: Before Fred Smith could deliver his first overnight package, he had to have trucks, drivers, airplanes, and facilities throughout the country, all at enormous fixed costs (indeed, those large fixed costs almost bankrupted FedEx in the early days). Yet the typical firm will not add an additional person until it is assured of a large "utilization" rate (usually between 60 to 80 percent). This has several debilitating effects; but perhaps the two worst are that it continuously keeps the firm running at an "overworked" pace, and that in turn limits the firm's capability to go out and acquire even more profitable customers. It also leaves very little time and resources to be devoted to new growth areas and new service offerings for existing customers. In other words, the focus is on capacity utilization and the *current* year's income statement, rather than investing in research and development and building the firm's balance sheet. Clearly, it is this latter investment that determines the firm's *future*.

Let us look now at the second element in the old theory—efficiency. Efficiency is a word that can be said with perfect impunity, since no one in his or her right mind would dispute the goal of operating efficiently. In fact, it is well known that in free market economies, efficiency is critical since it ensures that a society's resources are not going to waste. It is also well established that different levels of productivity largely explain differences in wages across countries. An American farmer will earn more plowing with a tractor than a Cuban farmer with an ox and hand plow; the American farmer is more productive, hence earns higher wages and more profits.

In a service firm, efficiency has always been measured based on the number of hours required to complete various jobs and average utilization rates achieved by the team members. In fact, if you were to study the average hours realized and the average productivity rate per person, you would find the hours average between 1,038 to 1,152, and the utilization rate is from 61.45 to 72.18 percent. These numbers are typical for as long as firms have kept such statistics. Even with the adoption of technology, there have been no major movements in these two measurements. As Ric Payne pointed out in his white paper on the future of the accounting profession:

> [T]here does not appear to have been any impact on productivity as measured by the proportion of hours charged to total hours available. Across-the-board productivity, by this measure seems to have been in the 60 to 70 percent range since the beginning of time. The inescapable conclusion is that restroom visits, watercooler chats, administration, marketing, and the myriad of other so-called nonproductive activities consume the same amount of time irrespective of whether a quill pen or a computer is used.
>
> To put that another way, technology has not contributed to an increase in the average number of hours people spend working on engagements even though it has obviously increased their output.
>
> It seems to the extent that technology has freed up time for the average practitioner, that practitioner has gone out looking for more low-level work and has been willing to bid prices down to win it. If technology adoption had in fact facilitated a shift toward more valuable analytical and advisory services then we could expect to see higher net profit margins being earned and a smaller proportion of revenue coming from compliance services. Neither of those things appears to be happening (Payne, 2002: Part II, 2).

Given these facts, it is curious that when asked in seminars around the world which of three *levers* an accountant would pull if he or she could only select one from the preceding equation—people power, efficiency, or hourly rate—efficiency is chosen more than half of the time. There is no doubt that increasing efficiency—or at least not sliding into inefficiency—is important. But the pendulum has swung too far in the direction of efficiency over everything else. It seems that innovation, dynamism, customer service, investments in human capital, and effectiveness have all been sacrificed on the altar of efficiency. It is critical to bear in mind that a business does not exist to be efficient; rather, it exists in order to create wealth for its customers.

PAUL This is a crucial point to which we'll return many times. Note that it is a matter of mind-set—the way we think. A business that operates from the "create wealth for its customers" mind-set does things fundamentally differently; that is to say, behavior is driven by belief.

Given that is true—the way we behave is governed by our beliefs—consider where so much effort and time is wasted. What many training programs are attempting to do is to modify behavior. It does not work, particularly long term.

In fact, many governments try behavior modification, too. Country A does not like what Country B is doing, so it tries to modify its behavior with, for example, sanctions or even cannons and bombs. Now, in the face of a cannon, you may well modify your behavior, but only while the cannon is there. But if the cannon hasn't helped you modify your belief, your mind-set, then you will not modify your behavior in the long term. That is precisely why this issue of how you think and what theory you use to construct your actions is so very important. We're talking about modifying your belief.

But let's get back to efficiency.

RON Peter Drucker is fond of pointing out that the last buggy whip manufacturers were models of efficiency. So what? What happens if you are efficient at doing the wrong things? That cannot be labeled progress. In fact, one indicator that an industry (or profession) is in the mature or decline stage of the *service life cycle* is when it is also most likely at the apogee of its theoretical level of efficiency.

The point is this: In industry after industry, the history of economic progress has not been to wring out the last 5 to 10 percent of efficiency, but rather to change the model in order to more effectively create wealth. From Walt Disney and Fred Smith to Bill Gates and Larry Ellison, these entrepreneurs did not get where they are by focusing on efficiency. (One looks in vain to find a comparable figure in the accounting profession. The only person that comes to mind is Henry Bloch, founder of H&R Block, who certainly changed the way tax services were delivered to millions of Americans, earning some $3 billion in revenue in fiscal year 2001 from that market.) All of these entrepreneurs created enormous wealth by delivering more effectively what customers were willing to pay for, not by focusing on efficiency. It is time for the profession to comprehend that its unrelenting pursuit of efficiency—whether in billable hour quotas or realization goals—exacts an enormous toll when measured in lost innovation, declining levels of customer service, foregone opportunities to cross-sell more services, and negative morale of team members. Of course, the problem is that these losses don't get counted anywhere since most firms do not have an effective method of capturing this type of information. These costs—and the concomitant loss of effectiveness in servicing customer needs—dwarf any efficiency gains you may achieve by being a taskmaster with your team members or by strapping a timesheet and a stopwatch around their necks.

Last, but certainly not least in terms of influencing the professions in myriad ways, is the hourly rate. Ever since I started my career in public accounting in 1984 with KPMG in San Francisco, I was repeatedly told by my partners and managers: "Ron, you don't have an inventory, you don't have tires our clients can kick; nor do you have a display case to show your wares; the only item you have to sell is your *time*." You soon learn that your entire professional career will be judged under the lens of billable hours, utilization rates, and your effective hourly rate. Every promotion is a badge of honor, since your hourly rate increases. Not only do you internalize this attitude, you begin to communicate it to your customers, telling them how important time is in everything you do for them, since it is an integral component of your price.

The hourly rate is a direct cousin of the Du Pont Return on Investment formula, and is also a form of cost-plus pricing. But the real ancestor of the hourly rate is the Labor Theory of Value, first posited by Karl Marx in the late 1800s. This theory was almost immediately shown to be false—in terms of its ability to explain, predict, or prescribe—as a method of determining value in a marketplace. My first book, *Professional's Guide to Value Pricing* showed the fallacy of this theory, and offered a better theory: the Subjective Theory of Value. That is, ultimately, the person paying for it—not the seller's internal overhead, desired profit, or labor hours—determines the value of anything. Value, like beauty, is in the eye of the beholder.

PAUL Interestingly, while reading my favorite newspaper in France—the *International Herald Tribune*, there right in front of me in the May 14, 2002, edition published in Marseille, an article beckoned. Written by David Leonhardt, the headline screamed: "Big League Baseball Tips Its Hat to Adam Smith." Let me quote directly from the article:

> The executives who run the Colorado Rockies may not know how to put together a good Major League Baseball team, but they seem to be at the forefront of economic theory.
> They have taken the radical step of acknowledging that their fans would prefer to watch the Rockies play the New York Yankees, who have won four of the last six World Series, than the Pittsburgh Pirates, who have not made the playoffs in 10 years.
> The Rockies are charging more for the three games next month against the Yankees than for games against the Pirates. A seat in the upper deck down the right-field line, for example, costs $23 for the Yankees and $15 for the Pirates (Leonhardt, 2002: 8).

Beauty is indeed in the eye of the beholder, isn't it? But then Leonhardt looks at another industry that, in his view, doesn't "get it"—Hollywood. Let me quote again:

> Based on the prices of movie tickets, Hollywood seems to think that moviegoers are no more excited to see *Spider-Man* than they are to see *Sorority Boys*. Both movies cost the same in any given multiplex.
> The people who set tolls in San Francisco, meanwhile, charge $5 to most drivers crossing the Golden Gate Bridge, whether they do so at 2:00 A.M. Sunday or during rush hour Monday morning. A newspaper costs no more the day after a big event than any other day.
> All of this clashes with basic economics, which hold that prices are supposed to rise as demand does. When they do, as Adam Smith argued more than 200 years ago, societies allocate their goods and services effectively and thrive (Ibid: 8).

Ah, therein is the key point, of course: "societies allocate their goods and services effectively and thrive." Leonhardt drives the point home this way: "In the public sector, the Port Authority of New York and New Jersey began charging $5 to cross the George Washington Bridge, among other bridges, at rush hour, and $4 at other times.

After the tolls changed, fewer cars used the bridges during morning rush hour and more did so from 5:00 A.M. to 6:00 A.M. when the roads are less crowded. And because of the altered traffic flow, drivers spent less time waiting on the bridges" (Ibid: 8).

Leonhardt ends his article with an interesting twist. He comments on how entertainers such as the Rolling Stones are now aware of *value pricing*, charging up to $350 per ticket (the scalpers were selling them at that price, after paying $100 for them). He concludes: "Tickets to the Yankees and Rolling Stones, as well as space on the road at the most convenient time, will increasingly go to the affluent" (Ibid: 8).

We will have more to say about that later. For now, let's remember that beauty is always in the eye of the beholder and get back to our discussion on hourly billing.

RON The deleterious effects of hourly billing are virtually endless. But perhaps one of the most pernicious effects is what it does to the attitude of the professional. You begin to believe that all you have to offer your customers is time, and then you begin to behave as if logging hours on a timesheet is more important than actually servicing the needs of customers by delivering results. You see how behavior follows belief yet again. It tends to create a stultifying belief that we are defined by our hourly rate; and since one hour is not distinguishable from that of a competitor's, we also begin to think of ourselves—and the services we offer—as commodities. Furthermore, since entry barriers to establishing a firm are relatively low, many new practitioners will price at a low hourly rate and justify it because their overhead is so low. But what does your internal overhead have to do with how much value you provide to your customers?

PAUL It's an answer we need to verbalize—"Nothing!"

RON The offense of believing that internal overhead or hours has anything to do with value is serious. Professionals should not be judged largely on how many hours they bill, but on the results and wealth they create for their customers. No customer in the world buys time, so how can that possibly be what professionals are selling? Scrutinize any survey of why people leave a CPA and how they select a new CPA, and nowhere will you read, "Because I (dis)like their hours." This pricing paradigm is not worthy of the professions, and it is time we throw it on the ash heap of history, because, quite simply, it is no longer relevant in an intellectual-capital-based economy. It is an idea from the day before yesterday. It is time for the professions to *price on purpose*. We explore that topic at greater length in Chapter 7.

For now, consider revenue. Since professional service firms have such large contribution margins (defined as revenue per person less direct cost per employee), averaging between 59 to 67 percent—they are not like grocery stores that operate on a 1 to 2 percent bottom line—the prevailing attitude seems to be that when marginal revenue is added to the top line, a larger and larger percentage will flow to the bottom, given that most firm costs are fixed, at least in the short and medium term (in theory, all costs are avoidable in the long run). And certainly this is true, marginal revenue can drive the profitability of a firm. Given this thinking, many firms will gladly accept additional customers that demand the same type of services the firm offers to its regular customer base; and as long as it can achieve its average hourly rate, the firm will be satisfied.

Not much thought is given, however, to the *profitability* of that marginal business. It is one thing to get *more* business, it is quite another to get *better* business. The "bigger is better" mentality is an empty promise for most firms. Acquiring more customers is not necessarily better. Growth simply for the sake of growth is the ideology of the cancer cell, not a strategy for a viable, profitable firm. My associate Dan Morris explained that, when he started his firm, he had a "fog the mirror test" for all potential new customers. Here's how it worked: if he placed a mirror in front of them and it fogged (and they had a checkbook), they qualified as a tax customer (if it didn't fog, by the way, they qualified for estate work). Where did this ideology come from? You can certainly see the algebraic effect by looking at the practice equation, and perhaps that has affected professionals' thinking over the decades. Yet there are two more insidious reasons for the belief that any customer is a good customer.

The first reason probably dates back to that timeless debate about being a generalist versus a specialist. After accountants began preparing tax returns in the 1940s, the demand for tax services and planning increased dramatically. Since it is relatively easy to prepare another tax return, the marginal customer always added to the firm's bottom line. Indeed, even today, in firms with as high as $1 to 10 million in revenue, we see $500 to $1,000 tax returns being prepared, always with the justification that, "Yes they're small customers, but we make money on them."

Yet the debate between the generalist and the specialist is over, and the latter won. The accounting profession is one of the last professions to have specialized; doctors started in the 1940s, lawyers in the 1950s. Even auto mechanics, toy stores, pet stores, baby stores, clothing stores, and furniture stores have all specialized, carving out niches that they serve best. Finally, sometime in the late 1970s and into the 1980s, accountants began to realize that specialists are higher up on the value curve, and thus we have seen the growth of many specialty practice areas, from consulting and elder care to estate planning and litigation support. This is not to say that your firm should have only one niche; many firms have multiple areas of expertise. What it does say is that you need to diligently stick to the niches you have strategically decided to pursue—and select your customers with care—and don't let growth or market share tempt you to deviate from your plan. Think of the incandescent lightbulb and laser beam. Both take the same amount of energy to operate, but one can bore a hole through metal because of its intense focus.

The second reason for the belief that any customer is a good customer also dates back to the post-World War II days. When demand and customers were plenty, marketers began to think that market share was the ultimate Holy Grail. Procter & Gamble exemplified this better than any company, choosing to sell as many boxes of detergent and tubes of toothpaste to as many people as possible. Beginning in the 1990s and into the current century, this attitude is starting to change. Traditional marketing and sales leaders, such as Procter & Gamble, Ford, and General Electric, began to switch their focus from top-line revenue growth and market share to increasing profitability. For instance, between 1995 and 1999, Ford raised prices, and even though it lost two points in market share, it reported record earnings for that period.

Perhaps better known, Southwest Airlines is a leader in the low-fare travel niche, and it has remained focused like a laser beam on that niche. As former CEO Herb Kelleher pointed out: "Market share has nothing to do with profitability. Market share says we just want to be big; we don't care if we make money doing it. That's what misled much of the airline industry for 15 years, after deregulation. In order to get an additional 5 percent of the market, some companies increased their costs by 25 percent. That's really incongruous if profitability is your purpose." (Freiberg, 1996: 49).

If market share explained profitability, General Motors, United Airlines, Sears, and Philips would be the most profitable companies in their respective industries. Yet they have all turned in mediocre profitability records. Growth in profitability usually precedes market share, not vice versa. Wal-Mart, for example, was far more profitable than Sears long before it had a sizeable market share. It seems that profitability and market share grow in tandem with a viable value proposition that customers are willing to pay for. The road to hell is paved with the pursuit of volume. Don't make this mistake. More often than not, less is more, as we will demonstrate.

SUMMARY AND CONCLUSIONS

We have exposed the flaws of the traditional practice equation theory. Although the preceding discussion is not meant to be comprehensive, it nevertheless sets forth a compelling case against the traditional paradigm. With the growth in the labor pool of accountants decreasing, the technology curve flattening, and utilization rates stuck between 62 to 75 percent from the dawn of time—not to mention the focus on efficiency compromising the profession's innovation and effectiveness—the items of leverage appear to be disappearing. But are they really, or are we not looking at the right things to leverage? In other words, is there a better theory for the professional service firm of the future? We believe there is, and our task in the remainder of this book is to prove this new theory's superiority over the old one, and even to have you adopt it as your own. Even better, if the theory we posit is someday replaced with a better theory, we will have contributed to the advancement of the professions—and nothing would please us more.

3

A PARADIGM WORTHY OF A PROUD PROFESSION

People like to think that businesses are built of numbers (as in the "bottom line"), or forces (as in "market forces"), or things ("the product"), or even flesh and blood ("our people"). But this is wrong. Businesses are made of ideas—ideas expressed as words.

—James Champy

There was once an immigrant tailor who came to this country and opened up a shop. He sewed buttons, stitched hems, made suits, and did all those other things that tailors do. One day his son, who was an accountant, dropped by for a visit. While he was there, he noticed two cigar boxes sitting next to the cash register. One was labeled "paid bills" and the other was labeled "unpaid bills." The son chastised his father for keeping his records in such an unprofessional manner because the old man didn't know what his profit was.

The father lovingly put his arm around the shoulders of his son and told him that when he came to this country many years ago, the only possessions he had were his clothes. Now he had a home, a car, a good business, good health, a daughter who was a college professor, a daughter who was an engineer, and a son who was not too sharp as an accountant. The old tailor then said, "When I add up all of my blessings and subtract the clothes on my back, what remains is my profit" (quoted in Stieber, 1998: 5–6).

RON Professionals tend to get so absorbed by the technical aspects and enveloped in the arcane knowledge of what they do, it rarely occurs to them to stop and think about why they are as successful as they are.

PAUL Yet some do stop and think. One such practitioner is Mark Spofforth, former chairman of the General Practitioner's Board, and chairman of the Technical Group at the Institute of Chartered Accountants of England and Wales (ICAEW) in London. In an introduction to a special seminar for his clients, Spofforth had this to say:

Our clients see us in different ways—as advisors, allies, friends, bean counters, protection from the taxman; we play all sorts of roles. But over the last 20 years, my profession has become obsessed with the intricate detail of accounts, producing change after change in a drive to produce a set of accounts that will satisfy the tax man, the banks, the Companies House, the government—everybody it seems. Everybody except the people who really matter in nearly every one of the businesses we look after—the owners and the managers.

The result is that, to the public, chartered accountants are boring bean counters obsessed with the detail of double entry, searching for the elusive Holy Grail—that is, a correct set of accounts.

What we have forgotten is that accountancy is a language, a means of communication, and a means of informing. It is all very well to construct from that language a work of great literature, but most of the people we are communicating with do not even understand our arcane language. We have got to get back to using it for the purpose it was invented: to help us to measure, interpret and analyze, make decisions, and solve problems.

And it is a very powerful language. It can describe the actions of every business in every industry in the land, however disparate. It covers government and the public sector. It can assist the child with pocket money or Microsoft with its megabucks. It is very, very powerful.

And what we have forgotten in our profession is that we are experts in this language and that gives us a great deal of power to help. We train by visiting company after company, looking at how they run the business from the shop floor up. We look at systems, their control, and how successful they are. We gain experience all through our working lives about what mistakes not to make, about the clever tricks that businesspeople use to build their firms. We understand how to structure deals, how to structure businesses, and how to make profits.

And what do we do? We use all that experience to produce the perfect set of accounts that end up in the filing cabinet at the clients' offices or at Companies House. What a waste! It's got to end.

The pace of change in the world has accelerated dramatically. Not just because of computer technology, but also because of better education, calls for greater social accountability, and because with the growth of world markets, trade is becoming truly global.

Some companies now have a turnover greater than the Gross Domestic Product (GDP) of some small countries. The competition is heating up. Communication is faster than ever before. We are deluged with data, with regulations, with new laws. And the smaller companies need to know what to do with all that data, all that information—there's too much of it to assimilate, too much to read, too much to do, and not enough time [to do it].

So we, the accountants, have got to stop spending so much time producing and checking clever numbers. We've got to start using our expertise in interpreting the numbers. We've got to start to teach the language, to spend more time in sharing our expertise in business, more time in helping to grow small businesses, helping them to achieve their objectives with the least stress. And we can do it.

Even if we don't have the answer to the problems ourselves, as knowledge professionals we know where to go to get it. Business development is a journey, and our job is to make the travel as smooth and comfortable as possible.

The press is having a field day spreading doom and gloom about another recession, about a slowdown in the economy, about the country not being able to afford its public spending targets. Our job is to help small businesses to not only survive a downturn in the economy, but to expand and grow through it.

Research shows that the biggest barriers to growth facing small business are a lack of revenue, a lack of a planned strategy for growth, and a lack of funding for that growth.

What Spofforth said gives another perspective on how we lose sight of the fact that the sole reason we exist is to serve customers outside of our walls.

RON Interestingly, if someone outside of our walls were to study the Practice Equation introduced in Chapter 2, that outsider would come away with the impression that professionals are successful because they have learned how to leverage people very efficiently and they have trained their customers into believing they are purchasing their time. This is a profound misunderstanding of exactly what makes professionals successful, and it has focused the profession on attempting to leverage precisely those things that do not explain its success.

Professional firms are not successful because they leverage people, because they constantly enhance efficiency, or because they raise their hourly rates every couple of years. All of these activities are nothing but means to the ultimate ends of serving the needs of their customers, hence creating more wealth for them than the cash price they willingly pay the firm. In Chapter 2 we asked whether the profession was leveraging the right things in order to grow and enhance profitability for the firm. Considering the Practice Equation from that chapter, the answer is a definitive no.

WHY ARE PROFESSIONALS SUCCESSFUL?

RON Surely professionals are not successful because they sell hours, because no customer buys hours. This is a very simple concept, but a profound one nonetheless. For approximately two generations, the profession has genetically encoded its members with the core belief that they only sell time. But, again, customers don't buy time; they mostly buy results, expectations, good feelings, hope, dreams, a preferred vision of the future, and solutions to problems. No customer seems to care how long it took the manufacturer to produce his or her car. The notion that all professionals have to offer the customers they are privileged to serve is their time is not only ludicrous, it is humiliating, and not worthy of a noble calling. A profession exists in order to "profess" something, be it a respect for truth and justice in the case of law, science and healing in medicine, moral tenets and teachings in religion, and helping customers achieve their goals in accounting. No firm of the future should "profess" to sell hours, to leverage people (how demeaning), and to increase efficiency at the expense of everything else.

You did not, nor did any of your colleagues for that matter, enter the profession with dreams of having the most billable hours in the firm, or the highest hourly rate, or the largest realization percentage. No, you entered the profession in order to help other people; but you soon learned that since helping your fellow human beings could not be measured very accurately—because it has to do with "soft, touchy-feely" things—it had been replaced by more "hard" measures of efforts and activities, which usually bear little relationship to the results achieved for customers. Is this the best our profession has to offer dreamy-eyed students wishing to make a difference in the world? Are these antiquated measurements laudable for a noble profession? Could this be one of the reasons for the precipitous decline in the number of students entering accounting?

In the final analysis, professionals are successful because they help people achieve their objectives. Mostly, this is a human endeavor and cannot be measured via a satisfaction survey or on a timesheet. Helping customers achieve objectives is done through leveraging your firm's intellectual capital, not mindlessly piling people into a pyramid and trying to leverage hours (which are fixed anyway).

The old theory is no longer relevant to the drivers of success in firms of the future. Buckminster Fuller (designer, cosmologist, philosopher, mathematician, and architect—he designed the geodesic dome) once said, "You can't change anything by fighting or resisting it. You change something by making it obsolete through superior methods." (quoted in Vance and Deacon, 1995: 78) It is time to replace the Practice Equation described in the previous chapter with this new model:

$$\text{Profitability} = \text{Intellectual Capital} \times \text{Price} \times \text{Effectiveness}$$

Let us explore each component of this equation; then we will discuss why it is a better theory for explaining the success of firms operating in today's marketplace realities and those of the future.

We start with *profitability*, rather than *revenue*, because we are not interested in growth merely for the sake of growth. As many companies around the world have learned—some the hard way, such as the airlines, retailers, and automobile manufacturers—market share is not the "open sesame" to more profitability. We are interested in finding the right customer, at the right price, consistent with our niche, vision, and mission, even if that means frequently turning away customers. I have coined a corollary to Gresham's Law (bad money drives out good) from monetary economics, affectionately known as Baker's Law: *Bad customers drive out good ones.*

PAUL If there was just one phrase from this book that readers should pin up on their walls, it would be that one: "Bad customers drive out good ones." In every gathering of accountants I'm asked to address, I always ask the question: "How many of us have customers we wish we didn't have?" I've never yet seen such a gathering where fewer than 99 out of every 100 raised their hands in the air (most of them in what you might call an enthusiastic way, along with another part of their anatomy—their eyes, literally in the top of their heads, as if to say, "Yes, I have them and what a drag it is.")

You know the customers they're thinking of, the ones who don't pay the bills, the ones who sap your energy rather than build it, the ones you simply don't like being with—the list goes on and on.

Or consider this: Imagine you could put the work you do into these three categories:

- I really love doing this type of work.
- I can tolerate it.
- If I'm brutally honest, I hate it.

How much of your typical week would be in the bottom two?

It may come as no surprise to read that, for many accountants, the number in those bottom two categories is frequently around 80 percent. Or, to put it another way, they're only loving what they do 20 percent of the time. Yet they smile through it because they're getting paid. As David Maister points out in his book *True Professionalism: The Courage to Care about Your People, Your Clients, and Your Career*, there is another "profession" that says, "Pay me the money and I'll fake it" (Maister, 1997). Some call it the oldest profession in the world.

So why does the profession prostitute itself so frequently? Maybe it's because many (most?) in the profession have been, as one practitioner in the United Kingdom put it to me, "indiscriminate" about the customers they work with. To put that more bluntly, if it looks like the customers have a checkbook, they take them on. Some don't.

Take Tom Weddell of the Newburgh- and Poughkeepsie-based practice, Vanacore, DeBennictus, DiGiovanni, Weddell (try answering the phone there!).Weddell, forty-two years old and the youngest of the partners, had been appointed managing partner just six weeks before he attended a four-day program I presented in Chicago. Weddell *really* got the message. On the way home from the program, he said this to his partners, "Clearly, there's so much for us to do to implement this material. I want to know right now if you're with me."

It was a completely general question with no implied reference to "reorganizing" the firm's customer list. "Well, yes, of course," they replied. "Are you certain?" Weddell asked. "Yes, we're really with you, Tom."

So the next day, Weddell went into his office early. He got a full list of the firm's customers and copied it 27 times (the number of team members he had at that time). He gave it to each member with the instruction, "Circle everyone's name on this list whom you don't like dealing with and give it back to me by 11:00 A.M., please." That was his only criterion. The other partners had no idea he'd done this at the time (Weddell presumably was taking them at their word that they were "with him").

That afternoon, Weddell took every customer whose name was circled and fired them (nicely). He even recommended another accountant they might like to try, who would welcome them with open arms. By 4:00 P.M., the job was done. Weddell had gotten rid of the customers—along with $64,000 worth of revenue.

When Weddell told the team what he'd done, they cheered! At 4:15, the other partners, who by now realized what had happened, called a meeting. In essence, their message was, "We're not sure we're with you, Tom!" But three months later, the partners were absolutely sure.

Weddell showed me his financials and pointed to the additional $300,000 worth of revenue the practice had generated in the period. And he made this wonderfully simple point; "We couldn't have gotten that unless we'd created $64,000 worth of space."

Do you have any customers taking up space? Many accountants are trying to be all things to all people. Yet they're advising their clients to be "selective" when those clients choose customer segments. The answer really does come back to that earlier comment about accountants choosing their clients "indiscriminately." Want to prove it? Take out your latest firm brochure (if you're still one of the people who believe in brochures) and mark anywhere on it where it specifically says something like, "You've got to be special to be one of our clients." I doubt you'll find it. Even your brochure or your website probably implies that all customers have to do is breathe and you'll take them on.

Of course, if the accountant is still stuck in what Bob Elliott (former chairman of a now-defunct AICPA group looking at the future of the profession) called "the death spiral of low-level tax work," then maybe being discriminate is hard. But when we as a profession finally realize we have so much more to offer than any other profession in the area of helping our selected clients grow their business, we'll have the courage to be truly professional. Bad customers (and the criterion for bad can be simply that you don't like them) drive out good ones.

After years of "preaching" that message, I've never known any firm to regret that they took action in the way that Tom Weddell did. You won't either. Bad customers drive out good ones.

RON Adopting that belief means you need to become much more selective about whom you do business with, even though that marginal business may be "profitable" by conventional accounting standards. After decades of studying professional service firms, we have learned that the most important costs—and benefits, for that matter— don't ever show up on a profit and loss statement. Accepting customers who are not a good fit for your firm—either because of their personality or the nature of the work involved—has many deleterious effects, such as negatively affecting team member morale and committing fixed capacity to customers who do not value your offerings. Because this is such an important subject, we have devoted Chapter 8 to exploring it; there we offer a powerful analogy for you to consider in managing your fixed *adaptive capacity*. For now, suffice it to say we will focus on *profitability*, not simply topline revenue. When it comes to customers, less is usually more.

Your firm's ability to create wealth outside of itself ultimately depends on your capability to create, disseminate, innovate, and leverage *intellectual capital (IC)*. There are many definitions of IC depending on which authority in the field you read. For our purposes in this book, we define IC as composed of three primary components:

- *Human capital (HC)*. This comprises your team members and associates who work either for you or with you. As one CPA leader said, "This is the capital that leaves in the elevator at night." The important thing to remember about HC is that it cannot be owned, only contracted, since it is completely volitional. In fact, we consider professionals to be knowledge workers who own the means of your firm's production, and knowledge workers will invest their HC in those firms that pay a decent return on investment, both economic and psychological. In the final analysis, your people are not assets (they deserve more respect than a copier machine and a computer) and they are not resources (to be harvested from the land like timber when you run out); ultimately, they are *volunteers,* and it is totally up to them whether or not they get back into the elevator the following morning.

- *Structural capital.* This is everything that remains in your firm once the HC has stepped into the elevator at the end of the day, such as databases, customer lists, systems, procedures, intranets, portals, manuals, files, technology, checklists, and all of the explicit knowledge tools you utilize in order to produce results for your customers.

- *Social capital.* This includes your *customers*, the main reason a business exists; but it also includes your suppliers, vendors, networks, referral sources, alumni, and reputation. Of the three types of IC, this is perhaps the most overlooked and least tapped by the firm, and yet it is highly valued by customers.

This is not a new theory, created during the dot-com revolution. In fact, IC has nothing at all to do with technology per se. Intellectual capital has always been the chief driver of wealth creation. Wealth does not exist in tangible resources—such as timber, land, real estate, oil, and so forth—but in ideas and their creative expression. Consider, for example, that oil was completely useless—in fact, if you were a farmer it was an absolute nuisance—until the combustion engine was invented. If it were not for the piston engine and the electrical needs of the industrialized world, the Middle East, which has been sitting on oil for thousands of years, would be nothing more than sand dunes, rocks, and caves.

Professional service firms have few tangible assets; certainly their balance sheets don't measure the most important factor at generating wealth, that is, IC. Yet it is this factor, more than any other—that is, it is the *means*—that produces the *ends* that customers purchase; and the fact is, most of it—human capital—exists in a form that cannot be owned, controlled, or managed. Firms of the future have to understand the profound importance of intellectual capital in order to focus on the right characteristics to uphold, and provide sustenance to, so they can achieve their objective of serving others. These three components will be explored at greater length in the next chapters.

There are four Ps of marketing: price, product, place, promotion. Of these, *price* is the most complex; it is your firm's only opportunity to *capture* the value you create through your value proposition. If you think of the four Ps of marketing as a farmer might, *product* is your crop, be it wheat, corn, fruit, and so forth, or some combination thereof. *Place* is the land where you plant your crop; and *promotion* is the fertilizer and water for your crop. Price is the harvest, when you reap what you sow. However, unlike farmers, who are for the most part (there are exceptions) *price takers*, professionals are *price makers*, since there is no fixed price for intellectual capital.

Yet professional pricing has been a sorely neglected topic until very recently. In fact, pricing in most industries has been neglected, usually relegated to some rule of thumb, or cost-plus pricing formula. This is beginning to change, thanks to some very innovative leaders in this movement (Tom Nagle and Reed Holden would certainly top the list of those who have forced pricing onto the organizational charts of many companies). It is time for professionals to *price on purpose* as well, and this has already started to happen.

For too long the profession has let its price be solely or largely predicated on the arbitrary rule of thumb of some multiple of wage expense or on an overhead plus desired net income calculation. Both of these pricing mechanisms are relics of Karl Marx's Labor Theory of Value, and are completely obsolete in an innovative, dynamic, and intellectual-capital-based marketplace. The firm of the future prices its intellectual capital based upon the value to the customer, not the internal labor cost of its human capital or the profit desires of its owners, and certainly not the labor hours involved in creating it. We'll explore this topic in greater detail in Chapter 9.

In the firm of the future, *effectiveness* takes precedence over efficiency. A business does not exist to be efficient; it exists to create wealth for its customers. An obsessive compulsion to increase efficiency (doing things right) reduces the firm's effectiveness at doing the right things. The pursuit of efficiency has hindered most firms' ability to pursue opportunities, hence the firms spend most of their time solving problems. As alluded to earlier in Mark Spofforth's seminar introduction, the cost accounting mentality has for too long pervaded the mind-set of professionals, blinding them to the customer's real needs and desires. One cannot grow a firm and continuously cut costs and increase efficiency.

PAUL Paul Cook, the founder of Raychem, put it really well when he said, "You cannot cut your way to success. In the final analysis, you cannot continue to reduce costs and grow." And then of course there's the Price Waterhouse study (done before they were PricewaterhouseCoopers) that points out that the value you can add to a business through cost-cutting is mathematically limited to zero. It goes on to observe the obvious (yet frequently missed) point that, economically, the limit is far less than zero since you can't cut costs to zero—even in the Internet age.

RON It is not that efficiency is bad, per se, it is that it has been pursued at the expense of nearly everything else. To add insult to injury, the efficiency measures that do exist in the professional service firm—billable hours, realization rates, utilization—all are *lagging* indicators that measure efforts and activities, not *leading* indicators that measure results and define success the same way the customer does. It is time for firms to develop testable hypotheses in the form of *critical success factors* and *key performance indicators* that measure the actual results of their work the same way customers do.

As opposed to efficiency, implicit to effectiveness is that there is no such thing as a free statistic. Just because we can measure something accurately does not mean we should. Also implicit to effectiveness is that imprecise measurements of the *right* things are infinitely more valuable than precise measurements of the *wrong* things. This will no doubt shock some of you, especially those trained well in cost accounting. But controlling costs, and accounting for them, does not ensure success. Professionals are not machines subject to the laws of electromechanical engineering. They are human beings who don't check their emotions at the door; they are subject to fears, doubts, variable levels of self-esteem, uncertainty, anger, rage, and a whole range of other emotions that cannot be captured by traditional efficiency measurements. In other words, *humans are messy*. Focusing on effectiveness does not eliminate these issues, but it does take them into account far better than efficiency metrics, which can be desensitizing and inhumane at times.

This Practice Equation correlates with our vision of the firm of the future. Professionals are the ultimate knowledge workers, using their hearts and minds, not their brawn and hands. This equation recognizes the importance of intellectual capital, the price thereof, and the effectiveness of the workers who produce it, as well as the customers who purchase it. It may not yet be a perfect theory, but it is far superior to the alternative discussed in Chapter 2.

COGNITIVE DISSONANCE

RON I have a love/hate relationship with this equation. On the one hand, I think it is a superior model for the firm of the future because it recognizes the realities of the marketplace in which professionals operate and it focuses on leveraging the right things. It takes into account the importance of dynamism, innovation, and a whole host of other human activities that are simply not captured in the old equation. On the other hand, because it is nothing more than an algebraic equation, it is an incredible simplification of the components that comprise the typical professional service firm.

When we look at equations, we tend to think of each component comprising a separate part that can be individually manipulated and controlled, a very one-dimensional view of a business made up of human beings. What the equation does not explain is how to raise prices or how to increase effectiveness, nor does it explain the interconnections and interdependencies of the various components. Certainly the equation can describe an abstract feature such as effectiveness, but it does not really enhance one's understanding of how change occurs in the firm as a whole. In other words, it can explain the *ends* (profitability), but not the *means* (how does one measure effectiveness?). Any equation assumes a certain cause-and-effect relationship, and tends to lead us to believe that these sequences are sequential and linear and not subject to the perpetual feedback of prior causes. Under the old equation, if you charge more hours, revenue grows; but in the day-to-day realities of a firm, trying to work your team members more hours is going to have a whole host of unintended consequences that will ultimately affect the goal of increasing revenue. No equation can capture the richness of these interrelated means.

Another problem with the equation is that it presents the characteristics of a firm as nothing but the sum of the parts; if you change one aspect, you invariably change another by an equal amount. But in a living, breathing, organic system such as a firm, parts and wholes are not linked so linearly. Thus, a small change in one of the parts can have a profound and dramatic influence on everything else. Think of the effects of a toxic manager who belittles and intimidates his or her team members. He or she may achieve higher efficiency in one aspect of the equation, yet so totally destroy morale and motivation that the ultimate outcome will be a reduction in firm effectiveness, customer service, and profitability.

Any equation is similar to the difference between a map and a territory: one is a two-dimensional explanation and the other is full of complex and rich interconnections that could never be captured on paper. Somebody once said that the difference between studying a living entity on paper is like performing an autopsy on dolphins versus swimming with them. Certainly both activities will give you a better understanding of dolphins, but which one will let you observe the rich and contextual feel of a living creature? Clinical pathologists implicitly understand this difference, as they instruct physicians to never treat a test result but rather treat the patient.

The careful reader—perhaps the reader with scientific or marketing training—will note that the equation also does not answer the important question of why we are in business, as it appears to put profitability above all else. This is serious omission. The fact that a business needs to make a profit is a tautology, and is in fact quite irrelevant. Most important, a business must create and retain customers, add wealth to their lives, and give them more in value than the cash they are giving up. The equation also does not answer the all-important question of where profits are derived. Because of these shortcomings, the remainder of this chapter deals with these issues since they are of profound importance to professionals operating in the firm of the future.

In any event, while you could observe that the new Practice Equation has weaknesses, in a book (or seminar), we must break things down in separate components in order to deal with them more effectively. We cannot do everything at once. This is the advantage of a theory, because while it will never capture the true essence of a living firm, it can be studied in its quantitative and qualitative parts, and our understanding of how those parts are interdependent can be better understood as a result. A theory need not be elegant nor capture the entire essence of the phenomenon it is trying to explain; all it is has to do to be effective is allow us to predict, explain, or prescribe the behavior we observe. To this end, the new Practice Equation is clearly superior to the old one.

WHY ARE WE IN BUSINESS?

Business must be run at a profit, else it will die. But when anyone tries to run a business solely for profit . . . then also the business must die, for it no longer has a reason for existence.

—Henry Ford

Why are we here? I think many people assume, wrongly, that a company exists solely to make money. We have to go deeper and find the real reasons for our being. As we investigate this, we inevitably come to the conclusion that a group of people get together and exist as an institution that we call a

company so that they are able to accomplish something collectively that they
could not accomplish separately—they make a contribution to
society, a phrase which sounds trite but is fundamental.

—David Packard

There is only one boss: the customer. And he can fire everybody in
the company, from the chairman on down, simply by
spending his money somewhere else.

—Sam Walton

RON All of the entrepreneurs quoted here built businesses that still exist; and as you can see, they did it by focusing on the customer, not profits.

PAUL Dave Packard and Bill Hewlett drove that message home incessantly. There is, if you will, a higher purpose.

Which brings to mind my friend Lloyd. Lloyd looked like he had everything. Based in New York, at thirty-four years old, he was a vice president of a major worldwide merchant bank and commanded a salary well into the six figures. Then three months ago, Lloyd decided there was more to life for him. He resigned from the bank to spend a year with a fledgling financial institution in Haiti, working with underprivileged people at a salary just enough to live on. He planned to follow that with a year in Kurdistan. Before he left for Haiti, he described his move as moving "from success to significance."

This is a growing trend. Some accounting firms are getting that "higher purpose" set in their minds and creating some wonderful "significance projects" to make it happen. One of the best I've seen is at Linkenheimer CPAs in Santa Rosa, California. Partner John Jones introduced me to the firm's KiddAccounts Children's Money Program. Jones explained that the basic goal of the program is to teach elementary schoolchildren to think of their money as more than something they immediately spend, to convince them it's okay to think and talk about money and how to use it, and to help them understand they really can be smart about money.

Interestingly, the program was the result of some brainstorming at the firm's annual retreat. "We were talking about how to approach practice development. Someone suggested the then seemingly far-out idea that it might be interesting to talk to children for a change instead of to clients and prospective clients. Why not do something of significance and value for the community?"

At that point, the firm's partners could have said, "Submit some plans and a budget." Had they done that, it's unlikely the idea would have gone anywhere. Instead they simply said, "Go for it." Steve Miksis, a manager with the firm, volunteered to make it work. He put together a small team, and together they developed a special kid-friendly workbook called "Tracking My Money," featuring a character called Lester Lynx to lead the kids through the workbook. Lester guides the kids through the budget process and helps them work with a specially created, oversize one-dollar bill that the kids cut up into categories.

The program is taught in three weekly lessons. Miksis (or another member of the team, from clerk to partner) visits the classroom for 45 minutes in the first week, engaging the kids in discussion about the four parts of a dollar. At the end of that first meeting, the firm gives each student his or her own book to take home. Homework materials are left with the teacher; and the children complete the exercises during week two. A young accountant on the Linkenheimer team then returns on week three to lead discussions about what it means to be a smart spender; the size and power of the children's consumer market; and how advertising affects how they spend. And, of course, at the end of the program, the children receive a certificate to prove they participated in the KiddAccounts program.

Does it work? Yes, on many levels. Research conducted by the firm shows that two-thirds of the children (typically eight- to ten-year-olds) take home the workbook and begin to use them. One boy even complained that he couldn't use the workbook because his father had taken it away from him—"My Dad is using it himself," the student reported.

After a local journalist observed the program in action and published a feature story in the local newspaper, the phones started ringing at Linkenheimer, with calls from both other schools and accounting firms. Linkenheimer now licenses the entire program to other firms across the United States (and, yes, they're interested in hearing from firms around the world too: simply e-mail John Jones at jjones@linkcpa.com for more information).

Naturally, clients now regularly call the firm to praise the program. Jones explains: "I ran into a prospective client I had been talking with for some weeks. He told me that we were obviously a very different firm and that what we were doing with the schools was wonderful. That individual and his business are now clients."

But Jones has much more significant things to say:

> It's possible that we could have made more money this year had we continued to go about business development using more traditional methods, but who's to say? I still think that, in the long run, the firm is better off with this community project as part of what we do. Every business needs a spark to succeed. Profit and net income are by-products of a lot of other things. You can't manage them directly. It seems to me that companies that have an inner life, a kind of vitality, are much more likely to secure and sustain higher profits. This project has created a spark in the firm.

For "spark," read "significance." Going from success to significance is a meaningful way to do business.

RON Think of it this way: Profit is merely the oxygen for the body; it is not the point of life. Profit is nothing more than a lagging indicator of what is in the hearts and minds of your customers. One of the many things I struggled with over the new Practice Equation was the exalted position it gives to profitability, as if that were the entire purpose of a professional service firm. This section addresses—emphatically—why that is not true.

As Peter Drucker has indefatigably pointed out, "There is only one valid definition of business purpose: to create a customer" (quoted in Flaherty, 1999: 131). This is known as the *marketing concept*. The purpose of any organization—from a governmental agency to a nonprofit foundation to a corporation—is to create results *outside* of itself. The result of a school is an educated student, as is a cured patient for a hospital. For a professional firm, a happy and loyal customer who returns is the ultimate result.

The only things that exist inside of a business are costs, activities, efforts, problems, mediocrity, friction, politics, and crises. There is no such thing as a *profit center* in a business; there are only *cost* and *effort centers*. In fact, as Peter Drucker wrote, "One of the biggest mistakes I have made during my career was coining the term 'profit center,' around 1945" (Drucker, 2002: 84). The only profit center is a customer's check that doesn't bounce. Customers are absolutely indifferent to the internal workings of your firm in terms of costs, desired profit levels, and efforts. Value is created only when you have produced something the customer voluntarily, and willingly, pays for. For example, Sears Roebuck became the purchasing agent for the middle-class family; and cosmetic companies, as Revlon founder Charles Revson pointed out, sell *hope*. What makes the marketing concept so breathtakingly brilliant is that the focus is always on the outside of the organization. It does not look inside and ask, "What do we want and need?" Rather, it looks outside to the customer and asks, "What do you desire and value?"

In fact, what is routinely called "capitalism" is more accurately described as "consumerism," wherein the customer is sovereign—that is, those with the gold, rule. While the marketing concept has existed for decades, it is regularly ignored in professional service firms, which get so caught up in their own rules, regulations, pronouncements, and internal efficiency quotas they tend to ignore the sole reason for their existence. It is perhaps why we always see the look of fear from many professionals when we suggest conducting a customer advisory board to elicit the opinions, thoughts, and ideas from their best customers. It is as if they are scared to death of what those customers might actually say—not to mention that the firm won't heed their advice once it is offered. Furthermore, barriers are erected that discourage customer conversation and connection, either through hourly pricing for phone calls and meetings or staying locked up in the office in order to bill hours. We lose sight of the fact that the sole reason we exist is to serve customers outside of our walls.

One organization that does understand producing results, rather than measuring and counting efforts, is the Salvation Army. Drucker has said that it is the most effective organization in the United States. "No one," he says, "even comes close to [the Salvation Army] in respect to clarity of mission, ability to innovate, measurable results, dedication, and putting money to maximum use" (quoted in Watson and Brown, 2001: 16). The Salvation Army began in the United States on March 10, 1880, 15 years after being founded in England by William Booth. Today, it has an annual budget exceeding $2 billion and a workforce (employees and volunteers) of 3.4 million; and that number understates the value of the extra contributions by Army staffers, which *Forbes* magazine estimates, if taken into account, would rank the Salvation Army among the biggest companies in the Forbes 500. Not bad, consider-

ing that, of the original firms listed on the 1896 Dow Jones Industrials, only General
Electric is still in existence. The Salvation Army provides a range of services, and
regards needs as opportunities and problems as future assets. It operates more than
1,600 thrift stores; provides some 65,000 individuals a place to sleep every night;
responds instantly to disasters, and offers relief; and delivers long-term drug and alcohol rehabilitation (at effectiveness rates that make government agencies blush). In
addition, it also provides "state-contracted counseling for former prisoners on parole
or probation; day care for children and seniors; community sports and recreation
programs; medical services; job training and placement; missing person services;
summer and day camps for kids; and visitations to people in institutions" (Ibid: 22).
Of every dollar collected, at least 83 cents goes to these services, with only 17 cents
going for overhead and administration (a number that would make any governmental
agency a defendant in a fraud case).

How does this organization achieve these spectacular results, especially when you
consider that the workforce's average pay is less than $400 per week (not including
Army benefits of housing and transportation, and that's only after 10 years), that they
are not micromanaged, and that not one of them completes a timesheet? As Robert
Watson pointed out in his book on the Salvation Army, they "engage the spirit."
People work hard, real hard, when they believe they are making a contribution beyond
just the bottom line. Here is some of the wisdom from Watson's remarkable book, *The
Most Effective Organization in the U.S.: Leadership Secrets of the Salvation Army*:

> Can a charity really teach leaders who have to operate in the "real world" of business?
> If we truly believe that we all aspire to achieve our best selves beyond mere material
> concerns and that the organizations we build are simply extensions of our aspirations,
> then the difference between for-profit organizations and nonprofit ones is about account-
> ing policies, not about proficiency and effectiveness. The bottom line is this: An organ-
> ization is an organization is an organization (Ibid: 14).
>
> As individuals, Salvationists are as unremarkable as any other man or woman you
> pass on the street. Not smarter, not stronger, not possessed of greater resources. Two
> things distinguish us, and both are available to anyone: an openness to God's grace
> and a commitment to demonstrating it through service to others. Hoard our assets?
> We exhaust them in the effort to reach more and more people. Lower our expectations? We
> are out to save the world. Trust no one? Our best customers—and future partners—are
> drug addicts, prisoners, the enfeebled, and the desperately poor (Ibid: 33).
>
> If we, as Salvation Army leaders, are confident we're in harmony with our spiritual
> mission, we can make just about every other decision by answering questions such as
> these: "What does this have to do with helping hurting people?" and "Is this the best use
> of our resources to help people we're pledged to serve?" If we can't define a policy or a
> proposal or even a longstanding program on those terms, it has to go. Managers in other
> enterprises can generalize these test questions to this one: How is this decision going to
> affect the lives of our customers? That's it. If you can't demonstrate that what you pro-
> pose is going to create value for people, it's probably the wrong choice (Ibid: 75–76).

This is sage advice, and all professional service firm leaders—or those who want
to be leaders—could benefit from reading the story of this organization, as it has many
lessons to teach us. Your firm exists to serve real flesh-and-blood people, not some

mass of demographics known as "the market." As Stanley Marcus (the son of one of the founders of Neiman-Marcus) used to love to point out, no market ever purchased anything in one of his stores, but a lot of customers came in and bought things and made him a rich man. In the final analysis, a business doesn't exist to be efficient, to do cost accounting, or to give people fancy titles and power over the lives of others. It exists to create results and wealth outside of itself. This profound lesson must not be forgotten.

Perhaps one of the reasons we lose sight of this truth is because the language of business is drawn largely from war and sports analogies. In sports, a competition is usually zero-sum, meaning one competitor wins and the other loses. This is not at all relevant in a business setting. Just because your competitors flourish does not mean you lose. There is room for both FedEx and UPS, Airbus and Boeing, Pepsi and Coke, Ford and General Motors; and while their sparring might be mistaken as some war, as John Kay points out, "Not in Pepsi's wildest fantasies does it imagine that the conflict will end in the second burning of Atlanta [Coca-Cola's head office] (quoted in Koch, 2001: 73).

Business is not about annihilating your competition; it is about adding more value to your customers. War destroys, commerce builds. Both sides to a transaction must profit or it would not take place, a point made as far back as Adam Smith in the 1700s. Marketplaces are conversations, derived from the Greek marketplace, the *agora*. It is where buyers and sellers meet to discuss their wares and share visions of the future, where supply and demand intersect at the equilibrium point with a handshake. It is as far removed from war as capitalism is from communism—and perhaps this analogy, too, needs to be tossed onto the ash heap of history.

STUDY SUCCESS: IT LEAVES CLUES

RON Let's go further: Suppose the top partners of all the top 100 firms were randomly reassigned to their competitors; do you think you'd see any major differences or innovations in how customers were served? Consultants to the professions have the opportunity to observe literally thousands of different firms, and over time they begin to share the same operating orthodoxies with every firm they consult with. Is it any wonder we begin to believe we are nothing more than commodities, offering the same services, at basically the same prices, at the same level of service as the firm across the street?

I have learned many things from Peter Drucker, the preeminent management consultant and thinker, but perhaps nothing as profound and enduring as what he wrote in his autobiography *Adventurers of a Bystander*:

> I never heard well enough to be a musician. But I suddenly perceived that I myself would always learn by looking for performance. I suddenly realized that the right method, at least for me, was to look for the thing that worked and for the people who perform. I realized that I, at least, do not learn from mistakes. I have to learn from successes. It took me many years to realize that I had stumbled upon a method. Perhaps I did not fully understand this until, years later, I read—I believe in one of Martin

Buber's early books—the saying of the wise rabbi of the first century: "The good Lord has so created Man that everyone can make every conceivable mistake on his own. Don't ever try to learn from other people's mistakes. Learn what other people do right" (Drucker, 1994: 75).

I have since adopted this method, and indeed, it does work. All of the teachings in this book share success with you, and not just success from the professions, but success from other industries and the entrepreneurs that created them. The new Practice Equation was inspired by companies such as Microsoft, Disney, and FedEx, as well as the teachings of Stanley Marcus, J.W. Marriott, Charles Revson, Henry Ford, and too many others to mention. It is not simply benchmarking, it is benchmarking on steroids, and applies to any endeavor you may undertake in your life. If I wanted to learn the successful traits of a marriage I wouldn't bother talking with Elizabeth Taylor; and if I wanted to become a professional golfer, I would hang around the PGA tour, not the hackers on the municipal golf course on the weekend.

Adam Smith brought this profound insight into his seminal book *An Inquiry into the Nature and Causes of the Wealth of Nations* (1776). He wanted to explain why some countries were wealthy, not why most countries were poor (notice the title isn't *An Inquiry into the Nature and Causes of the Poverty of Nations*). Poverty needs no explanation, nor do we learn much from studying it, since it is the natural condition of humans since they emerged from the cave. What would we do once we discovered the *root causes* of poverty? Create more of it? What needs to be explained is *wealth*, not poverty. What separates a good social scientist from a mediocre one is this understanding. Charles Murray in his 1984 book *Losing Ground* (explaining how the welfare state has failed) pointed this out with respect to why teenagers have babies (a condition, like it or not, that is most certain to end in both mother and child living in poverty). He pointed out that studying teenagers who have babies wouldn't provide the insights needed to understand the phenomenon, because you will hear reasons such as "babies are cute," "sex is fun," and "I wanted someone who would love me unconditionally." Rather, you would be better off to study why the majority of teenagers *don't* have babies (parental opprobrium, social castigation, interferes with college education, etc.). These reasons provide the missing elements into ameliorating the problem. P.J. O'Rourke, the former foreign correspondent for *Rolling Stone* magazine and currently the Mencken Research Fellow at the Cato Institute, sums it up more humorously in the beginning of his book, *Eat the Rich*: *A Treatise on Economics:*

I had one fundamental question about economics: Why do some places prosper and thrive while others just suck? It's not a matter of brains. No part of the earth (with the possible exception of Brentwood) is dumber than Beverly Hills, and the residents are wading in gravy. In Russia, meanwhile, where chess is a spectator sport, they're boiling stones for soup (O'Rourke, 1998: 1).

We will follow this approach in this book, studying successful practices from organizations that are effective at what they do, and our scope will be as far as it is wide. Wisdom is timeless, and many of the lessons shared herein are from what I call the "entrepreneur heaven," populated by those creative and imaginative risk takers who launched enterprises that many of us still patronize to this day, who had the vision and fortitude to test their ideas in the free market, and be judged solely—and either rewarded or rebuked—by their customers. While this characteristic cannot be captured in an algebraic equation, it is certainly one of the traits of effectiveness.

WHAT BUSINESS ARE YOU IN?

RON What business are you in appears to be a disarmingly simple question, yet as Peter Drucker points out: "Nothing may seem simpler or more obvious than to answer what a company's business is. A steel mill makes steel, a railroad runs trains to carry freight and passengers, an insurance company underwrites fire risks. Indeed, the question looks so simple that it is seldom raised; the answer seems so obvious that it is seldom given. Actually 'what is our business' is almost always a difficult question that can be answered only after hard thinking and studying. And the right answer is usually anything but obvious" (quoted in Flaherty, 1999: 108).

All business students are familiar with the story of the railroad magnates who defined themselves as being in the *railroad* business, thereby missing the opportunities in bus and airplane transport, on which they might have capitalized if they thought of themselves as being in the *transportation* business. A similar analogy could be made with Black & Decker: If they think of themselves as in the drill and drill bit business (and they are in much more than this, I'm only using a narrow example), when what the customer wants is a hole, not a drill or a drill bit, then they will most likely miss the opportunities in laser beams, which can also put holes in things. If Walt Disney had defined his company's core ideology as making animated cartoons, he never would have made movies and built theme parks, vacation resorts, cruise ships, and so on. He defined Disney as being in the business of "selling happiness." This defining process is done in part by looking outside of the business to figure out how the customer benefits from what is purchased, the realities that exist in the marketplace, and from internally understanding its core ideology—what it stands for.

Many professional service firms have never even considered this question because it seems so deceptively simple; yet having a core ideology is essential to creating a firm that will live on into the future. In their landmark book *Built to Last: Successful Habits of Visionary Companies*, James C. Collins and Jerry I. Porras, explain the importance of sticking to your core ideology:

In their 1992 book *In Search of Excellence*, Peters and Waterman counseled "Stick to the knitting," meaning, in their words, "the odds for excellent performance seem strongly to favor those companies that stay reasonably close to the businesses they know." On the surface, such a precept does not square with the evolutionary perspective we've presented. Indeed, if 3M had defined its knitting as mining or sandpaper, then 3M wouldn't be what it is today—nor would we have those fabulous Post-it tape flags that have helped us keep organized while writing this book. From our standpoint, thank goodness 3M didn't stick to its knitting! Furthermore, Norton stuck much closer to its knitting than 3M—and just look at the results. Zenith, too, stuck much closer to its knitting (television and radio) than Motorola—right into decline. J&J had no consumer goods experience when it began selling baby powder. Marriott had no background in hotels when it branched into that business. HP had no expertise in the computer business in the 1960s when it launched its first computer product. Disney had no knowledge of the theme park business when it created Disneyland. IBM had no background in electronics when it moved into computers. Boeing had virtually no experience in the commercial aircraft business when it did the 707. Had American Express stuck to its knitting (freight express), it probably wouldn't exist today [let alone own accounting firms].

  We're not saying that evolutionary progress equals wanton diversification, or even that a focused business strategy is necessarily bad. Wal-Mart, for example, has thus far remained resolutely focused on one industry—discount retailing—while simultaneously stimulating evolution within that narrow focus. Nor are we saying that the concept of "stick to the knitting" makes no sense. The real question is: *What* is the "knitting" in a visionary company? Our answer: its core ideology (Collins and Porras, 1997: 186–87).

As you can see, core ideology is an important question for any firm to answer. One could argue that if the accounting profession had obstinately "stuck to its knitting," it never would have branched out into tax preparation, let alone consulting. But if you define your core ideology as "helping our customers achieve their business objectives," then tax and consulting work are natural extensions of auditing services. In 2000, at a conference titled "The New Entertainment Era," sponsored by the Cato Institute, Christie Hefner, chairwoman of Playboy Enterprises, made the following remarks that go right to the heart of how important it is to understand what business we are in:

  It has been said that a brand name is like a theme park and your product is the souvenir. If the brand is really good, then it isn't just the identifiable logo of a product. It is an attitude, a point of view, something that people identify with. Some people have argued that even some of the most successful brands today, Coca-Cola and Levi's, will ultimately die if they remain captive to a single product. When my father started *Playboy* in 1953, he certainly didn't envision building an empire, but he had some very good instincts about things that would turn out to be very important in terms of ultimately creating a brand. And one of those was the idea of a magazine representing not just a package of entertainment but a lifestyle promoted and personified by Hef himself—the Playboy mansion and Black Bunny plane. [When I took over the company in the 1980s], we decided that the most leverageable asset of our company was not its publishing expertise but our brand, and that our growth would not come by launching or acquiring other magazines, as many others had done. In retrospect, that seems like a fairly obvious opportunity, but I would point out that today there is a hugely popular music TV network, but it's not called Rolling Stone—it's called MTV. There is a hugely popular sports network, but it's not called Sports Illustrated—it's called ESPN. And there is a hugely popular news network, but it is not called Time—it's called CNN. So we have reconfigured the company, from one in which the magazine was at the heart to one in which the brand is at the heart (Excerpted from the *Cato Policy Report*, January/February 2001, p. 6).

I am not arguing here for "branding" your firm, as there are a whole host of problems with that strategy, as many marketing consultants to the profession have pointed out for a long time (especially Bruce Marcus and Troy Waugh). I agree with their opinions on branding: beyond the Big 4 accounting firms it is very hard to brand a small local firm, since customers identify with the people they have relationships with, not with a brand name. If you doubt this, why is it when someone leaves a smaller firm, he or she is able to take away the customers he or she serviced?

PAUL Look at it another way: Would your clients really notice if you died today? Truth is, they probably would. They'd send messages of condolences to your family and friends; they'd support the people who needed their support; and (depending on the state of the weather on that day) they'd turn up at your funeral—or at least the wake! And then guess what? They'd go to someone else in your firm and say, "So who's going to do my work now?" And someone would step up to the plate and do the work that you used to do. What's even more interesting is this: the clients would be delighted with what the new person does.

Assuming that scenario, two key questions arise: Why don't I run the firm now so that it doesn't depend on me? Why don't I run the firm now as if I had expired? Put more simply: Why don't I run the firm now to match the actual reality of what would happen if I died? When you do that, you can then treat the fact that you're still alive as a bonus, but—and it's a big but—you modify what you do. In fact, it might even pay you to metamorphose into a bumblebee.

Let me explain why by relating a story Walt Disney told of being asked by a child if he drew Mickey Mouse. He had to admit he did not draw anymore. "Then you think up all the jokes and ideas?" the child prompted. No, he said, he didn't do that, either. Finally, the child asked, "Mr. Disney, just what do you do?" He answered, "Well, sometimes I think of myself as a little bee. I go from one area of the studio to another and gather pollen and sort of stimulate everybody. I guess that's the job I do."

Good thinking Walt! And of course, we miss him just like your clients will miss you, too. But we love the legacy (the bits of pollen, if you will) that Disney left behind— empowered people sharing a truly magic culture and passion for what they do.

Isn't that really what we all want? We'll talk about that in more detail later.

RON Looking at the bigger picture, we're arguing here that your core ideology and vision are an important component in defining exactly what it is your firm stands for, who it serves, what it does, and most importantly, what it will not do. Having niches is completely consistent with this vision, as firms can no longer be all things to all customers. As Art Bowman, editor of *Bowman's Accounting Report* and *Bowman's 100,* says, "For many years it has become clear, the firms that are focused make the money. We find every year the divide between the haves and the have-nots in the accounting industry gets wider because of this one issue (quoted in Waugh, 2001: 264).

Spend the time necessary to answer the question "what is the business?" for your firm. Develop a core ideology, based upon the realities that exist in your customers' lives and how they benefit from what you do. Whatever you determine, understand that your firm, no matter how small or big, is an intellectual capital company, and that is what it ultimately leverages to create value and wealth for your customers—and success for you.

WHERE DO PROFITS COME FROM?

A ship in harbor is safe—but that is not what ships are for.

—John A. Shedd

RON In seminars around the world, we have presented to participants the following factors of production in any economy, and the type of income derived therefrom:

Land = Rents

Labor = Salaries and Wages

Capital = Interest, Dividends, and Capital Gains

We then ask a deceptively simple question: Where do profits come from? Inevitably someone will joke, "billable hours." Of course, considering that accountants have been living under the old Practice Equation for two generations, perhaps that answer is no joke. Nonetheless, the real answer is that profits come from *risk*. The word "entrepreneur" comes from the French word, *entreprendre*, meaning "to undertake." It's the basis for the English word "enterprise." The great French economist J.-B. Say coined the word to mean "venture capitalist" or "adventurer." But not just entrepreneurs make profits; so do established enterprises.

When a business engages in innovation, it is taking a risk. In Italian the word "risk" derives from *risicare*, which means "to dare," which implies a choice not a fate, as Peter L. Bernstein points out in his outstanding study of risk, *Against the Odds*. In Arabic "risk" means "earning one's daily bread." In other words, risk is good. There are four responses when confronted with risk: avoid it, reduce it, transfer it, or accept it. In the final analysis, a business cannot eliminate risk, as that would eliminate profits. The goal is to take calculated risks and choose them wisely. The problem in many professional service firms is that they are playing in order not to lose, rather than to win. By setting a nice comfortable floor on their earnings (via the cost-plus pricing mechanism of hourly rates, derived from adding a desired net income to their overhead), they have placed an artificial ceiling over their heads as well. This is self-imposed, and it comes from the attempt to avoid risk and uncertainty (which is very costly in terms of lost opportunities). Risk avoidance is the antithesis to a successful enterprise, where the goal should be to maximize opportunities rather than to minimize risk.

Peter Drucker classified risk into three categories: the affordable, the nonaffordable, and the compulsory. First, there was the risk a business could afford to take. If it succeeded at the innovation, it would not achieve major results; and if it failed, it would not do great corporate damage. Second, there was the risk a business could not afford to take. This risk usually involved an innovation that the company lacked the knowledge to implement, and usually would end up building the competition's business. Third, there was the risk a business could not afford not to take. Failure to undertake this innovation meant there might not be a business several years hence (quoted in Flaherty, 1999: 172).

Naturally, in this book we advocate the third type of risk taking. That is, taking those risks that will spur the firm to higher levels of effectiveness and profitability. Too often in professional firms, risk taking is seen as a negative, a reckless use of resources that are better spent on partner draws. Nothing could be further from the truth. Committing a portion of today's resources to future expectations certainly entails risk, but since that is the source of profits—not to mention innovation, dynamism and economic growth—it is a process that must become systemic in the firm of the future's culture. Economywide, profits may constitute only 10 percent of what the American economy produces, but in terms of creating an incentive to effectively produce the other 90 percent, they are essential. And profits are derived from risk; complacency is not an option.

This, by the way, is another point you may care to note about the new Practice Equation, as it makes it look as if profitability appears by effectively leveraging IC at the right price, but misses the importance of risk. We must always remember that profits, ultimately, are derived from risk taking, and no equation, no matter how complex and intricate, will ever be able to capture the essence of an entrepreneur.

SUMMARY AND CONCLUSIONS

This chapter has laid the groundwork for the rest of the book. We have covered a lot of material and have presented some radical—Latin for getting back to the root—ideas. We have argued that the old Practice Equation is not worthy of our noble profession, that it leverages the wrong things, and doesn't explain the elements that comprise our success. The new Practice Equation does all of these things and is a worthy model for a proud profession. And while there are still shortcomings in the equation—it doesn't answer why we are in business, what business are we in, and where profits come from—it is a starting point for understanding the drivers of success for the firm of the future.

Professional firms are intellectual capital organizations, and it is time they began acting as if they understood this fact, rather than trying to constantly enhance efficiency by treating their human capital as if they had no mind of their own, redolent of the days of Frederik Taylor's time-and-motion studies. Humans are not simply machines that exist to bill hours, and the old Practice Equation keeps us mired in this mentality. We believe we can—must—do better than the opportunities presented by an antiquated model.

When we first publicly presented and contrasted the new Practice Equation with the old one, a CPA explained at the break why she thought the new equation was so superior to the old. Essentially, she said, "Your equation presents so many more factors that enable a firm to achieve its objectives than the old one did. It is like being freed from a cage that has restricted our firm for decades."

It is our fervent hope that this new paradigm has a similar affect on all who study it, and will change their behavior as a result. The old paradigm is indeed far too restricting, and it doesn't represent the realities of the current marketplace in which professionals operate. The firms of the future must lead the profession by following a model that is worthy of its proud heritage.

4

INTELLECTUAL CAPITAL: THE CHIEF SOURCE OF WEALTH

An investment in knowledge pays the best interest.

—Benjamin Franklin, *Poor Richard's Almanack*

In 1974, then nineteen-year-old Bill Gates and twenty-one-year-old Paul Allen founded a company called Traf-O-Data to read computer cards from machines that monitored traffic flow for local municipalities. In its first year, the company that was ultimately to become Microsoft generated $20,000 in revenues and had three employees. Presently, depending on the day, Microsoft's market capitalization ranks higher than all but nine nations' gross national product (Spain ranks just above it), with 40,000 employees in more than 60 countries and annual revenues of $20 billion.

RON How, in a little more than one generation, did Gates and Allen build a company that exceeds the value—in terms of market capitalization—of behemoths such as General Motors, Ford, Boeing, Sears, Lockheed, Kellogg's, Safeway, Marriott (including Ritz-Carlton), Kodak, Caterpillar, Deere, USX, Weyerhaeuser, Union Pacific, and others—again, depending on the day of analysis—*combined*? Certainly Microsoft's success cannot be explained by the old Practice Equation, as explained in Chapter 2. It did not leverage billable hours and create a pyramid business model. What it did leverage is intellectual capital (IC), the chief source of all wealth.

That is the central tenet of this book, and one the new Practice Equation is designed to explain. We posit that today's professional service firm is no different from Microsoft, in that its chief source of wealth is its ability to create, generate, disseminate, and sell IC. Microsoft encodes its IC into software, and professional service firms embed their IC into the product and service offerings delivered to customers to help them achieve their business and personal goals. From an economic perspective, it is the IC that is generating the wealth, not the means of producing the IC (billing hours versus developing software code). The ability of IC to generate wealth is not well understood, especially by a profession that is rooted in the old Practice Equation of hours and realization rates. The role IC plays in generating wealth is not well understood, or accurately measured, for that matter. Generally Accepted Accounting Principles (GAAP) do a horrendous job of valuing IC, as most of the cost of creating IC is treated as a period expense for GAAP purposes. This explains how Microsoft's GAAP assets, as reported on its balance sheet, account for less than 10 percent of its market capitalization. The point here is not to make an argument for better measurements, a subject we will return to later; the fact is—and this causes major cognitive dissonance among accountants—the most important things in life cannot be measured. Thus, we don't necessarily need better *measurements*, we need better *understanding*.

Today, intellectual capital is sometimes thought of as nothing more than another buzzword (witness that it is on the list of random business buzzwords used in the "random mission statement generator" on Dilbert's website, www.dilbert.com/comics/dilbert/career/html/ questions). As pointed out in Chapter 3, however, IC is not about the "new economy." IC has always been the chief driver of wealth, as economists have argued since the term "human capital" was first uttered (sometime in the 1960s). Wealth doesn't reside in tangible assets, or money; it resides in the IC that exists in the human spirit, and since this is so hard to measure (how does one measure the ambition of Steve Jobs to "change the world"), we tend to ignore it until it becomes so obvious—as in the case of Microsoft—that we have to recognize that our old theories of wealth are no longer relevant.

Ideas have consequences, but ideas are everywhere. It is knowledge that is rare, and it is those with the right knowledge who are able to generate enormous wealth by taking the risks necessary to capitalize on it, from Bill Gates and Paul Allen to Andrew Carnegie, Thomas Edison, and Walt Disney. Even Adam Smith's famous pin factory contained the idea of "division labor," an enormous wealth-generating idea, followed by ideas such as Scientific Management and the assembly line, the latter certainly capitalized on by Henry Ford.

THE PHYSICAL FALLACY

RON For centuries, economists have been explaining the "physical fallacy"—that is, the belief that wealth resides in tangible things, such as gold, land, raw materials, and so forth—and it seems as if we still do not understand this basic economic concept. We seem to think that *matter* is more important than *minds*, while it is the exact opposite. Taiwan, Hong Kong, and Singapore have no "natural resources," yet they all have a higher standard of living than Russia and Indonesia, both rich in natural resources.

From a corporate perspective, a revealing episode in the early career of Walt Disney may illustrate the physical fallacy on a smaller and more human scale.

Back in the 1920s, when Disney first emerged as a cartoonist, his early successes led him to found a studio and to employ other artists to draw the thousands of pictures required for animated cartoon movies. Disney Studios was particularly successful with an early cartoon character called Oswald Rabbit, whose copyright was held by a movie distributor, rather than by Disney. This distributor decided to eliminate the need to pay Disney by hiring away his cartoonists and both producing and marketing the product. From the standpoint of the physical fallacy, Disney was superfluous. He neither drew the cartoons nor transported the films to theaters nor showed them to the public. The distributor, with the Disney staff and the copyright on Disney's character, expected to profit from his coup. But without Disney's ideas, the previously valuable character suddenly became worthless as a moneymaker at the box office. What had really been sold all along were Disney's ideas and fantasies. The physical things—the drawings, the film, and the theaters—were merely vehicles. It was only a matter of time before another set of vehicles could be arranged and the ideas incorporated in a new character—Mickey Mouse— which Disney copyrighted in his own name.

Many of the products which create a modern standard of living are only the physical incorporations of ideas—not only the ideas of Edison or Ford but the ideas of innumerable anonymous people who figure out the design of supermarkets, the location of gasoline stations, and the million mundane things on which our material well-being depends. It is those ideas that are crucial, not the physical act of carrying them out. Societies, which have more people carrying out physical acts and fewer people supplying ideas, do not have higher standards of living. Quite the contrary. Yet the physical fallacy continues on, undaunted by this or any other evidence (Sowell, 1980: 71–72).

The physical fallacy explains why Andrew Carnegie once stated in total confidence: "You can take away our factories, take away our trade, our avenues of transportation, and our money—leave us nothing but our organization—and in four years we would reestablish ourselves" (quoted in Branden, 1998: 35). It is no different in a professional service firm. Your wealth-creating capacity resides in your IC—that of your human, structural and social capital.

THE SCARCEST RESOURCE OF ALL

RON The distinction between ideas and knowledge may be subtle, but perhaps management consultant Sid Caesar clarified it best when he quipped: "The guy who invented the first wheel was an idiot. They guy who invented the other three, he was a genius" (quoted in Stewart, 2001: 90). Specific knowledge is rare, despite all of the glib generalities of knowledge being everywhere. Thomas Sowell points out the difference between "general expertise" and highly specific knowledge with this historical example:

One of the classic disasters of government planning involved the British government's attempts to grow peanuts in colonial Rhodesia after World War II. Although this scheme turned out to be a costly failure, ordinary farmers around the world had been deciding for generations where and how to grow peanuts, each on his own particular land, whose individual characteristics were known directly from personal experience. Why was this government plan to grow peanuts such an economic disaster, when poorly educated or even illiterate farmers have been able to do what highly educated experts were not able to do? The farmers had highly specific knowledge, which is often far more important than general "expertise" (Sowell, 2000: 250).

In his seminal work on knowledge, *Knowledge and Decisions*, Sowell delineates various kinds of ideas by their relationship to the authentication process: "There are ideas systematically prepared for authentication ('theories'), ideas not derived from any systematic process ('visions'), ideas which could not survive any reasonable authentication process ('illusions'), ideas which exempt themselves from any authentication process ('myths'), ideas which have already passed authentication processes ('facts'), as well as ideas known to have failed—or certain to fail—such processes ('falsehoods'—both mistakes and lies)" (Sowell, 1980: 4–5).

In a business enterprise, two sources of profit are possible: an *economic* profit and an *epistemological* profit, the latter of which has the ability to advance specific knowledge. The market, meaning the sovereign consumer, is the authentication process Sowell alludes to, at least as it relates to product and service offerings. Any offering not valued by consumers will be ruthlessly repudiated in a free market environment, whereas ideas tossed around capriciously by social scientists—such as Marx—have no swift or certain authentication process, especially if they can appeal to enough people's emotional predispositions.

The interesting thing about the difference between an advanced civilization and a primitive one is not that each person has more knowledge but actually that he or she requires far less. A primitive savage must be able to produce a wide range of goods and services for him- or herself and his or her family, whereas an auto mechanic today can get by with just knowing his area of expertise, as he will rely on the specific knowledge of others to provide his wood, food, clothing and medical services. A photographer during the Civil War had to have far more knowledge of the photographic process than today's digital camera user.

Another way to think of your firm is as an organization that knows how to do things. Knowledge, unlike physical and financial assets, is what economists refer to as a *nonrival asset*, meaning more than one person can use it at a time. When United Airline's assigns a Boeing 777 to the San Francisco-London route, that same plane cannot be used for the San Francisco-Tokyo route, but you reading this book doesn't exclude someone else from reading another copy of it, at the same time even. When I give you the tie off my shirt, now you have it and I don't; but when I give you an idea—or valuable knowledge—now we both have it, can expand upon it, and make it even more valuable. This is why Stanford economist Paul Romer—a leading thinker in knowledge and growth economics—has called knowledge the only unlimited resource, as it grows with use. Thomas Stewart, a leading thinker and writer on IC at *Fortune*, sums it up this way: "Sell me a cake and you no longer have it. Sell me the recipe and we both have it. Where intellectual assets and intangible outputs are concerned, you can have your cake and eat it, too. But you cannot take it back. A seller can repossess a car, but not a fact" (Stewart, 1997: 171). Do you think Chef Emeril Lagasse understands this concept?

This was precisely Sam Walton's strategy with Wal-Mart: he substituted *knowledge* for *inventory*. If you think about it, inventory *is* a substitute for knowledge. If you knew exactly how many steaks, cans of beans, and other food items you were going to use in the next month, you wouldn't need a pantry full of these items. If a soldier knew exactly how many bullets he or she was going to fire before going into a battle, he or she could lighten his or her load by not carrying any extra. It is our lack of knowledge that necessitates inventory. By giving his suppliers real-time information, Walton was able to diminish the enormous transportation, distribution, and carrying costs associated with inventory, and pass along these savings to the end customer.

Japanese automobile manufacturers did the same thing when they created just-in-time (JIT) inventory systems, largely as a result of their physical space limitations and lack of resources that could be tied up in inventories. In the publishing business, Alfred A. Knopf's sardonic line is "Gone today, here tomorrow," pointing out the high return rate of most books. "Do you keep a copy of every book you print?" a lady asked British publisher Jonathan Cape at a London cocktail party. "Madam," he replied, "I keep thousands" (quoted in Vanderbilt II, 1999: 188).

Perhaps one of the best examples of leveraging IC in order to create wealth was given by a straight man for a very funny woman—Desi Arnaz, Lucille Ball's husband. *I Love Lucy* was certainly one of televisions first great sitcoms. Arnaz was born in Cuba in 1917, but it wasn't until the 1950s that Arnaz took a risk that was to have an enormous payoff. In return for a salary cut of $1,000 per each of 39 episodes, CBS gave the pair sole ownership rights over the show, since in 1951 most television shows were shot live and only preserved on kinescopes. Hence, television executives back then thought that yesterday's shows had as much value as yesterday's newspapers. *I Love Lucy* was the first show that was filmed, not shot live, so there was something worth selling after the original broadcast was over. Today, nearly half a century later, a single episode goes for $100,000. Jerry Seinfeld learned from success, and has banked $225 million from the sale of syndication rights for his sitcom.

Considering the wealth inherent to stories and songs, supposedly the most ephemeral of products, it's not surprising that Scarlett O'Hara and Rhett Butler are worth far more than cars made in the same year as *Gone With the Wind*, 1939.

When the discovery of new valuable knowledge and technical know-how combine, you have the leverage necessary to generate new wealth for your customers. As Walt Disney explained when asked about the secret to his success: "There's really no secret about our approach. We keep moving forward—opening new doors and doing new things—because we are curious. And curiosity keeps leading us down new paths. We're always exploring and experimenting . . . we call it *imagineering* [a term Disney coined]—the blending of creative imagination and technical know-how" (Disney Institute, 2001: 111). Specific knowledge may be scarce, but within your firm there resides all sorts of specific, applicable knowledge. The goal is to leverage this knowledge and use it to create new knowledge that can be validated in the marketplace by your customers. In turn, this becomes your firm's IC, composed of human capital, structural capital, and social capital. This is the ultimate fulcrum for the firm of the future.

THE THREE TYPES OF IC

Ron The wealth-creating ability of intangible assets over physical assets is indisputable as we move from capital-based enterprises to knowledge-based enterprises. An excellent example of this is American Airline's Sabre reservation and information system.

On October 11, 1996, AMR Corporation, the parent company of American Airlines, sold (an equity carve-out) 18 percent of its Sabre subsidiary in an initial public offering that valued Sabre at $3.3 billion. On the previous day, AMR had a total market value (including Sabre) of about $6.5 billion. Thus, a reservation system generating income from travel agents and other users of its services constituted half of the market value of AMR, equaling the value of the world's second largest airline, owning 650 airplanes (in 1996) and other physical and financial assets, including valuable landing rights. A $40 million R&D investment in Sabre during the 1960s and 1970s mushroomed into a market value of $3.3 billion in the mid-1990s. By October 30, 1999, Sabre's share in the total market value of AMR increased to 60 percent, demonstrating the value creation potential (scalability) of intangibles relative to that of intangibles (Lev, 2001: 24).

While the airplanes owned by American Airlines show up on its balance sheet, Sabre was nowhere to be found. A teacher once asked Yogi Berra, "Don't you know anything?" and he said, "I don't even suspect anything." GAAP's deficiencies in measuring intellectual capital notwithstanding, for our purposes we are going to separate a firm's IC into three categories, as was discussed in Chapter 3, and as originally proposed by Karl-Erik Sveiby—a leading thinker in knowledge theory—in 1989:

Human capital

Structural capital

Social capital (customers, suppliers, networks, referral sources, alumni, etc.)

We will explore each of these in greater detail in the next three chapters. The crucial point to understand at this juncture is that it is the *interplay* among the three types of IC that generates wealth-creating opportunities for your firm. Human capital, for example, can grow in two ways: when the firm utilizes more of what each person knows and when people know more things that are useful to the firm and/or its customers. And since knowledge is a "nonrival" good—meaning two people can possess it at the same time—knowledge that is shared is knowledge that is effectively *doubled* throughout the organization. That is why former Hewlett-Packard CEO Lew Platt said: "If HP knew what HP knows, we would be three times as profitable."

Since knowledge can be found almost anywhere, and it does not have to be newly created, it is critical that we incorporate social capital into our firm's IC, because defining our knowledge solely by our human and structural capital is too inward-looking. The boundaries of a firm do not just keep knowledge in; they keep it out as well. By expanding our definition of IC to the social environment within which a firm operates gives us many more opportunities to leverage our knowledge. This is why British Petroleum gives a "Thief of the Year" award to the person who has "stolen" the best ideas, and Texas Instruments has a "Not Invented Here, but I Did It Anyway" award for ideas taken inside or outside the company. Knowledge companies constantly celebrate learning, not just the application of knowledge to the services it offers its customers. Professional service firms have to do much more than merely extract eight hours of work from their human capital; they have to leverage their minds as well. This requires a different level of thinking and a totally different set of metrics to measure the effectiveness of firm learning.

Most knowledge is created and owned by people, and thus resides in the human capital of any firm. Converting human capital into structural capital is one of the major roles of a chief knowledge officer (CKO). All of the Big 4 accounting firms have now hired a CKO; and by 1997, a fifth of the *Fortune* 500 also have created this position. John Peetz, former CKO for Ernst & Young, summed up his knowledge mission this way: "For us knowledge management is critical. It's one of our four core processes—sell work, do work, manage people, and manage knowledge." As Thomas Stewart further explained, "In his self-written job description, Peetz outlined three responsibilities for a CKO: evangelizing about the value of sharing knowledge; running and backing projects that find, publish, and distribute knowledge around the firm; and managing a staff of about 200 people, mostly in the firm's Center for Business Knowledge in Cleveland, and a firmwide infrastructure of Web sites" (Stewart, 2001: 82).

I have serious reservations about "managing people," especially since we are talking about professionals, whom I firmly believe cannot be "managed" in the traditional sense. Nonetheless, the essential role of a CKO is to capture the knowledge that exists within the minds of the people who work in his or her firm. As Ikujiro Nonaka and Hirotaka Takeuchi point out in their book *The Knowledge-Creating Company: How Japanese Companies Create the Dynamics of Innovation*, "The individual is the 'creator' of knowledge and the organization is the 'amplifier' of knowledge" (Nonaka and Takeuchi, 1995: 240).

This is no easy task since we must draw a distinction between *explicit* and *tacit* knowledge. Explicit knowledge can be documented and kept somewhere, in a manual, filing cabinet, Web site, intranet, and so on. This type of knowledge usually comprises a firm's structural capital. Tacit knowledge is a different animal. *Tacit* in Latin means "to be silent or secret." This is why it is so hard to explain how to ride a bike, or to swim, or play golf like Tiger Woods. You could read all of the explicit knowledge—in books, for instance—on the subject, but until you actually did it, your understanding would be severely limited. Explicit and tacit knowledge complement each other, as in Latin *explicit* means "to unfold"—to be open, to arrange, to explain. Germans say *Fingerspitzengefuehl*, "a feeling in the fingertips," which is similar to tacit knowledge (Stewart, 2001: 123). Another useful way to think about the difference is that information can be digitized while knowledge is intrinsic to humans. It is usually a totally different experience to read an author's book than it is to have a chance to talk to him or her about it. The latter will give you a much richer, contextual feel for the explicit knowledge documented in the book, and in some cases may even be more valuable. Or consider the difference between reading a customer file—tax returns, financial statements, and so forth—and talking with that customer in person.

This type of knowledge transfer is a "social" process between individuals, and is especially important in professional service firms where so much of the IC is "sticky" tacit knowledge. Nonaka and Takeuchi postulate four different modes of knowledge conversion:

1. From tacit knowledge to tacit knowledge, which we call socialization;

2. From tacit knowledge to explicit knowledge, or externalization;

3. From explicit knowledge to explicit knowledge, or combination; and

4. From explicit knowledge to tacit knowledge, or internalization (Nonaka and Takeuchi, 1995: 62).

All four are important to capture in a firm, but how much time does the average firm spend in documenting and sharing what it knows when its primary metric is how many billable hours did you have last week? How often do firms take the time to mentor their colleagues on the importance of learning and sharing knowledge? "He's learning me all his experience," as Yogi Berra said about Bill Dickey. No doubt this gets done in most firms, but it is on an ad hoc and as-needed basis, rather than as a systemized, measured part of the performance criteria of team members. There is simply no mechanism in most firms to reward continuous learning, the sharing of tacit knowledge with peers, or externalizing tacit knowledge to explicit knowledge by writing an After-Action Review (a report borrowed from the U.S. Army, which will be discussed in further detail in Chapter 6) on complex engagements. Because most firms are so caught up in charging hours and working on their income statements, they are not building their balance sheet—and the primary asset is the knowledge that exists in the firm. Yet capturing this type of knowledge would be incredibly valuable to the firm in terms of leveraging, ability to delegate to less-experienced team members, and as a way to increase the structural capital of the firm just in case certain human capital investors decide not to return to work.

Managing explicit knowledge is certainly easier than managing tacit knowledge, since the latter exists in the heads of professionals and professionals are difficult to manage, to say the least. Nor is it possible to capture 100 percent of the tacit knowledge that exists in each team member's head, but that's not the goal. The goal is to capture a majority of it and place it somewhere (for example, in a file, on an intranet, a Web portal, etc.) where anyone else in the firm can get it when they need it. This way we are not constantly reinventing the wheel, but rather trying to figure out the most effective way to place the other three wheels in such a manner so we can get to our destination. Thomas Stewart gives this artful advice for managing explicit knowledge: "Assemble it; validate it; as much as possible, standardize and simplify it; keep it up to date; leverage it; make sure everyone who needs it knows that it exists, where to get it, and how to use it; automate and accelerate the processes of retrieving and applying it; add to it; sue any bastard who steals it" (Stewart, 2001: 124).

Consultant Stan Davis likes to make his clients think about creating "smart products," and to that end he poses an exercise: "What would a Coke machine like to know?" (Ibid: 146). Some of the more obvious answers would be its inventory and the phone number of its distributor so it could restock when needed, its physical location, the repairperson's phone number to call when it's broken or malfunctioning, and whether or not the money fed into it is real or counterfeit. Today, there are some vending machines equipped with technology that enables you to purchase a Coke with your cell phone. Another important piece of knowledge—and Coca-Cola actually announced this policy in a press release, but then decided to repeal it after it got negative publicity—is the temperature outside so it could adjust the price of drinks on hot days. The point of the exercise is to try and turn tacit knowledge into explicit knowledge. Your firm can do the same thing, with some creative thought.

IS ALL THIS STUFF GOOD?

RON Before we leave this important topic of IC and delve more into the details of each component in the next chapters, it is necessary to explain something that may, at first impression, not seem obvious. When IC is discussed, it is normally done in a very positive context, and most of the examples that we use are from successes in leveraging IC, such as Microsoft or the Sabre reservation system. Naturally, not all R&D projects, or new products, are successful, and in fact, the failure rate is astonishingly high. Most new drugs fail, as do most consumer products and books published. Investments in intangibles contain much higher levels of risk and more uncertainty than in tangible assets. If my software product fails, those costs are usually gone for good, unless I can somehow leverage the knowledge I gained into another attempt (this is the second form of potential gain from a venture, the *epistemological* profit mentioned earlier—meaning an advancement of knowledge). But if I purchase an office building or a mall, and it fails, I can at least recover a portion of my investment.

But that is not the main point to make here and now. What is important here is that there is such a thing as *negative* human capital, *negative* structural capital, and *negative* social capital. Certainly this sounds counterintuitive, but it is nonetheless true. Not everything we know is good. Think of the IC that a thief has; it is knowledge in the sense that he or she knows how to perform his or her craft just as much as United Airlines knows how to fly planes and transport people around the world. But that does not make the knowledge valuable; and with respect to thieves, the social loss they create is a societal negative.

Think of countries that doggedly adhere to the principles of socialism or Marxism, even though both of these theories of social organization have been repudiated by empirical evidence. There has been enormous negative social capital built up over the past four decades in Castro's Cuba, just as there was in the former Soviet Union. As the latter struggles to make its transition to a free market economy, these negative legacies are being felt (lack of secure private property rights, no efficient judicial system to adjudicate disputes, no efficient banking and credit system, and so forth). When President Ronald Reagan was asked what he thought of the Berlin Wall during a visit to Germany, he gestured at the wall and said succinctly, "It's as ugly as the idea behind it" (Morris, 1999: 461).

Examples of negative intellectual capital in your firm would include a rigid adherence to old methods that are hindering your people from achieving their potential. High on this list would be the billable hour, cost-plus pricing, timesheets, lack of delegation, and other forms of negative IC that have embedded themselves into the culture of not just individual firms, but the profession as a whole. These ideas have been leveraged throughout each type of knowledge discussed herein—human, structural, and certainly social—and have become part of our tacit and explicit knowledge systems. One of the duties of this book is to point out that these legacy systems are indeed *negative* forms of IC and need to be replaced in the firm of the future.

SUMMARY AND CONCLUSIONS

In this chapter we have discussed that the chief source of wealth in any economy is intellectual capital; and for purposes of discussing the firm of the future, we have separated IC into three specific components: human, structural, and social capital. We have alluded to the fact that IC is not accurately measured in standard GAAP financial statements, and that our ability to capture the value of intangible assets is severely limited. Throughout history, the "physical fallacy" was an idea that reigned supreme; that is, the notion that wealth is embedded in physical tangible assets. We also discussed how specific knowledge is the scarcest resource of all, and that it is the *interplay* of the three types of IC—human, structural, and social—that generates wealth. Finally, we explored the distinction between explicit and tacit knowledge and how important it is for firms to capture, utilize, and leverage both, and how some forms of IC can indeed be negative and harmful.

The ultimate drama in economics is acted out in the area of human capital, which we will turn to next as it relates to the effective functioning of the firm of the future.

5

HUMAN CAPITAL: YOUR PEOPLE ARE NOT ASSETS, THEY ARE VOLUNTEERS

The most valuable of all capital is that invested in human beings.
—Alfred Marshall, *Principles of Economics*, 1890

*In the knowledge society, the most probable assumption for organizations—
and certainly the assumption on which they have to conduct their
affairs—is that they need knowledge workers far more
than knowledge workers need them.*
—Peter Drucker (quoted in David Boyle,
The Sum of Our Discontent, 2001)

The term *human capital* was first used by Nobel Prize-winning economist Theodore W. Schultz in a 1961 article in *American Economic Review*. His basic thesis was that investments in human capital should be accounted for in the same manner as investments in plant and machinery. This wasn't exactly a new concept, but it did lead to an intersection of the economics and accounting profession, at least in theory. The economists were basically saying that accountants should treat investments in people the same as they treat investments in things; but we accountants never learned the lesson, and went on treating employees as nothing but expenses.

RON The obvious challenge is that investments in tangible, physical assets can be counted and comprehended, but those in people cannot. It is as if accountants would value the average human being at $3 since that is the approximate worth of our various chemical components. It's hard to see the label when you are in the wine bottle. Human capital is like the dark matter of the cosmos: we know it's out there but we can't measure it. Once again, Peter Drucker was at the forefront of thought when he coined both the terms *knowledge society* and *knowledge worker* in his 1968 book, *The Age of Discontinuity*. He posited it was the G.I. Bill of Rights—which made available higher education to some 2,332,000 veterans, and was certainly the largest single investment in human capital up to that time—that caused the shift to a knowledge society. Presently, less than one-fifth of the labor force is employed in blue-collar occupations, whereas approximately two-fifths are so-called knowledge workers.

Professionals don't contribute just work, but also knowledge to the firms that employ them—they are knowledge workers in the purest sense. If it were just physical exertion that mattered, we would expect to see younger workers earning the most since that is the point in life at which physical strength is at its apogee. In reality, what we see is that, as knowledge workers age, their incomes rise, and this is consistent with the theory of human capital postulated by Schultz and other economists since. Rising income can be thought of as increasing *profits* from investments in human capital, even though we may term this income *wages* from an accounting sense. The importance of human capital should never be underestimated, even in the noneconomic sense, as the following example from Thomas Sowell's splendid book *Basic Economics: A Citizen's Guide to the Economy*, points out:

> A failure to understand the importance of human capital contributed to the defeat of Germany and Japan in World War II. Experienced and battle-hardened fighter pilots represented a very large investment of human capital. Yet the Germans and the Japanese did not systematically take their experienced pilots out of combat missions to safeguard their human capital and have them become instructors who could spread some of their human capital to new and inexperienced pilots being trained for combat. Both followed policies described by the Germans as "fly till you die."
>
> The net result was that, while German and Japanese fighter pilots were very formidable opponents to the British and American pilots who fought against them early in the war, the balance of skills swung in favor of the British and American pilots later in the war, after much of the German and Japanese human capital in the air was lost when their top fighter pilots were eventually shot down and replaced by inexperienced pilots who had to learn everything the hard way in aerial combat, where small mistakes can be fatal. Economic concepts apply even when no money is changing hands. German and Japanese air forces were less efficient at allocating scarce resources that had alternative uses.
>
> Uneasy as some people may be with the idea of thinking of human beings as capital, this is not a denigration but an enhancement of the value of human life. In addition to the intrinsic value of life to each individual, that individual's value to others is highlighted by the concept of human capital. The old military practice of going to great efforts to save cannon in combat, while using soldiers as if they were expendable, has since given way to using very expensive high-tech weapons, as in the Gulf War of 1991, in order to minimize casualties among one's own military personnel, who represent very valuable human capital (Sowell, 2000: 341–42).

PAUL The "fly till you die" comment is particularly appropriate here. In many firms, the apparent motto is "account for your time until you have no more left."

RON Historically, people have felt uneasy about the buying and selling of labor, mostly as a legacy of slavery (an institution that existed on every inhabited continent). Nevertheless, the majority of personal income is derived from salaries and wages, thus by thinking in terms of human capital investors lends dignity and respect to the value of each person. The word *human* comes from the Latin *Hominem*, for man, and the word *capital* from the Latin *caput*, meaning head. In other words, all capital springs from the mind, as we explored in Chapter 4. In a strict sense, a professional service firm's knowledge is created only by individuals—albeit some are outside of the firm's employ—thus no knowledge can be created without people. Attracting and retaining today's knowledge workers is one of the major challenges facing firms of all sizes, according to Management of Accounting Practice (MAP) surveys dating back many years, always ranking in the top three in terms of importance. There are several reasons why attracting and retaining talent has become a major issue today, causing consternation among firm leaders around the world.

One reason is life expectancy; the average knowledge worker today will outlive their employer, with an average productive work life of approximately 50 years compared to the average organizational life of 30. This translates into the average knowledge worker having many more jobs—and even careers—than those of their predecessors a century ago. Another reason is the precipitous decline among people entering the profession in college—an approximately one-half decline in students majoring in accounting—and an increase in the exodus of professionals from public practice to private, government, nonprofit, and the education sectors. The flattening of the traditional pyramid model of the firm, along with advances in technology, have also contributed to the decline in the talent pool of professionals.

Perhaps another reason—and this is part speculation and part conjecture, based on observing the profession over the past 20 years—is that firms do not seem to understand the worth of their people. They treat them as if they were assets—or worse, resources—rather than as investors of human capital who own their own—hence the firm's—means of production. And like most investors, they will go where they can earn a fair *economic* return—measured in wages, fringe benefits, and other pecuniary rewards—as well as where they are well treated and respected—the *psychological* return, if you will. Yet thinking of your people as assets is demeaning; people deserve more respect than a phone system or computer. Assets are passive, bought and sold in the marketplace at the whimsy of their owners; conversely, knowledge workers have ultimate control over their careers. If workers are assets, what does that make managers and partners? Buses have drivers and planes have pilots, but does that put employers in the driver's seat when it comes to their people? Hardly.

Thinking of workers as resources—from the Latin *resurgere*, "to rise again"—is even worse, implying that people are no different from, say, oil or timber, to be harvested when you run out. Peruse a corporate annual report, or talk to partners in professional service firms from anywhere in the world, and inevitably you will hear "people are our greatest asset" (or "resource"); even Michael Eisner, chairman and CEO of Disney, has been recorded as saying, "Our inventory goes home at night." That's a new twist—people now are inventory to be turned over! One consultant suggested that we capitalize all salaries and wages on the balance sheet to reflect the fact that workers are part of the firm's capital. I'm skeptical: knowing the average accountant, they would start a depreciation reserve, and that view of their people is no better. Why do we insist on perpetuating this belief that people are resources to be mined rather than human capital to be developed?

A Chinese proverb teaches the beginning of wisdom is to call things by their right names. Your people are not assets, resources, or inventory, but human capital investors seeking a decent return on their investment. In fact, as we will argue throughout this book, your people are actually *volunteers*, since whether they return to work on any given day is completely based on their own volition. Consider for a moment how people decide which volunteer organizations to contribute some of their talent. The choice is usually based on a desire to contribute to something that is larger than themselves. They work hard for these organizations—some would say harder than at their jobs—

because they are dedicated to the cause and they have the passion, the desire, and the dream to make a difference in the lives of others. All for zero monetary pay. Why? This is not just an economic decision, it is a psychological and emotional decision.

Yet with all this evidence of human behavior, many firms still treat their people as if they will slack off if they're not held accountable for every six minutes of every day. Is this any way to inspire people to be their best? Is this any way to instill a spirit of service and dedication to serving customer goals and aspirations? Or is this nothing but antiquated thinking about the nature of Man being lazy and slothful unless forced to work? Your people may hang their hat at your firm, but where is their heart?

This is a serious issue in firms, but it is "below the radar screen" of most partners. For too long firms have thought of their people as expendable, that if they didn't bill enough hours, then out with them—in effect treating them exactly as resources to be harvested again or inventory to be turned. These methods are no longer effective at creating a lightning rod in order to attract—and develop—talent.

PAUL Think of it from another perspective for a moment, that of the customer. Fred Crawford and Ryan Mathews put it this way in their book *The Myth of Excellence*: "[Our research showed clearly that] consumers are looking for values, not just value" (Crawford and Mathews, 2001).

Isn't it precisely the same for team members? They want a firm that values them as people, not some expendable resource whose actions are logged every six minutes. Try this exercise to really make the point. Write the very best ad you can, one designed to attract new team members (not that ads are the best way to attract people, but do the exercise for our purposes here). In your ad explain how challenging the position is, how great the firm is, how wonderful the salary will be. Even throw in that the firm has a day care center for kids if you like. Then, at the bottom of the ad, include this note, "We ask you to account for every six-minute period of your time." That little phrase says so much about how you value your people—in short, you don't!

In the next sections of this chapter we will deal with the issue of attracting, retaining, and rewarding human capital. Increasing the size of the labor pool—how to attract more people into the accounting profession—is an issue we discuss in Chapter 12.

BECOMING A LIGHTNING ROD FOR TALENT

RON Why is it easier to get into Harvard or Princeton than to be hired by Southwest Airlines, which only accepts 4 percent of its 90,000 applicants each year? Here is how Herb Kelleher explained it to the American Compensation Association in 1995 when he was CEO at Southwest:

> It starts with hiring. We are zealous about hiring. We are looking for a particular type of person, regardless of which job category it is. We are looking for attitudes that are positive and for people who can lend themselves to causes. We want folks who have a good sense of humor and people who are interested in performing as a team and take joy in team results instead of individual accomplishments (Prusak and Cohen, 2001: 93).

Southwest does not hire for skills—it will train people in what they need to know—but for attitude, which is very difficult to train, or change. Kelleher got it precisely right when he observed: "We hire attitude, we teach functionality."

Attracting good people and hiring are two of the most important jobs to which everyone in the firm can contribute input and ideas. Partners spend more of their time—or at least they should—making people decisions than any other. No other decisions have as many repercussions throughout the firm or have lasting significant effects than hiring choices. The Heritage Foundation, a think tank in Washington, DC, has this axiom as it relates to new administrations making personnel choices: "People are policy." You would expect to find a high level of commitment and energy devoted to this task, but in the average professional firm, you do not. Typically, the average firm is batting 0.333 on its hiring decisions; that is, one-third turn out to be good decisions, one-third are minimally effective, and one-third are abject failures. It is rare in any other area that firm leaders would accept this level of performance.

The point is this: Intellectual capital organizations are *people* companies, and dealing with people will always be full of challenges. When you hire someone, you don't just get his or her hands and labor, you get his or her emotions, desires, dreams, aspirations, expectations, and hearts—if you do it right. The issue of attracting human capital investors is a *marketing* issue, and most firms do not seem to understand this (other than, perhaps, the larger firms). As in all marketing, the marketing function does not look *inward* and ask, "What do *we* want and need?" On the contrary, it looks *outward* and asks, "What do *you* want and need?" There is an enormous difference between these two approaches. The latter changes the mind-set from one of *allocating* resources to *attracting* investors. Silicon Valley works on the operating principle of attracting rather than allocating resources. If an idea has enough merit, it will attract capital and resources, in the form of venture capital or an entrepreneurial leap of faith. Think tanks also work on this principle. They gather ideas from anywhere, not just those they themselves generate, and put them out in the arena of ideas to do battle. In effect, firms have to do the same to win over people as they do to gain new customers: show them why the firm is their best competitive alternative.

Knowledge workers are not like workers from the Industrial Revolution who were dependent on the employing organization to provide the means of production (factories and machines). Today, knowledge workers themselves own the firm's means of production—their intellectual capital—in their heads. Similar to the four Ps of marketing—which we will discuss further in Chapter 9—the investor metaphor forces the firm to place its emphasis on value, not costs.

Because knowledge workers are investing their intellectual capital with firms that will pay a fair return, rather than asking "how much is this person worth to the firm?" the real questions should be: "How much is the firm worth to this knowledge worker? How can the firm add to this person's IC, and develop it even further?" These are the important questions to answer to create lasting success. Even with all the talk of a so-called free agent workforce, and the boon in self-employment, people still need organizations to produce the goods and services customers will demand.

Viewing new hires as IC investors is a much better paradigm for making the best hiring decisions. While partners in almost every firm lament that "you can't find good people" (and here I love Paul's response to change the "you" to "I"), the simple fact is, you're not always going to be able to hire the best people. Statistically, this is impossible, as the labor pool is not composed of 100 percent top talent. Bill Joy of Sun Microsystems has come up with this law: "Most of the smartest people are never in your own company." But your competitive advantage lies not necessarily in attracting the best talent, rather in a superior ability to *develop* those you do hire. Usually when people talk about their firms, they always mention how good its people are. This is a natural, and even healthy, viewpoint. But the important question that flows from that is, "Good for what?"

PAUL Indeed, the reality is that most people in the profession simply are not making themselves attractive to great people. Moreover, we inadvertently tell people we think *we* are unattractive by the ads we run. Take a look at them: they're all the same; relatively dull and boring and offering promises that don't ring true or build confidence. The classic question here is, "If I were a great person, would I respond to this?"

A better idea than using ads is to ask the great people already on the team to go out and find more great people—after all, they probably had dinner with some of them last night. Were the team members saying, "You should work at our place; it is truly an amazing place to be."

But suppose you don't go down that route (although you should) and decide to stick with ads: Let's discuss what makes an effective ad to encourage great people to join your firm. To start, great headlines make the difference. For example, a headline that reads: "Wanted, people with passion, people with heart" will get passionate people reading, then responding (if the rest of the ad is consistent with the message). Here's a good example:

> **We Want an Accountant Who Can Help Us Create Beans Rather Than Simply Count Them. Can you do that?**
> Our accounting firm is not the boring place most people think of when they think "accounting firm," because we are what is called a "Results Accountants" firm. We're doing far more for our customers—more than historical figures, more than "bean counting." We focus on helping our customers with the growth and development of their business through applying new skill sets. We use exciting software tools and new resources to help our customers create history, rather than just report on it. So if you're not the "standard" accountant; and if you want a fun, team environment, customer interaction, rewards, challenges, success, and constant learning; and if you have strong technical competencies, then send us your story.

The exciting thing about this ad is that it is not going to encourage hoards of people to responding; it is going to get the good ones. And so your selection process gets easier.

How should that selection process be run? The simple answer is, by the team—totally! There are several obvious reasons, not the least of which is that since the new hire(s) will be working with the team, they should be the ones doing the choosing. (Another reason is they'll be far tougher than you ever will be!)

Of course, you need to give the team guidance. And a great way to do that is to systematize the questions. Here are some we know work really well:

- What goals have you set yourself? (Great people have no difficulty answering this question precisely; less-qualified people will waffle on it.)
- What was your best and worst experience at your last job?
- How do you define a successful career?
- What type of person is the hardest for you to get along with?
- What major contribution do you think you'll bring here?
- What would your teachers say about you?
- Tell me about three books or articles you've read recently.

Then give the team a framework to evaluate the candidate. Include areas such as:

- Energetic
- Optimistic
- Disciplined
- Has street smarts
- Presents self well
- Is goal-oriented

Now assume that you've selected someone. What then? Well, some great people we know send engagement letters to new hires before they start, such as this:

> Welcome. We're glad to invite you to join the team.
>
> We have a buddy system in place, so on Monday when you start, you'll meet with Michelle Dalton in the lobby for a two-hour tour of the office. She will make sure you get to know some of the people you'll be working with.
>
> Between now and then, it's really important that you go to your local bookstore and get two books (which we live by here). One is Stephen Covey's *7 Habits of Highly Effective People* and the other is *The E-Myth Revisited* by Michael Gerber. If you have difficulty getting the books, please let John Jones know and we'll get copies from our library to you.
>
> Then, on the day you start with us, after you've taken time with the team, I'd like to see you in my office for 45 minutes so that we can get to know each other and so that you can give me your impressions of the books. I'd really like to know what in them meant the most to you.
>
> Again, congratulations for joining us. It's going to be great working with you.
>
> Managing Partner

You can see immediately how such an approach motivates great people to be even better from day one. Then those great people go get more great people and so on.

And of course, a letter like this speaks volumes about where the practice is and what it values. The professional knows instantly that when he or she joins a practice like that it *is* a different place.

A version of that letter is used by Tom Weddell at Vanacore, DeBenedictus, DiGovanni & Weddell. The following is part of the document that Weddell uses to attract new talent. Note some of the wording it uses, but more importantly, note the sense it conveys, the values it talks about.

Vanacore, DeBenedictus, DiGovanni & Weddell, LLP is a progressive public accounting firm that offers a wide variety of career opportunities in Tax, Accounting, Auditing, Business Development Consulting, and Technology. We are an Equal Opportunity Employer and offer a competitive salary and benefit package. Listed below are the Top 10 reasons to join our team, followed by current employment opportunities. Check them to see if your skills match our needs.

Top 10 Reasons to Work for Vanacore, DeBenedictus, DiGovanni & Weddell

1. A company that recognizes the individuals' talent by providing increased responsibility commensurate with ability.

2. A company committed to growth through expansion of services, resulting in additional employment opportunities.

3. An infrastructure where individuals are coached by a mentor, increasing the probability of success.

4. An established system where the individual receives feedback on performance.

5. A formal, annual appraisal system.

6. A Human Resource Committee composed of almost every level in the organization that helps shape firm policy.

7. A Bank of Overtime hours that can be used for additional time-off.

8. A comprehensive benefits package, including a 401(k) plan with employer contributions.

9. Consideration given to employees wishing to work flex- or part-time based on business needs and needs of the employees.

10. A company where celebrations are the norm, and not the exception.

A Special Place to Build a Career
Get the Best of Both Worlds

If you're an ambitious individual with an entrepreneurial spirit, Vanacore, DeBenedictus, DiGovanni & Weddell offers you a special place to build your career.

We're large enough to provide the challenge of diverse, high-quality clients, yet small enough to give you the personal attention that will help you achieve your full potential. You'll gain extensive experience in the full range of accounting, tax, and consulting services. From the start of your career, the easy accessibility to partners—and all our professional team—assures valuable guidance.

Our emphasis on personal attention is reflected in our client relationships. Vanacore, DeBenedictus, DiGovanni & Weddell's goal is to provide the best possible service, carefully tailored to the client's individual needs. We believe our commitment to the development of each team member helps us accomplish this.

Vanacore, DeBenedictus, DiGovanni & Weddell offers the professional challenges you seek and the personal support you need to meet them. That's the best of both worlds.

Grow with Vanacore, DeBenedictus, DiGovanni & Weddell

Since its founding in 1969, Vanacore, DeBenedictus, DiGovanni & Weddell has experienced consistent growth. The firm now ranks as the largest privately held CPA firm in the Mid-Hudson Valley, employing approximately 50 professionals and support team members, offering a full range of accounting, auditing, tax, and business development consulting services.

To help new graduates bridge the gap between school and work, our orientation program combines training, practice, and, of course, plenty of personal attention. We stress the value of being a well-rounded professional, so we make sure you obtain significant experience in auditing and both business and personal taxes. Within your first year, you'll be involved with the senior-level management of our clients. With our approach, you'll be challenged to learn a lot—and learn it quickly.

Throughout your career with Vanacore, DeBenedictus, DiGovanni & Weddell, extensive internal and external educational opportunities will be provided. We feel strongly that the personal knowledge and growth of our team directly benefits the firm and our clients.

Vanacore, DeBenedictus, DiGovanni & Weddell believes in rewarding performance. We offer a comprehensive compensation program, which is evaluated regularly to assure its competitiveness within the industry.

Employer of Choice: Team Member Comments

The following comments were given by VDDW team members when they voted us the Employer of Choice in the Hudson Valley. If you are interested in becoming a member of this dynamic team, please submit your resume, with salary requirements, in confidence to Tom Weddell, Vanacore DeBenedictus DiGovanni & Weddell, Box 10009, Newburgh, NY 12552-0009.

"There are two critical aspects for me when it comes to a place of employment:

- *Quality of work performed*
- *Working atmosphere*

Most firms cannot find a proper balance between these two aspects. VDDW manages to promote a positive working environment without losing any quality in the work that is produced. That fact makes VDDW a truly unique and exciting team to work for."

"I was amazed at how during this past busy season team members came through with unexpected support and sensitivity in what I dreaded to be at least the very worst season. To my amazement the VDDW team members proved to be wonderful supportive people to work with and count on."

"VDDW is my Employer of Choice because the culture is one where 'work hard, play hard' is really a philosophy. It means a lot to have an employer actually say what they mean and have their actions support their philosophies. I am grateful to be part of this team."

That last comment really says it all, doesn't it?

RON Even the most talented people have weaknesses along with their tremendous strengths; and since the firm is hiring to produce for its customers, it has to capitalize on each person's strengths and, in effect, make irrelevant—or downplay—his or her weaknesses. This creates an environment of meritocracy, one that does not squander resources on trying to solve problems but that pursues opportunities. Like a good sports coach, firm leaders need to work with people's strengths, develop them further, and put them in positions that downplay their weaknesses. This is no easy task, which is why coaches of professional sports teams are such a rare breed of leaders. They do exactly that, day in and day out. And if one of their team members fails after several attempts, they usually take the blame, and rightfully so. That is what being an effective leader is all about. A leader's job is not to motivate his or her professionals—they are already highly motivated to perform their best for the firm and the firm's customers; rather it is to not *demotivate* them. Firm partners and managers earn the cynicism of their team members. Who starts a new job with a negative attitude? Professionals tend to be fiercely loyal to their chosen profession, but rather less loyal to any one employer. Loyalty has to be earned, through providing them a fair return and helping them develop their IC in an environment that is conducive to continuous learning and that grants them the dignity and respect that professionals deserve.

This is why I like the metaphors of knowledge workers as both IC investors and, ultimately, volunteers. Leading knowledge workers in the firm of the future—in terms of effectiveness and leveraging their IC—is the challenge facing the professions. One area we can study that teaches many lessons is the nonprofit sector. For someone to volunteer his or her precious time and money, nonprofits have to have an inspiring mission, high goals, and expectations of their people, and be held accountable for performance and results. This is not a cottage industry, as it is sometimes thought by many in the business world. America's voluntary sector employs some 7 percent of the population, one that received, in 1998, approximately $175 billion in donations.

People volunteer not for the money, but for the sense of inner peace and accomplishing meaningful work that impacts the lives of others. I firmly believe that workers in the private sector are motivated by exactly the same desires, and that if the firms are structured right, even "ordinary" professionals can achieve extraordinary results. Noting that volunteerism had grown so much, and that many more for-profit executives were spending a portion of their time-off doing charity work, Peter Drucker asked them why. "Far too many give the same answer: 'Because in my job there isn't much challenge, not enough achievement, not enough responsibility; and there is no mission, only expediency'" (quoted in Watson and Brown, 2001: 45). This is a profoundly sad commentary on the state of the business world today (no wonder Dilbert is so popular, with his images of cynicism and disdain for everything corporate). Charitable organizations view themselves as real communities, whereas many professional firms are nothing more than payroll ledgers.

Man does not live by bread alone. No matter how well we pay our people, if we don't give them that sense of mission, the vision of achieving a better future, we will not capture their pride and their hearts (see Paul's comments earlier regarding his friend Lloyd's "success to significance" comment). It is true, we may get some 2,000 hours out of people per year, but will we tap into their potential to achieve great things? Here is how Robert Watson of The Salvation Army explains it:

> You have to make the most of the link between pride and performance by continually clearing away the stuff that interferes with people connecting what they do in the organization with how it's received on the outside. That's why we keep sending out desk-bound officers and employees to experience programs and to talk to beneficiaries firsthand. Here's the important thing about that kind of pride. You can't "instill" it in an organization, as we so often hear. Pride is earned. It grows from performance in line with expectations everybody agrees on. And you risk losing the bonus pride affords an organization when you let your practices slip out of alignment with your purpose, no matter how compellingly you advertise your intentions. The first to notice the misalignment, even before customers, will be employees (Ibid: 101).
>
> [Explaining the grueling schedule of the average Salvation Army couple, Watson says]: For all this labor, which often starts early and finishes late each day, and which provides precious little time-off, this couple may draw less than $400 per week (not including Army benefits of housing and transportation). That's after 10 years as officers and includes allowances for two young children, whose concerns also have to be taken into consideration. . . . This kind of exhausting schedule, with its simultaneous demands for broad skills and narrow focus, seems made to order for management burnout. There's always too much to do and too little time and resources. Yet our officers sign on for life and work happily and productively well into their retirement. How could you possibly compensate people for this kind of effort if you couldn't offer access to soul-deep satisfaction that was intrinsic to the job? (Ibid: 211)

How many lessons are here for the professional service firm of the future? I will always remember the seminar I took at Disney University in Orlando, Florida, September, 1997. The class went to the Magic Kingdom, where we watched the Lion King puppet stage-show version of the animated movie, a spectacular display. When it was over, there was not a dry eye in the house. When we returned to the classroom, the instructor made a comment that says it all: "I am so proud to work with Disney because my fellow colleagues did that." Samuel Goldwyn is credited with saying: "The key for an actor is sincerity, because if you can fake that, you can fake anything." But you can't fake sincerity, or pride, or being loyal to a team, let alone a firm. Former Secretary of Labor, Robert B. Reich, said he used a simple *pronoun test* when visiting a company: "I ask frontline workers a few general questions about the company. If the answers I get back describe the company in terms like 'they' and 'them,' then I know it's one kind of company. If the answers are put in terms like 'we' or 'us,' then I know it's a different kind of company" (Prusak and Cohen, 2001: 93). Take a moment to think about that: Which pronouns are being used in your firm right now? Then ask yourself, how often your team members celebrate their many successes with each other, and take pride in their work? Too often leaders in firms take the credit for their team members' development, a practice tantamount to parents commending their children for their fine upbringing. The firm of the future is a real community, not a consortium of sole practitioners sharing overhead under one roof.

If you think back to your first job as a professional, why did you select one firm over another? Was it the money? Was it the benefits? Or was it something far less measurable, and far more intangible, like the people and the culture? Why did you leave your first job? Again, money or benefits? Or lack of respect, challenge, or pride in your work? These are vital questions that get to the heart of why knowledge workers choose to invest in one firm over another. Yet how often do firms think in these terms?

While attracting human capital to the firm is one of the most important jobs facing the partners, the irony is that the top people in the firm are also the busiest and thus least likely to play a role in this vital area. But organizations such as Southwest, General Electric, Disney, Starbucks, Nordstrom, among others, make recruiting a top priority and devote ample resources to the task. They spend a lot of time thinking about their ideal candidate, one who fits a certain profile—and that is usually based on attitudes, not so much credentials and skills, as Herb Kelleher pointed out. Some firms even take into consideration family members in job interviews since they've learned that family dynamics play a major role in career choices and are part of the social capital of the firm. Firms of the future chart their retention rates and learn not only from their failures but also their successes. Why are people leaving the firm? What are the criteria the people who joined the firm say were the most important in terms of selecting your firm over the alternatives? Those people will also act as talent scouts, constantly on the lookout for talent, and perhaps even hiring that talent prior to having any work for them. I know this latter idea sounds heretical, but we've found that putting capacity before revenue is important in order to achieve quality growth in a firm. Yet most firms wait till the last minute to scout out talent, when they are already operating at nearly full capacity. Hiring in a rush results in many hiring mistakes. Far better to plan ahead, and perhaps add capacity first, then go out and cross-sell more services or attract new customers (or both), and you will already have the capacity in place. Also, be alert for economic downturns. While the professional services world may be more resistant to economic shocks than the general economy, many people migrate out of the private sector back to the public sector when times are tough, and that makes for good recruiting opportunities. In any event, place recruiting on the top of the priority list for the executives in the firm, perhaps even making it a requirement for advancement to the partnership. Better yet, make recruiting an imperative for everyone in the firm. Which would you rather have in a competitive world, a personnel department looking for talent or everyone in the firm scouting for it? No other job is as important to the future development of the firm.

PAUL And you can't simply pay lip service to recruitment. You have to do something, to have something in place that demonstrates your belief. For example, at Results Accountants' Systems (RAS) we started by creating a fabulous ad to attract team members. The ad directed respondents (and there were hundreds of them) to call a special number. When they called, they heard a recording (done by a team member) saying how great it was to work at RAS. The recording then briefly described the job. Next, the recording asked the prospective team member to leave a two-minute message explaining why he or she wanted the job, what relevant characteristics he or she had, and the kinds of contributions he or she could make to the firm.

The team then reviewed those recordings, ultimately selecting about a quarter to a third of the respondents to come to a special "preview" evening, which was really like a professionally prepared seminar. That evening, one of the team members would present the history of RAS and talk about its future, emphasizing throughout the role of the team and our corporate values. Up front, prospective team members were told that if it sounded too much for them, they could leave at the break.

After the break, each prospective team member was asked to stand up in front of the audience and give a one-minute presentation on why he or she was right for the job. (Current team members stood at the back of the room taking notes.) At the end of the evening, all prospective team members were told that they would hear from someone at the firm early the next morning whether they would be asked to proceed to the next step of the process. When the prospective team members had left, the team compared notes and developed a short list of possible candidates—perhaps 5 to 10 percent of the group.

The next step—held over the next three evenings—consisted of the team members working with the candidates, showing them the intellectual technology we had developed, working with it, honing it. And each night the candidates were given homework.

By the final night, the candidates had been whittled down to no more than four. And that night, each of them had to present a case study to the team. Based on that case study, the team selected its next team member.

If it sounds like a grueling process, it is. Talk with any team member who has gone through it and he or she will talk about the excitement of it, the challenge of it, and, interestingly, the camaraderie that developed. The people who made it through were truly volunteers in a sense.

RON Another salutary effect of thinking in terms of attracting human capital as investors—or better yet, as volunteers—is a rather counterintuitive supposition: It is *people* who have value, not *jobs*. There is not a market for jobs, per se, but there is a market for people. Hence, the issue is one of pricing people, not jobs, correctly. Jobs may appear to be fixed in most firms, but in reality they are not. Jobs in any dynamic economy are not zero-sum. Jobs are limited only to the extent of the knowledge worker's imagination, not a scarce commodity at all. It is individuals, not jobs, who perform above—or below—average. It is individuals who leave jobs and decide to invest their IC elsewhere; jobs do not. The firm of the future needs to think of knowledge workers as having areas of assigned responsibility, or team memberships, or certain customer-centered areas of focus. The notion of a fixed *job* for a knowledge worker is becoming outdated.

If you were to study the myriad surveys that have been conducted over the decades of why professionals select one firm over another—and indeed, why over time they show loyalty to any one firm—you would find essentially four factors taken into consideration (subject yourself to these categories, especially as to why you chose your first firm, and perhaps why you left it, to see if they make sense):

Intrinsic rewards: These are the awards that are inherent in the work itself. Factors such as the challenge of the work, the level of commitment to the organization's mission and values, an environment that encourages creativity, fun (yes, fun) and innovation, and the social culture of the firm. These factors are precisely why people give their hearts, bodies, and minds to the volunteer organizations they work for. The satisfaction comes from a job well done and from making a difference in the world.

Opportunity to grow: How is the firm going to help the person develop his or her intellectual capital? Is it going to offer room for growth and improvement? Will it invest an appropriate level of resources into educating the person in order to enhance his or her IC? How will the relationship with the firm enhance not only the workers' professional skills, but help them become better personally as well?

Recognition of accomplishments: How does the firm recognize outstanding performance, including promotion and involvement in the strategy and direction of the firm? How does it spread the recognition to other members of the firm, or the community? Does the firm have "storytellers," those individuals who pass on the legends and lessons of the past so they can inspire future workers to greatness? Does the firm have a culture of celebrating success, or does it spend most of its time solving problems and mitigating crises?

Economic rewards: This is the composition of wages, benefit, and other extrinsic aspects the worker receives from the firm. Today, more and more, there is a stronger emphasis on work/life balance, something the large firms don't pay enough attention to, though this is starting to change. Is there a strong correlation between the effectiveness of the workers, their value to the firm, and their compensation?

Think back over your career and try to remember a boss—I don't like that word, let's substitute *leader*—that you truly respected, one you looked up to and admired; perhaps he or she was even a mentor. The relationship with the leader may be the most important factor in determining whether someone stays or leaves a firm. As an instructor at the Disney University pointed out, "People don't leave companies. They leave leaders in those companies." Dale Dauten wrote a splendid little book, *The Gifted Boss: How to Find, Create, and Keep Great Employees*, which I would encourage you to read. Here is some of his best advice:

The old school is to hire someone you need by offering 20 percent more money. Well, try offering 100 percent more freedom or 100 percent more excitement. . . . Gifted bosses and great employees want the same things from a workplace:

- Freedom from . . . management, mediocrity, and morons.
- A change.
- A chance. (Dauten, 1999: Preface, 74).

Let us start to create an environment worthy of people's investment. My favorite one-dimensional test for creating a culture that is worthy of the respect and dignity of the people you are trying to attract is to simply ask: Would you want your son or daughter to work in your firm?

PAUL Or, along similar lines, would *you* work for you? When you begin to consider the HC question, you do so knowing that since 1995 (at least!) the major cry from practitioners has been, "You can't get good people these days." When you first hear that cry, you acknowledge with a gracious, "Yes, it is difficult isn't it?" But after a while you take a different approach, one that recognizes the implied "I am a victim of circumstances" in the phrase.

I remember one practitioner bemoaning his lot. "All this is very well, but you can't get good people these days," he whined. I suggested he try saying the sentence again but in the first person, replacing "you" with "I." Then it came out, "All this is very well but *I* can't get good people these days." George Bernard Shaw would have been proud of that. He once said: "People are always blaming their circumstances for what they are. I don't believe in circumstances. The people who get on in this world are the people who get up and look for the circumstances they want, and, if they can't find them, make them." The point is, of course, that good people are going somewhere; they're just not going to you. The moment you realize that, you're forced to ask yourself two key questions:

- Why are good people not coming to me?
- Would I work for me?

Sadly, the honest answer to the second question from many practitioners is a grudging "No!" And little wonder in many cases. The work is uninteresting, repetitive, and nonresults-oriented, and the place where the work is carried out equally so. On top of that, probably you're asking workers to account for every six-minute period of their day (with a timesheet and stopwatch metaphorically strapped around their neck).

Everyone understands about "differentiating" our services in some way to make them attractive to a buyer. Yet few understand it from a team member perspective. Surely, prospective team members are buyers, too, in a sense. They've got multiple choices. Why should they give their hearts, their minds, and indeed their souls to you? And why on earth would they want to become so-called staff?

All of us need to recognize the awesome power of words and labels. They can work positively or negatively for you. For example, just ask someone close to you how they are today. Frequently, they'll respond, "Not bad." What an awful response that is! It's setting up a not-bad day as opposed to a great day. Let's face it, if you're not bad, you must be good. And making the simple change from "I'm not bad" to "I'm good" is profound in terms of the effect it has. (Yes, you can take it to extremes as in "I'm terrific but I'm getting better!")

That's one of the reasons why, every team I've created has banned the use of double negatives—the brain cannot get its head around it, if you see what I mean. It's also the reason that every practice I've ever worked with bans the use of the word "staff." Consider the implication of asking a practitioner-owner to describe his or her firm, and hearing something like: "We have 3 partners and 18 staff." At the extreme, it's saying, "We, the partners, understand the way things work, you 'the staff' don't." So as a first step to recognizing the value of your HC, change the label. From today, you have "team members."

Then perhaps you can take some additional steps to make you attractive to talented people. Consider the case of Harry Rosenberg in Melbourne, Australia. But first take this quick multiple-choice quiz: A team member takes maternity leave. Six weeks after the baby is born, the team member calls you, tells you she wants to come back to work as soon as she can, but implying that she has to bring the baby to work with her. Would you say:

1. "Terrific, we'd love to have you both here."
2. "We'll pay for the baby to be looked after while you work."
3. "Oh I'd like to allow that, but I don't see how it's possible."
4. "I'll get back to you by the end of the week."

I suspect that few of us would select the first answer. Yet that's precisely what Harry Rosenberg did. And the effect has, he says, been amazing. I've seen it for myself too, and I'm impressed enough to recommend it as a key team-building strategy. Let's talk some more about it so you can understand why.

First, you have to understand that central to Rosenberg's firm is the TLC package. No, it doesn't stand for tender, loving care, but for Team, Lifestyle, and Care package. And the basis of the package is that team members come *before* customers. Now isn't that interesting—team members come before customers.

Rosenberg puts it like this, "We recognize that in order for our team members to provide the best possible service to our clients, we must look after them in exceptional ways." The TLC package is itself an impressive 30-page document given to all new (and, obviously, existing) team members. It talks about care and appreciation of team members, about continuous improvement, about empowerment, about business performance, about the critical importance of a team approach.

The document details the firm's commitment to be a learning organization; and it is underpinned by twice-monthly training sessions held by an outside consultancy firm alternated with an accountants' breakfast meeting. Together, they keep the firm focused on issues. Most important is that the TLC document contains a strong commitment to "walk the talk."

Now, back to the baby. When Rosenberg got the phone call from the team member (we'll call her Karen), to whom the firm had said farewell just eight weeks earlier, the "walk the talk" commitment was uppermost in his mind, so it took only an instant before he responded positively to Karen's request. "I'm not sure how we'll do it, but I know we'll work it out somehow," he recalls saying.

Here's how they did it: The 35-member team fitted out a special office for Karen and her baby. (Rosenberg remembers that he quipped it be at the other end of the floor from his office.) All the team rallied round in many and varied ways to make Karen and her infant comfortable and welcome. Most notable, according to Rosenberg, was the way the baby's presence inadvertently brought everyone into "living" the TLC culture.

He illustrates by describing one male member of the team. "John was always head down, tail up," Rosenberg says. "You'd ask him a question and he'd never even look up to answer. It was work, work, work, and more work for John; it was rare to see a smile. Then one day I walked into a team meeting and noticed John bouncing the baby up and down on his knee; and John with a huge smile on his face. I even noted he had some baby sick on the back of his shirt, but it didn't bother him one bit. He kept the baby happy and contributed to the meeting at the same time as if nothing had happened. And he's kept that smile ever since."

The firm is achieving its stated goal of being "the practice I'm proud to be a part of." You can see and feel it, and you can see and feel the impact that the baby and the TLC package have had every time you go into Rosenberg's office. It begins with the welcome you get at reception and flows through to the way you're asked if you'd like some refreshments and continues even to the computer screen on the reception desk that automatically displays a PowerPoint presentation filled with motivating quotes.

And its apparent on Rosenberg's face, and in the numbers, too: The firm rates fifteenth in terms of revenue per team member in the top 100 practices in Australia. "I've never been happier in my 30 years of practice than now," Rosenberg says. It sounds like a great recipe for success to me.

I found a similar recipe cooking in Northfield, Illinois, at the firm of Lipschultz, Levin and Gray. Former managing partner Steve Siegel found a truly unique way of doing business, one that many (if not all) practices would do well to emulate. Siegel explains that the office used to be what might best be called "traditional." One day in a team meeting (more about them later, too) a member observed that Siegel's door always seemed closed. "It's putting up barriers we don't need," the member said. Siegel, an open and exciting man, fired back, "So what do you feel we should do?". Discussion ensued and the firm (a.k.a the team) decided to literally knock down all (yes, all) of the dividing walls between offices to create a totally open space. There are no fixed desks and no offices (save one conference room reserved for clients, which itself is very different). There are even two red-painted telephone box structures in the middle of what is essentially open space for private phone calls.

One result is that the office has reduced its space requirements from 16,000 square feet to just 6,000 (and that, too, has gone straight to the bottom line). But, according to Siegel, that's just the smallest part of the bottom-line effect. Visitors to the firm's offices notice the change immediately (although the office reception is fairly conventional save for the projector screen running constantly changing business-focused motivational quotes). But further inspections reveals a "parking spot" for the specially designed wheel-equipped desks and "to-go's" (custom-designed filing drawers also with wheels). Everything, in fact, is on wheels!

When the team arrives in the morning, they wheel their "offices" to wherever they want to be located that day; for example, next to a workgroup preparing something for a particular client. The result is that, when you go in, it's impossible to tell who's a partner and who isn't. Two immediately obvious effects are that nobody can hide and the workgroups are enormously productive.

And the firm does not have partners' meetings in the strict (and boring) sense of the word. Imagine that, a multipartner firm with no partners' meetings. There's just no real need for them, according to Siegel, because, of course, the communication levels are so extraordinarily high.

Some would say, "Thank goodness! It must be a better place." Others might think, "It must be an out-of-control, low-profit, nonfocused, terrible place to work." The "others" would be categorically wrong. Steve Siegel has found a truly unique way of doing business, which has resulted in rapid growth the likes of which they'd never experienced. The effect has been nothing short of remarkable. On my visit, every one of the CPAs with me that day wanted to fill out employment application forms.

RETAINING YOUR FIRM'S HUMAN CAPITAL

Motivate them, train them, care about them, and make winners out of them . . .
we know that if we treat our employees correctly, they'll treat the customers right.
And if customers are treated right, they'll come back.

—J.W. Marriott, Jr., Chairman and President, Marriott Corporation

RON FedEx's internal value statement is: "People-Service-Profit," forming a virtuous circle. Excellent companies have learned that when they put their people first—yes, even before customers—they will take care of its customers with excellent service, which ultimately drives profit. There is a strong correlation between employee relations and customer relations. How a firm treats its people internally will mirror very closely how its people treat external customers. As James C. Wetherbe explained in his book *The World on Time: The 11 Management Principles That Made FedEx an Overnight Sensation,* "The rights and value of a single human life," begins the FedEx manager's training guide, "have become the central focus of social evolution in the industrialized world . . . FedEx, from its inception, has put its people first both because it is right to do so and because it is good business as well." And FedEx employees have responded in kind. At the end of one pay period in the difficult early days of the company, employees received a memo along with their paychecks. The memo, from Fred Smith, stated that they were welcome to cash their checks, but, he suggested, it would be helpful if some of them waited just a few days. To this day, some of those checks remain uncashed. Their owners display them proudly, as a badge of honor, in frames on their FedEx office walls. Do you employees feel a similar sense of loyalty to your company? (Wetherbe, 1996: 15).

Professional service firms can lament the fact that Generation X or Y is not as loyal as their parents, but loyalty is a two-way street: it must be earned. No business deserves any loyalty, either from its customers or its workers, until it does something to earn it. Loyalty is not dead in the business world, but a *reason* to be loyal may be ailing. The question firms should be asking their people is "Does the firm *deserve* your loyalty?" Measuring job satisfaction is not enough, anymore than measuring customer satisfaction is enough to ensure loyalty. Your firm can score very high on customer—or team member—surveys, and both may still defect for a better alternative. Customer and team member satisfaction is simply no longer enough. What counts is not *present satisfaction*, but rather *anticipated satisfaction*, which is another word for *expectations*. If customer or team member perceptions fall below expectations, you have a defection in your future. Satisfaction measures the past; deserved loyalty measures the future. Are professional service firms doing enough to earn the loyalty of their team members? Consider this December 1999 study of 6,357 workers by Randstad North America, which offered these top reasons given by employees for staying with their present employer: affection for coworkers (71 percent), a pleasant work environment (68 percent), an easy commute (68 percent), challenging work (65 percent), and flexible work hours (54 percent) (Kanter, 2001: 205). Another survey of human resource professionals showed that "68 percent agreed that telecommuters at their companies are no more difficult to manage than on-site employees. As of 2000, an estimated 11 to 22 million Americans telecommuted at least one day a week" (Ibid: 213). Obviously, telecommuting is much easier to achieve among knowledge workers, so why do firms keep insisting on hurdling a 200-pound body downtown in rush hour traffic when all you really need is the nine-pound brain?

The large firms understand the economics of team member loyalty, which is why they have started to discuss the concept of *knowledge handcuffs*. Another study, this one by Aon Consulting, showed that the "single most effective way to strengthen employees' loyalty is to increase their opportunities for growth" (Stewart, 2001: 28). What is the incentive? One of the Big 4 firms found they save $25 million for every 1 percent decline in team member defection. The halcyon days of the revolving door and the "up or out" strategy are over. In today's hypercompetitive environment, shrinking labor pool, and labor seller's market, it simply no longer makes sense to churn through your most important source of IC—your team members. Why, then, since we know what motivates team members to stay with a given firm (this issue has been studied to death by myriad companies, foundations, governmental bodies, and other organizations) do so few firms act on this information? Consider this survey released at the American Institute of CPAs Staffing Forum in Broomfield, Colorado. The study, which was conducted by the PCPS Staffing Task Force in November and December 2000, surveyed 558 nonpartner employees of PCPS Member firms from all 50 states and Puerto Rico to ascertain the components of employee job satisfaction among highly valued staff members (as reported in *The Practicing CPA*):

> While respondents cited comp time and bonuses as the top reasons for joining or staying at a firm, only 58 percent of firms offer these benefits. This indicates that by and large, firms are not offering benefits employees actually desire. Dependent medical and disability also rank high on the wish list.
>
> Of the employees polled, 88 percent ranked "respect for work/life balance issues" as critical for remaining with a firm. Today's employees have different priorities and want to believe their employer understands the importance they place on balance in their professional and personal lives.
>
> Although 75 percent agree that management encourages career growth and possible owner status and fully two-thirds believe they are being groomed for a senior position in the firm, only 37 percent are very interested in becoming an owner. In other words, only

roughly one-third of those employees being groomed for ownership even seriously plan to pursue the opportunity. Current firm owners should be aware of this and plan for the future accordingly, perhaps by adopting an alternative succession plan.

Of those who are not interested in becoming an owner, 75 percent say it does not hinder their professional success, but only 31 percent say their firm has identified alternative career paths.

Performance reviews of the respondents are typically both verbal and written; 62 percent agree that a review at their firm entails a productive, give-and-take dialogue between management and the employee where both can express their thoughts and concerns comfortably. Only 45 percent of respondents have a "mentor" within the firm.

Of the respondents, 92 percent are happy being a part of an accounting firm, but only 69 percent would make the choice again. Popular alternative careers include teaching, law, computer technology, medicine and engineering.

What can you do to recruit and retain top talent? An overwhelming number of respondents identified feedback, access, and recognition as key motivators. When asked, "If you could tell management at your firm one thing, what would it be?" respondents replied:

- More staff meetings! Let us know what is going on.
- Listen to your employees.
- Look for new ways that the firm can succeed.
- Improve the management skills of the partners.
- Hire more confident staff.

And when asked what would motivate them to work smarter and/or harder, respondents ranked the following in order:

1. Bonus or incentive pay
2. Recognition for a job well done
3. Annual salary increases

What comes through loud and clear in this survey, and others that report very similar results, is that the average accounting firm is overmanaged and underled. More meetings, recognition, access, better communications, opportunities for success, and more confident team members? Why do firms insist on grooming individuals for partnership when over one-third of them have no interest in the position? These are the characteristics not of firm managers, but firm leaders. Almost anyone can *manage* a professional service firm; it is the leader who takes it somewhere, who develops a preferred vision of the future everyone can imagine. All leaders need followers, no doubt, but all firms need leadership. No firm will rise above the level of its leadership. And by leadership I don't mean a dictator, a Moses type who comes down from a mountain retreat with the firm's vision. I mean *servant* leadership, the type of leader who facilitates and inspires people to perform at their best. It is the antithesis of management. In a knowledge firm, there are no superiors and subordinates, only younger and older workers. Yet leadership skills are the Achilles heel at most firms. Let us be honest: Many partners couldn't lead a trail of ants to a picnic lunch. According to Warren Bennis, one of the leading thinkers in the field of leadership development, followers look for three things from their leaders: direction, trust, and hope. We discuss direction in Chapter 11, where we also address the vision and core values and ideology of the firm. Suffice to say here, offering a clear direction of where the firm is going is something all firm partners must do to inspire their team members. Isn't this precisely what volunteer organizations of all sorts do? Each of them has a core mission and set of values that people believe in and work hard to achieve. This is also the hope, that is, the preferred vision of the future.

It is the trust issue I'd like to concentrate on here in terms of its effect on human capital investors. Empirical evidence suggests that workers behave less cooperatively and generously when they think their employers do not trust them. There is nothing more demeaning to knowledge workers than to feel they are not trusted. But I firmly believe knowledge workers are not manageable; in fact, I don't even like the word "manager." And since Paul and I have had many discussion about how "words mean things" and convey certain mental images and generate feelings, let us look at the origin of this word "manager." Even Peter Drucker, the father of modern management, no longer likes to use this word, explaining: "I'm not comfortable with the word 'manager' anymore, because it implies subordinates. I find myself using 'executive' more, because it implies responsibility for an area, not necessarily dominion over people" (Drucker, 1999: 188).

We don't know what the new word should be—I, too, prefer "executive" or "servant leadership"—but that is not the main point here. The point is trust, and most professionals, in our experience, really don't trust their team members. Hence the inglorious timesheet. When it is all said and done, the timesheet is not used for cost accounting, it is used for pricing; a secondary reason is to monitor and control the team. I have encountered many partners in firms of all sizes who ask, "If we didn't have timesheets how would I know what my team was up to?" Well, if you don't trust them to do a good job for the firm and the firm's customers, why did you hire them in the first place? The minute you feel the need to closely supervise a knowledge worker, you have made a poor hiring decision. Never one to let me get away with sloppy thinking, Ric Payne asked me, "Are you really suggesting that if you remove timesheets, trust will increase? Or that in firms with timesheets, there is less trust?" Yes, I am. Absolutely. This boils down to a leadership issue, not a pricing issue (we have alternatives to the timesheet for pricing) or an efficiency issue (we have alternative measures that track effectiveness and efficiency) and the timesheet is a relic of the early Industrial Revolution when managers truly didn't trust their workers and made them account for each minute, or used it as a tool to squeeze the last 2 percent of efficiency from an already beleaguered workforce.

I am not suggesting we replace the timesheets with *license*—that is, doing as one pleases. I am suggesting we replace it with *autonomy*, from the Greek words for "self-governance." Timesheets inhibit communication, innovation, creativity, and leadership, and in return we get a bureaucratic, lagging indicator. I don't think the trade-off is worthwhile (we discuss this further in Chapter 10). As Ikujiro Nonaka says: "Allow employees time to pursue harebrained schemes or just sit around chatting, and you may come up with a market-changing idea; force them to account for every minute of their day, and you will be stuck with routine products." Consider the employee handbook from Nordstrom shown in Exhibit 5.1: surely this is a service leader whose team members deliver outstanding service to its customers.

EXHIBIT 5.1   Nordstrom Employee Handbook

**WELCOME TO
NORDSTROM**

We're glad to have you with our Company.

Our number one goal is to provide
outstanding customer service.

Set both your personal and professional goals high.

We have great confidence in your ability to achieve them.

Nordstrom Rules:

Rule #1: **Use your good judgment in all situations.**

There will be no additional rules.

Please feel free to ask your department manager,
store manager or division general manager
any questions at any time.

n o r d s t r o m

Don't professionals deserve the same respect that the team members of Nordstrom get from their executives? Isn't it about time to free the professional from a bureaucratic holdover from the turn of the last century that is stifling our creative abilities and focusing on nothing but present production at the expense of research and development of new products and services to build our future? Isn't it ironic that in a profession of knowledge workers we spend so little time thinking, because we are too busy trying to meet this month's billable hour quota? Unfortunately for the profession, the timesheet is so engrained into our culture it is stifling innovation, creativity, and customer service. The last new services offered—and developed from the ground up—by the accounting profession as a whole to the general public were the compilation and the review, in 1978. A 24-year innovation curve? I am not blaming this solely on the fact that we maintain timesheets, but I truly believe there is a connection between the profession's ruthless quest for efficiency at the expense of effectiveness and innovation. Few knowledge workers yearn to be managed. One of the jobs of a leader is to create an environment where the average workers can flourish, utilizing their strengths and developing their potential as true professionals, all the while contributing to a firm they deeply care for and feel passionate about.

Servant leaders also require feedback from the entire team on how well they are performing in their jobs. Yet we have found very few firms where the partners are willing to conduct 360-degree feedback from the entire team. Why? Your people are already saying what they think about you anyway, but behind your back. Isn't it better to get the feedback candidly and honestly so you can strive to improve, or perhaps be removed? Lack of communication among partners and the team members almost always comes up in every survey I have read or private conversations with team members I have held, and this lack of communication is costing firms a substantial amount of lost opportunity. One problem is that these costs do not show up anywhere on the firm's financial measurements, so they are ignored, but that does not mean they are not there. Firm leaders need to foster an environment conducive to open and honest feedback, instead of making their team members feel like the former Russian who, on discovering his pet parrot was missing, immediately ran to the KGB office to report that his parrot's political opinions were entirely unrelated to his own. Firm leaders can—they *must*—do better.

THE IMPORTANCE OF CONTINUING PROFESSIONAL EDUCATION

RON I have spoken to thousands of partners who say they don't spend more than the minimum on their people's continuing professional education. This is astonishing, because it is precisely continuous learning that will enhance not only an individual's IC, but also the firm's. When you look at companies like Accenture, and other major accounting and consulting firms, they tend to spend approximately 6 percent of their *gross revenue* on education and training (this compares to a U.S. national average of 1.5 to 2 percent of *payroll expense*). How else are these firms expected to enhance their repository of IC? They can't go out and buy a better widget machine; they can't add robots to increase efficiency. They can invest in technology, but that is just a tool. What counts is what knowledge workers know, and perhaps one of the metrics should be what do they know this year that they didn't last year? Continuing education is a major driver of knowledge worker retention, and not just a curriculum that concentrates on technical skills, but one that provides a full, rounded source of learning and challenge. Marketing, selling, service, communication, listening, and leadership skills are all underinvested in by most professional firms. Most major companies—from Merck, 3M, P&G, Motorola, GE, Disney, Nordstrom, Marriott, and IBM—have their own internal "universities" because they recognize the importance of developing their people's human capital. Peter Drucker says, "I think the growth industry of the future in this country and the world will soon be the continuing education of adults. Nothing else is growing as fast. . . . I think the educated person of the future is somebody who realizes the need to continue to learn. That is the new definition and it is going to change the world we live and work in" (quoted in Beatty, 1998: 147).

One of the objections to this suggestion is that if you train and invest in your people, they will leave—and possibly become an even stronger competitor. This is no doubt true, although you face the risk of them leaving in any event. In fact, based on the empirical evidence, you are increasing their chances of leaving if you do not educate them. But let us deal with the objection directly, and acknowledge that it is true. Let me pose a better question: What if you do not invest in their education and they *stay*? The problem with this cost is that it does not show up anywhere on the firm's internal measurement systems. I posit to you that this loss far outweighs both the cost of education and the risks of people leaving.

Nobel Prize-winning economist Gary S. Becker, a leader in developing Human Capital Theory, says "I focus on the allocation of time to three activities: the production of nonmarket commodities (nonmarket time); the production of human capital (investment time); and the production of earnings (labor market time) (Becker, 1983: 5). Obviously, firms of the future will have to have a healthy respect for these three categories, and not make their team members feel as if they are not spending enough time in the production of earnings when they are investing in their human capital.

Consider education in the context of the new Practice Equation versus the old. In the short and medium run, education has a negative impact on a knowledge worker's efficiency. Does this mean we should not invest in it? This is precisely why we have replaced efficiency with effectiveness. It is simply absurd to think investing in education harms a firm's ability to deliver a superior value proposition to its customers, especially in the long run. In fact, one could argue that continuing education is essential for a firm to even have a long run.

What is your firm doing to develop the human capital it will need in the coming decades? Are you investing in your people's intellectual capital and developing their balance sheets, or are you consuming your seed corn and eating your future today because you're focused on nothing but the income statement (labor market time)? No other decision will have as significant an impact on your future as the willingness of your human capital to continue their investment in your firm.

REWARDING YOUR FIRM'S HUMAN CAPITAL INVESTORS

RON It is never easy to discuss compensation issues in a generic setting, since no two firms have the same compensation culture. Some firms are very entrepreneurial in nature, rewarding their high performers very well, while other firms take a more egalitarian approach. It is appropriate to offer some general guidelines from firms that appear to achieve extraordinary results from their team members. In doing so, we will raise some questions about rituals that have developed.

The first ritual to question is the annual appraisal process. Peter Drucker has been making the point for decades that abnormal psychologists developed this tool, and they focused the superior to look for weaknesses and shortcomings, giving priority to standards of pathology over health. Here is how Drucker explains the process in *The Effective Executive*:

> Again and again the same executives who say that of course they appraise every one of their subordinates at least once a year, report that, to the best of their knowledge, they themselves have never been appraised by their own superiors. Again and again the appraisal forms remain in the files, and nobody looks at them when a personnel decision has to be made. Everybody dismisses them as so much useless paper. Above all, almost

without exception, the "appraisal interview" in which the superior is to sit down with the subordinate and discuss the findings never takes place. Yet the appraisal interview is the crux of the whole system.

Appraisals, as they are now being used in the great majority of organizations, were designed by the clinical and abnormal psychologists for their own purposes. The clinician is a therapist trained to heal the sick. He is legitimately concerned with what is wrong, rather than with what is right with the patient. He assumes as a matter of course that nobody comes to him unless he is in trouble. The clinical psychologist or the abnormal psychologist, therefore, very properly looks upon appraisals as a process of diagnosing the weaknesses of a man (Drucker, 1993: 83–84).

The problem is precisely that the annual appraisal tends to focus on weaknesses and not strengths. But good leaders—like good coaches—design performance processes and tasks around a person's strengths, and ignore—or make irrelevant—their weaknesses. The Peter Principle—which says that people get promoted to their highest level of incompetence—may make for funny Dilbert cartoons, but in reality, there is nothing funny about it. We should promote people based on their strengths, not their weaknesses. Yet this basic truth is not carried out very often in professional service firms, and part of the problem is that the appraisal process is flawed.

Another problem with the process is the "annual" aspect of it; a year is far too long a time frame to evaluate and give feedback to any worker, but especially a knowledge worker. We should be reviewing our team members quarterly, or better yet, after every engagement. (The same principle applies to our best customers: Shouldn't we be meeting with them *at least* quarterly, if not more often? Our team members are certainly no less valuable, and I will argue they are more valuable, than any one customer). This is the role of the leaders in the firm, but many are far too busy working on current production to invest the time necessary to develop their team members. It's that Michael Gerber adage again: We must be working *on*, not *in*, the business. To do otherwise is enormously costly.

When senior people are working *in* the business, it means the managers and partners are doing work that should be delegated to a lower level in the firm—surgeons piercing ears again—but more important, it doesn't give team members the necessary guidance and coaching they need to develop their human capital and become more valuable to the firm. Someone who receives a stellar annual review one year is subject to the *Sports Illustrated* jinx; that is, when an athlete makes the cover of *SI* one week, he or she usually does poorly the next. The explanation for this is not a jinx; rather the athlete has usually performed at a peak level, which puts him or her on the cover in the first place. Inevitably, then, the next week's performance, even if above average, will fall below the standard that earned the athlete the original accolade. No doubt we need to acknowledge superior performance, and even reward it monetarily and in other ways—but we need to take a balanced view of a knowledge worker's contribution and development over the course of his or her tenure with the firm. (In Chapter 10 we offer specific team member key performance indicators (KPIs) that you can use to provide feedback and assessment on the performance of your people.)

Any organization of humans—be it a school, a nonprofit agency, a governmental unit, or a business—is going to have a bell curve of high, average, and below-average performers. One study found wide differences in performance for complex jobs (attorneys, physicians, and cartographers, for instance), where the top 1 percent of producers generated 2.27 times the output of average producers (Davenport, 1999: 66). Given human nature, not much can be done about this distribution, but what we can do is not exacerbate the problem of below-average workers by designing systems around their performance at the expense of placing a ceiling over the heads of the superior performers. Public schools do this all the time. They "dumb down" the standards for the slowest learners, while letting those with above-average abilities stagnate and get bored. A business organization should not do this to spare the feelings of the less effective team members; rather, it should design processes and compensation systems that take into account different levels of performance. As Thomas Jefferson said, "There is nothing less equal than treating nonequals equally." Not adequately rewarding your high achievers is a prescription for their defection, as it is precisely the high achievers who are the most desired by your competitors. Over 71 percent of the firms in the *Inc.* 500 list of young, entrepreneurial and fast-growing companies were started by individuals who duplicated or modified innovations at their former employers (quoted in Lev, 2001: 13). In a professional service firm, high achievers defect with customers.

I learned this lesson from a large accounting firm for which my company was doing some educational seminars. This firm had created some very innovative tax products that had the potential of generating very large revenue, since the price was based on the percentage of tax savings achieved by the customer. We were discussing how the partners (in a group of nothing but partners) who sold these products should be compensated. When the senior partner suggested a bonus of 50 percent of the revenue, a small, but very vocal, minority vehemently objected to the idea. When I asked why, they said it wasn't fair, that the firm needed tacklers and blockers, too, that it was wrong to compensate only the person who landed the sale.

Another suggestion was to give a percentage of the ultimate commission to that partner's particular team—or office, as the case may be—to be divided among them in the bonus pool. This was also met with objections, although fewer. Keeping the football analogy going, I asked the most vocal of the partners if he thought the quarterback of an NFL team should make the same as the center? He replied, "This isn't a football team, it's an accounting firm." Check, and mate. In most companies the salespeople are the highest paid, sometimes even higher than the top executives. Why is it anathema to the professional service firm culture to reward top playmakers extraordinarily? So I did some research on the NFL for this partner, pointing out that in 1998 the top-paid players at virtually every position in the NFL earned more than $3 million. Quarterbacks—like Dan Marino of the Miami Dolphins—made $7.5 million, while every team had some players who earned the league average of $131,000 a year. This is quite a range of salaries for people playing on the same team, and even some at the same position. Michael Jordan earned over $30 million in 1998, and rightfully so since *Fortune* magazine estimated that he had produced over $1 billion in revenue for the NBA during his career. People have value, not positions.

If you want high performers, you have to be willing to pay for them, and this requires that firms stop viewing jobs as caste systems—as if there were a union pay scale depending on the job classification—and start rewarding the value of your team members' human capital contributions. Firms should strive to create a meritocratic environment that rewards risk taking and innovation, rather than rigid, union-type jobs that reward seniority, mediocrity, and complacency. When was the last time you met a wealthy union member? It is not uncommon, for example, for salespeople working the floor of Nordstrom to earn over $100,000 per year; and as they say, "Your performance is your review." Why do professional service firms insist on putting artificial ceilings over the heads of their team members, therefore defining performance standards down? Remove those barriers and allow your team to reach for new opportunities and heights.

Another characteristic of successful firms we have studied is a greater emphasis on team bonuses—or individual bonuses—over pay raises and salary increase plans. This type of compensation scheme fosters teamwork and firm performance and removes the feelings of unfairness that so often come up when certain members think they are not being fairly compensated based upon the results they achieve. Money may not be the ultimate motivator, but there has to be a correlation between performance and pay in order to retain a firm's top talent. Many management theorists still cling to the view that Abram Maslow, or Fredrick Herzberg postulated in the sixties and seventies that pay was nothing more than a "hygiene" factor, especially once someone obtained a certain level of financial security. But Maslow and Herzberg's own research came to no such conclusion, and studies since have found that pay can be a motivating factor—albeit certainly not the only one—in achieving high performance.

Promotions are another signaling device to your team members, who watch very closely the behaviors that are rewarded when someone advances. Be careful who you promote, and what behaviors they display, since what gets rewarded gets done. If it is based on cleverness, flattery, or politics, then the firm is destined to sink to those traits, since they'll be perceived as the way to get ahead.

Public recognition of high performance is also a cultural trait in most successful companies, such as Disney, Marriott, and FedEx. The distribution of rewards must be done publicly, and they must be considered credible and meaningful. An old military saying has it that a man wouldn't sell his life for $1 million, but would gladly risk it for a ribbon or Medal of Honor. Super Bowl champions display their rings with pride, long after the money they earned has been forgotten.

WHEN HUMAN CAPITAL TURNS NEGATIVE

RON Recall the axiom: Bad customers drive out good ones. Let me suggest that bad team members drive out good ones, as well. They have a toxic and demoralizing influence on the performance of the firm. It is never easy to admit a hiring mistake, but when it's necessary to fire a professional, in a lot of cases, it is because the hiring decision was wrong in the first place. The onus is on the firm's leaders to decide who sits on the bus, to use Jim Collins analogy; and if they are on the wrong seat on the bus—because they are displaying weaknesses rather than fully utilizing their strengths—then the leaders must move them to a different seat. All firms need good people, and of course you have to understand precisely what it is they are good for. In today's labor market, we must try to retain human capital by finding a place in the firm where their strengths can be put to highest use. That onus is also on the firm's leaders, and they should take is seriously. If the virtuous circle that FedEx's slogan—People-

Service-Profits—embodies is true, and I believe it is, then we simply have to put the good of the firm's people first, even at the expense of expediency (I've seen firms wait until tax season is over to let someone go—this is simply *wrong*) or customers, because it is the *right* thing to do. It's not easy, but dealing with people never is.

When it comes time to let substandard performers go, it is a task that must be carried out with dignity, respect, and precision (sometimes a surgeon must cut in order to cure). We do people no favors when we let them languish in a job they are not capable of performing well or for which they have no heart. How do you know when it is time to let someone go? Ask yourself if you would hire this person again. Think how you would feel if this person came to you and said he or she was leaving to pursue another opportunity.

It is simply unacceptable to other team members to keep people in the firm who are not meeting expectations. The negative effects on morale of doing so are significant, and will ripple throughout the firm. Poor performers are not good role models, do not make good mentors, and may even be damaging customer relations. If the leaders don't make these tough decisions regarding the most important form of IC in their firms, who will? To keep poor performers in place is to risk the success of the firm. Comedian Steven Wright once wryly noted, "The problem with the gene pool is, there's no lifeguard." In a professional service firm, the leaders and executives are the lifeguards, and it is incumbent upon them to make sure the firm's genes are healthy. This is also why many firms involve the entire team in making hiring decisions (and even hold them accountable for new team member performance, as well as it being a promotion criterion). Better to have many lifeguards surrounding the pool than just a few.

There is another dimension to letting people go, and it involves the customer. In survey after survey of why customers defect from professional service firms, one reason always comes up: Let team member contact lapse, or the rotation of team members on the customer's account. And while it is not typical for a poor performer to walk away with customers, it can (and does) happen. Many firm partners worry incessantly that their team members could develop strong relationships with their customers and "take them with them" if they leave. There are some strategies a firm can use to diminish this risk (you can never eliminate it; no one owns a customer). Try rotating team members on customer jobs, while maintaining the same managers and partners; use customer service teams; introduce multiple team members to all customers so they can get to know more people in your firm; and offer more services to your customers so that different talent in your firm can develop relationships with them.

Most important, don't let team member turnover catch your customers offguard. Notify them early; make sure the partner or manager personally introduces the replacement; follow up with the customers to assure they are satisfied. This is an area of major weakness in most firms, because they are not thinking like a customer. From the customers' vantage point, they have several concerns when someone new is assigned to them: Does this person know as much as the replacement, or are they going to have to escort them down the learning curve? What does this turnover say about the internal quality of the professional service firm? Is it having trouble keeping good people? (Never forget, the customer usually does not know that the person let go was a poor performer). A firm can lose a lot of creditability if it does not manage the transition properly with the customer. The key here is good (and early) communication.

SUMMARY AND CONCLUSIONS

We have covered a lot of ground in this chapter, and rightfully so, since human capital is the most important component of the firm of the future's intellectual capital. It is time for firm leaders to start treating their people with the respect and dignity worthy of a proud tradition, and to stop viewing employees as simply problems, procedures, and costs. People are not assets—and won't be replaced by computers no matter how far advanced artificial intelligence becomes—or inventory, or resources; they are individuals entitled to a sense of mission and purpose in their lives, who congregate in firms in order to make a difference in the lives of others. The universal need of every worker is to perform meaningful work, in a community with others of like mind, in order to make a difference in the world. This is the lesson of the not-for-profits, to which all firm leaders need to pay heed. The real aspiration of a firm is to make people *better*, not just make them *better off*.

Characteristics like passion, desire, obsession, motivation, innovation, creativity, and knowledge may not show up anywhere on a firm's financial statements, but they are the traits that will ultimately determine the fate of the firm. Knowledge work is nonlinear and not subject to the cadences and rhythms of an assembly line; rather it moves by iteration and reiteration. We simply cannot treat people as if they are machines that supposedly check their minds and emotions at the door when they enter the firm. We must stop thinking in terms of management and operational efficiency metrics. Knowledge workers deserve better than these outdated modes of thinking.

Oscar Wilde once noted, "To have to do laborious work like sweeping floors and adding up numbers is depressing enough; to take *pride* in such things is absolutely appalling." Oscar was wrong. Professionals *want* to take pride in their work, they *want* to do a good job for their firm and its customers, and they *want* to grow and reach new possibilities in the process. It is the firm leaders—and its executives—that will determine the fate of human capital investors. Attracting, retaining, and rewarding human capital is the single most important role of leadership.

Dan Morris flies his firm's flag over his office building (below the American flag, of course) with its name and logo in three colors. Recall that those who first called themselves *liberals*—in the classical definition of the word—had in mind three liberations (which explains why the appropriate liberal flag is always *tricolore*). They intended, first, to liberate humans from tyranny and torture; second, to liberate humans from poverty; and, third, to liberate humans from censorship and other oppressions of conscience, intellect, and art. It is time we hoist a new flag over the firm of the future and usher in a new order of the ages, one that respects the dignity, and earns the rewards, of its human capital investors.

6

STRUCTURAL CAPITAL:
IF ONLY WE KNEW WHAT WE KNOW

*The only irreplaceable capital an organization possesses is the knowledge
and ability of its people. The productivity of that capital depends on
how effectively people share their competence with those who can use it.*

—Andrew Carnegie,
*Unlocking Knowledge Assets:
Knowledge Management Solutions from Microsoft*

Hollywood is a town that thrives on intellectual capital, always looking outside itself for material to leverage into movies and other forms of entertainment, from novels, comic books, plays, videogames, and television shows. Walt Disney Co. has decided to leverage its own structural capital in a new and innovative way, as described in this article from the *Orlando Sentinel*, by Richard Verrier:

Walt Disney Co. is developing three movies based on classic theme-park attractions, adding a new twist to an idea the company exploited a half century ago. The movies— The Country Bears, Pirates of the Caribbean, and Haunted Mansion—are inspired by the iconic Disney attractions and will be released this year and next. The movies mark a new chapter in the history of film and a new strategy for Disney, which until now has modeled its theme-park rides and shows mainly on its own movies, from *Snow White and the Seven Dwarfs* to *Lion King*.

Walt Disney built Disneyland in 1955 as a physical home for the cartoon characters he and his animators created on screen. Walt Disney's idea of synergy or cross-promotion, which other media companies now mimic, reaches new heights in the upcoming movies. The titles will already be familiar to millions of Americans who have visited Disney's parks in Orlando, Florida, and Anaheim, California, providing Disney with a ready-made audience at a time when studios are competing fiercely to market their movies. By shining the light back on the company's classic attractions, the movies also will help promote Disney's theme parks. "This just seemed to be so natural that we'd be crazy not to pursue it," Disney Studios chief Dick Cook said. "These are Disney icons. They just lend themselves to movies." Cook should know. The studio executive began his 31-year career at Disney as a ride operator, and his wife once worked at the Country Bears Jamboree show in Anaheim. "These films are the definition of the kind of films we want to do," he said. Disney may produce more such movies if the first three are successful, Cook said. His experiment comes as Disney is testing new waters to improve its box-office performance with more family-oriented fare tied to the company's roots. Disney, challenged by rival hits such as *Harry Potter and the Sorcerer's Stone* and *The Lord of the Rings*, is seeking to reclaim its reputation as a leader in family movies. Disney's new strategy also underscores how movies increasingly are becoming vehicles to market products, from videogames to cars, film historians say. "There's a tremendous paucity of new ideas today," said Rick Jewell, associate dean of the School of Cinema-Television at the University of Southern California. "The studios are not willing to take enough chances with new material." Company executives dismiss that idea. "There would be no point in making these movies if you didn't think they had the right to exist on their own terms; otherwise they'd be commercials, not movies," Disney studios production chief Nina Jacobson said. "The truth is Walt was one of the greatest minds of the twentieth century, and there are reasons why these rides are so popular and people remember them. If you have access to this great cultural iconography, there's no shame in going back to it." Though Disney produced a made-for-TV movie in 1997 based on the Tower of Terror attraction at Disney-MGM Studios in Orlando, the studio has never developed a feature film from a theme park attraction. . . . The parks will help spread the word, and movies should give the attraction a lift. "It does help raise awareness for our attractions," Walt Disney Parks and Resorts spokeswoman Leslie Goodman said (Verrier, 2002).

RON The genius of this strategy is how Disney is leveraging its intellectual capital—specifically, its structural and customer capital. Disney has a rich history of flouting the conventional wisdom, especially when you consider where its founder located his two most popular theme parks—in orange and walnut groves (Disneyland in Anaheim, California) and swampland (Walt Disney World in Orlando, Florida). The oft-repeated mantra in real estate—location, location, location—can be overcome by intellectual capital, when you consider that Disney purchased 29,500 acres in Orlando for an average price of $200 an acre. Today, that same acreage is valued at $1 million per acre. With respect to the Sentinel article quoted, certainly Disney is enhancing the movies described to include more than the ride attractions, but the fact is, the idea stems from rides built nearly 50 years ago; and considering that millions of people of all ages have experienced these attractions, the leverage here is enormous. And this enormous leverage translates to huge revenue gains.

Yet most professional services firms don't use leverage this way. They think only of leveraging people or, even worse, leveraging hours. What they need to focus on is leveraging their IC.

The Intellectual Capital Management Gathering, a group of leading companies in the forefront of managing their IC, met in January 1995 and defined IC this way: "Knowledge that can be converted into profits" (Lev, 2001: 155). Karl-Erik Sveiby defines *knowledge management* (KM) as: "the art of creating value from intangible assets ("value" being both financial and nonfinancial)."

Though not enamored with the term *knowledge management*, for reasons discussed in Chapter 5 on human capital, because we are concerning ourselves with structural, not human, capital in this chapter, we will use the term since it is in the mainstream of business lexicon and will make it easier for those of you who want to further your understanding—by doing more research—of this important field.

Knowledge management is, of course, nothing new. Standard operating procedures documented in a manual accomplished the same thing, long before computers were available. Libraries around the world house stores of structural capital. For our purposes, structural capital—your firm's systems, procedures, technology, databases and other processes you use in order to get work done—is the knowledge that does not go home at night, as opposed to your firm's human capital, which does. Structural capital is important because it prevents—or should prevent—firms from re-creating the wheel. But as Thomas Stewart points out, "'Reinventing the wheel' is the inevitable phrase, and most companies are so good at it you'd think they were suppliers to Schwinn" (Stewart, 2001: 223). All of the major accounting firms, consultancy firms, and many Fortune 500 companies now have chief knowledge officers, whose job it is to create knowledge, capture knowledge, and organize that knowledge in such a manner so it can be accessed by those who need it, in the format they need it, precisely when they need it. It is not necessarily *what* you know that counts, it's *when* you know it. Making it easier for your firm's human capital to tap into the structural capital of the firm is essential if you want to maximize your operating leverage.

Any KM system should deal with capturing the tacit knowledge that exists in your firm's human capital and placing it where those who may need it in the future can reuse it. Professional service firms have vast reservoirs of tacit knowledge, but since it resides in the heads of their people, it never makes its way into the firm's structural capital. It would have done Walt Disney no good to dream of creating the *Pirates of the Caribbean* unless he shared his knowledge and vision with his so-called imagineers to turn his dream into a reality. KM is not about creating another database, or intranet portal; rather it is about sharing knowledge throughout the firm, in a reusable format, in order to leverage what the firm knows more effectively.

Firms need to define their key technical know-how in each department, decide on a place where it should reside, and determine how to articulate it. In their book *Unlocking Knowledge Assets: Knowledge Management Solutions from Microsoft*, Susan Conway and Char Sligar outline the key elements of an effective KM system:

Storage. The system should include a repository to put knowledge assets (KAs). It might also have document tracking and version control, security, search, and rating capabilities.

Publishing. The system should allow several people to view and access information while restricting who can create and publish the information. It might include tracking and search features.

Subscription. The system should allow users to set rules regarding the information that will be automatically "pushed" to them. It might also be able to differentiate formats for certain participants, have an updating feature, and so on.

Reuse. The system should provide a many-to-many publishing environment. It might include rating, restricting, and tracking features.

Collaboration. The system should allow several contributors to work together to create a single piece of content and manage revision tracking. It might identify experts and their online availability, discussions, and so on.

> **Communication.** The system should capture and manage all forms of information exchange, including e-mail, phone, instant messaging, and face-to-face dialogue, and allow for spontaneous communication (Conway and Sligar, 2002: 17).

Microsoft, perhaps the preeminent intellectual capital organization in recent history, has more than 2.5 million intranet pages, and 2,000 intranet Web sites in order to achieve the preceding. It is what Bill Gates describes as "thinking work, through blending a business's processes and corporate culture with the enabling technology to foster an innovative environment" (Ibid: 4).

Make no mistake, KM is not simply a new technological tool that we are suggesting you add to your firm's capacity; this is a *cultural* change in the way you view what it is your firm is creating, disseminating and selling. Professional service firms are no different from Microsoft—both are the epitome of pure, undiluted, IC organizations.

PAUL This is the mind-shift we want you to make: "My professional service firm is the epitome of a pure, undiluted IC organization." Write that out and perhaps even stick it on your office wall to remind everyone who enters your office of that truth. Consider what a mind-shifting paradigm it is. While your competitors down the road are stuck in the myopic view that the levers of revenue and profitability are hourly realization rates and people power, you now know that is not the case, because your firm is the epitome of a pure, undiluted IC organization. And of course that means that in your firm (and in every firm of the future) knowledge capture, use and reuse is the *critical success factor.*

RON Think about the typical firm: How many times does that firm have to redo work because the person who did it originally couldn't be located (perhaps they left the firm's employ) or didn't take the time to document the *tacit* knowledge he or she learned so it would become *explicit* knowledge and part of the firm's structural capital? How often do firms invest in their human capital, perhaps by sending them to additional educational courses, but then never capture the knowledge learned?

Adding a sophisticated KM software program to your firm is not going to create any long-term sustainable advantages unless you start to understand the importance of leveraging knowledge. All innovation and creativity depend on knowledge, yet the average firm is so busy billing hours, it devotes no time or attention to this critical resource. The missed opportunities are enormous, both in terms of lack of innovation and creativity, along with lost profitability from not climbing higher on the customer's value curve.

LEVERAGING IC AND CREATING THE WORLD'S SECOND LARGEST CURRENCY

RON Humorist Art Buchwald gave this advice to Judith Martin ("Miss Manners") when she was starting her career at the *Washington Post*: "Never sell anything only once," he told her, explaining that the material he used in his newspaper columns he repackaged and resold in hardcover books, then in paperback, then told and sold again on talk shows and in paid speeches. That's what distilled knowledge is all about" (quoted in Stewart, 2001: 145).

The airlines certainly learned this lesson. Launched exactly 21 years ago at the time of this writing in May 2002, and as reported in *The Economist*, May 4, 2002), American Airlines launched the AAdvantage frequent-flyer program, which has become its own currency as of late and almost instantaneously duplicated by all airlines. At the end of April 2002, collectively, close to 8.5 trillion miles remained unredeemed; valued at the midpoint market value of between 2 and 9 cents apiece, the global currency is worth $500 billion (compared to notes and coins in circulation around the world, frequent-flyer currency could be said to be the second-largest currency after the dollar). These miles are fought over in divorce battles, and two-thirds of passengers polled said they see their miles as the next best thing to actual cash. One in three Americans now collect them, and roughly one-half of all miles are earned on the ground (through affinity programs with credit cards, hotels, rental car companies, telephone calls, etc.), generating approximately $10 billion for the airlines in 2001. US Airways now offers a deal whereby for 10 million miles you can purchase a seat on the first private spacecraft to take passengers into space in 2004. All this wealth created from leveraging a reservation system, plastic cards embossed with a customer's name and a frequent-flyer number, and empty plane seats. This spectacular wealth generation was not created by an industry that believes it sells passenger seat miles, or worse, passenger seat hours.

The contrast with "physical" capital couldn't be more revealing when examining the real leverage embedded in professional service firms. As mentioned earlier, if an airline assigns a Boeing 777 to the San Francisco-London route, it cannot be used at the same time for the San Francisco-Tokyo route. However, the airline's reservation system, which is based on its structural capital and its social capital (customer and supplier capital), can conceivably handle an unlimited number of customers. This is precisely why intellectual capital is a nonrival asset, as opposed to physical or financial capital.

At some point you might start to experience another interval of "cognitive dissonance," because we're using examples from the airline industry. After all, as many commentators have noted, since World War II, the airlines industry as a whole has essentially broken even. So why use the airlines as a model of success? It is a good question, and one frequently asked, so it behooves us to address it now since we will be using the airlines in many more examples throughout the book.

Even though not all the airlines are the most profitable businesses, some carriers certainly are, and others have had record years, and when they have, they have followed the same strategies in the areas of pricing, capacity utilization, marketing, and other ways to deploy their intellectual capital. An argument could be made that if the airlines were not adept at these functions, they would not exist. Another way to look at this is to be grateful the professional services sector isn't as intensely competitive as the airline industry, since legal and accounting firms operate on profit margins that would be the envy of any airline. Further, since the airlines have large fixed costs— and relatively low marginal costs—they offer many valuable lessons to the professional service firm in these areas. In specific areas—pricing and capacity utilization in particular—the airlines offer many "best practices," so it is important to understand why they do what they do. I'll admit a certain fascination with the industry, mostly because I spend so much of my time on airplanes, and I constantly find myself asking, "Why do they do it that way?" and "How could this facet of their operation be applied to a professional service firm?"

This constant questioning is a form of benchmarking (a buzzword coined in the last decade or so), a practice that has been around forever. Just as the founding framers of the United States Constitution looked at the historical record of other civilizations and took the best ideas from each, and just as Henry Ford got the idea for his automated assembly line by visiting a slaughterhouse, the opportunities to learn from other industries is endless. My first book, *Professional's Guide to Value Pricing*, was a comprehensive benchmarking study of pricing in other industries and centuries-old economic pricing theory. By looking at the best of the best from alternative pricing models in existence, the concepts of fixed-price agreement, change orders, bundling, and others, were developed. In fact, one of the most successful—and essential—tools in implementing value pricing in a professional service firm is the change order, a pricing tool originally developed by contractors. Professionals have no monopoly on intelligence, as the change order is perhaps the most sophisticated pricing tool ever developed, for reasons we will explore in Chapter 9.

The point is this: We can (no, we must) learn from other intellectual capital organizations how to best leverage our own knowledge assets. William Cobb, the father of the famous Value Curve, cites the following as an example of a firm that has successfully leveraged its intellectual capital:

> Linklaters of London has created an expert system to provide very complex legal services that can be accessed through the Internet called "Blue Flag." Traditionally, a client would hire Linklaters to do a one-time survey of the law and produce the resulting memorandum. This would cost approximately £125,000. With Blue Flag, that same fee (plus £40,000 for annual maintenance) buys access to the same information, for an unlimited number of surveys (Cobb, November 2000: 4 at www.Cobb-Consulting.com).

Cobb explains that it took a team approximately two years to develop this form of intellectual capital, during which time, of course, the efficiency of the professionals involved—as measured in billable hours—deteriorated. No doubt the airline industry suffered the same efficiency drop when developing the frequent-flyer program. Does this mean we shouldn't invest the resources necessary to innovate and create new product and service offerings? Apparently the professions have answered this question with a resounding "Yes."

Consider this: The last truly new service offering produced from the ground up in the CPA profession was the Statement on Standards for Accounting and Review Services (SSARS), effective in 1978. All of the other new services the profession has offered to the marketplace—from eldercare to Webtrust and from XBRL to Systrust—are merely extensions of services offered by others. In other words, the CPA profession has a 24-year—and counting—innovation curve! This is unacceptable; and one of the reasons for it is our incessant focus on efficiency and billable hours at the expense of effectiveness and innovation. No doubt efficiency affects your firm's income statement, but it is your innovation, dynamism, and creativity that build your balance sheet. How else could Disney create spectacular wealth on swampland, or the airlines devise the world's second-largest currency?

CONVERTING TACIT TO EXPLICIT KNOWLEDGE

RON William Cobb further points, "Most firms cannot get their lawyers to use the same forms much less share ideas." This is an incredible waste of the most important asset the firm of the future needs to leverage—its intellectual capital.

The philosopher Michael Polanyi first defined tacit and explicit knowledge. To illustrate tacit knowledge, he said, try explaining how to ride a bike or swim. Tacit knowledge is "sticky," in that it is not easily articulated and exists in people's minds. It is complex and rich, whereas explicit knowledge tends to be thin, like the difference between looking at a map and taking a journey of a certain territory. It is the difference between reading the employee manual and spending one hour chatting with a coworker about the true nature of the job and culture of the firm. In order for tacit knowledge to become explicit knowledge—that is, stored somewhere where it can be viewed, reviewed, and used by others—it must first be converted from the mind to another medium (a database, white paper, report, manual, video, picture, etc.). Tacit knowledge tends to be dynamic, while explicit knowledge is static; both are required for innovation and leverage to take place.

KM systems require *communities of practice* (CoPs) in order to leverage a firm's IC. These communities can be created through intranet sites, internal notes, databases, or Web portals. Each enhances the ability of knowledge workers to access the knowledge they need, when they need it. The system can even have a ranking of the usefulness of the various KAs, much the same way that amazon.com lets its customers review and rate the value of the books it sells.

It is an axiom of knowledge management thinkers that the best venue for exchanging tacit knowledge is around the coffeepot or the watercooler. Informal conversations among employees are rich with knowledge sharing. The old Industrial Revolution admonition, "Stop talking and get to work," changes to "Start talking and get to work" in an organization of knowledge workers. KM systems do nothing more than take some of this tacit knowledge and make it explicit by putting it in a location where people can find it when they need it. In a true KM system, each team member is a knowledge consumer and a knowledge producer. To a certain extent, professional service firms already acknowledge the importance of this kind of knowledge transfer. However, it is usually done on an ad hoc basis; it is not one of the requirements of the firm, let alone the measurement metrics. Far too often a firm will perform an outstanding job on behalf of a customer, and may even celebrate the resulting success; what it fails to do is capture what was learned so it can be leveraged in the future.

How can a firm capture all of its important tacit knowledge and turn it into explicit knowledge to be used by others facing the same jobs? Once again, through studying best practices. To that end, we turn to what at first may appear to be an unlikely source of a knowledge organization—the U.S. Army.

KNOWLEDGE LESSONS FROM THE U.S. ARMY

RON During the month of June 2002 I had two long conversations with U.S. Army personnel, one an active sergeant in the Army Reserves, and the second a retired 20-year major, who happened to be reading the same book I was—*Hope Is Not a Method*—on a flight we were on together. We talked mostly about the Army's policy of doing After-Action Reviews (AARs), which take place after every training event. Both officers assured me that the Army's goal is never to reinvent the wheel. In fact, the retired major expressed his incessant frustration with his company's inability to adopt the AAR in order to spread its knowledge internally (the main objection seemed to be "Why would we want to waste time doing that?").

After studying the Army's use of AARs, which originated in 1973, and thinking back on my own career in public accounting, I became convinced it is a practice that would have many salutary effects in the professional service firm of the future. Perhaps we ignore innovations in the military because its mission seems to be so divergent from that of a civilian organization. But this is far too parochial an attitude; and once again we discover a useful practice from another sector. In fact, because the AAR is such a useful method for turning tacit knowledge into explicit knowledge, not to mention to foster learning and sharing of knowledge throughout the organization, I will quote at length from Gordon R. Sullivan and Michael V. Harper's book *Hope Is Not a Method: What Business Leaders Can Learn from America's Army*:

An AAR takes place after every training event. Its purposes are simple: learning, improving, doing better the next time. The participants sit down with a facilitator called an "observer-controller" who has been with them throughout the event, and they discuss what happened. To do this effectively requires several things. First, there must be a fairly good basis for understanding what actually happened. . . . Soldiers call this "ground truth." Combined with ground truth, there must be a fairly unambiguous understanding of what should have happened, and that comes from having standards derived from doctrine.

Given those elements, it is possible to talk about an event in a way that focuses on improving team performance without getting caught up in individual performance, rank, position, or personality. By asking questions such as "What did you think I wanted you to do?" (as opposed to questions such as "How did you screw that up?"), one can get to the roots of both success and failure. This is not an easy process, and it generally takes a lot of time, maybe two to three hours to "AAR" a major event. The cost in time alone is heavy, but the outcome is a much more in-depth understanding of what happened. The return on investment, measured by improved performance, is very high.

The most difficult challenge is developing a culture that values this kind of learning. A colleague in industry once described an attempt to initiate a similar program in his company. He told me of a dialogue with a loading dock foreman who, in great frustration, finally said to him, "Look, I can either ship product or talk about it. Which do you want me to do?" The answer can only be "Both," but it is hard to make that answer a reality. It took a decade for the AAR process to become respected in the Army, for us to learn that you can do both—ship product and talk—and that carefully structured talking leads to more effective shipping or whatever. It is an investment that no one can afford not to make.

Today AARs take place in garrisons, on staffs, and in headquarters—everywhere soldiers gather to perform some task. My personal staff would hold AARs for me after a major event in which I had participated. I did not especially enjoy discussing the gaps in my own performance—especially when I felt pretty good about what I had done—but these AARs helped me improve, and they helped my staff learn to support me better.

For America's Army, the AAR was the key to turning the corner and institutionalizing organizational learning. You probably never become a learning organization in any absolute sense; it can only be something you aspire to, always "becoming," never truly "being." But, in the Army, the AAR has ingrained a respect for organizational learning, fostering an expectation that decisions and consequent actions will be reviewed in a way that will benefit both the participants and the organization, no matter how painful it may be at the time. The only real failure is the failure to learn (Sullivan and Harper, 1996: 191–93).

Imagine the benefits of having a library of AARs for almost any type of engagement the firm may encounter. Imagine further creating a culture that rewards professionals for taking the time to contribute to this stock of knowledge, and perhaps even determines its utility by tracking how many times particular AARs are accessed by others. Once your firm is comfortable dissecting the performance *after* each engagement, it will be better equipped to make plans and preparations *before* the next one. As a result, innovation, creativity, and risk taking will flourish as the firm constantly strives for improvement in an iterative process that respects and rewards learning. Here are the questions you need to ask in each AAR:

- What happened?
- Why did it happen?
- What should we do about it?

Each team member who worked on the engagement would participate in this process. The AAR is not a tool to fix blame or point fingers; it is a learning tool, designed to increase the effectiveness of the firm. Its role is to be *analytical*, not *critical*. It also fosters a true team environment and makes everyone responsible for the success of the engagement; moreover, it is a development tool that helps leaders to become more engaged in the success of their teams. If there are shortcomings, the AAR fixes the *problem*, not assesses the *blame*. Even if only one individual completes an AAR because there was no team on the engagement, it is still an effective way to spread learning and knowledge to other members of the firm.

The Army suggests you divide your time in answering the AAR's questions into 25–25–50: That is, 25 percent reviewing what happened, 25 percent reviewing why it happened, and the remaining 50 percent on what to do about it and how can you learn from it in order to improve. As Sullivan and Harper point out:

> Earlier we argued that, as we face our external environment, "We don't know what we don't know." As we face our internal environment, it seems that the opposite is too often true: "We don't know what we *do* know." As an important organizational asset, knowledge is usable only if can be identified and disseminated so as to contribute value. The challenge is to discover what is known in any part of the organization and, if it is valuable, make it known to all (Ibid: 206).

In my role as an educator, conducting courses and seminars around the world, I have always conducted an informal AAR, usually right after the event (or even during breaks and lunchtime, in order to make corrections and improve). Paul and I did this when we toured together, constantly offering each other tips on how to say something clearer, to give a better example, or to find a better way of structuring our material. These conversations were constant, and they effectively transferred an enormous amount of tacit knowledge between us.

There is enormous value in immediacy here. By the time you read an evaluation of a seminar, it is too late, you are reading history; and while it can shed some helpful light on how to improve, it is never as useful as an AAR would be right after the event. In fact, it is very similar to a timesheet—that is, they are both *lagging indicators*. What we want are *leading indicators* that can help us stay away from obstacles and problems or deal with them effectively when they do arise. To this day, within VeraSage Institute (the think tank I cofounded that is dedicated to teaching value pricing to professionals around the world), everyone who performs a seminar, speech, or course, completes an AAR with a team member, which has resulted in enormous improvements in the way we present ideas to our colleagues around the world. Without question, it is sometimes very uncomfortable to face your performance errors and mishaps; but how else are knowledge workers suppose to learn? By getting an annual review? Practical learning demands hands-on, experiential knowledge that only those closest to the engagement can capture and share. It's helpful to remember that McDonald's Big Mac, fried apple pie, large fries, McDLT, and Egg McMuffin were all invented by local franchisees, not as part of a corporate headquarter strategy.

No doubt AARs take time and will impair efficiency (at least in the short run). Once again, we can hear the objections from the profession on this note, which is myopically focused on efficiency rather than effectiveness and learning. Your firm's IC is the most important source of its long-term wealth-creating ability. It must be constantly replenished and created in order to build the firm's balance sheet. Constantly focusing on *doing* rather than learning, creativity, innovation, and knowledge sharing is the equivalent of eating the firm's seed corn.

Capturing the tacit knowledge that exists in the heads of your human capital and making it part of your firm's structural capital will ensure that your firm knows what it knows, and can deploy it quicker and at a lower marginal cost. It is IC that is the ultimate lever in the firm of the future, and firms have to begin to understand this fundamental economic truth of wealth creation.

SUMMARY AND CONCLUSIONS

We have explored the necessity of capturing your firm's tacit human capital and creating structural capital as a result, which will stay with your firm even if your human capital should depart. We also discussed why it is so important to leverage your structural capital to create wealth both for the firm's customers and itself. The new Disney movies based on popular ride attractions from its theme park, and the airline frequent flyer programs, are both excellent examples of this process.

Isn't it tragic that professionals are among today's preeminent knowledge workers, yet they are not really rewarded for thinking and reflecting because they are too busy doing and billing? Instead of asking someone who is reading a book at, say, one of the Big 4 firms, "Don't you have enough work to do?" wouldn't a better question be, "What are you learning from that book?" But that question requires we shift our focus from efficiency and billable hours to effectiveness, learning, and adding to our intellectual capital. The focus sends a mixed message to the firm's team members: Partners say they understand the importance of IC, innovation, and creativity, but they aren't really willing to make the investments necessary in order to create more of it and to leverage it effectively. Part of the problem is that our traditional metrics focus on precisely the wrong things (since the old theory of the firm is itself flawed), and we haven't taken the necessary time to study the success of other IC organizations—that is, until now. In fact, we posit the following argument: Most firms' legacy systems of measurements and reward systems—billable hours, timesheets, and other production oriented metrics—have actually become negative structural capital in the context of becoming a firm of the future. As with negative human capital, these types of antiquated capital must be extricated from the firm in order for the firm to achieve its latent potential.

Now that we have covered the human and structural capital components of your firm's IC, we turn our attention to what is perhaps the least leveraged—and perhaps least understood and underutilized—form of your firm's IC—its social capital.

7

SOCIAL CAPITAL:
MAN IS NOT AN ISLAND

Man is a social animal.

—Seneca, *De beneficiis*

Most people are familiar with the Archimedes saying, "Give me a lever long enough, and I shall move the earth." What is often forgotten is that he also said he needed not just a lever but "a place to stand." Without a solid ground—a family, neighborhood, a common corporate culture, social norms and customs—we move nothing, we do nothing, we become nothing. Yet, until recently, social capital is an area that has largely been ignored by businesspeople. We are just beginning to understand the importance of societal influences on human behavior.

RON Perhaps one of the reasons social capital has been ignored by economists, political philosophers, and businesspeople is the myth that capitalism depends on rugged individualists, entrepreneurs who constantly challenge the status quo with new ideas, services, and products that bring forth a "perennial gale of creative destruction," driven by an impersonal "invisible hand."

But an individual alone is not a corporation, and buying and selling are activities as ancient as the human race, and do not have much to do with capitalism. What does make capitalism unique is the fact that it is an organizing ethos, a corporate enterprise, a collective effort. It is far more dependent on social order, and is more social in nature, than its enemies—or its friends, for that matter—have yet to understand. The essence of capitalism is an organizing structure to house the division of labor, division of purposes, and a division of talents. That organizing structure is a *voluntary association*, registered in law as a *corporation*. The corporation transcends the life of any single individual, and it binds people cooperatively across time and space, voluntarily.

Corporate law was based on the law of the monasteries. The Benedictines were the first multinational corporations, selling wine, cheese, and honey all over Europe and the world. As Michael Novak explains:

> They also did it, interestingly enough, by being the first to be so efficient at it that they could live above subsistence. They lived on their own profits. They were such good farmers that they could give seven hours to prayer a day. They could work seven hours and pray seven hours because they were efficient businessmen and they sold across many nations. Corporate law developed out of monastic law because it was the only model for something that lived longer than any individual and it was given to something more than subsistence living (quoted in Younkins, 2001: 62).

No one raises their children to be *rugged individualists*. Rather, we raise them to work, play, and get along well with others of all different backgrounds. The sociologist James Coleman defines social capital as

> "the ability of people to work together for common purposes in groups and organizations; the ability to associate with each other, that is critical not only to economic life but to virtually every other aspect of social existence as well" (quoted in Fukuyama, 1995: 10).

A free market economy depends on the voluntary cooperation of many competing interests, not on the fable of the lone cowboy. Michael Novak cogently explains the American model:

> But what is the American model? Many commentators, especially those on the continent but also those Americans infected with continental ideas of a socialist, Rousseauian, collectivist cast, think that what dominates the American imagination is the individual, the lonely cowboy riding carefree on the prairie, the free and unconnected atomic self, the do-as-he-pleases outlaw on the frontier beyond the laws of the city. By contrast, Europeans, a visitor observes, tend to fear the independent individual; they visibly prefer people tied down by a thousand gossamer Gulliver's threads of tradition, custom, and unquestioning willingness to do things as they have always been done.
>
> A specter haunts Europe still—the specter of the free individual questioning the rationality of custom, tradition, and habit; the individual who is communitarian, but not wholly defined by his community.
>
> Nonetheless, despite its reputation, the American character is not the exact opposite of the European character—is not purely individualistic—but communitarian without being intensely communal. The true inner heart of America, as Tocqueville grasped right at the beginning, is the art of association. In America, fifty years after the ratification of the Constitution of 1787, Tocqueville observed thousands of associations, societies, clubs, organizations, and fraternities invented by a self-governing people unaccustomed to being told by the state (or even custom) what to do and when to do it. At the time of the revolution in France, he wrote, there were not ten men in all of France who were capable of practicing the art of association as most Americans practiced it.
>
> In the new science of politics, Tocqueville added, the art of association is the first law of democracy. This art does not belong to Americans only. It is rooted in the social nature of man. Its source does not lie in the authority of the state (as in France) or of the aristocracy (as in Britain), but in the capacity of all citizens to originate cooperative activities with their fellows, without being commanded from above. The American is not

the individual par excellence, but the practitioner of association par excellence. The American is through and through a social being. Virtually nothing significant gets done in America apart from free associations, of a virtually infinite number of kinds. In this view, the primary agent of the common good is civil society; the state is secondary (quoted in Younkins, 2001: 99–100: 99–100).

Even Adam Smith, the father of modern economics and the man who coined the term "invisible hand," understood the importance of social capital in creating the wealth of nations. In his first book, *The Theory of Moral Sentiments* (first published in 1759), Smith's opening paragraph begins:

> How selfish whatsoever man may be supposed, there are evidently some principles in his nature, which interest him in the fortune of others, and render their happiness necessary to him, though he derives nothing from it except the pleasure of seeing it (Smith, 2000: 3).

Smith explicitly understood that impersonal market forces don't force people to become impersonal. Economic life cannot be divorced from the customs, morals, traditions, and habits of the culture in which it exists. Smith poses a thought experiment in this book that is quite intriguing: Suppose you could save 100 million people at the expense of losing your little finger. Would you do it? Most people answer yes, and Smith suggests that this proves that people don't always act in their selfish and sordid interests. Instead, we desire the external praise of others, and we desire to attain the internal respect and praise of *ourselves*. We ultimately want to be *worthy* of our praise—in other words, we desire to be *praiseworthy*.

The development of human capital is obviously not an *individual* process but a *social* process. Human skills grow and develop only if one generation teaches the next. In a knowledge economy, at some point, your fellow worker's human capital becomes as important to your earning potential as your own. If he or she is uneducated, a ceiling will be placed on your potential. Nowhere is the concept of how social capital affects—negatively in this instance—the wealth of nations better illustrated than in the cost of the socialist experiment. As measured in the loss of human capital creation, including the work ethic, entrepreneurship, habits, customs, risk taking, creativity, and trust, the socialist dream is dead. Consider the human capital that has fled Cuba's negative social capital structure, as told by British historian Paul Johnson:

> In fact, the Cuban community in the United States grew and flourished. By the second half of the 1990s, it had founded 750,000 new businesses, become the richest and most influential political lobby after the Jewish lobby, and its 2 million members generated a Gross Domestic Product eleven times larger than that of Cuba itself, with 11 million inhabitants. Moreover, Miami, center of the new Cuban settlement, forming links with the entire Latin American society of the hemisphere, became in many ways its financial, economic, communications, and cultural center, hugely boosting American exports in goods and, still more, in services throughout the western half of the globe. In the long run, then, the grand beneficiary of the Cuban missile crisis was indeed the United States (Johnson, 1997: 867).

This is precisely why it is often wryly noted that Fidel Castro did more to develop the southern United States than did air conditioning. It also helps explain why the

Spanish philosopher Pedro Saenz Rodriguez said from exile in Lisbon a dozen years ago, "But if I wanted the American Constitution to prevail in Spain, I would import not the Constitution, but Americans" (quoted in Buckley, Jr., 2000: 241). It is also why, when asked what one book he would put into the hands of a Russian Communist, then-President Franklin Delano Roosevelt replied: "The Sears Roebuck catalog."

Culture matters. Cultures are not merely customs to be displayed in museums, but rather they are a particular way of accomplishing the things that make life possible. Social influences play a significant role in shaping human behavior. Author Alvin Toffler used to shock business conference attendees by asking them what it would cost in real cash terms if none of their employees had ever been toilet trained. Nobody knew, but they immediately understood the enormous subsidy provided by the transmission of social and human capital from one generation to the next. We are just beginning to comprehend the importance of social capital, and how it affects the development of people's individual human capital, and indeed their behavior, tastes, and preferences, as we will explore next.

IS THERE AN ACCOUNTING FOR TASTES?

RON You like bowling, I enjoy golf. You prefer white wine, I savor red. You always purchase Fords, I choose General Motors. The standard explanation for all of these human differences can be found in the English translation of the Latin proverb: "There's no accounting for tastes." But is that true? How do we acquire our various tastes? Is it custom, tradition, habit, or something else that explains individual preferences and why people behave the way they do? Gary S. Becker, a professor of Economics and Sociology at the University of Chicago, who in 1992 was awarded the Nobel Price in Economics, has an explanation for individual preferences that explains a great deal of human behavior. In his book *Accounting for Tastes*, he argues that, in modern industrialized countries—where basic biological needs for food, drink, and shelter have been adequately provided for—the necessities of life have little to do with the consumption habits of the average person. "Rather," according to Becker, "these choices depend on childhood and other experiences, social interactions, and cultural influences" (Becker, 1996: 3).

In addition to the pioneering work Becker has done in the area of human capital, where he has argued that spending on such items as education, training, medical care, and so forth should be classified as investments, not merely consumption, as governments and corporations are wont to do, in this recent book, Becker expanded on his definition of human capital to embody two components:

> My approach incorporates experiences and social forces into preferences or tastes through two basic capital stocks. *Personal capital, P,* includes the relevant past consumption and other personal experiences that affect current and future utilities. *Social capital, S,* incorporates the influences of past actions by peers and others in an individual's social network and control system. A person's personal and social capital form part of his total stock of human capital (Ibid: 4).

In other words, the fact that you have, for example, smoked in the past will, more or less, determine your future smoking consumption—that is now part of your personal capital. But what made you smoke in the first place? Perhaps it was peer pressure, which is part of your social capital, as Becker defines it. We all understand that word of mouth—and, with today's ubiquitous World Wide Web, word of mouse—advertising is the most effective. National surveys reveal that, three times out of four, most consumers rely on the advice of friends and family before making a purchase. Most successful professional firms have built their business almost solely on word-of-mouth advertising, and Becker's theory of social capital explains why it is so powerful:

> Men and women want respect, recognition, prestige, acceptance, and power from their family, peers, and others. Consumption and other activities have a major social component partly because they take place in public. As a result, people often choose restaurants, neighborhoods, schools, books to read, political opinions, food, or leisure activities with an eye to pleasing peers and others in their social network (Ibid: 12).

Psychologists refer to the *principle of social proof*, which states that one means we use to determine what is correct is to find out what other people think is correct. Social proof is a major motivator of individual behavior, and this explains why organizations such as weight-reduction clinics rely on public commitment and peer pressure to change behavior. It also explains why TV executives insist on using laugh tracks for sit-coms, even though most people say they don't like them. Experiments have found laugh tracks cause an audience to laugh longer and more often than they would in their absence. Bartenders will often "salt" their tip jars with a few dollars at the start of each evening to give the impression that tipping is proper behavior. Advertisers will often tout their product as the "fastest-growing" or "largest-selling," not to convince us the product or service is good, but to imply many others think so, which seems proof enough.

It has been estimated that the Tupperware Home Parties Corporation generates sales in excess of $2.5 million a day. This success is easier to understand when you consider Tupperware parties are usually thrown by friends rather than unknown salespersons. With this method, the hostess is relying on the attraction, affinity, warmth, security, and the obligation of friendship in order to make the sale. Mary Kay Ash used essentially the same strategy when she founded her cosmetics company, Mary Kay Cosmetics, in 1963, with her life savings of $5,000. When she passed away on Thanksgiving Day in November 2001, at the age of 83, she left a legacy with her corporation, which generates sales of more than $1 billion a year. Her company has made more women millionaires than any other organization in history; after the fall of communism, it even made headway in Russia. In 1995, Mary Kay's top Russian sales director earned more money than then-President Boris Yeltsin. Today, 850,000 women in 37 countries leverage the principle of social proof to create wealth for their customers, and in turn, for themselves.

Another important qualification of social proof, as pointed out by Robert B. Cialdini in his fascinating book, *Influence: The New Psychology of Modern Persuasion,* is that, "We will use the actions of others to decide on the proper behavior for ourselves, especially when we view those others as similar to ourselves" (Cialdini, 1993: 142). Witness teenagers whom adults tend to think of as rebellious and independent-minded. However, when you see them in a group, you realize how much they behave, talk, dress, and act the same as their friends and associates. They conform massively to their own peer pressures.

LEVERAGING THE SOCIAL CAPITAL IN THE FIRM OF THE FUTURE

RON A firm's social capital comprises the following elements:

- Customers
- Reputation and brands
- Referral sources and networks
- Suppliers and vendors
- Shareholders and other external stakeholders
- Joint venture partners and alliances
- Professional associations and formal affiliations
- Firm alumni

One of the advantages of looking at a firm's social capital in this manner is that it expands the boundaries of what a firm can leverage. The factors just listed give the firm "a place to stand" to use Archimedes' phrase. In a knowledge-based economy, the old lines of distinction between a customer, supplier, vendor, and so on become blurred. It does not really matter whether a person or an organization is both a customer and supplier or member of a joint venture, as long as he or she adds value in the economic chain. For instance, as an author, I am a customer, reviewer, and supplier to www.amazon.com, and—hopefully—creating value in each role. Enabling me to play multiple roles, Amazon is able to leverage its wealth-creating potential utilizing its social capital.

Customers are such an important part of the firm's social capital, we will deal with them in depth in Chapter 8. We will, however, discuss in this chapter a novel approach at leveraging all aspects of your firm's social capital by using the Concierge Service Model. But because this involves all components of the firm's external relationships, we will discuss this model last. First, let us take a look at each component of the firm's social capital.

REPUTATION, BRANDS, REFERRAL SOURCES, AND NETWORKS

RON An interesting legal and marketing question is who really "owns" a brand? Can you really control what external parties think of you and your firm? Should a business be allowed to sue a disgruntled customer who creates a *companyname*sucks.com Web site? No matter how much businesses would like to control the World Wide Web, the fact of the matter is the Internet was not created by businesses and it cannot be controlled by business, any more than it is controlled by the Department of Defense that originally created it. The Internet is a true conversation, connecting people with similar interests across all geographical boundaries. Companies no longer have a monopoly on what customers see and hear; consumers now can get the true story about any product or service from any other customer around the world, unfiltered by the marketing and public relations departments.

Perhaps one of the best illustrations of who really owns a brand is when Coca-Cola decided to remove Old Coke and begin offering New Coke. There was literally a customer revolt, proving beyond a shadow of a doubt that it is customers who ultimately decide the value of a brand. The Sears Roebuck catalogue was at one point in history a well-recognized brand; it is now extinct. Once an organization's brand and reputation begin to be perceived as adding no value, it is destined to become history. Your firm's reputation, and your individual reputation as a trusted and respected advisor, exists solely in the hearts and minds of the customers you are privileged to serve. Their impressions become your reputation.

As stated earlier in the chapter, most professional service firms are built by word of mouth and through referrals. These referral sources—whether they be bankers, attorneys, CPAs, insurance and real estate brokers, "A" customers, and so forth—have to be constantly cultivated and rewarded for sending you business. Building this network of contacts and referrals should begin in college and should never stop throughout a professional's career. As author Harvey Mackay pointed out: "If everyone in your network is the same as you, it isn't a network, it's an anthill." Yet most professional firms under invest in this vital aspect of social capital. Developing a referral network takes time and resources, and usually comes at the expense of traditional measurements of efficiency, such as charge hours and realization rates. Once again, the myopic behavior prevails over building a firm's intellectual capital.

Of course, the best source of referrals are your "A" customers, who are already loyal and enthusiastic about your firm's value proposition. This is where specialization in a given area or industry can provide truly outstanding leverage. We consult with one CPA in the Bay Area (whom I will call Mark), who has proven the absolute power of social capital in his practice. He has developed a niche in providing accounting, consulting, and tax services to dentists, who comprise some 97 percent of his customer base. It is said that "birds of a feather flock together," and dentists are no exception. They rely heavily on their peers' recommendations with respect to buying or starting a practice, purchasing equipment, securing liability insurance, selecting a lawyer, CPA, and so forth. Mark is as well known among all of the various dental service providers (dental schools, banks that make student loans and fund new practices, insurance brokers, equipment companies, etc.) as he is among the dentists themselves; and he does no marketing or advertising, yet his business grew in the early stages from 30 to 50 percent each year (it has slowed since, mostly because he has chosen not to take on very many new customers or grow his practice beyond where he is comfortable). When one dentist tells another, "If you need a CPA, Mark is your man," the sale is made before the new prospect even meets him. This type of specialization and niche marketing is going to become more essential in the future.

If you examine other professions, accounting is one of the last whose members have specialized. Doctors began to specialize in the 1940s, lawyers in the 1950s. Today, auto mechanics, pet stores, and toy stores all specialize. Unlike most CPAs—where the only thing their customers have in common is that they are customers—Mark taps into the supreme power of social capital in order to increase the profitability of his firm. Being so well niched in the dental profession has enabled him to expand his social influence and position well beyond what he could have achieved in a more diversified practice.

Another successful company that has taken full advantage of leveraging social capital, by creating a virtual marketplace where you can become both a buyer and seller, is eBay, the Web's premier auction site. Founded by Pierre Omidyar, whose fiancée was a committed collector of Pez candy dispensers, he thought of a creative way to help her trade with similar collectors. Today, eBay claims more than 2 million members who place over a million bids a day, giving new meaning to "garage sale."

PAUL The opportunity for professional service firms here is simply enormous, yet few exploit it. Again, it's a mind-set issue. The "flip" necessary in this case is to see your firm as a club—one to which an exclusive group of members (your customers) belong. This flip by the way, is precisely the mind-set that drives eBay and, in particular, Amazon.

The moment you make that flip you'll regard it as essential; that is to say there is no option but to consistently find ways to add value to your members. And, above all, you'll want to communicate with them frequently. Then, go further: Why not give them a place (either virtual or real) where they can visit?

Its staggering to realize how many firms do wonderful things with their customers and then don't leverage that "within the club." Consider (and then *act* upon) the simple idea of having a members night every month, where one of your customers tells the assembled multitude what great things they've done with you to solve a particular problem or to move to a new level in their business. And if that's too hard (which it shouldn't be), then at least do it in the virtual space of your Web site and through constant (yes, constant) communication via e-mail with your customers. Wouldn't it be great if each week (or day for that matter) I got a note in my inbox from my professional service firm saying, "We noticed this and this of interest this week and several of our customers did this and this." Most golf clubs do it better than the professional service firm. We're not talking about newsletters here; we're talking about reaching out to each customer in a unique and special way. Again, the opportunity here is *huge*.

Suppliers and Vendors

RON We often do not view those for whom we cut checks as being able to add value beyond what we purchase from them; yet, the organizations with which a firm does business sometimes have enormous wealth-creating potential when they are viewed as part of the firm's social capital. Suppliers such as consultants, noncompeting CPAs (or attorneys), financial planners, real estate agents, funeral directors, scientists, doctors, stockbrokers, insurance agents, veterinarians, charities, and so forth, all offer opportunities for a firm to create innovative and dynamic marketing programs. Perhaps a joint seminar could be run with any of the preceding professionals, or a joint article written in their respective trade publications.

Newsletters are also an untapped resource for your suppliers and vendors. Some firms charge for their newsletters, under the theory that things people get for free are not valued; other firms bundle them with their fixed-price agreements. But this concept scares most professionals, who believe it is an effrontery to charge for a piece of a firm's marketing literature. But that is precisely the point. If a firm charged for its newsletters, maybe it would contain something of actual value, rather than canned recitations of recently passed tax legislation that no one wants to read in the first place. If a firm's newsletter is truly valuable, then suppliers and vendors would gladly pay for advertising space to offer their products and services. Most view this as unprofessional. However, the true test is what customers are willing and able to pay for, and in the firms that offer this type of newsletter, the customers appreciate it. Further, your business customers will appreciate the opportunity to advertise their products and services to your excellent customer base, just as you appreciate the referrals they send you. The reason there is not more of this innovative approach is because we are stuck in the mind-set that it is "unprofessional," truly a relic attitude.

Shareholders and Other External Stakeholders

RON Obviously a firm owes a fiduciary responsibility to its owners and other stakeholders who have an interest in its longevity, such as bankers, landlords, and other parties with whom it has made commitments. The communities in which the firm is located also have a stake in its success. I am not arguing that these external stakeholders should have a say in the leadership of the firm, only that they have an ancillary interest in a thriving business community. Because a professional service firm directly impacts the success of multiple businesses in the community, its sphere of influence is quite large. Firms of all size need to be active and visible in their communities, whether by serving on the boards of charitable organizations or providing their team members with time off to participate in local charitable activities.

I recall reading that before Nordstrom would open a new store in a given community, it would make donations to various local charities in the community, thereby becoming visible as an active part of the social neighborhood long before it opened its doors. This created a bond with the community and demonstrated Nordstrom's commitment to maintaining its reputation as a good "corporate citizen."

Joint Venture Partners and Alliances

RON As firms continue to strive to offer a "one-stop-shop" experience to their customers, it becomes more apparent that no one firm can do it all. Thus, joint ventures and alliances with other professionals are becoming more and more common, possibly as a prelude to a true multidisciplinary firm. Observe the airlines use of alliances, such as United Airline's Star Alliance program, whereby it shares flights, gates, pricing, frequent-flyer miles, and other infrastructure with specific partners. From a historical perspective, accounting firms were the leaders of the alliance movement, since professional regulations in most countries required partnerships to be national (that is, owned by a citizen of that country). As a result, the major accounting firms, in response to the needs of their global customers who required quality and consistency in the level of service, globalized through forming alliances.

Cyrus Freidheim, a consultant with Booz-Allen and author of *The Trillion-Dollar Enterprise: How the Alliance Revolution Will Transform Global Business*, succinctly states why alliances are successful:

> Alliances can be a profitable way to expand a business. In an acquisition or merger, the partners take all—the good and the bad, the pretty and the ugly, businesses that fit and the baggage, the profitable and the unprofitable, the core capability, and the unwanted branch in Somalia. Any problems, liabilities, warts, and unfinished business of the acquired company are yours, for better or for worse, from this day forward.
>
> In an alliance, you can carve out the piece you like. You can take the prime cuts of meat and leave the liver and the hooves behind. Alliances are about combining capabilities of two or more partners. We take advantage of your strength in the market and my technology, or your cost position and my distribution. We do as Pepsi and Lipton did with iced tea—Pepsi's distribution and Lipton's product (Freidheim, 1998: 42).

Wal-Mart used this strategy by renting out space in its stores to McDonalds. Not only did this reduce its internal cost of running snack counters, it obtained a continuous cash flow; and the higher McDonald's sales rose, the higher revenue per square foot was achieved in each store. It also increased store traffic and no doubt brought in some customers who would not have otherwise entered. Today, more than 800 Wal-Mart stores have a McDonald's. Not only was this an effective leverage of Wal-Mart's structural capital (its physical buildings), it also promoted an alliance that enhanced its social capital.

Charles Schwab also leveraged its social capital by creating an alliance with more than 5,000 independent financial advisors in a network it calls Schwab Institutional, which manages more than $100 billion in assets. Schwab was built around a do-it-yourself investment strategy until it learned, in the 1980s, through market research, that a large percentage of investors wanted advice in managing their financial affairs.

PAUL There is, of course, another dimension to alliances that, sadly, most professional firms do not see. It's the dimension of taking a proactive stance, of being the organization that facilitates alliances between customers. To illustrate the point, ponder for just a moment this question: "Whom do you know who has contact with more businesses and greater potential to influence business than just about anyone else you know?" I hope you answered "No one other than me." Because try as I might, I can't find any profession that has greater ability to influence business than the accounting profession. The real concern I have is that it seems relatively few accountants truly understand that—very few in public practice act as if that were the case.

In particular, the public practitioner has the ability to "blend" clients in truly interesting ways. But, again, so few do it. To illustrate, consider the case of a small boutique winery in Queenstown, New Zealand, that I was fortunate enough to visit in March 2002. The winery is excellent—its Pinot Noir Reserve won the world Gold Medal for Pint Noir at the Wine Show in London the previous year. About 50 percent of its vintage is sold direct to people who visit the winery—some 125,000 of them each year. The remainder is sold, rather obviously, to local outlets and around the world.

Visitors who come to the winery for lunch receive a special printed invitation with their bill. Can you figure out what the invitation is for? To help you do that, imagine that the winery was your client, and that a local restaurant was your client, too. Consider that the restaurant buys wine from many sources including the aforementioned winery. Well, clearly, you as the accountant (or, more correctly, the *business advisor*) have a vested interest in making sure of two things: first, that your winery client sells more of his or her wine to the restaurant; second, that your restaurant client somehow capitalizes on the 125,000 people visiting the winery for lunch annually. Quick—put two and two together and get four! It should be obvious, then, that the invitation is a special card inviting guests to dinner at your restaurant client's establishment stating that when they order wine during dinner, they get a full 20 percent off the price of the wine (only wine from your client's vineyard, of course).

It's a remarkable win-win-win idea isn't it? Your restaurant client gets many more clients for dinner (the first win); when those additional people come, they order your winery client's wine (the second win, the customer); so now the restaurant has to order more of your winery client's wines (the third win, for the winery). And, of course, there's a fourth winner too: *you,* as both clients' businesses boom.

Notably, ideas like this don't work just for businesses that are relatively easy to relate. For example, consider the car dealer whose business adviser also had a client who mowed lawns. How on earth could you put those two together? Quite easily, when you start thinking in a different way. Here's what happened: The business advisor first suggested to the client that he needed to do something innovative to differentiate himself. The client agreed. "Why not," the business advisor suggested, "have someone visit each week's new customers and offer to mow their lawn? I have a client who's starting a lawn-mowing business so I know he'll be able to do two or three a week for free, provided he can leave a card suggesting that, since he mows the lawn so well, he should become their regular lawn mower. Of course, he'd say that the first mow is actually a gift from you so you'll look wonderful in the customers' eyes. And I bet they'll talk more about you, as in, "You'll never guess what happened after I bought a car from the XYZ Dealership in town; the people there are really special." The car dealer loved the idea. So did the lawn-mowing businessman. And, needless to say, so did the business advisor.

The point is to look at your client list in a totally different way. Instead of seeing it as a single-dimensional entity, think of it as having many, many dimensions as you ponder which clients could effectively piggyback each other. Or perhaps even more profoundly, do as we suggested earlier: think of your client list as a special club with you as the host. Part of your job is to make sure club members get together to "synergize" their business opportunities.

Again, few professionals have the opportunity that accountants and attorneys in public practice have to help people build far better, more profitable businesses. Make sure you grasp it with both hands.

RON As the professions move toward true multidisciplinary practices, as they have existed in Europe for decades, alliances of all kinds are going to become more common. This is not to say that mergers and acquisitions will be replaced with alliances, but rather that alliances will be an effective competitive strategy for the smaller firms in order to offer the same array of services their larger competitors can provide. Consider Freidheim's "seven main reasons that companies choose alliances over acquisition or internal action":

1. *Risk sharing.* Companies cannot afford the potential downside of the investment opportunity alone. Airbus Industries, an alliance of German, French, British, and Spanish aerospace companies, was created exactly for this reason. The oil industry has long used alliances to share exploration risks in such locations as the North Sea, the South China Sea, and Azerbaijan.

2. *Acquisition barriers.* Companies cannot acquire the right partner because of price, size, unwanted businesses, government resistance, reluctance of owners, or regulatory restrictions. The GM-Toyota alliance fits almost every one of those reasons.

3. *Market-segment access.* Companies don't understand their customers or don't have the relationships or infrastructure to distribute their products to a particular market. Lipton chose PepsiCo for this reason.

4. *Technology gaps.* Companies don't have all the technology they need and can't afford the time or resources to develop it themselves.

5. *Geographic access.* Companies aren't where they want to be and don't have the resources to get there. Corning joined forces with Samsung to enter and compete in the Asian market. In many cases, government regulations inhibit direct access. China is a good example. Few companies have the resources, commitment, or permission to go it alone in China. Most companies welcome the government's encouragement (or mandate) to get a local partner.

6. *Funding constraints.* Individual companies can't afford to develop or launch the venture alone.

7. *Management skills.* Companies need more talent to be successful. Oracle and Microsoft have several alliances with start-up technology companies to which they contribute management talent and access to their resources in exchange for proprietary access to the start-up technology (Ibid: 42–44).

It is apparent that several of these factors apply to the smaller professional firm. At the present time, the American Bar Association appears to be fighting the formation of multidisciplinary practices, similar to how the accounting profession initially fought American Express purchasing accounting firms. Nevertheless, ultimately the market will prevail; the consumer is sovereign, and they are demanding full-service financial, accounting, and legal firms. The ABA's attitude is a myopic, zero-sum view of the world. In short, accountants and lawyers are not as much *substitutes* as they are *complements*, much like autos and tires, hot dogs and mustard, and airlines and hotels.

Professional Associations and Formal Affiliations

RON Ric Payne, founder of the Principa alliance, discussed his views of professional associations in the Australian business magazine *BRW*:

As long as smaller, independently owned firms are able to deliver all the services that their larger competitors can offer, they will thrive in this environment and will carve out, and in my view retain, a very profitable niche.

The key here can be found in the words "are able to deliver all the services that their larger competitors can offer." One way to do that is to align your firm with a network that gives you access to a broader range of services so that you can position yourself as a multidisciplinary firm. In the future, I believe the most viable form of structure for professional service firms will be through formal networks. To put that another way, if you are not in a network you will be competing against one.

And if you are in a network, you had better avail yourself of all the benefits that that offers, because simply offering your clients what you have provided them in the past will not cut it (quoted in Baker, 2001: 254–55).

There are many networks in the accounting profession today that firms can join in order to offer a wider range of services in an expanded geographical market—networks such as BDO Seidman, BKR International, DFK, McGladrey Network, Moore Stephens, IGAF, CPAmerica, Leading Edge, Principa, among others. Belonging to any one of them is an excellent way to increase a firm's sphere of influence and add tremendously to its social capital. Associations not only share customers and projects, but also education, team members, marketing, and other functions of operating a firm. If your firm is not presently part of an alliance, seriously consider joining one. The investment will pay off in the additional intellectual capital you will acquire.

Firm Alumni

RON In a knowledge economy, where human capital investors own the means of a firm's production, it simply is not possible to retain them for life. But even when a knowledge worker no longer works *for* you, he or she can certainly still work *with* you. Professional service firms have actually long understood that an ex-team member is a valuable future customer. "The goal in not to retain employees," says Cindy Lewiton Jackson, director of global career development and alumni relations for Bain & Co., a pioneer of the concept of Alumni networks, "the goal is to build lifelong affiliation." Katie Weiser, global director of alumni relations at Deloitte Consulting, adds, "Our people will be movers and shakers wherever they land next. We're planting seeds for the future" (quoted in Canabou, May 2002: 28).

Former team members can benefit in many ways, as pointed out by Cem Sertoglu and Anne Berkowitch in the *Harvard Business Review*:

Rehires and Referral Sources. Companies used to go out of their way to avoid recruiting ex-employees. But that was always shortsighted. The facts are, it costs half as much to rehire an ex-employee as it does to hire a brand-new person; rehires are 40 percent more productive in their first quarter at work; and they tend to stay in the job longer. . . . Perhaps even more important, alumni are known quantities; the risk of a costly mishire is almost completely eliminated. Alumni are also a growing source of referrals. Some companies even offer alumni compensation for referrals who are hired.

Suppliers of Intellectual Capital. Former employees can be great sources of ideas and intelligence, helping their old companies to stay abreast of new trends, technologies, and even investment opportunities. . . . One major financial services company hires alumni as temporary workers during periods of high demand, and another company taps into the expertise of former employees as market research sources.

Ambassadors, Marketers, and Lobbyists. Former employees are just as likely to influence outside opinions about an organization as current employees—especially if they haven't been gone from the organization for very long. So building and maintaining goodwill with alumni can fortify the company's reputation, brand, and influence. . . . [Some] companies are starting to use their alumni networks as low-cost test beds for new products and marketing campaigns (Sertoglu and Berkowitch, June 2002: 20–21).

Establishing and maintaining an alumni network is more than just sending out an occasional directory and setting up a Web site with potential job postings. It should contain its own value proposition and give alumni a reason to stay in it, such as sharing of intellectual capital, subsidized educational programs, invitations to firm events, and special gatherings.

Consider Creating a University

Ron Many companies have reckoned they possess so much intellectual capital that they use internally to train their team members, why not leverage this IC to the outside world and create a university? From universities at Disney, Motorola, and Nordstrom to the Ritz Carlton Leadership Center and GE's Leadership Development Training, all these companies have found that offering educational opportunities to firm customers, referral sources, alliance partners, and so forth, is an excellent way to further broaden a firm's sphere of influence. Further, as Peter Drucker points out, continuing professional education will be one of the largest growth industries in this century, as it is increasingly difficult for any knowledge worker to stay abreast of current developments in his or her field of specialty. Other firms have established research institutes to provide leading-edge thinking in a variety of areas.

One firm in Buffalo, New York, Dopkins and Co., is establishing its own firm university in order to offer business education to its customers. Mark Koziel, Director at Dopkins Placement Services, detailed this institution, in the following sections.

Dopkins University: History

Over the years, Dopkins & Company, LLP, has traditionally offered a variety of business seminars to existing and potential clients. Topics have included "Succession Planning," "Financial Management Training," "Business Development," and "Sexual Harassment and Recruiting." Some sessions carried a nominal charge, while others were given as a means of thanking our clients (i.e., we were too sheepish to charge for them). We found that these seminars were popular, educational, and important to many of our clients. As a result, Dopkins & Company created Dopkins University, an interactive learning center for all employment levels within family-owned businesses. By conducting these seminars under the auspices of Dopkins University, we have been able to fine-tune the content of the seminars and deliver them consistently and at a consistent cost to our clients.

Why the Need

Family-owned businesses have a variety of different and very specific needs. However, most training offered by specialized training companies is generalized and designed to make small companies run like big conglomerate corporations. Also, national training companies come and lecture for a few hours, but provide no follow-up for implementation. This usually means that any good ideas provided to smaller companies are forgotten a week after the training. In addition, a large struggle for many family-owned businesses is in the lack of resources and personnel necessary to implement the changes that these training companies promote.

The most important need has come directly from business owners. Dopkins & Company was in the process of establishing a manufacturing consulting practice. We assembled an advisory board consisting of business owners of manufacturing enterprises so that we could determine their wants and needs. We initially thought we could provide help and information concerning process efficiencies, inventory control, and general plant issues. However, after listening to our advisory board, we realized the overwhelming request for assistance was in adding value to their customers. These businesses were *already* efficient in production because that is what they are good at. And, if they wanted to be more efficient, there were a number of existing manufacturing consultants with proven track records to help them better their efficiencies. The business owners wanted intellectual capital and a resource that understands small business issues to help train their people.

Lastly, family-owned businesses typically have little or no internal human capital support. The few that do have a dedicated HR staff are focused more on HR compliance, personnel issues, and recruiting. Training is usually the HR function that is left behind. While it is quite common for large corporations to have well-established internal learning centers they call universities, family-owned businesses typically cannot afford to offer the same type of learning center for their team members. The choice then is to send their team members to external training seminars, which are usually based on large corporate views or which, in actuality, provide no training at all.

The answer is Dopkins University. We are making a niche in the training market and satisfying a training need by focusing on the family-owned business. At Dopkins University, we can offer the local small business market an opportunity to enhance their intellectual capital at a reasonable cost. Also, we provide these businesses with an important tool—a local source that offers the opportunity for follow-up to ensure implementation of ideas generated from the training. Business owners can control the process by choosing the team members they feel would best benefit from the program.

Developing the Product

The selection of topics for the Dopkins University seminars came from a variety of sources. First, we looked to our clients. We specifically asked them for topics they felt were most important to the advancement of their team members' skills. Our second source was well-established corporate universities. We researched existing universities, their course offerings, and the success or failure of these courses. Finally, we looked at our own seminars and training programs and incorporated them into the development of our product.

Once we determined our courses, we categorized most of them into three learning tracks: a business owner learning track, a supervisor/manager learning track, and a general skills learning track. The business owner track was an important track to provide. Business owners typically will not attend sessions geared toward managers. Also, once the business owner is engaged and supportive of the university, he or she is more willing to send other team members to future sessions. Likewise, when managers and supervisors attend and are supportive, they typically become advocates as well. Courses offered in each of the tracks are shown in Exhibit 7.1.

EXHIBIT 7.1   Courses Offered in Each Track

Business Owners	General Skills
• Introduction of Economic Value Added to the Family Business • Advanced Financial Management Training for the Non-Financial Manager • Total Quality Management • How to Build a Team • HR Update for Business Owners • Succession Planning for the Family Business • Creating a Corporate Culture	• Customer Service and Awesome Service Training • Performance Evaluations—Giving and Receiving • Phone Right Training • Conflict Management • Selling Skills • Establishing E-Business • Communication Skills • Business to Business E-Commerce • Meeting Effectiveness • Business to Consumer E-Business • Problem Solving/Decision Making • Occupational Fraud and White Collar Crime • Career Planning • Fundamentals of Asset-Based Lending • Time Management • Recruiting in the Twenty-first Century
Managers/Supervisors	
• Introduction to Leadership • Performance Management • Communication • Conflict Resolution • Coaching • EEO/Sexual Harassment • Motivation • Team Skills/Problem Solving Skills	

We are now in the process of establishing a schedule for the courses. The business owner and manager/supervisor tracks will be offered as a semester over a 10-month period. The courses will be held once per month for four hours. The general courses will be offered four times per year on specific dates. Our goal is to have four tracks running by the end of the first year, meaning a new semester would start quarterly for a new group. By the end of the first year, we will have four business owner tracks, four manager/supervisor tracks, and four general sessions running at the same time. A "full" session would have 15 to 20 participants.

The investment for a semester track is $1,500 per person, which includes a total of 10 courses. The business owner track has seven "mandatory" courses and three courses—to be selected by the business owner—from the general skills track. The manager/supervisor track includes eight "mandatory" courses and two additional courses from the general skills track. The price for individual sessions is $195 per course.

The Benefits

For the firm, there are several benefits to establishing this program. First, we will actually get paid for the seminars and workshops we present. As accountants, we tend to give away our intellectual capital for free, yet there is tremendous value to our clients. Dopkins University will help build a consistent pricing strategy for our programs.

Second, Dopkins University can be a venue for training our internal team members. Ideally, we would like 15 to 20 client personnel at each session. Dopkins & Company, LLP team members who have not been through that particular program in house can attend the sessions filling the remaining five to 10 seats, and, in essence, the firm will be paid for our internal CPE efforts. Many of the programs were designed around systems that we have already implemented at the firm and have since helped implement with some of our clients. This also gives our own team members more familiarity with Dopkins University so they can assist in marketing this service to our clients and to potential clients.

Third, since the concept is unique, we can use our university as a differentiator in our recruiting efforts, letting prospective team member know that we want to invest in their career by offering strong career skill enhancements.

Fourth, we have increased the cross-selling of our services. Based on the topics being offered, several of our departments are represented: Audit, Tax, Asset Based Lending Consulting, Management Consulting, Computer Consulting, Placement, and HR Consulting. Any one of those departments now has a stronger chance of receiving additional projects based on the success of its program. Each program can be offered as a stand-alone session to an individual client for a fixed price. Also, business development work done by our management consulting team can offer the general track courses on a very regular basis to its business development clients. The business development clients are in several tiers based on our level of involvement. Some tiers offer courses as part of their monthly fee, while other tiers offer discounts on the courses.

Overall, we feel that Dopkins University has tremendous potential. From an internal perspective, we have 12 team members from seven departments involved with the university. This will help in the promotion of the program. We are increasing our level of commitment to our team members by offering these nontraditional programs on a regular basis. From an external perspective, we are offering a unique concept that will differentiate us from other firms. We are able to offer businesses a variety of training options by running the semester tracks, offering each program individually and offering a client-specific program. Finally, marketing the university to the community, as well as a strong feeder system through business development clients, offers an even greater chance for success. This is a concept we hope to see our profession institute so that the general business community sees their CPA as the "one-stop-shop" business consultant.

RON An excellent example of a research institute is the McKinsey Global Institute (MGI), which exists to cogitate over questions that reach far beyond whether any company will buy into a McKinsey proposal for consulting services. McKinsey associates—usually its best thinkers—serve one-year fellowships at the institute, and are measuring world economics from the broadest perspective they can create. Here is how James O'Shea and Charles Madigan describe MGI, in their book *Dangerous Company: Management Consultants and the Businesses They Save and Ruin*:

> If one thinks of McKinsey as its own kind of nation, then this is its intelligence agency, a well-funded think tank that studies world economics in depth, then issues reports available to anyone who wants them. They are free of charge, but worth their weight in whatever currency you want to spend. They buy goodwill and page after page of publicity for McKinsey and help create the consulting relationships that will carry The Firm well into the twenty-first century.
>
> All the big consulting companies have think tanks that grind out reports. [Led by the collapse of the Soviet Union and the move toward free markets and privatization] what we realized as a firm is that we were either going to have to invest to get better informed and to understand better what was happening in the world's economy and the global economy and really help our CEOs or we were going to have to get out.

The Firm had two options: It had to buy into the study of economics in a big way or it had to leave the field to the collection of academics and macroeconomists who were already talking to the business leaders of Europe. Ultimately what that meant is that it would have to abandon the potentially profitable path of consulting on economics and just stick to business.

Some of the partners were confused. *Why should McKinsey spend to create something new when it was already doing very well?* The answer rests partly in The Firm's inherent sense of curiosity about how the world operates, since it now operates on the same level. The unspoken answer, speculation invites, is that The Firm did not at all like the feel of being bested by a collection of economists and academics.

Why do anything different? That is always a challenge for successful organizations. Of course, what we tell our clients is that that is just the time when you invest and do something different to maintain that success. In a narrow sense, we were taking some of our own medicine.

And so the MGI was born and now runs on one-tenth of 1 percent of McKinsey's revenues. It is deeper than the CIA in the sense that it can call on McKinsey partners everywhere in the world for their special expertise. It is aimed at making certain McKinsey never again faces questions about the global economy from savvy CEOs for which it has no answers. On the surface, it might seem like an academic exercise. But if it follows the course of [The Firm], undoubtedly it will become a magnet, not only for clients eager to take advantage of McKinsey's special expertise, but also for the consultants of the twenty-first century who will want to make their start, and perhaps their careers, at a company that presents truly global opportunities (O'Shea and Madigan, 1998: 288–89).

One firm in the wine country of Napa County houses a wine research institute that publishes first-rate economic studies of that industry, available to all who ask. This has increased the firm's visibility and stature, and reinforced its expertise, within the wine industry.

PUTTING IT ALL TOGETHER: THE CONCIERGE SERVICE MODEL

RON My colleague, Dan Morris, CPA and Partner in Morris + D'Angelo, says social capital is the least leveraged of all of the intellectual capital in a professional service firm. He has borrowed a very old concept from the hotel industry in order to change this situation in his firm—the Concierge Service Model, mentioned at the beginning of this chapter. In effect, Morris wants his best customers to call him for *anything* they need, *anytime*, *anywhere*. The logic is not to offer a one-stop-shop, but a first-stop-shop, experience for your customers. It has been suggested that the only true scarce resource in today's information-rich and knowledge-intense economy is people's *attention*. The Concierge Model was devised to ensure that your best customers come to think of your firm first for any need or want they might have.

Morris's firm has helped people get Super Bowl tickets, reservations at five-star restaurants, theater tickets, a plumber, a new roof, an automobile, a doctor or dentist for newcomers to town, and so forth. The theory is that you already know someone in your network who can satisfy the customer's need or want. Is it not better to recommend them to someone in your network in order to leverage your firm's social capital? If you trust the people within your network, this will be a win-win situation all around—your firm will be offering higher value, your customers will appreciate the additional business you send their way, and the customers will be satisfied and, most likely, have their expectations exceeded. If no one in your network can satisfy the customer's need, chances are they know someone who can. And even if it turns out that no one can satisfy the customer, isn't it nice to know that your customer is thinking of your firm first for anything he or she may desire? You are putting "velvet ropes" around customers, helping to ensure they do not let a potential competitor enter outside the sphere of your influence.

This service mentality has the salutary effect of raising your firm's collective consciousness with respect to its best customers. You move through the following levels in order to provide a full-service concierge:

1. Awareness
2. Familiarity
3. Knowledge
4. Understanding

Once you move to the level of understanding your customers' wants, desires, hopes, aspirations, future goals, and so on, the Concierge Model becomes easier to facilitate. It does entail some risk, however; there is always the possibility the customer will not receive outstanding service, so you have to refer businesses that you know are excellent value providers, but your customers are (or should be) an excellent source for this talent. Don't let the risk overshadow the opportunity of offering this dynamic service model. It will increase customer loyalty; you can charge a premium price for offering this service; it will deepen your relationships throughout your social capital base; it will change the mind-set in your culture from a technical-answers to a total-solutions firm; and it will provide a competitive differentiation in the marketplace, enabling your firm to compete based on service, rather than merely on price. (You will be able to read much more about this dynamic service model, as Morris is presently working on a book based upon his firm's experience in offering it, and his teachings in this area, to be published by John Wiley & Sons, Inc., in the future.)

SUMMARY AND CONCLUSIONS

Your firm's social capital—its customers, reputation and brands, referral sources and networks, suppliers and vendors, shareholders and other external stakeholders, joint venture partners and alliances, professional associations and formal affiliations, and firm alumni—not only represent a lever to help you move the earth, but also provide a solid place on which to stand. As with other nonrival assets, a firm's social capital is not limited by physical time or space. In fact, it takes advantage of Metcalfe's Law of the computer industry and the Telecosm, which states the value of a network increases as the square of the number of users connected to it—that is, connections multiply value exponentially. Everyone in your firm's social network is a producer, consumer, and supplier of intellectual capital.

Gary Becker's theory—as well as that of others studying this area—of social capital recognizes the dominant role it plays in our lives and the lives of our customers and associates. No one exists in a vacuum. We are all heavily influenced by our family, friends, colleagues, neighbors, and so forth. The firm of the future will begin to leverage this inexhaustible source of intellectual capital to create value for everyone who comes into its sphere of influence, and it will become more effective in attracting the type of people it wants to work with and for, and improve the quality of its social, not to mention financial, life.

It is now time to turn our attention to the most important component in the firm's social capital—its customers.

8

YOU ARE YOUR CUSTOMER LIST

*It's axiomatic: You're as good—or as bad—as the character of your
Client List. In a very real sense, you are your Client List!*
                    —Tom Peters, *The Professional Service Firm 50*

A fisherman walks into a bait and tackle shop looking at an assortment of very flashy green and purple lures. He asks the owner of the shop, "Do the fish really go for these?" The owner replied, "I have no idea, I don't sell them to fish."

RON Building on Peter Drucker's marketing concept discussed in Chapter 3, which states the purpose of any organization is to create results outside of itself, this chapter explores what is perhaps the most critical component of any professional service firm—its customers. We will take a very holistic approach to exploring the importance of customers; and because this is a very complex subject, we have broken it down into these following topics:

- What customers really buy
- The value proposition
- What is beyond Total Quality Service?
- From zero defects to zero defections
- Baker's Law: Bad customers drive out good customers
- Adaptive capacity

If there is one lesson we have learned from successful professional firms around the world, it is this: Customer selection and retention is arguably the most important criterion a business can establish for long-term success. In a world of increased competition, customization, and specialization, firms can no longer be all things to all people. It is critical to define your target customers; what they need, want, and expect from you; and the value proposition you will offer them. The most successful firms turn away more business than they accept because they are diligent in prequalifying potential customers and have made the strategic decision not to accept any and all comers. Also, the firm of the future thinks about its capacity in a totally different way from the traditional metric of billable hours. We therefore lay out a model of *adaptive capacity* that enables your firm to maximize its profit potential from its fixed capacity.

WHAT DO CUSTOMERS REALLY BUY?

RON One of the problems professionals face in truly understanding their customers is that they tend to focus on the technical aspect of what they *do* for the customer, rather than how customers *benefit* by what is done on their behalf. Businesspeople are constantly being exhorted to *listen* to their customers; but perhaps a better strategy is to *become* a customer. This is not as difficult as it sounds, as all of us are customers every single day, and we understand why we buy things, what we look for in choosing a service provider, and how we feel about the overall experience with the organization. While many professionals don't necessarily have experience in purchasing accounting or legal advice for themselves, some do (e.g., controllers in industry have to hire CPA and law firms, and in-house legal counsel has to choose outside counsel). It is quite a learning experience to talk to these professionals about how and why they make the decisions they do, since they are sophisticated buyers.

It is a deceptively simple question: What are we getting paid for? Yet many professionals arrogantly assume they know what their customers want and believe they have been giving them exactly that for years. This is a myopic vision, and potentially harmful. A plethora of information is available on why people buy, how they buy, the decision process they go through, which firms ignore at their peril. Economist Shlomo Maital, who has been teaching economics to business executives for decades, has put forth in his book *Executive Economics: Ten Essential Tools for Managers* 13 forces that shape what people buy:

A Aptness
B Bandwagons and bubbles
C Cost, or price
D Demographics
E Elasticity, or sensitivity to price
F Fashion and fads
G Greed

H Habit
I Income
J Jazz (ultimately, value for money)
K Knowledge
L Loyalty
M Minds and money (Maital, 1994: 171).

Some of these factors explain why jewelers have long understood that people do not buy diamonds for the four Cs inherent in them: color, cut, clarity, and carat weight. Jewelers implicitly understand that people are really buying the reaction of others—the man pictures the reaction of the woman he loves receiving the diamond, while she imagines the reaction of her family, friends, coworkers and so on, when they see it. These factors also explain why movie attendance and book sales are dramatically affected by word of mouth: it's the so-called bandwagon effect.

Many theories attempt to explain why people buy what they do. Economist Thorstein Bunde Veblen (1857–1929) posited many in his book *The Theory of the Leisure Class* (first published in 1899), which Maital has drawn upon for some of the motivations of why people buy. Veblen referred to a "barbarian culture," citing trophies such as property or slaves, which were signs of successful aggression. In today's culture, luxuries are the major signal of status and class, which Veblen reasoned were purchased for two reasons: To show others you are member of the class above and to distinguish yourself from those below. Economists of the day did not take Veblen's book seriously, finding it obtuse and unsupported by any evidence. One Chicago economist said, "I congratulated him and asked if he had thought of having it translated into English."

In his book, *How to Win Customers and Keep Them for Life: Revised and Updated for the Digital Age*, Michael LeBoeuf, Ph.D., suggests customers have the following motivations for these various purchases:

- Don't sell me clothes. Sell me a sharp appearance, style, and attractiveness.
- Don't sell me insurance. Sell me peace of mind and a great future for my family and me.
- Don't sell me a house. Sell me comfort, contentment, a good investment, and pride of ownership [and a piece of the American Dream].
- Don't sell me books. Sell me pleasant hours and the profits of knowledge.
- Don't sell me toys. Sell my children happy moments.
- Don't sell me a computer. Sell me the pleasure and profits of the miracles of modern technology.
- Don't sell me tires. Sell me freedom from worry and low cost per mile.
- Don't sell me airline tickets. Sell me a fast, safe, on-time arrival at my destination feeling like a million dollars.
- Don't sell me *things*. Sell me ideals, feelings, self-respect, home life, and happiness (LeBoeuf, 2000: 22–23).

Successful salespeople do not necessarily ignore features in the products they are selling, but they almost always add "which means" to the end of every explanation of their product or service offering. A statement such as, "This car has a V-8 engine, which means it will last longer because it doesn't have to work as hard as a smaller engine" (Williams, 1998: 98). Advertising giant Leo Burnett used to say: "Don't tell me how good you make it; tell me how good it makes me when I use it."

Complete the following phrase: Don't sell me accounting (or legal) services, sell me _____. Notice how these "do-sells" apply not only to the physical product or service, but also to the feelings and experiences that go along with them. This is an essential part of a company's value proposition, which we discuss in the next section.

For now, let us concentrate on developing a theory of what people buy from their professional service providers. Abrams Little-Gill Loberfeld PC, from Chestnut Hill, Massachusetts, conducted extensive customer focus groups and produced a report (which they turned into an effective marketing brochure) entitled "Why Abrams Little-Gill Loberfeld? The Top 10 Reasons According to Our Clients," which spelled out the following reasons customers gave for selecting the firm:

Reason 1: They reduce my anxiety.

Reason 2: I have access to specialized knowledge and a wealth of experience.

Reason 3: I trust my CPA/business advisor.

Reason 4: The firm takes a personal interest in my business, my family, and me.

Reason 5: My CPA/business advisor provides valuable information.

Reason 6: They meet all of my expectations.

Reason 7: The firm has helped me create new opportunities.

Reason 8: I like the results they achieve.

Reason 9: They utilize the latest technology.

Reason 10: The members of the firm care about the community.

Now you could say that these are really reasons why people *stay* with the firm rather than why they bought initially. Put that thought on hold and simply consider that, armed with these 10 reasons, the firm now has a far better chance of using these reasons (in its marketing materials) to attract precisely the kind of customers it wants.

Notice particularly how none of the 10 reasons deals with price? Or the technical quality of what the firm produces? This has important ramifications for developing the firm's strategic pricing policies (which we explore in Chapter 9) and for developing the firm's value proposition. Peter Drucker has advanced the notion that the patient knows the symptoms, but the doctor knows the meaning. But both must be heard in order for a value-added relationship to develop. Doctors must not complain that the patient didn't attend medical school; conversely, it does no good for the CPA or attorney to complain that the customer "just doesn't understand the value of what we do." It is our job to make them understand the value of what we do, and we can do that only by understanding—at a very deep and meaningful level—the motivations of why customers select and stay with the professionals they do.

Michael LeBoeuf distilled his summation of customer statements and posited the following theory to explain what people really buy: "Despite all of the untold millions of products and services for sale in today's marketplace, customers will exchange their hard-earned money for only two things: good feelings [and] solutions to problems" (LeBoeuf, 2000: 23). This is a good theory, and it has a certain utilitarian streak to it—that is, the notion that individuals spend their time (and money) pursuing pleasure and avoiding pain. It is the old marketing axiom that says you really don't buy drill bits, you buy the hole the drill makes. Understanding that simple fact could help a company (such as Black & Decker) get into the laser beam business, since they too put holes in things. It also explains why so many people purchase lottery tickets; they are really buying a low-cost dream. Charles Revson, who created the Revlon cosmetics empire, introduced color-coordinated nail polish and lipstick during the Great Depression. Many commentators hailed the bright colors as "trashy," but by providing a fashion statement—and good feelings to millions of women—he was able to convert a product with low margins into a very profitable product. Indeed, he knew he was selling hope. Upjohn ran an ad for Rogaine that read: "Gentlemen, start your follicles." Rogaine does not sell hair (it cannot legally make that claim, since it does not work 100 percent of the time); but it does sell hope, and its advertising reflects this motivation.

Professionals are excellent at solving customer problems; it is, after all, what they are trained to do. But merely solving problems is no longer enough; we must also provide the good feelings that are a part of the customer's experience in dealing with our firms.

The point is also that the process of solving the problems is just as important to the customer as the results achieved. Focusing on the total customer experience—solving the problem and creating the good feelings—demonstrates not just *competency*, but *distinction*. But the utilitarian view posited by LeBoeuf does not help a firm custom-tailor its service offering to its various customers. It is easy to get caught up in hairy hypotheses that are long and complicated, but I prefer to shave with *Occam's razor*—a medieval philosophical concept that states that it serves no purpose to achieve a result with many assumptions rather than with a few. Which is why I prefer Theodore Levitt's theory of what customers really buy: *expectations*. Levitt was a marketing professor at Harvard Business School and the editor of *Harvard Business Review*. His expectations theory is useful because it forces the firm to focus on the utility the customer is trying to maximize. No two customers have the same expectations, therefore each one has to be treated differently.

Levitt's theory also emphasizes the importance of ascertaining the customer's expectations *before* accepting him or her as a customer, or doing work for an existing customer. Since the customer judges a firm's performance as a function of how he or she perceives the firm's performance divided by what he or she expected, it is a critical step in the service delivery process to understand exactly what those expectations the firm will be graded on are. Before each engagement, the firm must (yes, must) ask the customer: "What do you expect from us?"

Asking this question allows the firm to manage—to a certain degree—the customer's expectations. If a customer has unrealistic expectations, better for the firm to find out before it begins any work, rather than after it has committed firm resources to an unreasonable customer. Southwest Airlines is a master at managing customer expectations. Customers understand very well that it is a no-frills airline, with no assigned seats, no food service, no first class, and so on. However, since the airline has lowered customers expectations in these areas, when it achieves a stellar on-time arrival record and does not lose your luggage, all at a price comparable to driving yourself or taking the bus, most customers walk away with their expectations exceeded—and, more importantly, they come back to fly Southwest again. Compare these expectations to buying a first-class ticket on, say, United Airlines. The customer's expectations of every aspect of the flight are totally different.

Harvard Business Review has been reporting for years that customer satisfaction is no longer enough; a business must strive to *delight* its customers. Studies conducted by *HBR* reveal that 65 to 85 percent of customers who chose a new supplier said they were satisfied or very satisfied with their former supplier. It is hard enough to meet a customer's expectations, let alone exceed them, if a firm does not know exactly what they are. Becoming a customer and experiencing what they do, is a good way to learn. The next-best alternative is to constantly question customers as to their expectations.

After being warmly referred by another customer, a CPA met for the first time with a CEO of a company who needed a full-disclosure financial statement compilation. During the meeting, the CPA asked the CEO, "If you decide to hire us, what do you expect from us?" The CEO was a little taken aback by this question—probably because no other CPA had ever asked him that before—and began to explain that he really wanted the CPA to develop a relationship with his banker. It seems his company had a rather cyclical cash-flow cycle and, during certain periods of the year, his company would be in violation of the banker's loan covenants. He told the CPA: "If my banker is comfortable with my CPA, I'll be able to sleep at night." This was the *customer's expectations,* and the CPA focused on this aspect of the relationship immediately. Because he was able to exceed the customer's overall expectations by developing an excellent relationship with the banker, he was also able to command a premium price for the financial statement compilation. If all a firm ever focuses on is the technical aspect of the job—in this case, the compilation—and never looks for the *value drivers* that reveal the deeper understanding of exactly what the customer is buying, the firm is destined to be treated like a commodity, with no viable difference between itself and the competition.

Because expectations are *dynamic*, not *static*, it is also imperative that the firm continuously ask the customers what they expect, at least annually, if not in shorter intervals—after every project, for instance. A firm should never rest on its laurels and assume it knows exactly what the customer is up to, as this humorous story from Sheila Kessler, a management consultant and California Baldridge Quality Award examiner, illustrates in her book, *Measuring and Managing Customer Satisfaction: Going for the Gold*:

> Motorola noticed a radical increase in its pager revenues in Korea. When investigating how people there were using them, Motorola found that young women sometimes carried as many as seven pagers tucked into their waistband. Each pager represented a different boyfriend who was paging the woman—an exclusive communication link. The number of pagers a young woman wore was a status symbol (Kessler, 1996: 179).

In his book, *The World On Time: The 11 Management Principles That Made FedEx an Overnight Sensation*, James Wetherbe posed a very thought-provoking question:

> I travel quite frequently, and I never check my luggage. Never. When I speak at an out-of-town meeting or seminar I need my suits and my slides. That's why I always carry my own bags. To send them in the care of the airline has been, far too often, to send them directly into a nameless abyss.

And that cautiousness raises an intriguing question: Why do I "absolutely, positively" trust FedEx to do on its planes what I never trust other airlines to do on theirs? For one thing, I can't think of any other airline that has an internal information system to track and assure on-time delivery of baggage. There is no such passenger carrier today. Maybe that will change, sometime (Wetherbe, 1996: 141).

Today, almost every major carrier has an internal tracking system for passenger luggage, modeled on the one developed by FedEx. This is a major lesson. Businesses compete against *any* organization that has the ability to raise customer expectations. FedEx brought a new standard to the passenger airline business, just as anyone who visits Disneyland or Walt Disney World has his or her expectations raised when it comes to customer service. Once people experience premium service, they want more of it and are less and less tolerant of those organizations that do not deliver on the promise. This expectation dynamism, though, requires that firm leaders constantly look beyond their own four walls to learn from other industries.

PAUL Tom Connellan expresses the point this way in his book *Inside the Magic Kingdom*: "If someone else delights customers better than you do, irrespective of what business they're in, you suffer by comparison." He then adds, "The competitor is *anyone* the customer compares you with." Put that in this very simple perspective: If the customer has called FedEx just before calling you, and your phone is answered (as is in many firms) somewhat more tardily and less friendly than at FedEx, you instantly suffer by comparison. Or, say, the customer has just returned from a wonderful stay at a Ritz-Carlton and is now sitting in a creaky old chair across from you at your somewhat untidy desk . . . well, you get the point.

RON Unfortunately, under the old way of doing things, as people rise within a firm, their focus becomes more and more internal, dealing with problems and crisis within, rather than recognizing opportunities and possibilities outside.

Learning from customers is an ongoing process and requires many different listening posts to accomplish. It is not enough to send out an annual "how are we doing" customer satisfaction survey, as most people do not fill these out, as they tend not to spend their waking hours cogitating on how their professional service providers can do better. Thus, such surveys have limited usefulness right from the start. Further, most of the questions are biased and may not deal with the issues the customer is concerned about. Instead, Marriott, for one, has learned to engage customers in dialogues at many different levels, often surveying their business customers on the concierge level during cocktail hour through informal chats. The data may not be as scientific and precise, but there is no doubt to Marriott the information conveyed is much more relevant to customers' true concerns and experiences. When one Chicago Marriott had budgeted $20,000 to upgrade the black-and-white TV sets to color in the bathrooms located on the concierge level, based upon actual conversations with engineering and concierge-level team members, they learned not many people requested the upgrade. What they did want, based upon insistent requests from guests, was irons and ironing boards. Disney is another company that has mastered surveying and listening to its customers. At the Disney University course on customer loyalty, instructors teach that the most significant factor that determines whether a family will return to a particular resort hotel comes down to one item (and this Disney executives were shocked to learn, according to the instructors): the swimming pool. Since then, Disney invests heavily in each new resort's pool.

Focusing on the customer's individual expectations forces the firm to individualize its service delivery to that particular customer's wants and needs. No two customers should be treated equally. Customers want to be treated *individually*, or better yet, *specially*. This is inherently easier to accomplish in service organizations than in manufacturing, although with the recent trend toward "mass customization" of everything from Levi jeans to baby dolls, bicycles, and children's books, this is changing.

One brainstorming idea used by Richard Branson, founder of Virgin, is to ask the following question: "What are 10 things you would never hear a customer say about our company or our industry?" Supposedly, before Branson invests in a new industry, he has his executives come up with such a list. Things like, "airlines treat their customers with respect and dignity; hotel food is excellent; banking is fun," and so forth, help Virgin differentiate its value proposition from the established competition. Virgin Bride—a one-stop shop for holding a wedding—for example, was launched after one Virgin team member found it was a complete hassle to plan her own wedding.

We are not suggesting you launch new businesses as Branson does, rather that listening to your customers—and team members—is a crucial tool. Listening will also help you solve that perennial issue all firms desire: *cross-selling* your services.

It is a mantra in almost every professional service firm to cross-sell, yet most firm leaders are disappointed with the results of these efforts. Why has cross-selling not been as successful as it could be? Perhaps one of the reasons most firms are not satisfied with their cross-selling results lies in their belief that all they have to do to sell more services is to be the customer's "trusted advisor." But there is a more fundamental customer psychology and it is directly related to the words we use. People love to *buy* and *own*, but they hate to be *sold*. Think of the last time you purchased a big-ticket item—a car, stereo, new computer, house—did you call a loved one, friend, or colleague and say, "Guess what I was sold today?"

The point is, rather than focusing on what firms want to sell their customers, perhaps they should start focusing on the customers desires and needs. In almost every seminar we have conducted to professionals around the world, we ask this simple question: "When was the last time you paid an unannounced visit to a customer and asked the owner, "So, how's it going?" And when you did that, 6 out of 10 times (maybe more) what did you walk away with?" Almost everyone nods and says, collectively, "More work." Woody Allen once said 90 percent of success is showing up. Yet because most professionals are so focused on billing hours and because visits of this nature distract from that fundamental mission, they lose out on all sorts of cross-selling opportunities. Coupled with the fact that the compensation structure of most firms tends not to reward cross-selling behavior (and investments), we tend not to notice what does *not* get rewarded. And, of course, those lost opportunities do not show up in any of the conventional firm measurements or metrics of team member performance.

For all these reasons, rather than the term *cross-selling*, we prefer to use *cross-buying*, given that, as noted, people do not like to be sold. For customers to want to *buy* more from your firm, they first have to be aware of the full menu of your service offering. But we have heard many firm customers say, "I didn't know they offered that service." Whose fault is that? The firm's, of course. It is as if you ran a restaurant and were reluctant to pass out a menu describing all your courses, or not offer a dessert menu and wine list (the most profitable items).

PAUL We hear that "I didn't know you did that" phrase most often at client advisory boards. As we go around the room getting views, invariably someone will say, "I really liked it when John came over and did the business development review." And then we'll see a look of surprise all around, and someone else will ask, "What's a business development review? It sounds interesting. I didn't know you did that."

RON More alarming is that when many CPA firms see, for example, "consulting" or "professional services" on their customers' income statements and ask the customers what it was for, the reply is usually, "We hired so and so to do such and such." When the CPAs say, "We could have done that for you," the customer replies, "I had no idea."

But if, on an ongoing basis, you are striving for a deeper understanding of your customers' expectations, wants, and needs, you will be in a position to capture these additional services when they arise. According to Roy H. Williams, "A recent national survey tells us that 67 percent of all shoppers intend to return home with the item for which they are shopping, yet only 24 percent actually manage to do so. The other 43 percent tell your salespeople that they're 'just looking,' and your salespeople let them leave your store disappointed and empty-handed" (Williams, 1999: 153). This was a particularly sore subject for Stanley Marcus, the son of one of the founders of Neiman-Marcus. He ran the store from the late 1920s through the 1960s and never lost money in any single year. He became famous for many innovative creations, such as holding fashion shows, promoting his-and-her Christmas gifts, among others. After he sold his interest in the business, he became an author and consultant and his teachings hold many excellent lessons for the willing student. Here is what he had to say with respect to lost sales opportunities:

> Americans used to be known as the world's best salesmen. Recently, it has become difficult in most stores to encounter that quality of salesmanship, if indeed you can even find a salesperson. A few years back, I made up my mind I would not buy anything I did not urgently need unless a salesperson was convincingly persuasive. As a result of this self-imposed discipline, I have saved $46,734 (Marcus, 1995: 55).
>
> No one has been able to establish a gauge to determine how much business walks out of any institution because of salesperson failure. The problem is not the sales staff; it is management that has failed to educate its staff, to supervise its staff, and to establish and maintain standards and adequate compensation. It's tough, but so is training for the Olympics. To win the gold on the track or in business demands the consistent performance of participants (Ibid: 11).
>
> The volume of lost business to retailers and industry as a whole is appalling. Some merchandise can be sold without benefit of a salesperson, but many products require an introduction and presentation. If stores are dedicated to self-service, then it is incumbent on them to organize displays and stock for easy shopping, but if they profess to supply service and charge for it, then they must provide adequate, well-versed sales assistants.

Otherwise, they should resort to vending machines that can be more efficient and a lot less costly than human beings who don't know their stock or why a product is worth buying. Stores and sales staffs have been spoiled by years of easy selling. During the Depression, I learned that the best way to sell anything was to encourage the prospective customer to feel the article while I discussed the benefits he would receive from it. We treated every prospect as though we wouldn't see another all day. And some days, we didn't (Ibid: 56).

PAUL Of course, you can view the comments from Marcus through another lens—that of culture. Culture is not something that exists in the minds of partners. Culture is something you can feel when you're standing at a reception area. Culture is like the air we breathe, in the sense that it is all around us and is necessary to life. Culture is in the words we use, the way we talk to each other, and so on.

This was brought home to me one time in New Zealand. We had just arrived at an airport in the north of the country and were in a cab driving to a hotel to present a seminar. Three of us were in the cab, in addition to the driver—21-year-old Jodie, who organized the logistics of our trips and who was also the main receptionist; Rob, the general manager, and me. The taxi driver asked, "What do you all do?" As quick as a flash, Jodie responded, "We make businesses more valuable." What struck me was not that Jodie was repeating part of the mission statement we had in place, but the passion and meaning behind how she said it. She really believed it and, more importantly, was proud to be a part of a company that did that. It was culture in action. So consider how culture works in your firm. Imagine you're riding in the back of a taxi with your receptionist and the taxi driver asks, "What do you all do?" How will he or she (or you for that matter!) respond. Would he or she say, "I work for a firm of accountants?" And what about you: would you say, "I'm an accountant!"

RON Let us return to Stanley Marcus again. While he was obviously referring to merchandise sales, mostly in department stores, can there be any doubt the same admonition applies to professional service firms? (In Chapter 10 we explore alternative measurements for assessing the effectiveness of a firm's team members, including how to reward for cross-selling activity.)

Now that we have discussed what people buy, let us turn our attention to the firm's value proposition and how it plays an important strategic role in devising and delivering results to the firm's customers.

THE VALUE PROPOSITION

RON In the 1980s, British Airways (whose initials, BA, at the time stood for Bloody Awful among flyers) had always been subsidized to make up for its poor service and resulting losses. Margaret Thatcher ended that when she privatized the flagship carrier in 1987. Suddenly BA had to compete, and it started by rethinking its fundamental value proposition. It innovated the concept of Club World business-class service, which provided the business traveler—the most profitable segment in the airline industry—with a truly unique flying experience. BA's major insight was to focus on the totality of the traveler's experience, that is, how he or she experienced the airline from point of origin to destination. By the late 1980s, by focusing on the value proposition it was offering its customers, BA became the world's most profitable airline.

PAUL But it didn't last. And for reasons you need look no further than the very costly exercise BA went through in 2000 to repaint its entire fleet, including tail-fin designs commissioned from well-known artists around the world. The idea behind the effort was to remove the Union Jack from the tail fins, to give the world the message that BA was "the international airline." Margaret Thatcher (who, like most people, hated the new look), summed it up well, when at the official launch, she covered the trendy tail fins on the model planes with her scarf and said she'd refuse to fly the airline until it put the Union Jack back on.

Probably, however, BA executives had loved the redesign undertaking (imagine going home and telling your friends you'd commissioned some famous artist to paint your tail fin!), but it was of absolutely no value to customers. Furthermore, customers thought BA had really lost its reason. And of course it had!

RON Fortunately, more companies now realize it is not enough to focus on simply the value of the product or service being offered, but that they have to take into consideration the total ownership experience from the customer's vantage point. They have to provide a total value proposition that, when compared with the customer's viable alternatives, offers a better deal. The originator of the value proposition, Michael J. Lanning (a former Proctor & Gamble executive and consultant with McKinsey), defines it this way in his book *Delivering Profitable Value: A Revolutionary Framework to Accelerate Growth, Generate Wealth, and Rediscover the Heart of Business*:

> Essentially, a value proposition is the *entire set of resulting experiences*, including some price, that an organization causes some customers to have. Customers may perceive this combination of experiences to be in net superior, equal, or inferior to alternatives. A value proposition, even if superior, can be a "trade-off," that is, one or more experiences in it are inferior while others are superior (Lanning, 1998: 55).

When most firms think about their value proposition, they usually include the following elements:

- Trusted advisors
- Long-term history
- In the profession for the long term
- Good reputation and/or brand name
- Technical expertise
- Knowledgeable and experienced professionals
- Utilizes latest technology
- Committed to our customers

PAUL Interestingly, a few (just a few) professionals actually put those elements on their business cards to attempt to differentiate themselves. It's actually not hard to include them on business cards. At almost every seminar I run, I ask attendees to "raise your hands if you have competitors." Of course, every hand goes up. Then I ask them to get out their business cards, after which I collect maybe five or six at random. Usually I pick those cards that are most enthusiastically thrust at me by those who believe they have a great card. Almost without exception, the cards are the same. Sure, some have wonderful (to the accountant) graphics with logos most likely designed by the senior partner's spouse years ago. And some have "artsy-fartsy" typefaces that, unfortunately, are impossible to read. And some even have embossed lettering. But in the middle of the cards is essentially the same thing: the name of the person, and underneath, the big statement, "Accountant." Wow! Isn't that exciting.

However, three cards were very different. I'll tell you about two here and describe the third later. First, Rick Stalling, who had gotten the point from a previous program that we needed to break the mold, had redesigned his card to read:

Rick Stallings, CPA

Chief Destruction Officer

a.k.a. Captain Chainsaw, Future Framer, Delta Man

If it ain't broke, break it!

Well, it does get your attention!

And so does Tom Weddell's. At a seminar, Weddell apparently had been greatly affected by a video I showed of geese. Accompanying the video were these words (what we called "Lessons from Geese"):

Observation: As each goose flaps its wings, it creates uplift for the birds that follow. By flying in a V-formation, the whole flock adds 71 percent extra flying range.

Lesson: People who share a sense of community can help each other get where they are going more easily . . . because they are traveling on the trust of one another.

Observation: When a goose falls out of formation, it suddenly feels the drag and resistance flying alone. It quickly moves back to take advantage of the lifting power of the birds in front.

Lesson: If we have as much sense as geese, we stay in formation with those headed where we want to go. We are willing to accept their help and give our help to others.

Observation: When the lead goose tires, it drops back into the formation and another goose flies to the point position.

Lesson: It pays to take turns doing the hard tasks. We should respect and protect each other's unique arrangements of skills, capabilities, talents, and resources.

Observation: The geese flying in formation honk to encourage those up front to keep up with their speed.

Lesson: We need to make sure our honking is encouraging. In groups where there is encouragement, production is much greater. Individual empowerment results from quality honking.

Observation: When a goose gets sick, two geese drop out of formation and follow it down to help and protect it.

Lesson: If we have as much sense as geese, we will stand by each other in difficult times, as well as when we are strong.

Not only did Weddell have all of that printed on his card, but he included pictures of geese flying in a V-shape. Then came the line: "At Vanacore, DeBennictus, DiGiovanni, Weddell, we help you fly further and safer than you ever thought possible." Now you may not want to be that bold; and in any event, we're not really talking about business cards per se here. We're talking about value propositions. But let's agree that once you've got one, you do need to communicate it.

The next step up the chain to differentiate is to be aware of and use the value propositions that Ron mentioned earlier. But that's not as clear-cut a step as it sounds, as Ron is about to explain.

RON Note that none of the characteristics listed previously describe the *experience* the customer will have with the firm. No doubt, many of those characteristics are essential, but they are not related to customer experiences. It is very difficult to catalogue all of the various experiences a customer will have with a professional service firm. In fact, this is an exercise the firm needs to conduct in order to enhance the value of the total experience for its customers. However, some generalizations can be made. The experiences a customer will have in interacting with a firm generally revolve around three areas:

- Quality
- Price
- Service

A firm must look at the interaction of all three of these variables and decide which combinations of each it will deliver to its customers. Focusing on any one is not enough, since the three are interdependent, not mutually exclusive.

Mercedes-Benz (now DaimlerChrysler) always touted its high quality to the marketplace, since it essentially started the automobile industry and had built up a reputation for excellence in engineering. But in the early 1990s, Lexus and Infiniti came along and offered customers a superior value proposition, not just in terms of price (indeed, a Lexus was not materially cheaper than a Mercedes), but rather in the totality of the ownership experience. Between 1985 and 1992, Mercedes market share dropped from 11.6 percent to 6.4 percent, with total units sold in the United States dropping from approximately 100,000 in 1986 to 59,000 in 1991. Resting on your laurels in terms of technical quality alone is a prescription for losing customers. The

Japanese even have a term for this: *atarimae hinshitsu*, which means *quality taken for granted.*

No professional service firm can compete on quality alone; it is merely *a table stake,* that is, the minimum you need to play the game. Who is going to stay with an incompetent professional? Besides, customers cannot easily judge the technical expertise of the professionals they use, any more than you can be confident in the technical competence of your doctor. What customers do know is how they are treated—the bedside manner of the doctor—and based on the empirical evidence, this treatment determines whether the customer remains loyal.

Neither is price enough to attract customers; if it were, books.com would have been a raging success, since it sold books cheaper than Amazon. Instead, books.com is now gone, disappearing even before the dot-bomb of 2001. Think of Southwest Airlines: By its own definition, it is the low-fare leader in the airline industry, but would that be enough to retain customers if it did not provide good-quality flights and excellent service? If everyone were price conscious, we would all be driving Hyundais. Customers are not *price*-sensitive; they are *value*-sensitive.

Professional firms tend to think about their value propositions in terms of a SWOT analysis—strengths, weaknesses, opportunities, and threats. A SWOT analysis is indeed a useful concept for firms to work through, but it does not address customer experiences explicitly. The same can be said for benchmarking best practices. Unless you can relate these tools to what the customer actually experiences when dealing with your firm, they are half-measures at best. Lanning describes a benchmarking study that was focused on the customer's experience:

> Consider a U.S. regional bank that benchmarked its mortgage approvals against car dealers. Not a vague comparison of customer service, this analysis benchmarks the speed with which customers can get approved for credit in the range of $100,000. For a Mercedes dealer, the collateral on an $80,000 asset drives off the lot, is difficult and costly to repossess, and depreciates instantly in resale value. With a $120,000 mortgage, the house can't leave town and usually appreciates in value. Yet the bank takes two weeks to approve the mortgage, while the car dealer approves a loan in two hours. There are technical differences, but two weeks versus two hours? The regional bank stands to learn something valuable about how to provide a better experience (faster mortgage approval) from such benchmarking, because it is focused on a particular resulting experience (Lanning, 1998: 257).

Many banks departmentalize their service offerings, from checking and saving accounts, business and personal loans, mortgages, and so on. Yet most customers would rather have a single contact within the bank to handle all of their needs. Professional service firms have traditionally followed the same strategy. Accounting firms, for instance, have audit, tax, and consulting divisions, each with its own methods of operation and, usually, different relationship partners. This is fine from an internal strategic position, since this is how firms are structured in terms of work flow, personnel, technology, and so on. But customers do not experience a *strategy*, they experience the *execution* of the strategy.

Focusing on the value proposition—and the resulting experience the customer will have—forces the firm to utilize those items that provide the most latitude in creating an overall positive set of experiences for the customer. Since there is not much latitude in working with technical quality, that leaves price and service. The former provides an enormous opportunity to establish a competitive differentiation to your firm's customers by adopting innovative and creative pricing strategies. By customizing your services into a fixed-price agreements and utilizing change orders, your firm will be able to remove fear, uncertainty, doubt, and risk from your customers. This is an enormous positive competitive advantage, one we explore in greater detail in Chapter 9.

The latter characteristic—service—is limited only by your firm's imagination. It is excellent service that separates the best firms from mediocre firms. Companies with an excellent service record are, for the most part, price *makers*, not price *takers*, in their respective industry. Think of Disney, FedEx, Nordstrom, Lexus, Ritz-Carlton, Four Seasons, and American Express: all of these companies charge a premium, they do not let their competition dictate their price, and they consistently offer a superior service experience to their customers. Another reason service excellence is such a critical component of your firm's value proposition is because your competitors can match technical quality and price fairly easily. If they do not have the expertise in-house, they can go buy it (or rent it); and there is *always* some firm, somewhere, willing to do what you do for a lower price.

PAUL And those firms "somewhere" may not necessarily be in your country, let alone your town. But why not think of those firms not as competitors but as additional (and lower-priced) resources that you can use. There is now a very significant trend in the United Kingdom and, perhaps surprisingly, in America, to outsource the preparation of tax returns to (of all places) India. The data are e-mailed to India and the completed returns are transmitted back the same way within 48 hours. How you price that part of the process is up to you, but why on earth would you want to price it lower (even though the cost might be one-tenth what you'd charge)?

One practitioner I know very well (Greg Hayes in Sydney, Australia) drove this point home to me. Whenever Hayes's customers would achieve some predefined goal, he would order a special plaque, similar to those Successories motivational plaques you often see these days (www.successories.com). He'd then put an engraved plate on the bottom, which might typically read: "Presented to Alan Smith and his team at ABC by the team at Hayes Knight Partners in recognition of the tremendous achievement of the bimonthly target." All told, Greg's plaques might end up costing $200 a piece.

These plaques would then be hung up all over the client's workplace, adorning corridors and offices alike. I commented to Hayes once on the amount of referrals the firm must get from stuff like this. He said, "Yes; and remember, it's hard to give plaques like this if you're the lowest-priced provider." Point made. (We get more into pricing in the next chapter.)

RON Competitors may be able to match (or beat) your price, but what cannot be very easily matched—or even observed, for that matter—is your firm's service quality, the "bedside manner" your professionals have with your customers. Moreover, as we explore later in this chapter, most professionals lose customers not over price or quality issues, but over service-related issues. Overall, then, service excellence is an enormous fulcrum to use to develop your firm's value proposition and create superior experiences for your customers.

Moments of Truth

Utilizing the *moment of truth* (MOT) method is one of the most effective ways to develop your firm's value proposition. The term has its roots in *the hour of truth* in bullfighting, to signal the third and final hour, the killing of the bull. In a business context, MOT certainly has a more prosaic meaning, but in terms of delivering excellent experiences to customers, and hence lengthening a firm's life, it is potentially just as fatal as to the bull. Karl Albrecht, who is probably the modern founder of the Total Quality Service movement in the United States, defines the moment of truth as follows: "Any episode in which the customer comes into contact with the organization and gets an impression of its service" (Albrecht, 1992: 116).

Jan Carlzon, former president of Scandinavian Airlines, led the failing airline to become one the most profitable airlines in Europe. His book, *Moments of Truth: New Strategies for Today's Customer-Driven Economy*, explains how he accomplished this transformation using the MOT philosophy:

> Each of our 10 million customers came into contact with approximately five SAS employees, and this contact lasted an average of 15 seconds each time. Thus, SAS is "created" 50 million times a year, 15 seconds at a time. These 50 million "moments of truth" are the moments that ultimately determine whether SAS will succeed or fail as a company. They are the moments when we must prove to our customers that SAS is their best alternative (Carlzon, 1987: 3).

For a professional service firm, a MOT could be a phone call from a customer, an office visit, a chance meeting on the street, an invoice received from the firm, or even a letter from the Internal Revenue Service (who will the customer think of first?). Taken individually, each MOT is a minor event. Over time, however, each interaction is like a pebble placed on a scale, with one side being service excellence and the other being service mediocrity. Eventually, that scale will begin to tip in one direction or the other. Generally, there are three possible outcomes to each MOT:

- Neutral experience (rarest)
- Positive experience (moments of magic)
- Negative experience (moments of misery)

PAUL Thinking about moments of truth is an enormously useful exercise. Better, of course, is *doing* something about it. Consider, for example, what a customer experiences when he or she comes into your place of work. Does it look like everyone else's office, or is it set up so that it is instantly apparent that this is a very different environment? We'll talk more about that in a moment when we discuss transformations and experiences but for now consider the impact of walking into Peter Byers's offices in New Zealand.

Byers's value proposition is very simple yet effective. His card says it simply and well: "An accounting firm that helps you build your financial position by making your business far more valuable." But then he makes it come alive with wonderful graphics. On the front of the card is a dandelion in full bloom and the words: "Great things come." Upon opening the card are two more pictures, the first of a smaller flower with the words, "From doing small things," followed by a larger flower with the words, "in a great way."

So when a customer receives Byers's card (a moment of truth) he or she immediately gets a positive impression. But it doesn't stop there. When the customer goes into his office, it comes as no surprise to see every wall adorned with larger versions of the pictures on his business card. It's a great way to share the culture.

We've already spoken about the Chicago-based firm of Lipschultz, Levin, and Gray. It got it right, too. It created positive moments of truth (and let you know how different the firm is) by creating a stunning office environment and conveying important cultural and value messages at the same time. Customers who walk into their offices in Northfield see what initially looks like a typical accounting environment. But as they turn left, they are amazed to see their personal or business name up on a huge projection screen above very distinctive furniture.

On a first visit, customers always ask about the interesting chairs. The response is: "These chairs are made especially by a client of ours. We love to work closely with our clients in this way and share with them ways to build their business. We're looking forward to doing the same with you."

RON Few customers come into contact with an organization and walk away with a neutral perception. When developing your firm's value proposition, it helps to map out each potential MOT with the customer and be as inclusive as possible. Even mundane things such as how accessible your parking is affects a customer's overall experience of dealing with your firm. Disney used the MOT mapping strategy and discovered that many children visiting its EPCOT Park at Walt Disney World were disappointed there were no Disney characters wondering around as there are in the Magic Kingdom. Disney has since placed characters in all of its parks, creating literally millions of magic moments for its guests. Saturn utilized the strategy to help develop its policy of one-price, no-hassle car-buying experience.

The key here is to understand absolutely that the MOT forces the firm to focus on the *outcome*, not the *activity*, of each encounter. A few years ago, before the IRS put a Power of Attorney check-off box on the U.S. Individual Tax Return, Form 1040, one firm utilized the MOT to come up with the strategy of having each customer sign a power of attorney so the firm could handle any correspondence on behalf of the customer, usually before customers had opened the letter themselves. The genius of this was that it turned a moment of misery—since most customers are deathly afraid of the IRS—into a moment of magic. At his firm, Morris + D'Angelo, my colleague Dan Morris, e-mails all draft tax returns using the Acrobat portable document file (pdf) format, insisting the customer review and sign off—and pay the invoice—before the return is finalized and filed. This may shock some as an onerous process, adding an extra layer of complexity to processing tax returns, and no doubt it does; however, it also adds a personal touch to the rather impersonal process of tax work: it gets the customers involved in their tax return; catches errors earlier, thereby lowering rework costs; speeds up payment; and creates literally hundreds of MOTs the firm can leverage into additional cross-buying opportunities.

Each MOT in your firm is an opportunity to deliver exceptional value to your customers and make them feel special, cared for, and appreciated. Every contact is an emotional connection and exchange with the customer; and if you thought intellectual capital was hard to measure, try empathy. Karl Albrecht and Ron Zemke articulate this core principle of service excellence: "When the moments of truth go unmanaged, the quality of service regresses to mediocrity" (Albrecht and Zemke, 2002: 55). No MOT should ever be taken for granted, for no matter how small it may be, in the long run, each one determines the destiny of your firm.

WHAT IS BEYOND TOTAL QUALITY SERVICE?

RON It may be premature to discuss what is beyond service excellence, considering that the modern-day founder of the Total Quality Service movement in the United States, Karl Albrecht, has pronounced the revolution dead. One of the problems with quality service is it is easier to discuss than deliver. Though we supposedly live in a *service* economy, the level of customer service, by some indicators, has actually dropped in recent years. Here is how Albrecht sums up the movement's fate:

> As management movements go, customer focus had an unusually long run—nearly ten years (Albrecht and Zemke, 2002: 2).
>
> Two primary factors, we believe, led to the fade-out of the customer focus movement. One was the aggressive promotion of competing management methodologies, particularly TQM [Total Quality Management], as solutions for the problems of service quality. The other was the "too hard" factor; that is, the disappointment and disillusionment felt by many executives when they realized that "customer service" was not the panacea or the quick fix they'd been led to believe it was. When they discovered that it involved such distasteful realities as financial investment, long-term commitment, constant attention to detail, service-oriented leadership, culture-building, perpetually listening to customers, and even changing the business design, many of them signed off (Ibid: 3–4).

One company that has never lost sight of its customer service focus is Southwest Airlines, still one of the most profitable airlines in the United States today. It has always believed, "We are not an airline with great customer service. We are a great customer service organization that happens to be in the airline business" (Freiberg and Freiberg, 1996: 282). Southwest never fell for most of the management fads from recent decades because it felt that those techniques lacked spirit and heart. This stance has certainly not impaired the company's success at attracting and retaining good people who deliver fantastic customer service, not to mention at achieving productivity and effectiveness levels that are the envy of the industry. Jack Welch, former CEO of General Electric, used to say, "The problem at too many organizations was that the employees perceived the boss as their primary customer." "If," he continued, "you think of an organization as a pyramid, and everyone is looking inside and up to the boss, the customers see nothing but the employees' rear ends" (quoted in Wetherbe, 1996: 95).

Be that as it may, we still think it is important to discuss a trend that an astute observer can witness taking place in the marketplace today, as it is a level beyond Total Quality Service. Granted, you have to look at specific companies to find this trend, but it is worth exploring in order to broaden the horizons of the firm of the future's value proposition. Let us start by posing these two questions:

- What is next for organizations that already provide unsurpassed customer service?

- What do companies such as Disney, Ritz-Carlton, FedEx, and Nordstrom, among others, see as they peer into the future and strive to offer a value proposition to their customers that prevents them from falling into the so-called commodity trap, while still enabling them to maintain their leadership role as price makers, not takers?

One fascinating hypothesis comes from Joseph B. Pine II, and James H. Gilmore, in their book *The Experience Economy: Work Is Theatre and Every Business a Stage*, wherein they put forth a futuristic value curve for businesses, with the following echelon of customer value:

- If you charge for *stuff*, then you are in the *commodity* business.

- If you charge for *tangible things*, then you are in the *goods* business.

- If you charge for the *activities you execute*, then you are in the *service* business.

- If you charge for the *time customers spend with you*, then you are in the *experience* business.

- If you charge for the *demonstrated outcome the customer achieves*, then and only then are you in the *transformation* business (Pine and Gilmore, 1999: 194).

What is interesting about this proposed hierarchy is not only where professional firms are on it, but where their greatest potential is on the curve. Most firms would think of themselves as service providers, offering intangibles to their customers; and no doubt this is true. Very few accounting and law firms view themselves as being in the experience business, let alone the transformation business. Visiting a professional firm is not often thought of as an enjoyable experience and is certainly not equated with visiting Las Vegas or a Disney Theme park.

It is interesting to speculate how professional service firms could be in the experience business. This does not mean to charge for the time—as in billable hours—the customer spends with you, but rather charge for the experience you create for the customer. As crazy as it may seem, imagine what would happen if you charged an admission price to enter your firm. This is not as uncommon as you might think. Already top hotels around the world are charging an entrance price just to come and look at their décor; and wineries in the Napa Valley are charging for tasting.

What would you have to do differently in order to provide a value proposition worth paying for? Think of the difference between entering a Disney Theme park and one of its retail stores in a mall. Although the mall store provides good service, it is nowhere near the standard of an amusement park experience. One of the reasons for this, perhaps, is that Disney does not charge you to enter the store. What would it have to do differently to induce customers to pay an admission? Would it result in a better and more lasting experience? Our conjecture is that it would.

You can apply this thinking to a *minimum* price for all new customers. What is going to be included in your firm's standard offering in order to entice a customer to pay a minimum to do business with you? It is an interesting experiment and one worth thinking about seriously. However, the main point we want to make is that the firms of the future—and the future of the profession—is poised at the top of value curve, since they are already offering their customers transformations, even though they may not think of themselves as doing so. To prove this, let us first define what is meant by a *transformation*:

> While commodities are fungible, goods tangible, services intangible, and experiences memorable, transformations are *effectual*. All other economic offerings have no lasting consequence beyond their consumption. Even the memories of an experience fade over time. But buyers of transformations seek to be guided toward some specific aim or purpose, and transformations must elicit that intended effect. That's why we call such buyers *aspirants*—they aspire to be some *one* or some *thing* different. With transformations, *the customer is the product!* The individual buyer of the transformation essentially says, "Change me." So transformations cannot be *extracted*, *made*, *delivered*, or even *staged*; they can only be *guided*. Being in the transformation business means charging for the demonstrated outcome the aspirant achieves—the transformation itself—not for the particular activities the company performs (Ibid: 171–72; 177; 192).

Think of the difference between a fitness center, one that charges for membership, versus personal trainers. The latter earn more because they take personal responsibility for the *outcome* of their customer's fitness regimen. And because they take responsibility for the demonstrated outcome the customer achieves, they are more selective about whom they accept as customers, as well as more diligent in performing an up-front analysis of each customer's expectations and willingness to change. This is a critical analysis, because if the customer is not willing to follow the trainer's advice, his or her attempt at transforming the customer is bound to fail. The point is, today's sophisticated customers are demanding more from their professionals than merely providing services and a good experience; they want transformations and they hold the professional accountable for guiding the transition.

A business is defined by that for which it collects revenue. *You are what you charge for.* As we discuss in Chapter 9, your price is the only opportunity your firm has to capture the value it creates for the customers it serves. Price is an integral part of your value proposition and therefore must be based on the value as perceived by your customer. Taking responsibility for the transformation of your customers—guiding them from where they are to where they want to be—is the ultimate expression of your firm's value-creating potential, and this is how a firm should be judged and perceived by those who pay its price.

Professionals, especially CPAs and attorneys, already enable many transformations for their customers. For example, they can help their clients become millionaires, retire at a specific age, finance a child's education, grow and enhance the value of a business, and carry out a customer's last wishes through estate and gift planning. These are inherently personal transformations, guiding the individual to fulfill their preferred vision of the future. There is no similarity between this offering and a commodity or even a bundle of intangible services. You are literally touching your customers' soul, forging a unique relationship with them that is virtually impervious to outside competition and commanding prices commensurate with the value of the results you are creating.

PAUL "Transforming the experience" came home to me recently in two quite distinct ways. In the first, I was in a meeting with managers of a major resort holiday company (Bourne Leisure) in England. We were discussing the outcomes they wanted from an upcoming three-day program. They explained how, some 18 months previously, they'd taken over a very large company (the holiday component of the former J. Arthur Rank) and had gone from a 2,000-member team to one of 15,000. Not surprisingly, there were challenges. "Some of our team members just don't seem to be understanding what we're trying to communicate about focusing on the customer and so on," they told me.

During the discussion, it became very apparent that the customers were experiencing the result of that miscommunication. So we devised a program that we called "Transforming the Experience." Nothing remarkable-sounding in that, until you realize its implications, on two related levels.

One: It is impossible to transform the experience for your customer unless you first (and continuously) transform the experience for your people, too. After all, it's your people who are serving the customer. Two: The customer must see the commitment, the passion, and the excitement in your people. Without working on and with your people, without working on your culture, if you will, attempts to transform and/or create wonderful experiences for your customers will be transitory at best.

VirginBlue Airlines in Australia understands that well. Richard Branson and, in particular, his Australian CEO, Brett Godfrey, have created an airline based, perhaps not surprisingly, on Southwest Airlines (why not copy a great model, after all?) But Branson and Godfrey took their airline further.

The first most obvious example is when the plane taxis from the gate. If you happen to be on the left-hand side of the plane and look out your window, you'll see all of the ground crew *and* the people who checked you in standing in line waving goodbye. It's amazing to see (and experience!) Once in the air, and after the no-frills meals have been served, crew members move to the face-painting area, where they paint cute faces on the children and on some willing adults, too.

Of course, that might not go down too well in your office environment, but you can learn from VirginBlue in other ways. For example, when the airline was just getting underway and had to use temporary hangers for check-in and disembarkation, those cavernous hangers were completely decorated with wonderful large posters promoting the importance of "you," the customer. (And, by the way, Virgin uses the term "guest," not "passenger." That simple word change does so much to underscore the culture similar to the effect of our using the word "customer" rather than "client").

One English practice has even learned from VirginBlue's "waving goodbye" scenario. In a team meeting at this practice, one 18-year-old asked this question: "When customers come to visit us, is it less expensive for us than when we go to visit them?" The answer was obviously yes, so the team member continued: "Why don't we use the money we're saving to create a special experience when they visit us? How could we do that?" The team brainstormed the idea for a while and came up with the remarkably simple plan of getting the customers' cars washed in the firm's parking lot. They even asked a mobile car cleaner if he'd be willing to do it at no charge in exchange for being able to leave his business card with the customers as a way of building his business. He agreed! (If the firm had had to pay for it, it would have been no big deal anyway, of course.)

Here's how this idea plays out: Prior to a customer's appointment, someone at the firm calls him or her with a reminder about parking. When the customer arrives at reception, the receptionist simply asks to hold on to the customer's keys—the assumption being in case the car needs to be moved. While the customer is taking care of business, the mobile car-wash man goes about his work and drops the keys back at the receptionist before the customer comes out.

Imagine what happens: The partner does not say goodbye to the customer at the desk, as normal. Instead, the partner takes the customer's car keys and accompanies him or her to the car. According to the partners of the firm, the "wows" they get (even in conservative England) are well worth the extra effort (or, if you prefer, well worth the *experience*).

Is Being a Trusted Advisor Enough?

RON In the aftermath of the Enron scandal and other assorted accounting debacles of 2002, there has been a lot of discussion about the trust factor in the accounting profession. Terms such as the *trusted advisor* have become common in mission and value statements at firms. In fact, many believe that trust is a *core competency* of the profession. I have a different perspective on this issue, which I have learned is very controversial (when sharing it with colleagues, it ignites quite a debate).

There is no doubting the importance of trust in business relationships. Accounting itself owes it origins to this very issue, since, from the late fifteenth century on, firms that were originally based on kinship and family ties grew to a size that made it imperative to hire outsiders. In addition, as personal finances became further separated from business finances, double-entry bookkeeping became a necessity in order for the principals of an enterprise to monitor the agents they hire.

In any economy, a high level of trust acts as an expedient to commerce, reducing the need for lengthy negotiations, protracted contracts, and costly litigation, or what economists refer to as *transaction costs*. Nobel Prize-winning economist Kenneth Arrow explains the function of trust:

Now trust has a very important pragmatic value, if nothing else. It is extremely efficient; it saves a lot of trouble to have a fair degree of reliance on other people's word. Unfortunately this is not a commodity that can be bought very easily. If you have to buy it, you already have some doubts about what you've bought. Trust and similar values, loyalty or truth-telling, are examples of what the economist would call "externalities." They are goods, they are commodities; they have real, practical, economic value; they increase the efficiency of the system, enable you to produce more goods or more of whatever values you hold in high esteem. But they are not commodities for which trade on the open market is technically possible or even meaningful (quoted in Fukuyama, 1995: 151–52).

With high levels of trust, commerce is more fluid, and transactions costs can practically be lowered to zero, as economist Thomas Sowell points out:

Commercial transactions that require trust and reliability are more readily concluded among people who share not only certain traits, but whose possession of these traits can be verified more easily. An extreme example of this are the Hasidic Jews of New York's jewelry industry, who give each other consignments of precious gems to sell, without the need for contracts or other costly safeguards that would be absolutely necessary if dealing with strangers. Lebanese traders in the interior of Sierra Leone likewise have had to depend on the honesty and reliability of other Lebanese traders in the port city, who sold their consignments of produce in the international market and shared the proceeds. The Chinese in Southeast Asia have also been noted for the large and complex transactions, which they conduct among themselves without written contracts (Sowell, 1994: 50–51).

You can't purchase trust; it is a table stake in a free market economy, and not just for professionals, but for *all* businesses. All transactions require trust; it is a basic expectation when conducting business. It certainly *is not* a core competency, because it is not an attribute you can do better—or at lower cost—than your competitor. Trust is complex and, obviously, there are different levels of trust, as it is a contextual concept. It is one thing to purchase a pack of gum at a convenience store, or get a shave from a barber, and quite another to trust a babysitter with your child. But it is a mistake for any firm to advertise or market its trustworthiness; it is frankly something that must be demonstrated and earned (one way to accomplish this is to offer a money-back guarantee on all of your work). Merely having trusting relationships with your customers does not ensure they will remain loyal.

I fly quite extensively on United Airlines; I trust them with my life, which certainly requires a higher degree of certainty and confidence in a complete group of strangers than in my accountant or lawyer. In the airlines, safety is simply a table stake—it is necessary, since it is hard to sell anything to a corpse—but it doesn't ensure customer loyalty or even profitability. If United's service ever begins to decline, I will defect. We witness the same response among customers of professional service providers. Moreover, no airline would advertise: "Fly with us, we won't kill you." The majority of transactions that take place in the worldwide economy are done under an umbrella of trust. Professionals are among the most trusted advisors. So what? This is a subtle point, but an important one. The profession—or any firm therein—does itself no favors by continuously trumpeting its level of trust.

Like your technical quality, it is merely a table stake. Those who talk about it injure it, and are perceived less believable.

Certainly you can lose customers if they lose faith or trust in you—and you will be the last to know—but that is not the reason the majority of customers defect from their professionals. As you will learn, most defections occur because of the service experience, not issues of integrity and trust.

FROM ZERO DEFECTS TO ZERO DEFECTIONS

RON I recall obtaining a new customer while in practice, the owner of a successful travel agency. Her husband had passed away the prior year and she never had to deal with the tax and accounting aspects of her business (her husband had been using the same CPA for over 20 years). When I asked (as I made a habit of doing) why she left that CPA, her answer was very laconic and poignant, and one I will always remember: "He showed no compassion."

From what I could determine, the CPA's work was technically proficient. My client had no complaints about his price or the quality of his work. She even trusted him. When I called him to ask for copies of certain documents, he was shocked that he had been replaced. It wasn't the *technical quality*, but the *service quality*, that made all the difference to her, not *what* she got, but *how* she got it.

During the 1980s, Total Quality Management (TQM) swept the business literature, and many companies rushed to institute a TQM program. (TQM is a body of knowledge that dates back to the late 1800s, as part of the agricultural revolution.) Yet applying TQM to a service business is no easy task, since it is a standards-based approach. Karl Albrecht has always been a strong critic of TQM, especially as it applies to a service business, as he pointed out in *The Northbound Train: Finding the Purpose, Setting the Direction, Shaping the Destiny of Your Organization*:

> Too many quality efforts begin as administrative, analytical, mechanistic, control-oriented, dehumanized, standards-based management attempts to "tighten up" the organization rather than loosen it up and empower the people to make their own individual quality commitments. This is why the doctrinaire, mechanistic TQM systems are ultimately doomed to failure (Albrecht, 1994: 32–33).

Albrecht then offers an example of an insurance company that invested heavily in a performance standard it considered important: a five-day turnaround in issuing policies, 90 percent of the time (Ibid: 139). This is the perfect project for a TQM model because it can be counted, measured against a standard, analyzed, constantly improved, and so forth. The only problem was, when Albrecht's consulting firm talked with the insurance agents and their customers, nobody cared about receiving their policies within five days.

What is the point? There is really no right way to do the wrong thing. As Peter Drucker says: "Nothing is so useless as doing efficiently that which should not be done at all." From a customer value proposition perspective, the breakdown here is easy to diagnose: TQM is an inside-out approach. The organization can internally count, measure, and analyze against almost any standard. But weighing yourself 10 times a day will not reduce your weight. TQM may provide a scale but not the guiding light for what should be weighed. We do not believe TQM is the answer to the profession's service deficiencies. Some firms have embraced it largely because it utilizes mathematical and statistical methods we easily understand. But we need to shift our thinking from "everything begins and ends with management" to "everything begins and ends with customer value." Counting and measuring things for the sake of counting and measuring things will not be the "open sesame" to attracting and retaining customers.

The alternative to TQM is Total Quality Service (TQS), which Albrecht defined as: "A state of affairs in which an organization delivers superior value to its stakeholders: its customers, its owners, and its employees" (Albrecht, 1992: 72). Notice how this definition is a goal condition to be sought, not a particular method of operation. Methods are developed as a way to achieve the goal, not as ends in themselves. The reason TQS is a better beacon than TQM for professional service firms is that it recognizes the subjective value of what is delivered, not the objective quality. Customers expect their financial statements and tax returns to be correct; TQS puts the focus and emphasis on the subjective value and the service quality, the ultimate arbiters of whether the customer remains a customer.

There is a sign in the textile plant of the Baldridge National Quality Award-winning Milliken & Company that reads: "Quality is not the absence of defects as defined by management, but the presence of value as defined by customers." Motorola, Inc., another Baldridge winner, has gained a worldwide reputation striving for six-sigma quality, which is 3.4 defects per million units of output. It is an impressive standard and Motorola has been able to achieve this in many aspects of its operations. But what happens when they achieve that impressive goal? Does that automatically earn them customer loyalty or guarantee profitability? Zero defects is not enough. In the long run, customers will begin to expect this result and competitors will be able to match this standard. What counts even more is how Motorola treats its customers, for as Donald E. Peterson, former chairman of Ford Motor Co., said upon bringing that company back from the precipice of poor financial performance: "If we aren't customer-driven, our cars won't be either."

In the 1990s, following the line of reasoning that being customer-driven was the ultimate goal of a company, many organizations began to calculate the lifetime value of an average customer. Consultants began asking their customers, "How much are you willing to spend to acquire a new customer?" Once this amount was determined, they would respond: "Then you had better be willing to spend *at least* that much to retain one." It was the dawn of the customer-loyalty economics movement, given voice by Frederick F. Reichheld and his book *The Loyalty Effect*, among others.

The automobile industry computed that a brand-loyal customer was worth at least $332,000 over the course of a lifetime; banking found $156 per year in profit; appliance manufactures figured $2,800 profit per customer over a 20-year period. Even the local supermarket calculated $4,400 per year and $22,000 over a five-year period of residence in a neighborhood. The theory was that businesses should look at the value of the relationship over the long term, rather than simply the math of the moment. You are more likely to handle a customer complaint differently, or resolve a dispute in favor of the customer, if you take into account his or her lifetime value.

This lifetime value paradigm also proved, empirically, that customer *retention* was more profitable than customer *acquisition*. Various studies showed that it cost between 4 and 20 times more (depending on the industry) to acquire a customer than it did to retain one. The American Institute of CPAs found it cost the average CPA firm 11 times more to acquire than retain a single customer. As a result, cross-selling became the mantra in most professional service firms, with the focus shifting from market share to *wallet share*. In other words, for a CPA firm, for example, the question was, "What percentage of the customer's audit, tax, and consulting budget went to the firm?" For many firms, the goal was to get the number as close to 100 percent as possible. Also, many firms began to invest resources in order to discover the needs and wants of their existing customers and sell more services to them, rather than combing the streets looking for new ones.

The loyalty movement created another positive effect, at least in terms of replacing the TQM paradigm: it focused the company away from zero *defects*, toward zero *defections*. For professional service firms, this focus makes imminent sense, since a service firm would never be able to achieve zero defects—to err is human, after all. And even if it did achieve this magical standard, customers would still defect over service quality. Like trust, technical quality is a table stake, the basic expectation of the customer. You do not return to a hotel because it changes the linens and vacuums every day.

While the lifetime value of a customer is important, we believe there is a better measurement the firm of the future should be cognizant of and attempt to compute: the lifetime value of the *firm* to the customer.

PAUL Isn't this a stunning reversal? This literally turns what we might call a "normal" inward-looking ratio right on its head. It asks, simply, "How valuable am I to my customer?"

RON This puts the emphasis not on selling more *core* services, but on increasing the amount of spending each customers does with the firm overall. As discussed previously, market share is simply the wrong measurement of success. What matters is to maximize the customers' spending by ensuring their *longevity* (over a lifetime), *depth* (capturing a greater share of the customers' wallet), *breadth* (obtaining revenues from complementary sources), and *diversity* of spending (striving for new service offerings in order to generate wealth for the customer).

This approach requires the firm to strive for customer loyalty, or what we are calling *zero defections*, of the type of customers it wants. There is an undercurrent of opinion that believes customers cannot be loyal to an organization, other than perhaps cottage-type businesses, such as hairdressers, stockbrokers, travel agents, or local restaurants. "How can a person be loyal to an airline or a hotel chain?" asks Karl Albrecht, who suggests that consumers merely have strong *preferences*, not loyalty. We disagree. If you study human behavior, people are loyal to their spouses, schools, neighborhoods, communities, not-for-profits where they donate money and services, and so forth. It is not so much that loyalty is dead in the business world, it is that a *reason* to be loyal is rare. Firms have to earn the loyalty of their customers, and that goes far beyond just being a trusted advisor and providing technically competent work. It requires providing service experiences that exceed the customer's expectations, as well as personal transformations to guide them in achieving their dreams. How does a firm increase the loyalty of its customers? Let us consider this question by analyzing why professionals lose customers.

Why Do We Lose Customers?

RON In the United States in the 1980s, a wave of "Buy American" campaigns swept the nation; and while these campaigns have always existed is some form, during this time period it was given extensive coverage because of the beating the U.S. automobile industry was taking from the Japanese. When surveyed, a majority of the people (between 60 to 70 percent) responded they would buy American not only because they felt a patriotic duty, but because it would be better for the country than purchasing foreign-made products. But the next time they walked into a car dealership, they drove home in a new Honda. Economists have a name for this dichotomy: *revealed preference*. This principle states: Watch what people *do*, not what they *say*, because it is what they do that reveals their true preferences.

Measuring customer loyalty should follow the same axiom: where does the customer spend his or her money, not what does he or she say on satisfaction surveys. Many companies learned the hard way that they could score high on satisfaction surveys and yet still have customers defect. That is because satisfaction measures the *past*, while loyalty attempts to measure the *future*.

Many firms have attempted customer satisfaction surveys with mixed results. As we have pointed out, there is no doubt you can learn some valuable things from them, but they are also fraught with dangers—low response rates, not addressing relevant issues, biased questions, and so forth. When conducting exit interviews, firms face the same challenges. Most customers are reluctant to give the firm the real reason why they left, so they tend to respond by saying, "You were too expensive." Yet, the revealed preference shows something quite different. Fortunately, many independent organizations and researchers—universities, the Big 4, consulting firms, private foundations, government agencies, think tanks, professional organizations, and others—have studied this issue extensively, and it is worth discussing some of their findings.

In their award-winning article, "How to Lose Clients without Really Trying," published in the *Journal of Accountancy*, August J. Aquila and Allan D. Koltin surveyed thousands of customers who had defected from their accounting firm. Here are the top seven reasons why they left:

1. "My accountant just doesn't treat me right." [Two-thirds of the responses].
2. CPAs ignore clients.
3. CPAs fail to cooperate.

4. CPAs let partner contact lapse.

5. CPAs do not keep clients informed.

6. CPAs assume clients are technicians.

7. CPAs use clients as a training ground [for new team members] (Aquila and Koltin, 1992: 67–70).

To corroborate this survey, the Rockefeller Corporation studied why customers defect and found the following:

1% The customer dies.

3% The customer moves away.

5% The customer has a friend [who provides the service].

9% The customer is lost to a competitor.

14% The customer is dissatisfied with [some aspect] of the service.

68% The customer believes you don't care about them.

PAUL You might want to read those ratios again, or better yet, put them in a pie chart. What you'll see immediately is that in nearly 7 out of 10 cases, people move away because they believe (rightly or wrongly) that you don't care. It's what I call "perceived indifference." And customers get that message of indifference on your part in so many ways, from the way your phone is answered (you don't have an automated recording directing people do you?) to more complex issues, such as you forgot that they never drink coffee.

That reminds me: Many firms in recent years have realized that offering coffee is a great way to generate a positive moment of truth. I'll always remember the second time I visited a firm using the coffee MOT. The receptionist (who had a sign on her desk with her name and her position—Director of First Impressions) asked, "Can I get you your skinnychino [a cappuccino with skim or low-fat milk] now Mr. Dunn?" I have to point out here that the receptionist was new—she hadn't been there on my first visit. So I asked how on earth she knew about my passion for skinnychinos? "It's a secret," she said. "But if you ask Mr. Pollins when you see him, I'm sure he'll explain." Mr. Pollins did explain: "Well, Paul, a team member suggested it actually. All we've done is add an extra column called 'preferred drink' to our customer database. It's amazing the reaction it gets."

So practitioners like this (and many more, we're pleased to say) have come to understand that if nearly 7 out of 10 people leave a professional because of perceived indifference, the opportunity obviously exists to create a perceived *difference*.

RON If we were turn the coin over and analyze which characteristics customers use to select an accountant, we would find these:

• Interpersonal skills

• Aggressiveness

• Interest in the customer

- Ability to explain procedures in terms the customer can understand
- Willingness to give advice
- Perceived honesty (Winston, 1995: 170)

Notice that *price* and *quality* are conspicuously absent from all of these surveys. The reasons cited on these studies have not changed much since they began, sometime around the 1950s. The fact of the matter is that most defections from professional service firms are the result of human failings and perceptions of indifference, rather than price or technical quality. In other words, it is how people are treated—or mistreated—that determines their willingness to remain loyal. This has important implications for your firm's value proposition, pricing policies, and key performance indicators (KPI). We will return to these surveys and look at them through a different lens when we discuss pricing and KPIs in Chapters 9 and 10. For our purposes here, and as it relates to the value proposition, it should be apparent that you want to compete based upon service, not price or quality.

Marketing professor Theodore Levitt offered this analogy in a 1983 *Harvard Business Review* article:

> The sale . . . merely consummates the courtship, at which point the marriage begins. How good the marriage is depends on how well the seller manages the relationship. The quality of the marriage determines whether there will be continued or expanded business, or troubles and divorce. The era of the one-night stand is gone. Marriage is both necessary and more convenient (quoted in Hart and Bogan, 1992: 182).

The analogy is not perfect, as the onus is really on the professional to instill a sense of loyalty in the customer; it's not a 50-50 partnership. Firms need to invest at least one-half of their advertising and marketing budgets for *retention*, rather than acquisition, which demonstrates the value the firm places on its existing relationships. No firm has a right to attract new customers if its existing customers are not delighted with its service, and this is especially true for our "A" customers, as this story from the June, 1994 issue *of CPA Quality Client Service* newsletter illustrates:

> Accountant Joe S. from Toledo tells this eye-opening story: "For over a year, I vigorously pursued a top executive. I wanted to steal his business from the Big 6 firm he had been using. I did everything I could to show this man how attentive and accommodating our firm would be, pulling out all the stops. Finally, we were set to have a lunch meeting at which I was sure I would get his business. As we sat down, across the room, I saw a partner from a Big 6 firm lunching with my best client.
>
> "At that moment, I realized that, in my quest for new business, I had all but ignored my existing clients. By working quickly to mend relationships, I was able to keep most of them. Now, my first priority is taking good care of my clients."

The lesson: Never take your clients for granted. Always let them know you care and that you appreciate their loyalty and their business. *If you don't invest in client relationships, your clients will have no reason not to think twice about experimenting with your competitors.*

Your firm's best customers are your competitors' best potential customers, and you should always act as if they are at risk. By providing Total Quality Service, a value proposition that differentiates you from the competition, fixed-price agreements wherein you bundle services and a 100-percent money-back guarantee, you can begin to lock the customer in *golden handcuffs*—increasing their switching costs—making it difficult for any other firm to offer more value. Customers will continue to patronize those businesses that give them a reason to be loyal, and your firm will motivate the behavior it rewards. Customer loyalty is worth rewarding. As the cited surveys make clear, professional services are built on relationships; that is, customers hire *people*, not so much firms. A Nordstrom team member expresses the attitude needed to ensure customer loyalty: "We are trained to make the customer, not the sale. We are trained to make customers."

To ensure zero defections, every firm must deal with problems when they arise. One of the characteristics that separate excellent service organizations from mediocre ones is how they handle, and even encourage, customer complaints, a topic we explore next.

Customer Complaints

RON The Chinese ideogram for the word *crisis* requires two brushstrokes to write. One brushstroke stands for *danger*; the other for *opportunity*. That is precisely what a customer complaint is; and the opportunity is actually greater than the danger, if handled correctly. Since it is virtually impossible for a professional service firm to remove defects from its work, handling complaints when they arise provides a competitive differentiation for your firm and enhances customer loyalty and goodwill if they are handled properly. Further, complaints that are handled quickly result in greater loyalty; and for that reason alone, one of the highest-value activities a firm can add to its repertoire of Total Quality Service policies is a proper complaint recovery system.

The empirical evidence proves the point. One organization that has done extensive research in this area is Technical Assistance Research Programs Inc (TARP.), now known as e-Satisfy.com of Arlington, Virginia. In its report "Basic Facts on Customer Complaint Behavior and the Impact of Service on the Bottom Line," by John Goodman, the following facts are reported:

- Only 1 to 5 percent of customers will escalate their complaint to a local manager or corporate headquarter.

- For large-ticket items, the complaint rate is higher, rising to 50 percent to front line and 5 to 10 percent of complainers escalating to local management or corporate. The existence of an 800 number at corporate HQ will, on average, double the number of complaints getting to corporate.

- Complaint rates vary by type of problem. Problems that result in out-of-pocket monetary loss have high complaint rates (e.g., 50 to 75 percent) while mistreatment, quality, and incompetence problems evoke only 5 to 30 percent complaint rates to the front line.

- Twice as many people are told about a bad experience than they are about a good experience.

- For major problems (those over $100) 91 percent of customers won't complain at all; they will just walk away. If they complain and it is not resolved to their satisfaction, only 19 percent will repurchase; if the complaint is resolved to their satisfaction, the repurchase rate increases to 54 percent; and if the complaint is *resolved quickly*, it jumps to 82 percent (www.e-satisfy.com, June 1999).

What is astonishing to realize from these statistics is that customers who complain can become more loyal than if they had no problem at all—if the complaint is handled quickly and resolved to their satisfaction. Marriott found the following percentages of intent to return when customers had a problem during their stay:

- No problems during the stay = 89 percent return rate
- Had a problem during the stay and it *was not* corrected to customer's satisfaction = 69 percent return rate
- Had a problem during the stay and it *was* corrected to customer's satisfaction, *before he or she left the property* = 94 percent return rate

This is why it is so important to resolve all customer complaints quickly, or at least take action to resolve them immediately. Complaints are not like fine wines; they do not age well. Customers complain because there is a gap between what they wanted to happen and what actually happened. Once they experience a problem, their expectation of having it resolved quickly is actually low (which is precisely why most customers do not complain—they think it will do no good), so a complaint is an excellent opportunity to improve their condition and turn the experience from a moment of misery into a moment of magic. You will redirect their focus to the *satisfying outcome*, rather than the original problem.

The golden rule when it comes to customer complaints: It is not *who is* right, it is *what is* right. Carl Sewell, author of *Customers for Life: How to Turn That One-Time Buyer into a Lifetime Customer*, has this advice: "Everything you need to know about handling mistakes you learned in nursery school: acknowledge your error, fix it immediately, and say you're sorry. Odds are, your customer, like your mom and dad, will forgive you" (Sewell, 1990: 164).

Hal Rosenbluth, CEO of Rosenbluth Travel, returns all commissions earned on any arrangements his company makes incorrectly, a policy almost unheard of in the travel industry. He explains the benefits of this policy in his book, *The Customer Comes Second and Other Secrets*:

> It's better to spend money refunding clients when they are not satisfied than to forfeit money in lost accounts for the same reason.
>
> Many of our service-guarantee refunds have been because of supplier error [airlines, hotels, rental car agencies, etc.], but we returned our commissions to our clients because we hold ourselves responsible for the entire process (Rosenbluth, 1992: 135, 204).

When analyzing customer complaints and firm defects, ask how, not why. Why questions tend to generate excuses and justifications, while how questions will lead to knowledge to correct the problem. "How can we prevent this from happening again?" is a much better question than "Why did this happen?" Also, follow this five-step recovery process to deal effectively with all customer complaints:

1. *Apologize.* Say *I am* sorry, not *we are* sorry.

2. *Make an urgent effort.* Fred Smith, founder of FedEx, followed the "Sunset Rule": "The sun will not set on an unresolved customer or employee problem that is not dealt with in some way."

3. *Show empathy.* Show understanding and compassion; fix the customer before fixing the problem.

4. *Compensate.* Be generous, show remorse; better yet, ask the customer how he or she would like the problem to be fixed (usually, the request is less than you would have given up).

5. *Follow up.* Learn how the customer feels about the situation; provide closure.

The Ritz-Carlton gives its team members great latitude in resolving customer complaints, with each one informally authorized to spend $2,000 on solving customer problems. In the Ritz-Carlton Basics, a set of 20 guiding principles every team member is held accountable for, number 13 states: "Never lose a guest. Instant guest pacification is the responsibility of each employee. Whoever receives a complaint will own it, resolve it to the guest's satisfaction, and record it." This "ownership" of customer complaints it quite effective, and every firm must take this attitude with respect to any customer problem.

Customer complaints can be more valuable than customer compliments because they provide the firm with information on aspects of their service delivery that need to be improved, a second chance to gain the customer's business, and an opportunity to actually increase the customer's goodwill and loyalty. Given these facts, firms should actually provide an incentive for customers to complain, and one of the most effective strategies to do that is the 100-percent money-back guarantee.

The 100-Percent Money-Back Guarantee

PAUL In 1997, when I first read Christopher W.L. Hart's breakthrough book *Extraordinary Guarantees: Achieving Breakthrough Gains in Quality and Customer Satisfaction* his words rang true to me. Here was something that made perfect sense to me—why force people to pay for things that, in the end, they didn't value?

But Hart went (appropriately) much further than that. One clue is in the first word of the title, "Extraordinary." He points out that guarantees that say, in effect, "we guarantee our workmanship" do absolutely nothing. But when you understand the concept of extraordinary, you begin to see that well-thought-out guarantees give you real presence in the marketplace.

Consider the case of the Bugs Burger Bug Killer Company (a real company based in Miami, Florida run by Al Burger). Burger, obviously, is in the pest control business, specializing in the hospitality industry. But Burger correctly determined that most people don't want to *control* pests, they want to *wipe them out*! So he developed this extraordinary guarantee:

> You don't owe one penny until all pests on your premises have been totally eradicated. If a guest spots a pest on your premises, BBBK will pay for the guest's meal or room, send a letter of apology, and pay for a future meal or stay.
>
> If you are ever dissatisfied with BBBK's service, you will receive a full refund of the company's services *plus* fees for another exterminator of your choice for the next year.
>
> If your facility is closed down due to the presence of roaches or rodents, BBBK will pay any fines, as well as any lost profits, plus $5,000.

Extraordinary isn't it? And Burger is so good at what he does that he's able to get insurance against ever paying out!

Of course, it's important to recognize that a guarantee *forces* you to be even better at what you do. And that, of course, is the point. Consider which pest control service you'd choose: the one that says, "We try our best," or Burger's almost regardless of his price.

And that, of course, is another point: Once you institute a great guarantee (and Ron has more to say about that soon) you should increase your price if only to cover the eventuality of someone calling you on the guarantee. Hart observes that, in all his research, he estimates fewer than 0.1 percent abuse or calls on the guarantee. Suppose that Hart's numbers are off by two orders of magnitude (100 times off): that's still only 10 percent who may call on the guarantee. That being the case, why is it that so many people base policies and procedures on the 10 percent of people who may seek to take advantage of you, as opposed to basing policies and procedures on the 90 percent (actually 99.9 percent according to Hart) who are honest?

Interestingly, when you read Ron's last point about complaints, it means that we should, in fact, put in systems that actually generate complaints.

RON Many professionals think it counterintuitive to offer incentives for their customers to complain, worrying that they would be inundated with angry customers; or that if they didn't respond effectively, they might lose the customer. These fears are unwarranted, however. Supplementing the research discussed previously, Theodore Levitt made this observation with respect to asking for customer complaints: "One of the surest signs of a bad or declining relationship with a customer is the absence of complaints. Nobody is ever that satisfied, especially not over an extended period of time. The customer is either not being candid or not being contacted (quoted in Albrecht and Zemke, 2002: 86).

According to the U.S. Office of Consumer Affairs, 37 to 45 percent of all service customers are dissatisfied with some aspect of the service they receive, but do not complain. Obviously, this is a risky situation, so we suggest you include the following service guarantee in all of your fixed-price agreements and engagement letters:

> Our work is guaranteed to the complete satisfaction of the customer. If [customer name] is not completely satisfied with the service performed by [firm name], we will, at the option of [customer name], either refund the price or accept a portion of said price that reflects [customer's name] level of satisfaction. We will assume you are satisfied upon final payment received under the terms of this agreement (Baker, 2001: 145).

PAUL Recognizing that we're actually transforming the experience, why not stop using the word "satisfaction?" Why not replace it with "delight?" Then the guarantee reads:

> Our work is guaranteed to the complete delight of the customer. If [customer name] is not completely delighted with the service performed by [firm name], we will, at the option of [customer name], either refund the price, or accept a portion of said price that reflects [customer's name] level of delight. We will assume you are delighted upon final payment received under the terms of this Agreement (Baker, 2001: 145).

RON Whichever way you phrase it, the advantages of this policy are many. It demonstrates to the customer that your firm is serious about Total Quality Service and providing a valuable experience for them. It puts your money where your mouth is. It is one thing for a firm to *tell* a customer how good it is, quite another to *show* them with a service guarantee. It gives your entire firm the impetus to exceed the customer's expectations, since now your money is on the line. This focuses the firm on the only true profit center it has: a customer's check that does not bounce. The service guarantee establishes a competitive differentiation and helps to sway the marginal customer to select your firm (especially in request for proposal (RFP) work). Because having a guarantee requires a higher level of trust, the firm will do a more diligent job of prequalifying all of its new customers and will document the expectations of each party much more thoroughly. A service with a guarantee is more valuable in the marketplace than a service without a guarantee—because it dramatically decreases the customer's risk—and this alone enables the firm to command a premium price over its competition (think of FedEx and Nordstrom). It also provides word-of-mouth advertising for the firm, as customers appreciate this policy and will be less reluctant to refer new customers. It gives the customer an incentive to complain, which as we have learned, is more valuable than the alternative.

With all that said, there is an even more substantial reason you should offer a service guarantee to all of your customers: *You already do*. If any one of your customers were to complain loudly enough, you would either write down or write off their invoice, according to his or her wishes. Or, you would ask the customer to pay only what he or she thinks is fair. Unfortunately, this is done *after* the fact, when you will receive no benefit from it. In effect, you have a *covert* service guarantee; we suggest you make it *overt* in order to gain a marketing and competitive advantage over your competition. Again, the idea is to have an overt extraordinary guarantee policy—one that you trumpet in the marketplace.

PAUL And why not go one stage further: let your team members decide which services or aspects of the service you can guarantee. The way to do it is simple. Start by developing a list of the key frustrations people feel about dealing with professionals (you probably know most of them already, but why not ask some customers through a client advisory board, for example). If your experience follows others on this path, you'll find that many frustrations involve time—for example, the turnaround time of documents, returns, and so on.

One firm we know lets their team members work on it, essentially asking, "Which systems would we have to put in place to guarantee a 10-day turnaround on returns?" The team decided that by modifying systems they could cut what was an average six-week turnaround time down to eight days. So they then felt comfortable offering a 10-day guarantee.

And to anticipate a question you may have, a question often asked in seminars, particularly business development seminars: "Should I guarantee that my client gets a certain quantum of extra profit by working with me?" the answer is an unqualified no. To do that misses the point. You can guarantee only that which you can control, and you clearly have no control over whether a customer *implements* your ideas to move to greater profit.

Again, the idea is to have an overt guarantee policy, one that you trumpet in the marketplace.

RON Baldrige Quality Award-winning firm Graniterock instituted such a policy, calling it "short pay." This provides, in essence, a line-item veto to customers and allows them to deduct any amount of the invoice in accordance with their subjective value of the service provided. It is not a refund or discount policy, it is a pure service guarantee, as the customer is not required to return the merchandise. Here is how owner Bruce Woolpert explained the advantages of this guarantee:

> You can get a lot of information from customer surveys, but there are always ways of explaining away the data. With short pay, you absolutely have to pay attention to the data. You often don't know that a customer is upset until you lose that customer entirely. Short pay acts as an early warning system that forces you to adjust quickly, long before we would lose that customer (quoted in Collins, 2001: 80).

Will some customers take advantage of Woolpert's policy? Probably (though as Paul has already mentioned, we know of no widespread proof of this). But consider Nordstrom, legendary for taking back merchandise that was not even purchased from them. It estimates that between 2 to 3 percent of its customers take advantage of this policy, yet 97 to 98 percent appreciate the policy and are more loyal—and pay a premium price—as a result. Do not let the tail wag the dog. If any one customer were to abuse your service guarantee, he or she has actually done you a favor by identifying him- or herself as a problem customer. Gladly refund his or her money and fire that person from your firm.

Do not misconstrue anything we have said here as meaning that "the customer is always right." That is patent nonsense.

PAUL We actually prefer to say, "the right customer is always right!"

RON Even e-Satisfy.com has shown through its research that up to 40 percent of expressed dissatisfaction is caused by the customer's own mistakes or unreasonable expectations. While the customer is not always right, it is no use to argue with him or her, since I've rarely seen anyone win an argument with a customer. The fact is, customers are entitled to their feelings and will act upon them, even if intellectually they are wrong. Sometimes the only course of action is to fire them—or, as Troy Waugh says, "outplace" them.

There is nothing worse for you firm's morale than to continue to serve customers who do not understand or appreciate the value you provide. Given a choice between continuing a relationship with a toxic customer and the effect it might have on the morale of your team members, observe whom former CEO of Southwest Airlines, Herb Kelleher, sided with, as this story from *Nuts! Southwest Airlines Crazy Recipe for Business and Personal Success* humorously illustrates:

> [A] woman frequently flew on Southwest, but was disappointed with every aspect of the company's operation. In fact, she became known as the "Pen Pal" because after every flight she wrote in with a complaint. It was quickly becoming a volume until they bumped it up to Herb [Kelleher's] desk, with a note: "This one's yours." In 60 seconds, Kelleher wrote back and said, "Dear Mrs. Crabapple, We will miss you. Love, Herb." (Freiberg and Freiberg, 1996: 269–70).

And this is a company that computes that, for the year 1994, only five customers per flight accounted for its entire profit (Ibid: 121). So why would Kelleher so nonchalantly fire a customer? *Because he stands up for his people and puts them first.* Once his response was published in the Southwest newsletter, what do you think happened to team member morale? If it comes down to a choice between your team members and an unreasonable customer, side with the team members, even at the expense of short-term profits. The team members will make up for the lost revenue, but you can hardly ever recapture the loss of dignity and respect team members suffer by forcing them to work with rude and unreasonable customers. Even better, like Tom Weddell and others, let your team members decide which customers to fire—you will be surprised how diligently they perform this task and then how motivated they are to make up the lost revenue.

Of course, one of the best ways to implement a policy of *zero defections* is to select the right customers in the first place, a topic we turn to next.

BAD CUSTOMERS DRIVE OUT GOOD CUSTOMERS

RON It is common in professional service firms to grade customers and focus attention on the "A" and "B" customers and even hold out incentives to the "C" customers to upgrade to "A" or "B" status. In this section, we offer two distinct methods of applying this customer segmentation strategy in a more sophisticated and rigorous manner. Along with your human capital selection, your customer capital criteria are the most important aspects of crafting your firm's success.

The traditional customer grading criteria are most likely familiar to you; they usually include:

- Amount of annual revenue
- Prompt payment history
- Potential for growth
- Potential for future referrals
- Actual referrals
- Profitability of customers
- Risk of having customer in portfolio
- Timing of work (fiscal or calendar year)
- Reasonable expectations
- Willing to take advice
- Profitable and not undercapitalized

Certainly these are important criteria and should be made part of any firm's prequalifying process. Ric Payne, chairman and CEO of Principa, advocates the following 12-point criteria for selecting customers:

- In business for at least three years.
- Pleasant, outgoing personality.
- Willing to listen to advice.
- Positive disposition.
- Technically competent.
- Business is profitable.
- Business is not chronically undercapitalized.
- Business is not dominated by a small number of customers or suppliers.
- Clearly established demand for the product or service.
- Business has a scope for product or service differentiation through innovative marketing.
- Business has scope for improved productivity through innovative management planning and control.
- Business has a strategic plan.

These are all good criteria to judge potential new customers; and certainly Paul's discussion of David Maister's personality criteria (see Chapter 3) should be foremost on the list as well. There is no point in working for and with people whom you do not like or are indifferent about. Bob Gaida, dean of the BDO Sales College, uses this two-prong criteria when qualifying potential customers: "Does the client have the ability to pay a premium fee and do they have a thirst for knowledge?" (quoted in Waugh, 2001: 114).

As good as these criteria are, I want to add one more. I have come to believe that *character* is more important than personality in judging new customers. The ancient Greek philosophers held the view that "character is destiny"; and being an inveterate student of human behavior, I find this reasoning compelling. The Greeks also spoke of *good habits* and *bad habits*. The good habits they called *virtues*, the bad habits *vices*. A person's character does provide a basis on which to predict behavior, which is why we say certain behavior is *in* character or *out* of it. In light of the accounting scandals in 2001 and 2002, the firm's reputation and the partner's peace of mind should be more important than profitability.

When a professional service firm accepts a new customer, it is not merely *closing* a sale; it is beginning a lifelong relationship. We select our spouses, friends, and other important relationships very carefully, why would we not perform a proper amount of due diligence before selecting a customer? If the customer is worth having, he or she is worth investing some time and resources in determining if he or she is a good fit for your firm.

It is no longer wise to accept new customers simply because they have a checkbook and are alive. Let us reiterate: The most successful firms in the world all have very rigorous prequalifying standards, and they do not accept all comers (in fact, they report they turn away more business than they accept). This is not out of arrogance, but from the recognition that the firm cannot be all things to all people. Saying no to a new customer is not necessarily easy, but it is vital if you want to accept only those customers who are pleasant to work with, have interesting work, and enhance your firm's intellectual capital. Complexity kills a business, and by accepting any customer—especially those who don't fit your value proposition—you are adding a layer of bureaucracy that will starve your best customers and put them at risk of going elsewhere. For instance, we see far too many firms take on low-price tax returns during busy season on the assumption that the marginal revenue contributes to profits (the old Practice Equation paradigm again). This may be true, in the short run, but the complexity it adds to the firm will distract it from offering higher-value services to its best customers. The Pareto Principle is always in effect—that is, 20 percent of your customers generate 80 percent of your profits, or even 5 percent generate 50 percent. In order to adopt the Pareto Principle, let us offer the following metaphor.

ADAPTIVE CAPACITY

RON In his essay on the art of poetry, Aristotle makes the following observation: "But the greatest thing by far is to be a master of metaphor. It is the one thing that cannot be learnt from others; and it is also a sign of genius, since a good metaphor implies an intuitive perception of the similarity between dissimilars" (quoted in Satinover, 2001: 66).

We would like to offer the metaphor of your firm as a Boeing 777 airplane, similar to Exhibit 8.1. Like the airlines, professional service firms have high fixed costs

EXHIBIT 8.1   Boeing 777

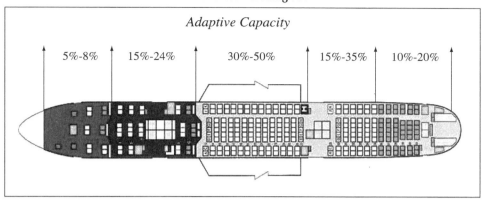

and fixed capacity. When United Airlines places a Boeing 777 in service, it adds a certain capacity to its fleet. Then it goes one step further, by dividing up that marginal capacity into five segments (the percentages shown are suggested capacity allocations for a professional service firm):

First class (5 to 8 percent)

Business class (15 to 24 percent)

Full-fare coach (30 to 50 percent)

Coach (15 to 35 percent)

Leisure and bereavement fares (10 to 20 percent)

Your firm has a theoretical *maximum capacity* and a theoretical *optimal capacity,* and it is essential to see how that capacity is being allocated to each customer segment. Your maximum capacity is the total number of customers your firm can adequately service (not how many hours you have), while the optimal capacity is the point at which customers can be served adequately and at which crowding out does not affect customer behavior. Usually, for most service firms, optimal capacity is between 70 and 90 percent of maximum capacity.

The airlines are adept in managing their adaptive capacity to maximize their revenue and profitability. There are many examples of this strategy in practice. For instance, I looked up a United Airlines next-day flight from San Francisco to London and the airline was able to accommodate me in first class, business class, or full fare coach. The airlines understand it is the last-minute purchaser who values the seat the most, hence they reserve a portion of each plane's capacity for their best customers. They do this even at the risk the plane will take off with some of those high-priced seats empty—and that revenue can never be recaptured since they cannot inventory seats. Why do they take that risk? Because the rewards of withholding capacity for price-insensitive customers comprise the majority of their profits. I was given the option of a first-class ticket on the San Francisco to London (Heathrow) route for $13,583, while business class was $9,230, and full-fare coach was $2,218. This is not cost-plus pricing, but rather value pricing. It is pricing commensurate with the value being received by the customer. It does not cost United four to six times less to fly a coach passenger than a first-class or business-class passenger. Rather, it has taken a risk by withholding some of its capacity so I could wait till the last minute to make my booking.

At the other end of the plane, the airlines allocate so many seats to coach, leisure, Priceline (or bereavement)-type seats, which they offer well in advance of the flight. However, no airline *adds* capacity to accommodate these customers. This point is critical, as too many professional firms will, in fact, add capacity—or reallocate capacity from higher-valued customers—in order to serve low-valued customers.

Furthermore, many firms will turn away high-value, last-minute work for its best customers because it is operating near maximum capacity, and usually at the low end of the value curve, for price-sensitive customers. This is common during busy seasons, where high-value projects will arise from customers, but the firm is at maximum capacity and cannot handle the marginal work. The lost profit opportunities caused by this are incalculable.

Many firms worry about running below optimal capacity and cut their prices in order to attract work, especially in the off-season. This strategy is fine, but you must understand the trade-off you are making. Usually, that capacity could be better utilized selling more valued services to your first-class and business-class customers. This way, the firm does not cut its price in order to attract price-sensitive customers, thereby sending a signal to the marketplace that it is willing to engage in this strategy and affecting the perception of its value proposition. According to most pricing consultants, pricing mistakes are usually the result of misallocating capacity to low-value customers due to the fear of not running at optimal (or maximum) capacity.

Of course, in any high fixed-cost environment, there are multiple strategies for managing capacity, both from the demand side (pricing) and the supply side (offerings). The firm wants to make sure that it can supply exactly what each customer demands, at the right time. Firms have several strategies for managing their capacity, including:

- Hiring part-time team members.
- Working overtime.
- Cross-training team members.
- Increasing customer participation in the service (think of ATM machines in banking).
- Sharing facilities and team members with other firms.
- Outsourcing.

All of these strategies work well for supply-side management. However, it is on the demand side where the profit-optimizing strategies exist for the firm. The conventional wisdom is that firms have to be at maximum capacity—where demand exceeds supply—in order raise your prices. But since when do you have to wait to be fully booked to demand a premium price? Do not confuse working *harder* (supply-side capacity) with working *smarter* (demand-side pricing).

This is precisely why the airlines, after being deregulated in the late 1970s, moved to a system of *yield management*, also referred to as *dynamic pricing*, or *revenue management*. Robert G. Cross, a lawyer formerly employed by Delta Airlines, described the situation he found at Delta in the mid-1980s, in his fascinating book *Revenue Management: Hard-Core Tactics for Market Domination*:

> Some flights that had been loaded with discount seats sold out well in advance of the departure. But on these flights, Delta would also turn away significant last-minute, full-fare traffic. This added up to a lot of lost revenue. Also, on numerous occasions we had severely limited discount fares and ended up sending flights out with empty seats that could have been filled with discount passengers. . . . I estimated that Delta was leaving as much as $200 million a year on the table, just from misallocating discount seat availability on its flights. This number was so mind-boggling, I didn't dare tell anyone. No one would have believed it!
>
> In one year's time, Delta realized an incremental revenue gain of $300 million solely from the new seat inventory control process. This $300 million accounted for half the $600 million turnaround Delta reported in fiscal 1984 (Cross, 1997: 42, 45).

If you have ever wondered why airline pricing is so complicated—with the carriers in the United States changing their prices approximately 12 million times each day—this is why. The gains from implementing a yield management pricing strategy are enormous, and professional service firms should adopt these methods as well. The optimal strategy for the firm is to be able to offer the right service, at the right time, to the right customer, at the right price. (We discuss value pricing in the next chapter.)

In terms of your firm's capacity, think of the five classes of airline customers as your "A," "B," "C," "D," and "F" customers. How much fixed capacity will you allocate to each class? What will be the criteria you use to ascertain where in your airplane each customer sits? Will you use the Maister personality criteria, Ric Payne's 12-point criteria, or some mixture of all, as discussed? One effective idea is to grade your customer base on both an *objective* basis—such as Payne's—and on a *subjective* basis—such as Maister's. Under each method, you will see how your capacity is allocated, forcing you to understand the trade-off you are making between serving various groups of customers. It is possible—indeed likely—you will have a first-class customer under one grading method and the same customer as a bereavement fare under another grading method. By viewing your firm as an airplane with a fixed amount of seats, you will begin to adapt your capacity to those customers who appreciate—and are willing to pay for—your value proposition.

Unlike an airplane, however, when a firm is operating under optimal capacity, its human capital need not sit idle. Since professional service firms are intellectual-capital-intensive, there are myriad activities that team members could perform in below-capacity periods, such as:

- Take time off (as part of an overtime bank, for example).
- Schedule continuing professional education courses.
- Catch up on reading, or teach fellow colleagues new knowledge learned from a book or article.

- Engage in practice development for the firm.
- Cultivate your social capital by engaging in networking.
- Spend additional time with your first and business class customers.
- Add to the firm's structural capital by completing After-Action Reviews on recently completed engagements (see Chapter 6).

All of these activities—and this is in no way a comprehensive list—add to the firm's stock of IC, which is hardly a waste of its idle capacity.

Firing Customers

RON What happens when your plane becomes filled with too many "C," "D," and "F" customers? Many consultants to CPA firms estimate, for instance, that the average firm contains between 10 and 40 percent of "F" customers. It is never easy, but it is necessary, to remove these customers from your firm. We suggest removing those customers whose personalities clash with the culture of your firm, or whose character is in question. Once that is completed, you can focus on removing other low-valued customers (such as the "Cs" and "Ds"). These customer are usually the ones who complain most vociferously about your price; and the debilitating effect is that we tend to listen to them the most and this affects how we price our "A" and "B" customers. And keep in mind that firing customers is not a one-time event, but a continual process. The most profitable firms annually cull through their customer base and "outplace" between 5 and 10 percent of their customers. One caveat: Be sure you have done everything within your power to turn a low-value customer into a high-value customer. The fact of the matter is, *your customers are not going to get better until you do.*

That said, how should you fire a customer? There are many strategies, some more effective than others. Many firms in the early days of implementing this strategy would simply raise their prices by a factor of two or four, and to their surprise, over half of the customers remained with the firm (a leading indicator of just how much money professional service firms leave on the table). Nevertheless, we strongly advise against this strategy. The goal is to remove the customers, not simply increase their price. Getting two or four times more from an "F" customer does not make him or her a "C," "B," or "A" customer (this is the ethic of the world's oldest profession, not of true professionals).

Another strategy is to write a letter. This is a useful strategy if you are firing a lot of customers at one time, but with a customer you have served for many years, clearly a one-on-one meeting is far preferable. A phone call or a meeting is the best—and most dignified—strategy. You may line up other professionals as potential referral sources (one of your "D" or "F" customers could be his or her "A" or "B" customer); or, some firms have even sold off these customers to other firms. Here is an example of a possible conversation you might have:

"Mary, we need to talk about how well we're working together. We need to be sure that the range of services we offer matches your needs. Here in the prac-

tice we want to work with people where we can add significant value to their business, rather than just crunching some numbers and filling in some tax returns for them.

"This means we are reducing the number of clients we work with and increasing the range of services we provide for them. We're working with them on growing their businesses by offering consultative services. Naturally, this means that our price levels are increasing, too. Many of our clients are comfortable with that extra investment because of the value we are giving them in return.

"Mary, unless I'm very mistaken, we simply can't provide you with that value. It seems to me that your needs would be better served by an accountant who just wants to stick to the numbers. How do you feel about that?"

The Forced Churn

RON The first item we look at in firms we consult with is the Pareto Analysis—a ranking of all customers from highest to lowest in revenue. Without fail, 20 percent of the customers generate between 67 and 85 percent of the revenue. This is the first step in ascertaining how the firm is allocating its fixed capacity to its different customer segments. When we suggest firing between 40 and 80 percent of customers, obviously there is strong resistance. The most common objection is that doing so would make the firm too dependent on the remaining 20 to 60 percent. However, given the realities of the Pareto Analysis, your firm is already dependent on these customers, and by focusing too many resources on the bottom 50 to 80 percent, you are actually putting the remaining high-valued customers at greater risk of defection by ignoring their needs and wants. Many firms have learned that *fewer* customers equates to higher profits, better service, improved team member morale, and less complexity in the firm.

That being said, it is difficult to fire that many customers at one time, so we have an alternative strategy. My colleague, Dan Morris and I were driving around Lake Tahoe one evening and he commented that he had read in the local paper that many older hotels, motels, and other buildings down by the lake, just on the California side of the state line, were being bulldozed. The article claimed that for every new room added, somewhere between two and three would be lost. Obviously, the developers were shifting up the value curve, by constructing higher-end hotels, time shares, condominiums, and so forth. This led Morris to comment: "Why shouldn't a firm remove somewhere between one and four customers for every new one added?" It was a provocative question and it led us to develop what we have since labeled the *forced churn.*

The cable and cellular phone industry track the *churn rate;* that is, lost customers are divided by new customers acquired (you can perform the calculation with both the number of customers and the revenue from the customer). As a way to upgrade your firm's customer base from "C," "D," and "F" customers, each time a new customer is obtained, you would fire somewhere between one and a half to four old customers. Of course, the exact ratio would depend on how many "C," "D," and "F" customers your firm has and what factor the partners are comfortable with. Not only would this free up capacity to serve the new customers, it would shift the firm up the value curve, allowing your "plane" to add more full-fare coach, business-class, and first-class seats.

The French have a wonderful saying that epitomizes this strategy: *Recueillez pour mieux advancer*, which translated means "Fall back, the better to advance." By implementing this strategy gradually, many firms feel more comfortable upgrading their customer base, and their sense of security is not jeopardized all at once.

THOUGHTS ON REQUESTS FOR PROPOSALS (RFPs)

RON In auction markets, economists refer to the dreaded *winner's curse,* whereby the winning bidder is often a loser. One of the ways to avoid the winner's curse is to bid more conservatively when there are more bidders. Thomas Nagle and Reed Holden explain why:

> To understand the curse, imagine first that you are one of two bidders and you win a bid with the lower price. You will probably be quite happy. Now imagine that you are one of ten bidders and you believe that your competitors are sophisticated businesspeople who know how to bid a job. Again you win. Are you still happy? What does it mean that you bid below nine other knowledgeable bidders? Perhaps it means that you were willing to take less profit on the job. On the other hand, it could also mean that you underestimated the cost to complete the work.
>
> The more bidders there are, the more likely you will lose money on every job you win, *even if on average you estimate costs correctly and both you and your competitors set bids that include a reasonable margin of profit.* The reason: The bids you win are not a random sample of the bids you make. You are much more likely to win jobs for which you have underestimated your costs and are unlikely to win those for which you have overestimated your cost.
>
> The only solution to this is, in effect, to formalize the principle of "selective participation." You do that by adding a "fudge factor" to each bid to reflect an estimate of how much you are likely to have underestimated your costs if you actually win a bid. Needless to say, adding this factor will reduce the number of bids you win, but it will ensure that you won't ultimately regret having won them (Nagle and Holden, 2002: 225).

This is where the firm's value proposition becomes a critical differentiation from its competitive bidders. By offering a service guarantee, and price guarantee (discussed in Chapter 9), and competing on Total Quality Service, your firm can maintain neutral pricing (or even a slight premium) over the competition. Be careful not to prepare RFPs for all askers, as many are used merely as a weapon against the customer's current professional in order to obtain a lower price. The better you know the customer and the more thorough you are at ascertaining both his or her needs and wants, the higher probability you have of securing your share of profitable RFP work.

Keep the winner's curse in mind as you prepare RFPs and be sure the potential customer is serious about doing business with you and is not just using your bid as a way to lower his or her existing price. Some firms have tested this commitment by charging for a proposal and then offering a full credit if the bid is accepted.

SUMMARY AND CONCLUSIONS

This chapter focused on your firm's customer capital, by looking at what customers really buy—expectations—and how important it is to exceed them. We emphasized how important it is to constantly monitor your customers' expectations, since they are dynamic, not static, and subject to ever-increasing standards from any organization that has the ability to raise them.

The value proposition discussed how your firm's price, quality, and service come together to create a unique offering for your customer and how your firm must continuously offer a superior alternative in comparison to your competition in order to create customer loyalty. We also speculated on what is beyond Total Quality Service—experiences and transformations—and how the firm of the future can take advantage of this movement.

Since the 1980s, the Total Quality Management—and reengineering—movement arose as a way for firms to increase their quality, moving toward a six-sigma, or zero defects, standard. The flaws in this strategy for a professional service firm are obvious, since to err is human; rather than focusing on zero defects, we proffered a zero defections standard, along with an effective customer complaint recovery strategy.

The most successful firms in the world today turn away more customers than they accept because they have a rigorous prequalifying process and they understand that, ultimately, bad customers drive out good customers. We suggested the metaphor of your firm's fixed capacity as a Boeing 777 jet, in conjunction with the concept of adaptive capacity, in order to segment your customer base by the value they place on your offerings. We believe the firm of the future is just as diligent in forecasting this capacity—in terms of its yield and load factors—as the airlines are today. And while supply-side strategies exist in order to accomplish this, we believe demand-side strategies are much more effective and more profitable, in terms of allocating your firm's fixed capacity.

Next we explore those demand-side procedures, embodied in the pricing strategies and tactics of the firm of the future.

9

YOU ARE WHAT YOU CHARGE

Ultimately, a business is defined by that for which it collects revenue, and it collects revenue only for that which it decides to charge.

—Joseph Pine II and James H. Gilmore
The Experience Economy:
Work Is Theatre and Every Business a Stage

Why did Xerox fail to capitalize on the innovations that its Palo Alto Research Center developed during the seventies? This included the computer technology that eventually led to the introduction of the Apple computer, which launched the personal computer revolution. But Xerox did not see the opportunity there in front of it. In *Dealers of Lightning*, Michael Hiltzik offers this hypothesis for the failure:

> In the copier business Xerox got paid by the page; each page got counted by a clicker. In the electronic office of the future, there was no clicker—there was no annuity. How would one get paid? The hegemony of the pennies-per-page business model was so absolute that it blinded Xerox to an Aladdin's cave of other possibilities (quoted in Hamel, 2000: 112).

RON A business is what it charges. Indeed, a business is defined by little else. Ultimately, it must offer a value proposition a customer is willing to pay for. Xerox's pricing paradigm prevented it from seeking new and emerging opportunities in the marketplace and the same myopia is inflicting damage on professional service firms worldwide. As the old Practice Equation dictates, professionals have been taught the value they provide is measured by the "hourly rate." Firms have taken their collective intellectual capital and commoditized into a one-dimensional billing rate. From a marketing perspective, this is a serious mistake, since price is one of the four Ps of marketing and deserves much more thought and creativity than merely rate multiplied by hours. This hourly rate mentality is another prominent example of the negative social and human capital that has developed among professionals in the past two generations.

It is the purpose of this chapter to supplant that negative human and social capital with positive pricing strategies firms of the future are using to capture the value they create. Prices comprise the language of business, indeed of society. They serve three crucial functions: First, they transmit information; second, they provide an incentive to use methods of production that are least wasteful and most valuable; and finally, they distribute income. Free market prices are essential to a well-ordered society, and should be protected as a form of free speech.

Once it becomes clear that no customer buys hours, it is self-evident that pricing by the hour is precisely the wrong measurement to establish the value provided to the customer. The firm of the future will *price on purpose,* for profitability, not market share. Pricing is an art more than a science. Of the four Ps of marketing—price, place, promotion, and product—price is the most complicated. It is the only chance a business has to *capture* the value it produces outside of itself, which is the marketing concept championed by Peter Drucker that was discussed in Chapter 3. Price does not create the value per se—although it can greatly influence the perception of it—but it does *capture* it, leaving the other three Ps to produce value for the customer.

Price also sends distinct signals into the marketplace, giving customers clues as to who you are, what you do, who you serve, and ultimately, how your firm perceives itself. Think of the message that a Mercedes versus a Chevy, or a Mont Blanc pen versus a Bic, sends into the marketplace; a large part of that message is embedded in the price. A firm's price creates an acoustic effect in the marketplace, which over the long term will speak volumes about the firm and its level of self-esteem.

For too long—approximately two generations—professionals have ignored the art of pricing, and have starved it of the intellectual creativity and resources it richly deserves. Professional service firms have even gone a step further by relegating the pricing function to an administrative or organizational task, delegating the art to a rote procedure of completing timesheets and inputting the results into time and billing programs. This is a serious mistake. Pricing is, always has been, and always will be, a *marketing* issue, ultimately determined by the customer. It is time to restore price to the exalted position it merits in the marketing strategy of your firm. The firm of the future does not have hourly rates, it has prices, set in advance of work being done. Let us first explore how we got to where we are.

A TALE OF TWO THEORIES

RON A professor visits a jewelry store to purchase a wedding ring for his fiancée. The jeweler informs him that he can have the inside of the ring engraved with the name of his fiancée for an additional $100. He said, "But that will reduce the resale value!" The jeweler was aghast. He said, "How can you say such a thing. You are a butcher!" "No," replied the professor, "I am an economist."

Oscar Wilde once wrote, "A cynic is one who knows the price of everything and the value of nothing." When it comes to hourly billing, this is prescience. Although Karl Marx's tomb inscription ("The philosophers have only interpreted the world in various ways. The point however is to change it.") appeals to young revolutionaries who set out to remake the world in their image, the real work of economists, social scientists, psychiatrists, and other students of human behavior is not to *change* the world, but to *understand* it. Until you understand why people behave as they do—and that is a Herculean task in and of itself—there is little hope in changing their behavior.

Ideas have consequences. As John Maynard Keynes wrote in the final passage of the *General Theory*:

> The ideas of economists and political philosophers, both when they are right and when they are wrong, are more powerful than is commonly understood. Indeed, the world is ruled by little else. Practical men, who believe themselves to be quite exempt from any intellectual influences, are usually the slaves of some defunct economist. Madmen in authority, who hear voices in the air, are distilling their frenzy from some academic scribbler of a few years back. . . . Soon or late, it is ideas, not vested interests, which are dangerous for good or evil (quoted in Buchholz, 1990: 219).

The idea that the amount of labor spent producing a product or service is responsible for its value has a very long history, and has confounded great economic thinkers up until the late nineteenth century. For example, the word *acre* in medieval English meant the amount of land that could be ploughed in one day. But it was Karl Marx who gave this theory prominence, which was subsequently labeled the *labor theory of value*. Here is how Marx explained his theory in *Value, Price and Profit*, first published in 1865:

> A commodity has *a value*, because it is a *crystallisation of social labour*. The *greatness* of its value, or its *relative* value, depends upon the greater or less amount of that social substance contained in it; that is to say, on the relative mass of labour necessary for its production. The *relative values of commodities* are, therefore, determined by the *respective quantities or amounts of labor, worked up, realized, fixed in them*. The *correlative* quantities of commodities which can be produced in the *same time of labor* are *equal* [emphasis as published] (Marx, 1995: 31).

This sounds quite reasonable, until you put this theory to the test of explaining how real people spend their money in the marketplace. Marx's theory cannot explain how land and natural resources have value, since there is no labor contained in them. Taken to its extreme, the labor theory of value would predict that those countries with the most labor hours—such as China or India—would have the highest standards of living. But this is demonstrably false; what we witness instead in those countries with less labor inputs and more entrepreneurship—and secure private property and other institutions conducive to economic growth—have vastly higher standards of living, including shorter hours for workers.

If Marx's theory were correct, a rock found next to a diamond in a mine would be of equal value, since each took the same amount of labor hours to locate and extract. Yet how many rocks do you see in the jewelry store at the local mall? Perhaps you will have pizza for lunch today: under Marx's theory, your tenth slice would be just as valuable as your first, since each took the same amount of labor hours to produce. One glaring flaw in Marx's theory was it did not account for the law of diminishing marginal utility, which states the value to the customer declines with additional consumption of the good in question.

Dating back before Marx, even Aristotle explained that a good could obtain a price because there was a need for it. To quote a representative from the school of Salamanca, Luis Saravia de la Calle (1544):

> Those who measure the just price by the labor, costs, and risk incurred by the person who deals in the merchandise or produces it, or by the cost of transport or the expense of traveling to and from the fair, or by what he has to pay the factors for the industry, risk and labor, are greatly in error, and still more so are those who allow a certain profit of a fifth or a tenth. For the just price arises from the abundance or scarcity of goods, merchants and money, as has been said, and not from costs, labor, and risk. If we had to consider labor and risk in order to assess the just price, no merchant would ever suffer loss (quoted in Fog, 1994: 79).

Although this is a closer description to the true source of value, it also misses the mark by stating that scarcity (or abundance) determines a just price. But scarcity does not determine value. I could autograph the book you are now holding in pink crayon, and testify to the fact it is truly one of a kind. I seriously doubt it would enhance the value of the book by even one-tenth of a cent. Just because something is scarce does not make it valuable; the item has to be desired by people as well.

Benjamin Franklin is often cited by businesspeople for his much-repeated saying, "Time is money." This little adage has certainly infected the way professionals view the value of the services they deliver; unfortunately, it is taken out of context. The sentence was written in 1748—over 100 years prior to Marx's labor theory of value—in a letter Franklin sent to a young businessperson just starting out, and who had sought Franklin's advice. Here is what Franklin wrote in its entirety on the subject of time in a letter entitled "Advice to a Young Tradesman":

> To my friend, A.B.:
>
> As you have desired it of me, I write the following hints, which have been of service to me, and may, if observed, be so to you. Remember that *time* is money. He that can earn ten shillings a day by his labor, and goes abroad, or sits idle, one half of that day, though he spends but sixpence during his diversion or idleness, ought not to reckon *that* the only expense; he has really spent, or rather thrown away, five shillings besides (quoted in Krass, 1999: 283).

Note that Franklin was not speaking of value, nor price; he was articulating the concept of *opportunity cost*. This is the idea (coined by the Austrian economist Friedrich von Wieser (1851–1926)) that every activity or product in the economy has an alternative use. It is an important economic principle, but a seller's opportunity cost has little to do with the value provided to the customer. In fact, Franklin's statement has been misinterpreted as validating the labor theory of value, yet it does no such thing.

Even Adam Smith, a seminal thinker and the founder of classical economics, was not immune from the visceral appeal of the labor theory of value. Unlike Marx, though, Smith understood the importance of profit as an inducement to entrepreneurs to take the risks necessary to bring goods and services to the market. Smith modified

Marx's theory into a *cost of production* theory, which basically said it was all of the costs of production—including Marx's dreaded profit—that determined the value of a commodity. Another seminal thinker and economist, David Ricardo, struggled with the anomalies of the labor theory of value up until the time he died, writing to a fellow economist about a month before he died, "I cannot get over the difficulty of the wine which is kept in a cellar for 3 or 4 years, or that of the oak tree, which perhaps had not 2+-[hours] expended on it in the way of labor, and yet comes to be worth £100" (quoted in Skousen, 2001: 108).

A direct derivative of the labor theory of value can be found among the thinking of cost accountants after World War I. One of the century's most influential accounting theorists was William Paton, who in a 1922 treatise described what he thought was the cost accountant's chief activity:

> The essential basis for the work of the cost accountant—without it, there could be no costing—is the postulate that the value of any commodity, service, or condition, utilized in production, *passes over into* the object or product for which the original item was expended and *attaches to* the result, giving it its value [Emphasis as published] (quoted in Johnson and Kaplan, 1991: 135–36).

But in a speech Paton gave at a conference in 1970, he repudiated this notion that costs attached to a product as it moves through the factory:

> The basic difficulty with the idea that cost dollars, as incurred, attach like barnacles to the physical flow of materials and stream of operating activity is that it is at odds with the actual process of valuation in a free competitive market. The customer does not buy a handful of classified and traced cost dollars; he buys a product, at prevailing market price. And the market price may be either above or below any calculated cost figure (Ibid: 139).

Though Karl Marx is dead, he still haunts us as the father of the billable hour, since it was his labor theory of value that was the dominant thinking until it was repudiated in the late nineteenth century. Prior to World War I, the industrial barons—such as Andrew Carnegie, Pierre du Pont, Alfred Sloan, and other engineers of the scientific management movement—were the leaders in pioneering cost accounting for their operations. The most significant contribution made to management accounting theory was the invention of the return on investment (ROI) measure. H. Thomas Johnson and Robert S. Kaplan provide the history of the ROI measure in their award-winning book *Relevance Lost*:

> The idea for the Du Pont return on investment formula originated, as far as we know, with F. Donaldson Brown, a college-trained electrical engineer and one-time electrical equipment salesman who joined the Powder Company's sales department in 1909 and became assistant treasurer of the company in 1914. None of Brown's surviving records indicates how he hit upon the idea for his return on investment formula. Interestingly, Brown had no formal training or experience in accounting.
>
> His experience in selling no doubt gave him an appreciation for the effect of turnover and distribution costs on a company's profits. Evidently, his mathematical,

engineering, and marketing skills gave Brown a unique perspective on the determinants of company performance that was not understood by most contemporary accountants. Brown's idea about financial planning and control had a profound impact on the Du Pont organization and later on General Motors. Yet his ideas did not become widely known among professional accountants until the 1950s, when a new generation of management accounting textbooks introduced them into the standard MBA curriculum (Ibid: 1991: 86–87).

The importance of the Du Pont ROI cannot be overemphasized, since it was the dominant theory taught to at least two generations of accountants and MBAs. Once the MBAs began to migrate into the professional service firms, they brought with them the idea that firms could perform cost accounting similar to the manufacturing industries. This is what led Wall Street law firms to use timesheets beginning in the 1940s. The theory was that by tracking time, the firms could perform cost accounting—not pricing—and determine if any one job, or customer, was profitable. It was the application of the ROI—a direct cousin of the labor theory of value—to professional service firms. No law or accounting firm came up with the idea of tracking time in a consistent and rigorous manner until the MBAs and other consultants brought them the idea.

The most comprehensive history of the billable hour is William G. Ross's *The Honest Hour: The Ethics of Time-Based Billing by Attorneys.* Here is how he describes the billable hour's history:

> During the 1950s and early 1960s, various studies indicated that attorney compensation was failing to keep pace with inflation and was lagging behind that of other professionals, particularly physicians. Starting as early as the 1940s, management experts concluded from various studies that lawyers who kept time records earned more than attorneys who did not. Management experts advised lawyers to raise their compensation by selecting a target annual salary and dividing that figure by the number of hours that they could bill to a client during a year and factoring in overhead costs in order to arrive at an hourly billing rate.
>
> Although many commentators have suggested that time-based billing dates from 1960s, many attorneys were actually using it during the previous decade. While even so large a firm as New York's Shearman and Sterling did not keep time records until 1945, time-keeping had become much more common by the 1950s than is now usually supposed . . .
>
> Between the 1950s and the middle 1970s, management experts extolled the benefits of timekeeping and exhorted law firms to institute time-based billings. As one commentator exclaimed in 1960, "Lawyers who *do* keep personal time records have a *net* income which is almost equal to the *gross* income of lawyers who *do not* keep time records. Need more be said!" (Ross, 1996: 16–17).

Notice how timekeeping was originally adopted for *cost accounting* purposes, and then became the method by which professionals *priced* their services. What was expected to be a way to track the inventory of professionals—time—became the inventory that was sold. It was a distortion of the intent of timesheets. Prior to pricing by the hour, both attorneys and CPAs charged fixed rates for everything they did, as Ross explains:

During the late 1930s and 1940s, more and more state and local bar associations adopted fee schedules because they provided a more objective means for attorneys to justify their fees to clients. Left to their own devices, many attorneys were uncertain about how to charge clients or were embarrassed to charge for minor work or to request a reasonable compensation for their services. Fee schedules gave lawyers the courage to charge higher fees. . . . By the 1950s, fee schedules existed in virtually every state.

Fee schedules were not obligatory, since bar associations recognized that mandatory fees might run afoul of the antitrust laws and that such fees would fail to take account of the special expertise of individual attorneys (Ibid: 14–15).

Despite the efforts of Karl Marx, Adam Smith, David Ricardo, Ben Franklin, the industrial barons, cost accountants, engineers, and MBAs, a better theory of value remained elusive until the Austrian school of economics posited the *subjective theory of value*.

A Better Theory of Value

When confronted with what appears to be an incorrect theory, the alternative is to replace it with a better theory. Many economists understood the labor theory of value was flawed, but were unable to construct a better theory to explain how people spend their money on the things they valued. It was not until three economists invented what became known as the *marginalist revolution* that the labor theory of value was replaced with a more appropriate theory. An Austrian, Carl Menger (1840–1921), a Brit, William Stanley Jevons (1835–1882), and Leon Walras (1834–1910), who was French-Swiss, were the three economists who independently developed the idea that value was determined, ultimately, by the consumer. Here is how Mark Skousen explains Menger's contribution in his book *The Making of Modern Economics: The Lives and Ideas of the Great Thinkers*:

Menger's discovery was labeled the "law of imputation." The law of imputation was a direct assault on the Ricardo-Marx labor theory of value. Menger wrote, "The determining factor in the value of a good, then, is neither the quantity of labor or other goods necessary for its production nor the quantity necessary for its reproduction, but rather the magnitude of importance of those satisfactions with respect to which we are conscious of being dependent on command of the good.

In short, Menger had reversed the direction of causation between value and cost. A consumer good is not valued because of the labor and other means of production used. Rather, the means of production are valued because of the prospective value of the consumption goods. The value of all producer and capital goods are ultimately consumer driven.

Menger wanted the German antitheoretical economists to know that the law of imputation was valid in all circumstances. "This principle of value determination is universally valid, and no exception to it can be found in human economy" (Skousen, 2001: 182).

In other words, as we've said before, value is like beauty—it is in the eye of the beholder. The subjective theory of value explains why people purchase items from eBay that have long outlived the lives of the original laborers who manufactured them. It explains the appreciation of housing, artwork, wine, entertainment, among other commodities. It prescribes that pearls are valuable not because people dive for them, but people dive for them because they are valued. It even explains the axiom from the oil business: "What you spend does not matter; what you find does." Yet, today, we find professionals are still being misguided by the labor theory of value, since they continue to teach each new generation, "You sell your time."

Cost-plus pricing became dominant because most firms implicitly understood their cost structures, and could easily calculate a fair rate of return. It is much easier to look inside of a firm and determine the cost than to look outside to the customer to determine the value. In fact, cost-plus pricing provides a nice, neat, objective formula on which to base these calculations. However, given the realities of the subjective theory of value, they have little to do with the value provided to the customer.

Cost-Plus Pricing: Epitaph

In their outstanding book, *The Strategy and Tactics of Pricing: A Guide to Profitable Decision Making*, Thomas T. Nagle and Reed K. Holden offer the following indictment of cost-plus pricing:

> The problem with cost-plus pricing is fundamental: In most industries it is impossible to determine a product's unit cost before determining its price. Why? Because unit costs change with volume. This cost change occurs because a significant portion of costs are "fixed" and must somehow be "allocated" to determine the full unit cost. Unfortunately, since these allocations depend on volume, which changes with changes in price, unit cost is a moving target (Nagle and Holden, 2002: 2).
>
> The only way to ensure profitable pricing is to let anticipated pricing determine the costs incurred rather than the other way around. Value-based pricing must begin *before* investments are made (Ibid: 3).
>
> The job of financial management is not to insist that prices recover costs. It is to insist that costs are incurred only to make products that can be priced profitably given their value to customers. . . . From Marriott to Boeing, from medical technology to automobiles, profit-leading companies now think about what market segment they want a new product to serve, determine the benefits those potential customers seek, and establish a price those customers can be convinced to pay. The companies challenge their engineers to develop products and services that can be produced at a cost low enough to make serving that market segment profitable (Ibid: 4).

If one were to lay the two theories of value—labor and subjective—side-by-side, it would look like this:

Cost-Plus Pricing—Labor Theory of Value

Product » Cost » Price » Value » Customers

Value Pricing—Subjective Theory of Value

Customers » Value » Price » Cost » Product (adapted from Ibid: 4)

Notice how value pricing turns the order of cost-plus pricing inside out, by starting with the ultimate arbiter of value—the customer. This is precisely why William

Paton repudiated his "cost-attach" idea from traditional cost accounting. Goods and services do not magically become more valuable as they move through the factory and have costs allocated to them by cost accountants. The costs do not determine the price, let alone the value. It is precisely the opposite—as Carl Menger pointed out—that is, the price determines the costs that can be profitably invested in to make a product desirable for the customer, at a profit for the seller.

When General Motors introduced the Corvette, it projected how many units it would sell and the priced was based upon the Du Pont ROI formula, whereby GM marked up each car with a desired profit. The Corvette did well, and no doubt cost-plus pricing can result in a profit for sellers, assuming they make a product desired by the customer. However, cost-plus pricing is not a *profit-optimizing* pricing strategy, and herein is its fundamental problem. When Lee Iacocca developed the Ford Mustang, he reversed the order of the usual car-making pricing up to that point. Rather than giving his engineers carte blanche to develop a sports car and then marking up the resulting costs—as GM did—he solicited the opinions of potential customers as to what features they would want in a sports car and what price they thought they would be willing to pay. He then went to his engineers and asked if they could manufacture a sports car with the desired features and sell it at this price and still turn a profit for Ford. The engineers developed the Ford Mustang (based on the platform of the existing Falcon), and it was launched in April 1964 at a price of $2,368. In its first two years, net profits were $1.1 billion, in 1964 dollars, far in excess of what GM had made on the Corvette. From an engineering perspective, the car was mediocre; from a marketing and profitability perspective, it was one of the most successful cars in automotive history. This led Iacocca to quip, "So many people have claimed to be the father of the Mustang that I wouldn't want to be seen in public with the mother."

This method of pricing—known as *price-led costing* as opposed to *cost-led pricing*—was successfully adopted by the Japanese in the automotive and electronics industry, and is one of the reasons they have been so successful in those markets. There is a long history of companies that became obsessively focused on cost, at the expense of providing a product or service of value to the customer. The fact of the matter is, you can make a pizza so cheap no one is willing to eat it. The obsession with cost-cutting can be counterproductive to fulfilling the real mission of any business: to create wealth for the customer. An obsession with cost accounting and cost cutting causes the business to be inward-looking, rather than outward-focused, and as a result all costs are viewed as democratic, and are subject to across-the-board cuts, without taking into account those costs that are essential for creating a superior value proposition versus those costs that add no value to the customer.

This is not to imply that a firm's internal costs are unimportant, or irrelevant, to the pricing decision, for they certainly are not. It is the order of those costs that are important and that need to be reiterated: The profit-optimizing firm will only invest in those costs that can be recouped through the value delivered to the customer, not the other way around. In other words, the firm of the future explicitly understands that its price determines its costs, and the firm does not let its costs dictate its price. There is another underlying truth in this statement: A firm's costs are estimated *before* it sets any price, not after, as is traditional with hourly billing. This puts the onus on the firm to quote prices to its customers *before* it expends any resources, similar to how every other business must operate.

Deleterious Effects of Cost-Plus Pricing

The manifestation of the labor theory of value—and its cousin, the Du Pont ROI formula—in the professional service firm is the computation of the hourly rate. Sometimes a rule of thumb is used to compute the hourly rate, such as three to five times the professional's salary, which is just another way of adding a desired ROI onto the firm's cost structure. But since a firm contains more costs than merely salaries and wages, the true formula for computing the hourly rate looks like this:

$$\text{Hourly Rate} = \frac{\text{Overhead} + \text{Desired Net Income}}{\text{Expected Billable Hours}}$$

Four pernicious effects result from this cost-plus formula. First, one way to increase the firm's revenue is to increase the overhead. Of course, this is one reason that cost-plus pricing has become extinct in government contracts, the contracting industry, and most other businesses: it misaligns the interests of the buyer and seller. Raising overhead with no concomitant increase in value to the customer is a recipe for disaster.

Second, no customer believes it is his or her job to provide the professional with a decent standard of living. Customers do not lay awake at night wondering if their attorney is making enough money. That is not their job. On the contrary, it is the professional's job to provide a service that is so good customers willingly pay a profit in recognition of what was done for them.

Third, the formula is a self-imposed ceiling on the professional's income, not to mention profit. And since most professional firms have realization rates somewhere between 60 and 95 percent, they are obviously not even obtaining the standard hourly rate. Even Thomas Jefferson, admitted to the Virginia bar in 1767, and an extraordinary attorney—and thinker—by any account was not immune from this self-imposed limitation. He often charged at £500 per year, but usually collected far less, with his best year being 1770, when he realized £213 (Kimball, 1995: 75).

Finally, the formula does not take into account the intellectual capital of the firm; worse, it commoditizes the firm's IC into one homogenous hourly rate. It simply represents the firm as a bundle of overhead costs and desired profit wishes of the partners, without looking to the value that is created for the customers.

In short, the customer does not care about any one of the numbers in the formula, yet consider how much time professional service firms waste justifying to the customer the result of the formula—that is, the hourly rate. The formula is totally inward-looking, whereas all of marketing should be outward-looking, to the customer, and price is an integral component of marketing.

One of the fiercest defenses of this formula is that it essential for proper cost accounting, to enable the firm to measure how much profit is being made on each job or each customer. But the formula is *not* cost accounting, it is *profit forecasting*, and professionals—CPAs especially—should know better. Cost accounting does not allocate a profit. The formula is nothing but a *wish list*, and may or may not have any relationship to the value created outside of the firm's walls. The business graveyards are full of firms that had overhead and profit desires, but are long gone because they did not produce wealth for their customers. If you want true cost accounting, you must remove the Desired Net Income factor from the formula, and calculate a *true cost* per hour.

The formula has provided professionals with a false sense of security and objectivity with respect to their pricing policies. The labor theory of value can be measured and quantified, hence it feels quite comfortable to justify your pricing on that basis. In contrast, the Austrian's subjective theory of value cannot be precisely quantified: there are no easy formulas, no magical incantations that will help you achieve the right price, for the right customer, at the right time. It requires the firm to get into the hearts and minds of its customers, to look for the real value drivers in the buying decision, and to comprehend and communicate the value they are creating. It is not easy, and this is why all businesses, always and everywhere, struggle with price. Again, it is an art, not a science; but we can deepen our understanding of it by studying the success of other entities that have strategically used the four Ps of marketing in order to *price on purpose*.

Lessons in the Subjective Theory of Value

If the labor and subjective theories of value confounded brilliant minds such as Adam Smith, David Ricardo, and others, imagine how difficult it would be for businesspeople to comprehend, who do not spend a fraction of the time formulating these types of theories, and have to deal with the day-to-day difficulty of pricing in the real world. The subjective theory of value was a revolution in the economics profession, and it is, as Thomas Sowell put it, "a sobering reminder of how long it can take for even highly intelligent people to get rid of a misconception whose fallacy then seems obvious in retrospect" (Sowell, 2000: 338). But the history of business is the history of epiphanies, and sometimes the fog lifts and the right path becomes clear. This certainly happened with respect to pricing for Ben Cohen and Jerry Greenfield, founders of Ben & Jerry's ice cream. In an essay written in 1997 (before they sold the business on August 3, 2000, to Unilever, the British-Dutch food company), titled "Bagels, Ice Cream, or . . . Pizza?" they explain what they term was their "famous pricing epiphany":

> We were working our hearts out for the first two or three years, and every year we just barely broke even. The first year we were thrilled to break even. We'd made our overhead; we could see the light at the end of the tunnel.
>
> Then the next year came and we'd just broken even again, even though our sales had grown by $50,000. This went on for three years. Each year we would break even and say we needed only to do a little more business to make a profit. Then the next year we'd do a lot more business and still only break even. One day we were talking to Ben's dad, who was an accountant. He said, "Since you're gonna make such a high-quality product instead of pumping it full of air, why don't you raise your prices?"
>
> At the time we were charging fifty-two cents a cone. Coming out of the sixties, our reason for going into business was that ours was going to be "ice cream for the people."

It was going to be great quality products for everybody—not some elitist treat. We aren't just *selling* to people. We *are* the people! Ice cream for the people!

Ben said, "But, Dad, the reason we're not making money is because we're not doing the job right. We're overscooping. We're wasting ice cream. Our labor costs are too high—we're not doing a good job of scheduling our employees. We're not running our business efficiently. Why should the customer have to pay for our mistakes? That's why everything costs twice as much as it should."

And Mr. Cohen said, "You guys have to understand—that's human. That's as good as people do. You can't price for doing everything exactly right. Raise your prices."

Eventually, we said, either we're going to raise our prices or we're going to go out of business. And then where will the people's ice cream be? They'll have to get their ice cream from somebody else. So we raised the prices. And we stayed in business (quoted in Krass, 1999: 462–63).

Excellent advice from an accountant! Physician, heal thyself, as they say. Nevertheless, let us not confuse cause and effect. You will not be profitable simply because you raise your prices. You can raise your prices only if you offer a value proposition worth more to the customers than the cash they are parting with, which Ben & Jerry's ice cream obviously did (the profit margins on gourmet ice cream would make the so-called robber barons blush). Ben's father also made a brilliant point by stating you can't price for 100 percent efficiency. This, again, makes Peter Drucker's point that a business exists, first and foremost, to create wealth for its customers, not to operate efficiently. Many an efficient business has gone bankrupt because it did not create wealth for its customers. (We explore the fundamental difference between efficiency and effectiveness in the firm of the future in Chapter 10.)

Another lesson in the subjective theory of value was learned by Akio Morita, founder of Sony (named from the Latin word *sonus*, meaning "sound," and combined with the English word *sonny*, for "sonny boy"). In this essay written in 1974, "Moving Up in Marketing by Getting Down to Basics," he relates this lesson to the tape recorder that Sony had brought to millions of people around the world:

One weekend I took a stroll in my neighborhood and stopped in front of an antique shop. I am not interested in antiques, but I gazed at the various articles displayed in the show window. Out of curiosity I walked into the shop where a customer was asking the salesman various questions. And then the customer paid an amazingly high price for an antique that would not have attracted me in the least, and he walked out happily with it. I thought that our tape recorder was much more valuable, but he had gladly paid an even higher price for an antique.

I was surprised and intrigued by this behavior [so were the eighteenth-century economists]. It taught me a basic principle of sales. This principle is that no sale can be achieved unless the buyer appreciates the value of the merchandise. I would not have paid such a price to buy the antique piece, because I am not interested in such things. But the other person, who understood the value of antiques, was willing to pay the price.

The tape recorder was a tremendous technical achievement in the eyes of those of us who had struggled to create it. For us it had a very high value, and we thought that the price we had put on it was even less than its true value. But the general public looked on it only as an interesting toy. This meant that unless the customer understood that the tape recorder was a valuable device with a wide variety of uses, he would not pay the price. The principle was this simple, but we realized that we were ignorant of even this basic principle. We therefore embarked on the task of teaching people how useful the tape recorder was in practical life.

This experience taught us a basic lesson in the marketing of our product, which has guided our policy ever since. A company such as ours, which is constantly developing new products, must always have the capability of educating prospective customers. Otherwise new markets for new products will never be created. . . . We realize that marketing means increasing the number of persons who can communicate to customers the usefulness and value of our new products in the same way as we would ourselves (Ibid: 316–19).

Professionals Subject to the Laws of Economics

It is only within the past three decades that professionals have learned they are subject to the same economic laws of the marketplace as every other businessperson. It is interesting to note that the noun "professional" does not even appear in American dictionaries prior to 1861. In 1925, the first public opinion survey of vocational status revealed that doctors had passed lawyers and ministers, though not professors, in public esteem. To be a professional meant to *profess* something, from the word "professor"; and as more occupations sought the designation "professional," they tried to elevate their status above the *crass commercialization* of the market. This attitude is expressed in a 1933 State Supreme Court of Washington decision, which upheld an exemption of "professions" from an excise tax upon "business activities" on the grounds that:

A profession is not a money-getting business. It has no element of commercialism in it. True, the professional man seeks to live by what he earns, but his main purpose and desire is to be of service to those who seek his aid and to the community of which he is a necessary part (quoted in Kimball, 1995: 315–16).

Today, this thinking is truly obsolete. And it is more than a matter of semantics, since all businesses serve their communities. An airline, hotel, grocery store, or rental car agency each provides a needed, useful, and valuable service as any professional service. Businesses are based on *serving* the needs of others. Yet it took professionals decades to overcome the idea they were somehow better than the local merchant down the street. Former Chief Justice Warren Burger was an outspoken critic of lawyers advertising, claiming many of the ads would make a used-car salesman blush. Nonetheless, the 1976 U.S. Supreme Court ruled in *Bates v. State Bar of Arizona*, that it was an unconstitutional violation of the First Amendment for states to prohibit lawyers from advertising their services. If you were to read the advertisement that was the subject of this lawsuit, it is tame by today's standards. Prior to this decision the AICPA Code of Professional Conduct for CPAs explicitly prohibited advertising:

Solicitation to obtain clients is prohibited under the Rules of Conduct because it tends to lessen the professional independence towards clients, which is essential to the best interests of the public. . . . Advertising, which is a form of solicitation is prohibited. . . . Promotional practices such as solicitation and advertising, tend to indicate a dominant interest in profit.

It would come as a shock to most CPAs to learn they are not interested in profits. After the landmark *Bates* decision, the AICPA modified this rule:

A member shall not seek to obtain clients by advertising or other forms of solicitation that is false, misleading, or deceptive.

Then, in 1994, the U.S. Supreme Court ruled in *Ibanez v. Florida Department of Business and Professional Regulation* that the accounting profession could list dual credentials on letterhead in all jurisdictions. Most economists who have studied the effects of advertising on professional service firms have found no harmful effects, and in fact have learned most customers appreciate the advertising as a form of information. It is also interesting to note that where there is more advertising, prices are lower, which may explain the reluctance of professionals to begin advertising in the first place. As George Bernard Shaw said, "All professions are conspiracies against the laity."

Today, it seems a quaint notion to claim professionals should not market their services, especially with the influx of marketing professionals in many firms. The Management of Accounting Practice (MAP) movement began in Missouri over 30 years ago. I have had the good fortune to speak with Charlie Larson, one of the founders of the MAP movement, and he told me at the first MAP conference (which was prior to the *Bates* decision) there were audible gasps from the audience when marketing issues were mentioned. Since then, an annual MAP survey has been conducted that asks accounting firms the top issues they face; here, from *The CPA Letter/Small Firms*, published by the AICPA (January 2002, pg. C2) are the top five issues from 1999 through 2001:

1999 Top Five MAP Issues

1. Finding, hiring and retaining quality staff.
2. Marketing/practice growth.
3. Keeping up with technology.
4. Delivering high-quality service.
5. Succession planning/future owners and partner retirement.

2000 Top Five MAP Issues

1. Finding, hiring and retaining quality staff.
2. Keeping up with technology.
3. Fee pressures/pricing of service.
4. Succession planning/identifying and developing future owners/funding partner retirement.
5. Marketing/practice growth.

2001 Top Five MAP Issues

1. Finding, hiring and retaining quality staff.

2. Marketing/practice growth.

3. Succession planning.

4. Fee pressures/prices of services.

5. Succession planning/future owners and partner retirement.

Other issues that came out of the MAP survey (which is also broken down by firm size), not mentioned in the preceding are:

- Coping with seasonality/workload compression.
- Balancing personal/professional life balance.
- Determining and meeting client needs.
- Capitalizing on consulting opportunities.
- Balancing needs of the firm with staff needs.
- Attracting students to the profession
- Billing and collection.

Most of these are marketing issues, which illustrates professional service firms are subject to the same laws as every other business. The clarion call has been heard, and firms are beginning to pay more attention to the four Ps of marketing: *product*, *promotion*, *place*, and *price*.

The Four Ps of Marketing

In their course, "Pricing: Strategy and Tactics," at the University of Chicago Graduate School of Business, Thomas Nagle and Reed Holden teach the four Ps of marketing using the farming analogy. This is a powerful analogy because it treats the four Ps as an interdependent system whose components have to work together to achieve the maximum result. Take product—for professional firms, this is the technical aspect of what is done for the customer, be it tax returns, audits, lawsuits, wills, bankruptcy, estate work, consulting, and so forth. As share of wallet is beginning to replace market share, and as the professions are maturing, new services take on added importance to achieve growth. Product also encompasses the service, experience, and transformational aspects of what the customer receives as well. In the farming analogy, product is the seed, crop, and planting process.

Promotion has also become much more important in the professions, especially in the aftermath of the *Bates* decision. Prior to that decision, most firms spent virtually nothing on advertising, marketing, and promotion. Today, it is common for professional firms to spend between 2 to 8 percent of gross revenue on those items, and even to have in-house marketing departments—usually non-CPAs or nonlawyers—who assist in selling the firm's services. This was relatively rare even 20 years ago, and arose in response to the maturing market for professional services. Promotion has become much more sophisticated within the professions, especially with the emergence of firms owned by American Express and H&R Block as preeminent marketing organizations. In the farming system, promotion is the equivalent of fertilizing the soil and watering the crop.

Place is not just in which zip code your office is located, but rather which type of customer the firm is targeting, that is, your market niche. The professions started to specialize in the 1940s, with medical doctors leading the way, followed by attorneys in the 1950s; finally, CPAs began the movement in the 1980s. No firm can be everything to everyone, and specialization has become more important in order to segment various customers for the purpose of custom-tailoring a value proposition to suit their needs. Place in the farm analogy is the land where you plant and grow your crop.

Last, by no means least, is price, perhaps the most complex of the four Ps. Because value is subjective—and determined by the customer—pricing services is an art, never a science. In professional service firms for the past two generations, price has been relegated to an administrative or organizational issue—a rote task to be delegated to the time and billing program—rather than to the exalted position it deserves in the marketing mix. In the farming analogy, price is the harvest, when you reap what you sow. It is the only chance you have to capture the value from what you create. The other three Ps will generate internal costs—albeit they also create actual and perceived value—but only price will grasp the value you create. Other industries—from the airlines, hotels, rental car companies, and retail stores to manufacturing and sports teams—have invested enormous resources and intellectual capital in developing revenue management models and dynamic pricing simulations. For instance, a new automated pricing system at National Car Rental Systems Inc. in Bloomington, Minnesota, can make up to 40,000 price changes *per day*, and is credited with adding $56 million in profitability the first year it was put into service.

United Airlines, which made over 10 million price changes in 1999 alone, installed a new $20 million inventory management system called Orion. It is credited with adding $100 million per year in profits according to United's management. This form of pricing has come under severe criticism as of late, the charge being it does nothing to build customer loyalty, is capricious, and is difficult for team members to explain to outraged customers who are offered various prices, even within the same day, or hour. Frederick Reichheld, who has done seminal work in the field of customer loyalty economics, explains in his book, *Loyalty Rules! How Today's Leaders Build Lasting Relationships,* why he believes this form of pricing does not build loyalty:

> This price gaming does little to build customer trust or improve convenience. One of the few airlines that has avoided this approach is Southwest, which concluded that the yield management systems are unfair, complicated, and expensive to administer. So Southwest has one price for advance purchase and one fare for unrestricted purchase. Customers know that they are getting a fair deal. The accountants at the competition probably believe that Southwest is leaving a lot of money on the table with this unsophisticated pricing strategy that emphasizes fairness and simplicity over extracting maximum value from every customer, but they cannot deny that Southwest is the only consistently profitable major airline (Reichheld, 2001: 144).

I have tremendous admiration for Mr. Reichheld, but on this issue I respectfully disagree. Southwest was one of the pioneers of the peak, off-peak pricing structure. Furthermore, the airline does indeed engage in yield management and price discrimination. Researching a flight from Oakland, California, to Burbank, California, for one month away, I found six different airfares on Southwest's Web site, ranging from $29 to $95 one-way, all with various rules and restrictions. If I were booking the same trip for tomorrow, it would be priced at $95 one way. That is quite a range of prices, even though the overall fare is relatively low, and hardly the two fares Reichheld mentions. The airline industry is a marginal business, and Southwest knows that only several passengers per flight make up its profits. Why shouldn't it engage in yield management? Those different tickets are not the same value proposition to every passenger. If you did not have the luxury of being able to plan your trip one month in advance, you would be delighted that Southwest has reserved capacity to accommodate you at the last minute. That is not the same ticket as someone who booked a seat on the same flight over one month ago.

Reichheld is confusing simplicity for sameness, yet no two airline seats are the same; it all depends on when you purchase your ticket, whether you include a Saturday layover, what you are doing at your destination (business or leisure), and other rules that are in place in order to estimate the value each passenger puts on the flight. Holding up Southwest's pricing strategy as a model to emulate because it is simple is a non sequitur. Try flying Southwest overseas, or even across the United States, which is an arduous task—unless you don't mind stopping multiple times. Southwest has many lessons to teach, such as how to offer excellent service and how to manage customer expectations, but its pricing strategies are not that much different from other airlines, and confirm the value of yield management in driving profitability.

Consider the yield management pricing systems and the customer loyalty programs instituted by the airlines, and you soon realize these tools are sophisticated uses of the four Ps of marketing. Marketing is *communication* (or, perhaps better still, *conversation*) with your customers and potential customers. It is the process of matching the resources of your firm with aspirations of its customers, and pricing on purpose—and for profitability—are critical strategies to signal your firm's value proposition to the marketplace. It is one way to differentiate your firm from the competition, and eschew falling into the *commodity trap*. Far too many professional firms have repeated the conventional wisdom that they are nothing but commodities. But as we shall see, this is more conventional than actual wisdom.

ARE PROFESSIONALS COMMODITIES?

RON During the days of Prohibition 25 of Chicago's top bootleggers were rounded up in a surprise raid. During their arraignment, the judge asked the usual questions, including the occupation of each suspect. The first 24 all claimed to be engaged in the same professional activity, as an accountant. "And who are you?" the judge asked the last prisoner. "Your honor, I'm a bootlegger," he said. Surprised, the judge laughed and asked, "How's business?" "It would be a lot better," he answered, "if there were not so many accountants around."

G.K. Chesterton once wrote, "Competition is a furious plagiarism." Yet the fact of the matter is, there is *no such thing as a commodity*. Anything can be differentiated, which is precisely the marketer's job. Believing your firm—and the services it offers—is a commodity is a self-fulfilling prophecy. If *you* think you are a commodity, so will your customers. How could they believe otherwise? Yet how can the personal relationship between a professional and customer be nothing but a commodity. Consider this story from *The Tom Peters Seminar: Crazy Times Call for Crazy Organizations*:

> Transformation. Breaking the mold. Anything—*anything*—can be made special. Author Harvey Mackay tells about a cab ride from Manhattan out to La Guardia Airport: "First, this driver gave me a paper that said, 'Hi, my name is Walter. I'm your driver. I'm going to get you there safely, on time, in a courteous fashion.' A mission statement from a cab driver! Then he holds up a *New York Times* and a *USA Today* and asks would I like them? So I took them. We haven't even moved yet. He then offers a nice little fruit basket with snack foods. Next he asks, 'Would you prefer hard rock or classical music?' He has four channels. [This cab driver makes an above-average amount per year in tips]. (Peters, 1994: 235–36).

If a taxi cab driver can establish a rapport with a complete stranger in a 15-minute ride to the airport, what is possible with a professional relationship over the course of a lifetime? Note how the cab driver differentiated himself with low-cost items (newspaper, candy, and so on). It is not the cost that counts, but the value *perceived* by the customer; and in this instance, the little touches make all the difference. If a taxi cab driver can be this imaginative and creative, what is the professional's excuse? Peter's expounded on this theme in his later book *The Circle of Innovation: You Can't Shrink Your Way to Greatness*:

> But my sympathy and empathy run (*totally*) out when it comes to . . . professional services . . . of any sort. Oy vey! I've had Big Six accountants tell me that the audit is "becoming commoditized." I've had engineering-services professionals tell me that their business is being determined "entirely by price." I've had trainers lament that "leadership training" is now a commodity.
>
> And . . . it makes me sick. Look . . . *The delivery of a professional service is absolutely, positively nothing more than the delivery of you and/or me!* Is the person you see when you look in the mirror at 6:00 A.M. a "commodity"? No! It's Tom Peters. It's Mary Jones. It's Jeff Smith. It's Jane Doe. It is a person. Singular. With character. Unique skills. The delivery of professional services is the delivery of . . . Jane Doe, Tom Peters, and so on.
>
> If professional services become "commoditized," it means that you and I have become commoditized. I say again: The delivery of a professional service is the delivery of who you are, who I am. P-E-R-I-O-D. (Peters, 1998: 324).

The potential for competitive differentiation is limited only by your imagination. Many lawyers and CPAs lament that since their professions are mature, commoditization is inevitable, despite all the empirical evidence surrounding them that this is simply not so. Consider the candle-making industry, which has literally been in decline for the past 300 years. Yet Blyth Industries custom-tailors its candles for the specific location, companion, and occasion, growing from $3 million in sales in 1982 to nearly $500 million in 1996, with a market capitalization of $1.2 *billion* dollars in 1997. Candles!

Even the declining lettuce business has been differentiated by prewashing it, cutting it up and packaging it—along with some salad dressing on the side—to save the customer time. As a result, from the late 1980s to 1999, a $1.4-billion industry was created. Great Northern Wholeaves Lettuce, for one, has come up with the innovation of offering *ripped* (not cut) lettuce, giving restaurants a way to handle waste and save time. Wholeaves Lettuce commands a premium price. Lettuce!

Would you ever pay more for a share of stock—whose price is publicly listed and traded on the New York Stock Exchange—to one broker over another? After all, how can a share of stock be differentiated? It may be one of the few examples of a pure commodity. To answer that, visit www.oneshare.com, where you can purchase only *one* share of stock at a time, valued primarily as gifts for babies and teenagers. Included in the 10 best-selling shares, which you can have framed for an additional price, are Disney, Apple Computer, Coca-Cola, Harley-Davidson, Microsoft, Wal-Mart, World Wrestling Federation (WWF), Krispy Kreme Doughnuts, among others. You pay the market price for the stock (minimum $15), a $39 OneFee, and a frame ranging from $34 to $74 depending on your choice. A share of stock!

Procter & Gamble launched www.reflect.com where women can customize their own health and beauty products. In turn, P&G charges salonlike premium prices.

How fast is Starbucks growing? "I don't know for sure," quipped one comedian, "but I do know they just opened one in my living room." Opened in Seattle, Washington, in 1971, Starbucks—named after the coffee-loving first mate in Herman Melville's novel *Moby Dick*—has grown to over $1.7 billion a year in revenue. Howard Schultz, the founder, earned a business degree in 1975 and worked for Xerox until he joined Starbucks in 1982 as an employee. In 1987, he bought the Starbucks chain for $3.8 million and took it public in 1992. Here is how he explains the phenomenon that is now Starbucks:

> We never set out to build a brand. Our goal was to build a great company, one that stood for something, one that valued the authenticity of its product and the passion of its people. In the early days, we were so busy selling coffee, one cup at a time, opening stores, and educating people about dark-roasted coffee that we never thought much about "brand strategy."
>
> We built the Starbucks brand first with our people, not with consumers—the opposite approach from that of the crackers-and-cereal companies. Because we believed the best way to meet and exceed the expectations of customers was to hire and train great people, we invested in employees who were zealous about good coffee.
>
> If you look for wisdom on brand marketing, most of what you'll find is based on the Procter & Gamble model. That is, you go after mass markets with mass distribution and mass advertising, and then focus on grabbing market share from your competitors. That's the basic way of life for mature products in established markets.

At Starbucks, we have a different approach. We're creating something new. We're expanding and defining the market. We didn't set out to steal customers away from Folgers or Maxwell House or Hills Brothers. We didn't go for the widest possible distribution. We set out, rather, to educate our customers about the romance of coffee drinking. We wanted to introduce them to fine coffees the way wine stewards bring forward fine wines. Just as they might discuss the characteristics of a wine grown in a specific region or district of France, we want our baristas to be able to intelligently explain the flavors of Kenya and Costa Rica and Sulawesi.

Today, there's a lot of marketing rhetoric about adding value to products. At Starbucks, the value was there from the beginning, in the coffee itself. When your average sale is only $3.50, you have to make sure customers come back. And ours do—on average eighteen times a month (quoted in Krass, 1999: 301–4).

The success of Starbucks has been so meteoric, *Harvard Business Review* has labeled it the "Starbucks Effect":

Ten years ago, only 3 percent of all coffee sold in the United States was priced at a premium—at least 25 percent higher than value brands. Today, 40 percent of coffee is sold at premium prices. We've found plenty of evidence of the Starbucks Effect. When individual companies increase the perceived "premiumness" of a product through innovations in the product itself or the way it's delivered, the entire category can reap higher prices and profits (quoted in Vishwanath and Harding, 2000: 17).

If coffee beans and water can be differentiated—not to mention command a premium price—what is the excuse of professionals? Basic economics teaches it is very difficult to sell something that someone else is giving away for free. Yet notice bottled water. Water covers three-fourths of the Earth's surface. Could there be a larger commodity than water? You would not think so until you read these facts from www.bottledwaterweb.com, an industry portal:

Water, Water Everywhere
Walk down a grocery aisle in any town in the U.S., Canada, Europe, or Asia and there is a virtual tidal wave of bottled water brands. This $35 billion worldwide industry continues to grow as water quality concerns and fitness and health awareness increases. Bottled water sales in the U.S. rose 9.3 percent in 2000 to $5.7 billion, according to Beverage Marketing Corporation, a New York-based research and consulting firm.

PET [polyethylene terephthalate, the popular high-quality plastic bottle usually produced in smaller sizes—2 liters and under)] bottled water sales in 2000 reached about 1.7 billion gallons, and the segment is expected to grow at a compound annual rate of about 15 percent over the next five years, according to Beverage Marketing. In 2000, fruit beverage volume grew 1.4 percent, beer 0.8 percent, carbonated soft drinks 0.5 percent, and bottled water 9.9 percent.

Perhaps this is why Evian is Naïve spelled backwards. In any event, there is absolutely *no* excuse for professionals to think of themselves as commodities. As the research on why professionals lose customers (from Chapter 8) revealed, price did not make the list. Any firm can compete on price; it is truly a fool's game. In contrast, competing based on Total Quality Service, positive customer experiences, and transformations requires more thought, creativity, and investment. Creating a competitive advantage is never free. If you do not have the talent internally to develop a sophisticated marketing strategy, we recommend you go buy it. Either internally or externally, working with the four Ps of marketing is the only way to ensure your firm will not be caught in the self-fulfilling commodity-thinking trap.

Unless your firm decides to compete based on price—as had H&R Block, Jacoby and Meyers, Wal-Mart, and Southwest Airlines—you cannot create a loyal customer based solely on being the low-cost provider. If customers are attracted by your low price, they will easily leave for another firm that offers an even lower one. Cutting your price to attract a customer encourages customers to constantly ask for future price concessions—thereby subsidizing your worst customers at the expense of your best ones. In any case, the notion that customers get excited over a low price is not grounded in reality, as Roy H. Williams humorously points out:

> "I was charged a fair price" is not the statement of an excited customer, yet many business owners mistakenly believe they need only convince the public that they will be treated "fairly" to win their business. Phrases like "Honest Value for Your Dollar" and "Fair and Honest Prices" tempt me to say (with no small amount of sarcasm), "Yippee Skippy, call the press."
>
> If the most your customer can say when he walks out your door is, "I was treated fairly," your business is pitifully stale and you have virtually nothing to advertise. Why? Because the expectation of "fair treatment" is such a basic assumption in business dealings that most people take it for granted. What we really hope to find is the "delight factor" (Williams, 1998: 88).

As all of these examples illustrate, the firm's marketing function is to differentiate itself from the competition and develop a value proposition customers are willing to pay a premium price to receive. If your firm finds itself continually competing on price, it is taking the easy way out—since price is always the easiest way to make marginal sales gains. It is also the apparent factor on which to place blame for a firm's lack of awesome service and competitive differentiation. Constant write downs, write-offs, and price discounts signal you are targeting the wrong customer segments, not developing a viable value proposition that separates you from the competition, not getting your share of negotiation success, or offering too much service in your basic package. Do not let your firm acquire a core competency in cutting prices. In addition to the four Ps of marketing, the five Cs of value are essential to implement in order to capture the full value of your services.

The Five Cs of Value

The main function of your firm's marketing strategy is not simply to acquire revenue at any price, but to gain your share of highly profitable work. It is not enough to price based upon a customer's willingness and ability to pay, you must increase that will-

ingness by constantly communicating the value of your offerings. Thomas Nagle and
Reed Holden have developed the five Cs of value:

- *Comprehend* what drives sustainable value for customers.
- *Create* value for customers.
- *Communicate* the value that you create.
- *Convince* customers that they must pay for value received.
- *Capture* value with appropriate price metrics and fences (Nagle and Holden,
  2002: 164).

Every job for every customer has value drivers, and the firm's job is to understand
what those are. Why does the customer want you to provide the service? What is
the motivation for hiring you? Most professionals do not pay enough attention to the
actual motivations of the customer, thinking they already know why they are being
engaged to perform a service. Yet there are almost always motivations other than simply, "I have to get my tax return in by the due date," or "My banker is demanding a
financial statement review." It is not enough to focus on the technical product, you
must probe deeper to discover the customer's true expectations and desires.

Creating value for the customer is not merely providing high-quality technical
work, but also includes the level of service the customer experiences. It could also
include the transformation through which you are guiding the customer, from where
he or she is to where he or she wants to be. Bundling your services into a *fixed-price
agreement, offering a 100 percent money-back guarantee, providing payment terms,*
and *utilizing change orders* are all methods used to enhance the value of your offering. Since value is always subjective—and, ultimately, solely determined by the customer, not the amount of labor hours you put into the job, or your overhead, or your
profit desires—you have to get close to the customer to understand exactly what he
or she values.

Even if the firm does a stellar job in creating value for customers, there no doubt
will be instances where the customer does not understand the value. This places the
onus on the firm to communicate to the customer the full value of what it is delivering. Understand that most customers do not have an incentive to collect data on the
value you are providing, since they purchase infrequently. Your firm, on the other
hand, sells frequently; therefore, you should make communicating your unique value
a core competency among your professionals. Certainly the marketing function is the
main way to communicate to your chosen customer segments. After-Actions Reviews
and postmortem pricing analyses are also critical to perform if you are to formulate
more effective methods for communicating value. If the firm does not understand the
value of what it is providing, how will the customer?

Convincing customers to pay for the value is an integral part of any professional's
responsibilities. Of course, this job is much easier with the right customers, which is
why prequalification is so critical. It also requires negotiation skills, which most professionals are loath to even consider, equating it with car salesmen or being beneath
the status of a professional. But the fact of the matter is, you are going to have a price

negotiation at some point with your customer, either at the beginning of the engagement or at the end. It simply cannot be avoided, since price is a major factor in any customer's decision whether or not to purchase. You need to face this issue squarely, and be confident as to the value you are providing. Most of a firm's customers are adept negotiators, since this is precisely how they built their businesses.

Entrepreneurs negotiate everything, and many businesspeople actually enjoy the process. This is why it is not adequate to set your prices solely based upon the customer's willingness to pay. That turns the negotiation into a poker game. The willingness to pay should not be viewed as an upward constraint on your pricing, rather as a variable that needs to be managed. This is why many professionals open discussions with potential new customers by saying something like this: "We are not the cheapest CPA firm in town; and I just wanted to let you know up front we do not negotiate on price, only value."

The final duty is to capture the value you provide by utilizing the appropriate pricing strategy. This is where the billable hour method fails miserably, since it treats all jobs and all customers equally. There is no effective mechanism that allows prices to rise commensurate with value of the service, only with the labor time involved in production. Utilizing fixed-price agreements, change orders, and the Retrospective Price Clause (also known as the TIP clause, to be defined later) offer a much wider range of strategic pricing options the firm can implement to capture value.

FIXED-PRICE AGREEMENTS AND CHANGE ORDERS

PAUL I've said passionately in many other places that Ron's book *Professional's Guide to Value Pricing* is the best book ever written for the accounting profession. It still is making, each and every day, an enormous contribution. Ron placed the term *fixed-price agreement* (FPA) in the lexicon of the accounting profession. Thousands of firms have adopted FPAs as a core pricing strategy, and the results have been impressive. In this section we focus specifically on how to implement the FPA and change order process and look at adopting other useful pricing strategies.

Fixed-Price Agreements

Let us begin by reviewing a sample FPA for a CPA firm.

Sample Fixed-Price Agreement

November 19, 2003

Dear Customer:

In order to document the understanding between us as to the scope of the work that ABC CPAs will perform, we are entering into this Fixed-Price Agreement with XYZ, Inc. To avoid any misunderstandings, this Agreement defines the services we will perform for you as well as your responsibilities under this Agreement.

2004 PROFESSIONAL SERVICES

- ABC will perform the following services for XYZ during 2004:
- 2003 W-2s/1099s and 4th Quarter Payroll Tax Reports and Workers Comp Report
- 1st, 2nd, and 3rd Quarter Payroll 2004 Reports, Workers Comp Reports, and Fiscal Year Sales Tax Return
- 2003 Year-end Accounting Adjustments and Closing of 2003 books
- 2003 XYZ S Corporation Tax Returns
- 2004 Tax Planning
- 2003 Financial Statement Review (with PBC Schedules to be completed by XYZ by February 15, 2004)
- Unlimited Access 2004

Total 2004 Professional Services $X,XXX

- Unlimited meetings, to discuss operations of XYZ, business matters, tax matters, and any other topic at the discretion of XYZ or its employees and/or agents.*
- Unlimited phone support for XYZ personnel and/or independent contractors and agents regarding accounting assistance, transaction analysis, and the like.*

Because our Fixed-Price Agreement provides ongoing access to the accounting, tax, and business advice you need on a fixed-price basis, you are not inhibited from seeking timely advice by the fear of a meter running endlessly. Our program is built around one-price pricing, as opposed to hourly rates, and offers you access to the accumulated wisdom of the firm through CPAs with substantial experience, who can help enhance your company's future and achieve its business goals.

While the fixed price entitles your company to unlimited consultation with us, if your question or issue requires additional research and analysis beyond the consultation, that work will be subject to an additional price negotiation before the service is to be performed, utilizing a Change Order.

Unanticipated Services

Furthermore, the parties agree that if an unanticipated need arises (such as, but not limited to, an audit by a taxing agency, a financial statement review or compilation required as part of a lender financing agreement, or any other exogenous service not anticipated in this Agreement by the parties) that ABC hereby agrees to perform this additional work at a mutually agreed-upon price. This service will be priced separately to XYZ utilizing a Change Order.

Service and Price Guarantee

Our work is guaranteed to the complete delight of the customer. If you are not completely satisfied [or delighted] with the services performed by ABC, we will, at the option of XYZ, either refund the price or accept a portion of said price that reflects XYZ's level of satisfaction. Upon final payment of the terms in this Fixed-Price Agreement, we will assume you have been satisfied. Furthermore, if you

---

*Included in Unlimited Phone Calls and Meetings are the following services, to be provided by ABC to XYZ:

ever receive an invoice without first authorizing the service and/or the price, you are not obligated to pay for that service.

Payment Terms

XYZ and ABC hereby agree to the following payment plan:

January 31, 2004	$	XX
February 28, 2004		XX
March 31, 2004		XX
April 30, 2004		XX
May 31, 2004		XX
June 30, 2004		XX
July 31, 2004		XX
August 31, 2004		XX
September 30, 2004		XX
October 31, 2004		XX
November 30, 2004		XX
December 31, 2004		XX
TOTAL 2004 PAYMENTS		**$X,XXX**

Revisions

To assure that our arrangement remains responsive to your needs, as well as fair to both parties, we will meet throughout [weekly, monthly, quarterly, etc.] 2004 and, if necessary, revise or adjust the scope of the services to be provided and the prices to be charged in light of mutual experience. [Note: This is an optional clause, effective for new customers or veteran customers you are transitioning to an FPA].

Termination

Furthermore, it is understood that either party may terminate this Agreement at any time, for any reason, within 10 days written notice to the other party. It is understood that any unpaid services that are outstanding at the date of termination are to be paid in full within 10 days from the date of termination.

If you agree that the above adequately sets forth XYZ's understanding of our mutual responsibilities, please authorize this Agreement and return it to our office. A copy is provided for your records.

We would like to take this opportunity to express our appreciation for the opportunity to serve you.

Very Truly Yours,

By: _____

Allan Somnolent, Partner, ABC, CPAs

Agreed to and accepted:

By: _____ Date: _____

Customer, President, XYZ, Inc.

(Adapted from Baker, 2001: 186–89).

Explaining the FPA

RON Let us scrutinize each section of the FPA and explain why it is designed the way it is.

Professional Services. The FPA is designed in order to take advantage of the economics of bundling. It will easily accommodate the *needs* of the customer—tax compliance, financial statements, and so forth. Also, you want to get at least one *want*—such as a consulting service or an estate plan—in the bundle as well. This is especially important for veteran customers you are transitioning from hourly billing to value pricing, in order to move your offering up the value curve in the perception of the customer. It also makes comparisons with prior year's prices more difficult, since you have totally repackaged the price and terms of your services.

Be sure to explain all responsibilities of each party; for example, as the requirement in the Financial Statement Review that the customer is responsible for preparing the schedules by a certain date. The general rule is, the less sophisticated the customer, the more specific and detailed the mutual responsibilities should be outlined.

The "Unlimited Access 2004" service is designed to break down the "Berlin Wall" between most firms and their customers. How many times have you looked at a customer and said something to the effect, "Why didn't you call me before you did this? If we would have structured it this way or that way, we could have saved [or prevented] $XXX." This is all too common, and when we have asked customers of professional service firms in customer advisory boards why they did not contact their professional before undertaking some significant transaction, they usually responded with some variant of, "Tick, tock: I knew I'd be on the clock and don't like getting charged $100 for a phone call." Now that might not be the most rational response—the $100 probably would have been one of the best investments they could have made—but you cannot always rely on the customer to be intellectually rational. Emotions rule, and very few people like to be charged for phone calls.

When customers do not call, it is a lose-lose situation all around because the point at which the firm can add the most value to a transaction is *before* it takes place, not after. If the customer does not contact you until after, you can only mitigate any damages. This is not the highest point on the value curve. The Unlimited Access service is designed to provide an incentive for the customer to contact you *before* doing anything, precisely the time you can add the most value.

We are always asked whether customers will abuse this clause, and the answer is a resounding no. Remember, the FPA is designed for your best customers, those in the top 20 percent usually, and they are not likely to abuse your time. However, if a customer were to place excessive demands with phone calls and meetings, then you have a basis for increasing your firm's price in the FPA. After all, if they are calling on you that often, you must be adding more value than originally anticipated.

But the reality is that most phone calls or meetings initiated by the customer will result in your firm getting more work. And this is where the change order comes into use. How do you draw the line of demarcation between what is included in the

Unlimited Access service and a change order? The general rule is if you hang up the phone or walk out of a meeting and do not have to do any further work—no research, no further analysis, and so on—that is included in the Unlimited Access service. If you have to do something further as a result of the phone call or meeting, then you have a change order, and that has to be discussed *before* you do the work, as well as be signed and authorized by the customer.

Notice that the Unlimited Access service is not free; it is bundled in with the other services. Because the customer is paying for it, he or she is more likely to use it, which will translate to a higher wallet share since the firm will cross-sell more services. Furthermore, there is only one price for the entire bundle of services, rather than line-item pricing that makes it easier for the customer to shop each service. This changes the focus from negotiating each service to negotiating the value of the total offering. By focusing the customer on the *totality* of your service offering, you can command higher prices than individual item pricing.

Determining a price up front is essential if you want to capture the full value of your services. Frankly, this is how every other business prices, and since professionals are subject to the same laws of economics and price psychology as every other business, they, too, must quote a price before the work is begun. How many items do you, as a consumer, purchase without knowing the price up front? Not many. How else can the customer make the value-versus-price comparison without knowing the price? This issue is not about trust, it is about strategically pricing your services commensurate with the value you provide. There also exist psychological reasons for pricing up front.

The most significant is *pricing leverage*. Pricing leverage is defined as the party—the buyer or seller—who is more or less price-sensitive at some point in the transaction. The professional possesses the maximum leverage *before* the service is rendered because that is when the customer needs you the most. A service needed is always more valuable than a service delivered. This is the point at which you will command the highest price for your services. It is an interesting question why professionals suffer from write-downs and write-offs more than write-ups. One of the reasons is because they price their services *after* they are completed, when the customer possesses the leverage. When do you want to discover that you and the customer have vastly different assessments of the value of your work, before or after the engagement? If you learn this before, at least you have the opportunity to modify the bundle of services, change the payment terms, or withdraw from the engagement. Finding out afterward is a prescription for write-downs, write-offs and perpetual accounts receivable headaches.

There are only two reasons customers do not pay an invoice: either they are *unable*, or they are *unwilling*. If they are unable—perhaps due to an economic downturn, bankruptcy, or simply do not have the means—chances are the firm did not prequalify the customer rigorously enough. After all, who better than professionals to determine, whether a potential customer has the ability to pay for your services? If a customer is unwilling to pay your invoice, this is an issue of not meeting his or her expectations, and it is incumbent on the firm to learn what went wrong. You will discover these types of problems quicker when you engage in up-front pricing and set payment terms, as well as provide a 100 percent money-back guarantee, since that provides the customer an incentive to complain.

Many professionals object they cannot quote a price up front because they do not know how long a specific project will take. But this is Marx's labor theory of value, which is completely irrelevant. The fact of the matter is, your customers do not care how long it takes you to complete a project. They only ask about hours because professionals quote hourly rates, and what they are trying to compute is the total price. If you quote prices—and do not mention hours—the customer can focus on the value proposition, rather than an inflated hourly rate they cannot relate to.

Let me be blunt: If you cannot quote a price up front to the customer *before* the work begins, you have no business doing that work. I stand by this statement, even though many professionals I've confronted with it recoil. In the real world, prices are quoted up front, before any purchase decision is made. Would you fly on an airline that tried to charge you $4 per minute? Think of actuaries who have to set prices on earthquake, hurricane, fire, and other types of insurance in a world of uncertainty and risk. They do not have the luxury of tallying up their internal costs afterward, marking those up with a reasonable profit and sending out a bill. Why professionals do not believe they are subject to these same economic laws has always baffled me; but it does explain why they suffer more write-downs and write-offs than other businesses. No one can convince me that operating a professional service firm is more complicated than pricing disaster insurance or running an airline.

This is such an important point, I want to emphasize by sharing a dialogue I had with David Cottle—a well known consultant to CPAs—in a workshop I hosted for Accountingweb.com:

> **DC:** How about the research project for a long-term client who trusts you? You don't have a clue what you will find or how long it will take, but the client is willing to pay your hourly rate for as long as you feel is appropriate. What's wrong with hourly billing in that case?
>
> **RB:** David, hourly billing is never appropriate, and the relationship between time and price is simply not there. To believe it is to fall prey to Karl Marx's labor theory of value.
>
> **DC:** In the case I proposed, it seems fair to both parties.
>
> **RB:** No, what is fair to both parties is an agreed-upon price up front.
>
> **RB:** No client wants to be billed by the hour; they hate it.
>
> **DC:** But I have no clue as to how much research I will do.

This confusion between trust and pricing comes up all the time as a primary objection to pricing up front. Just because the customer trusts you does not negate the necessity of pricing up front. As I've analogized before, I trust United Airlines with my *life*, yet they provide me a price up front, *before* I fly. Pricing and trust are not necessarily related; in fact, I would argue you generate a higher level of trust by pricing up front because it avoids surprising customers with an invoice they are not prepared for. If you insist on pricing by the hour, after the work is completed, you will never command a value price for your services. This is the precise link that needs to be broken. Remember, your price determines your cost, not the other way around. You need to set the price and determine whether the necessary costs to complete it will generate a profit suitable to the firm.

Of course there will be projects where the scope is not well defined, but that does not obviate the need to quote a price up front. It does, however, require the scope be carefully crafted (perhaps you can break down the project into various phases) and landmarks be set to determine when one phase ends and another begins. This approach is useful, for example, in complex estate planning, where the firm will charge a minimum price to perform a needs and assessment diagnosis; and once the needs and wants of the customer are determined, phase two of the project can be scoped out and priced accordingly. Litigation can be handled in the same manner for attorneys, by offering a price for various phases—such as discovery, depositions, and so on.

Unanticipated Services. This is the change order clause, which is a way of communicating to your customers that yours is a firm that utilizes change orders for additional services that arise during the course of the year, or for scope changes on services already included in the FPA. This clause is essential for managing your customer's expectations and making your pricing policies transparent. The axiom to live by in a value pricing culture is "no surprises." The customers should never be shocked by an invoice or a price, because they have authorized it up front, *before* the work began.

The change order is also advantageous because most of them will deal with customer *wants*, not just *needs*. The majority of customer needs will be dealt with in the FPA, hence when additional services are needed, they will more likely deal with wants—such as a merger or acquisition, consulting service, estate planning, and so forth. An example change order is shown later in the chapter.

Service and Price Guarantee. The advantages of the service guarantee were outlined in Chapter 8; but to review briefly, a service guarantee will enable your firm to command premium prices—similar to FedEx and Nordstrom. To put a finishing point on it, upon final payment of the FPA, it is assumed the customer is satisfied. Normally, if any customer is not satisfied, you will discover this far ahead of the final payment due date.

The last sentence of the clause is the price guarantee, which forces the firm to price everything up front when it possesses the leverage. This is essential to creating a no-surprises culture in your firm. Literally no work is performed until authorized by a customer, period, no exceptions. Otherwise, you are risking firm resources on customers who may be unable—or more likely—unwilling to pay your price. This clause also sends the message to team members and customers alike that your firm is one that takes its pricing policies seriously, and prices on purpose.

Professionals are uncomfortable confronting the pricing issue up front with customers, but customers feel better knowing the price in advance—even if its just for the first phase of a project. Make no mistake about it, you will have a price discussion with your customer; the question is when will it take place, before or after the service is performed. Having it before assures that you maintain the leverage, which is essential in commanding premium prices.

Payment Terms.   Terms are price, and they should be negotiated before any work is performed, just as much as the overall price of the FPA (or change order) is. The sample FPA shows monthly payments, but payments could be on any basis—biweekly, quarterly, semiannually, and so on. In fact, get the customer involved in the timing of the terms, so as to coincide the terms with the cyclical cash flow of his or her business, as long as the FPA is cleared to zero by the end of its term (usually one year, but it can be longer). You should also require a retainer for all new customers in order to gain their ego investment to the relationship. If the customer is not willing to pay a portion of your price up front, why should you believe he or she will pay you in full when you are done? A retainer solidifies the relationship and demonstrates the customer is serious about doing business with you.

Specifying payment terms also has another positive aspect: they become part of your pricing negotiation. Organizations such as General Motors Acceptance Corporation and GE Credit make more money *financing* what they manufacture than they do *selling* it. Perhaps this historical digression will illustrate the importance of payment terms, especially to the customer. Despite the view that consumer credit is a recent phenomenon, it has actually been around for the past 200 years. As pointed out by Lendol Calder in *Financing the American Dream: A Cultural History of Consumer Credit*, in the United States, Cowperthwaite and Sons was reputedly the first furniture retailer in New York that sold furniture on installment terms in 1812; in the 1850s, buying "on time" (as it was known then), was introduced by sewing machine salesmen. Because of their success, other big-ticket items, such as pianos, organs, and the *Encyclopaedia Britannica*, began to be sold on credit.

It was the automobile, however, that truly expanded installment credit. By 1924, almost three out of four new automobiles were bought "on time," generating approximately $670 million of installment paper. The conventional wisdom is that the mass market for cars started when Henry Ford brought out the first Model T. In fact, it was when dealers began offering installment options to customers that allowed them to buy cars they couldn't afford to pay cash for. In reality, Henry Ford didn't lose out to General Motors simply because he offered only the Model T in black. Henry Ford had a puritanical streak and disapproved of installment buying (he also thought the country would not be able to function without Prohibition). Because he insisted on selling his cars in the 1920s for cash, he lost market share to General Motors, which established the General Motors Acceptance Corporation (GMAC) in March 1919. Most installments required one-third down, and the balance to be paid in 6 to 12 months. The short term was due to the large repair bills that would normally occur after the first year of owning a car. By 1926, almost $4 billion was loaned out by 1,600 to 1,700 financing companies for the purchase of automobiles. Ford finally capitulated and established the Universal Credit Corporation in 1928, shortly after introducing his Model A. Unfortunately, it was a strategy done too late, as General Motors had by then captured a dominant share of the industry that Ford was never able to retrieve.

Do not repeat Ford's mistake. Make payment terms part of your up-front negotiation with your customers, and get their commitment to abide by them. This will prevent your firm from acting as an interest-free financing institution for its customers.

Revisions to the FPA.   This is an effective clause both for veteran customers you are putting onto an FPA for the first time and for new customers with whom you may not have a complete understanding as to the nature and scope of their work. Agreeing to meet weekly, monthly, or on some other periodic basis ensures that you will have an understanding of your customer's expectations and that problems that arise will be dealt with expediently. This clause not only lowers the customer's risk, it lowers the firm's as well, since you will always have an opportunity to modify the price, terms, or scope of the FPA. Lowering the customer's risk is an essential element in overcoming the three pricing "emotions" we will explore shortly.

Termination Clause.   The FPA is an at-will agreement, meaning either party can terminate it at any time, for any reason (subject to professional responsibilities and state laws, of course). This is another way to lower the customer's—and the firm's—risk of doing business with you.

Because you are offering a packaged price, if either party terminates before the completion date of the FPA, one party will owe the other a sum of money, and you will have to work that out with the customer. That said, do not let the tail wag the dog; do not line-item-price your services out of fear of termination. The FPA is designed for your first-class and business-class customers—those who are in the top twentieth percentile—and these are precisely the customers who are *least* likely to defect.

Other Issues Regarding the FPA.   Note how the FPA is a rather simple document, yet it contains some relatively radical ideas (though, as mentioned earlier, "radical" is Latin for *getting back to the root*). You are offering a fixed price for a *bundle* of services, not line-item-pricing each service. Bundling is an excellent way to get clients not only to focus on the totality of your service offering, but to force them to acknowledge the value of your services. Witness the American Express Green, Gold, Platinum (and now) Black credit cards. If you are presently a Gold card member but desire some of the benefits of the Platinum card, you have to step up and pay the full price—American Express will not *unbundle* only those services you want from the Platinum level.

By establishing a minimum price in your firm for a core bundle of services—such as tax preparation, planning and Unlimited Access—you are communicating the value of your services in terms of the totality of your offering, a very effective way to lower price resistance. Many firms have used the Green, Gold, Platinum, Black strategy—calling it by various different names, of course—as a way to migrate the customer up the value curve. This is the same strategy as a small, medium or large drink; or the old Sears catalogue categories of good, better, best. If the pricing spread between A and B is greater than the difference between B and C, you have a greater probability of upgrading the customer. By establishing a minimum price for the bare essentials, you will also be able to capture a higher price from the services at the lower end of the value curve.

For instance, one CPA firm I consult with has a minimum price of $1,000 for personal tax return work. For this price, customers receive their tax return preparation and Unlimited Access. For perhaps $1,500, the customer would receive tax planning, and for $1,800, the firm provides audit representation in the event of an Internal Revenue Service audit. It is not necessary—nor is it desirable—to set standard prices for the levels beyond the minimum, since that would depend on the individual circumstances of each customer. The point, rather, is to offer customers a range of services and let them select the investment they are most comfortable with. As most marketers have learned, the majority of customers select from options B and C, since very few customers consider it desirable to buy the cheapest offering.

Incidentally, notice how American Express offers four levels of credit cards. It learned there was a segment of customers beyond the Platinum level who were willing (and obviously able) to pay for a higher level of service. The Black card was designed for those customers who wanted a 24/7/365 concierge-type service. This level is by invitation only, and all who are invited—as of this writing—have paid the $2,000 annual membership (it started out at $1,000). This is a credit card, and how many solicitations do you receive in the mail in an average week for a free credit card? American Express once again has taught us that even a credit card can be differentiated from the competition, if the value proposition appeals to the customer. People are not *price*-conscious, they are *value*-conscious.

Most FPAs—at least in accounting firms—are for one year, usually negotiated at the end of the calendar (or fiscal) year for the following year's services. You must meet and design the FPA with the customer; do not do them in a vacuum or treat them like a request for proposal. You want to obtain the customer's ego investment and commitment to the relationship and to the design, scope, and price of your services. Do not feel as if you have to accomplish this in one meeting; it may take two or three, which is fine since there is no better reason to meet with a customer than to discuss the value you are adding to his or her life.

The FPA is not for all of your customers, but only for those who demand more from you than just basic services. You may only ever have between 20 and 40 percent of your customers on an FPA, though those will comprise the majority of your revenue. For those customers not on an FPA, you still need to quote fixed prices, up front, and offer a service and price guarantee, but you can include those in your firm's standard engagement letter.

The FPA is *not* designed to replace your firm's standard engagement letter. You still need this letter as required by your insurance carrier or professional ethics. However, where the engagement letter discusses price, simply refer to the FPA, dated such and such; or in the case of a non-FPA customer, insert the price (and terms).

As stated earlier, most FPAs are for a one-year term, though we have seen multiple-year FPAs utilized in some accounting firms. This is an effective method of increasing the customers' switching costs, thereby increasing their loyalty. However, a one-year term is most typical. Also, we have begun to see what are being called *perpetual FPAs*, whereby the CPA firm covers the basic compliance and other needs of the customer on a fixed-price basis, which runs in perpetuity. This is an effective way to handle most of the customer's needs; then in the FPA meeting, you focus on the customer's *wants*, which are usually less price-sensitive. It also has the added advantage of removing the core services from the annual pricing negotiation so the customer only has to focus on the incremental value you are offering.

Finally, the FPA is designed to overcome the three pricing emotions every customer will experience at some point in the relationship:

- Price resistance
- Price anxiety
- Payment resistance

Price resistance is also known as *sticker shock*. This occurs, for instance, when you walk into an automobile dealership and notice the retail price is higher than you paid last time you purchased a car. It is usually an emotional response, since if you were to calculate the *real* (adjusted-for-inflation) price of the automobile, it might be approximately the same price you paid before, or even lower if you were to take into account the quality and features of the new model. In any event, sticker shock is more emotional than rational, and if you want to command prices commensurate with value, you have to learn to overcome it. Usually it can be overcome by explaining—or reiterating—the value to be realized by the customer. Perhaps you did not do an adequate job of explaining the value, and the customer is not challenging your price so much as doubting your value.

Do not let sticker shock stop you from quoting a price you believe is based on value. If you never experience any sticker shock, chances are your prices are too low. In fact, we prefer you to *induce* sticker shock, as it enables you to determine the customer's pricing points—and real value drives—much sooner. If a customer cannot get over sticker shock, this is an excellent indication he or she is not the right customer for your firm. The FPA will diminish price resistance somewhat—by bundling your services, offering the service and price guarantees, payment terms, and revision and termination clauses—but the task is primarily the professional's to overcome by utilizing his or her negotiation skills.

Price anxiety is also known as *buyer's remorse*. Anytime customers make a relatively large purchase, they will go through a phase of doubting their decision. This is normal, and you should expect the customer to sometimes question an FPA at some later point after its authorization. The FPA is designed to mitigate buyer's remorse by including the service guarantee and the revision/termination clauses. Staying in constant communication with your FPA customers and exceeding their expectations are other methods to reassure them they made the proper decision in engaging your firm.

Payment resistance is simply the customer's *unwillingness to cut the check*. By making payment terms an explicit part of the FPA negotiation, you will remove this pricing emotion. Since FPA customers are generally first class and business class—and have characters you trust—most will act in accordance with the agreements they sign. Many firms have established electronic fund transfers (EFTs) or automatic credit card authorizations to secure the payments in accordance with the FPA terms. Some firms have reported they receive full payment from some FPA customers who are earning frequent-flyer miles (a great way to leverage off the airlines structural capital).

In fact, most firms utilizing FPAs do not even send invoices to these customers. What would be the point? They know, and you know, exactly what is to be done, what the payment terms are, and what the price is, so why send a periodic invoice? Think of all the time you would save by not preparing and reviewing invoices, time you could spend strengthening your customer relationships and increasing your share of their wallet.

We also know firms that have *negative work* in process; in other words, they have received full payment in advance of performing any work. This is particularly the case in tax practices. I always point out in my seminars that United Airlines currently holds several thousand dollars of my money for future flights. There is really only two ways your firm will ever get paid before it does any work: It has to set the price up front, and it has to ask for the payment. Many firms do this when they send out the annual tax organizer, engagement letter, and a cover letter stating the price (as previously discussed), and a credit card authorization. When the organizers are mailed back, they contain the payment, in full. Think of the invoicing, collection, interest on financing accounts receivable, write-down and write-off costs you will avoid by employing this method. It is another salutary effect of up-front pricing.

Finally, the words you use when utilizing FPAs and change orders are very important. Words convey images, and you want to avoid words that conjure up negative associations in the minds of customers. That is why we do not use the word "billing." Who likes to pay bills? The word "fee" is associated with a government tax, escrow, or other type of surcharge, a very negative connotation. "Price," on the contrary, is an innocuous word, and one all consumers are comfortable with; it generates no negative associations.

When you are ready for the customer to sign the FPA, say, "Authorize the agreement," rather than "Sign the contract," since contracts conjure up images of courts, attorneys, disputes, and so on. We also prefer the word "customer" to "client" because the welfare state refers to "having clients," which does not describe the relationship professionals want to cultivate with the people they are privileged to serve.

Change Orders

Imagine you hire a contractor to build a game room in your home. After he walks around the house taking measurements and drafting preliminary plans for the job, chances are at some point you are going to ask what every customer wants to know: "How much?" If the contractor could not quote you a price up front, but said instead, "Well, I'm not sure, but I will keep fastidious track of the time and the cost of materials, and will bill you when I'm done." My conjecture is you would find another contractor. More likely he would quote you a fixed price for the job and you would enter into a contract.

Assume then, that on the first day his crew begins the job, while tearing out one of your walls, they discover dry rot and termites. They immediately stop work, inform you of the problem, tell you what the price will be to fix it, and let you decide how you want to handle the issue. This is what separates a contractor (or auto mechanic) from a professional. In contrast, professionals would simply plow ahead and fix the problem, with no input or authorization from you, track the time spent, and simply send the invoice when the work was complete. At that point, you would lose the pricing leverage and would be at risk for a write-down or, sometimes, a write-off. This is not an effective way to cross-sell your firm's services.

Notice you expect the contractor to quote you a price *before* he begins work, even while knowing that myriad problems could arise that would cause the job to go beyond the original estimate—what we term *scope creep*. Simply because you do not know everything that might arise on a particular customer engagement does not mean you are released from the obligation to set a price for the parameters you are aware of. It simply means you must define the scope of the job and be diligent about issuing change orders when scope creep occurs.

Change orders originated in the contracting industry, and are simply one of the most sophisticated pricing strategies ever devised (this should dispel, once and for all, the notion that professionals have a monopoly on knowledge and cannot learn from other industries). When the contractor makes you aware of the dry rot and termites, he is putting you in charge of making the decision on how to handle the problem. Drafting a change order produces the best of both worlds, from a seller's perspective. It keeps the customer in charge of the buying process (which is always imperative since no one likes to be *sold*, but they do decide to *buy*), while the contractor *retains* the pricing leverage.

Change orders should be used anytime scope creep appears in a project included in the FPA, which is why it is essential that the team members know exactly what the responsibilities of each party are and the scope of the project. It is team members on the front lines who are usually the first to spot scope creep, and once they do, they need to inform the manager or partner on the engagement of the problem, the remedy, and the resources required to solve the problem. This way, the manager or partner can contact the customer to determine how he or she wants to move forward. Do not allow team members to commit firm resources by providing work the customer has not yet authorized. A sure prescription for write-downs and ill will among customers, and for not maximizing your profit potential, is to perform work they have not agreed to.

Also, utilize change orders for projects that arise that are not included in the FPA, such as an audit, consulting service, and so on. The advantage of combining FPAs with a change order strategy is that, as noted previously, because the FPA deals with most of the customer's needs, change orders will mostly be used for wants, which are less price-sensitive to the customer. This allows you to utilize some innovative pricing strategies, such as the TIP clause, discussed later in this chapter.

We are always asked if customers get upset by the firm triggering too many change orders. The answer is no. The customers appreciate the communication and being given the authority of determining how to handle the issue. This is not to say you can get lazy regarding determining the scope of projects because you know you can rely on change orders. You still have to do proper planning and learn as much as you can about the customer's situation. By managing the customers' expectations from the beginning, and informing them that your firm utilizes change orders to implement the no-surprises policy, you will not experience resistance from them when you utilize this procedure. The following is a sample change order for a service that has not been included in the FPA.

Sample Change Order

Customer:

Date:

Project Description [and estimated completion date, if appropriate]:

_____

_____

Price: $_____

We believe it is our responsibility to exceed your expectations. This Change Order is being prepared because the above project was not anticipated in our original Fixed-Price Agreement, dated xx/xx/xx. The price for the above project has been mutually agreed upon by Customer XYZ, and ABC, CPAs. It is our goal to ensure that XYZ is never surprised by the price for any ABC service, therefore we have adopted the Change Order Policy. The price above is due and payable upon completion of the project described [or, payable up front, if agreed upon, or in installments—whatever you and the customer agree to].

If you agree with the above project description, price, and payment terms, please authorize and date the Change Order below. A copy is enclosed for your records.

Thank you for letting us serve you.

Sincerely,

Allan Somnolent, Partner, ABC, CPAs

Agreed to and accepted:

By: _____

Customer, President, XYZ

Date: _____

(Adapted from Baker, 2001: 204–5).

NEGOTIATING SKILLS

RON When you come to the point at which you have to set a price with a customer, there are no supply and demand curves tattooed on their forehead. You either get the price you quote or you don't. In a perfect world—for sellers anyway—each customer would pay their reservation price, that is, the maximum amount they are willing (and able) to pay for the product or service. Most customers are not willing to share this price with you (although Paul will tell you of an instance where he did precisely that). Economists call this situation *asymmetrical information,* that is, information concerning a transaction that is unequally shared between the two parties.

I recall wandering through a used bookstore in San Diego and coming across Stanley Marcus's book *Quest for the Best.* This book is out of print, and I had been searching for it for quite sometime (this was long before amazon.com and the Internet). I eagerly grabbed the book off the shelf, opened it and saw it had been autographed by Stanley Marcus himself, and was a first edition copy in very good shape. At that moment, I determined my reservation price to be $100; that is, I was willing to pay up to that amount for the book. When I noticed the price of $10, I was elated— and as an economist would tell you, I was also $90 wealthier, as I had been able to retain the consumer surplus from the transaction. I did not ask the owner of the bookstore if he wanted to split the difference between his stated price of $10 and my willingness to pay $100. If it is unethical for businesspeople to seek high prices, is it unethical for customers to buy at low prices?

Here is the lesson from this story: Had the bookstore owner known anything about me as an individual, could he have priced the book higher? Of course he could have. And would I have been any less delighted as a customer? Of course not. But he is constrained by the fact that he cannot develop a relationship with every customer that wanders into his store, since it would be cost-prohibitive even with today's sophisticated customer relationship management software. Professionals do not suffer from this limitation. You *do* know each of your customers, most likely fairly well, or at least better than the bookstore owner knows his or her customers. You should be able to lower the level of asymmetrical information that exists between them and you and determine the value drivers of each one. Setting a price is not simply a matter of negotiation, for once you base it on that you are providing your customers with an incentive to beat you up on price. And if you cut your price as a result, you are actually rewarding their behavior, and they will seek additional price reductions, as they will continue to drive down your price in future negotiations. Let us be frank: It is the customer's job to push your prices down; it is the seller's job to push back. The key is to negotiate not price, but value.

That is why designing the FPA with the customer's involvement and bundling your services is so important, because you are focusing on the customer's needs, desires, and wishes—which you both are attempting to *maximize*—not the price of each service, which of course the customer wants to minimize. The more you know about your customers, their specific situation, and the value drivers that are motivating them to engage your firm, the better able you will be to set a price commensurate with the value you are providing. This is a two-stage process: First, there are certain questions you should ask the customer; second, there are certain questions you need to consider from an internal perspective. Here are some questions you (or the team members who serve the customer) should ask the customer during an FPA meeting (or change order negotiation) in order to assess their needs, wants, and value drivers.

Questions to ask the customer:
- What do you expect from us?
- What is your current pain?
- What keeps you awake at night? What are your major challenges?
- How do you see us helping you address these challenges and opportunities?
- What growth plans (long- and short-term) do you have?

- Who are your major competitors? How are you different from them?
- Do you anticipate capital needs? New financing?
- Do you anticipate any mergers, purchases, divestitures, recapitalizations, or reorganizations in the near future?
- We know you are investing in Total Quality Service, as are we. What are the service standards you would like for us to provide you?
- How important is our satisfaction guarantee to you?
- How important is rapid response on accounting and tax questions? What do you consider rapid response?
- Why are you changing professionals? What did you not like about your former firm that you do not want us to repeat?
- How did you enjoy working with your former firm?
- Do you envision any other changes in your needs?
- Are you concerned about any of your asset, liability, or income statement accounts where we should pay particularly close attention?
- In what ways do you suggest we best learn about your business so we can relate your operations to the financial information and so we can be more proactive in helping you maximize your business success?
- If we were to attend certain of your internal management meetings as observers, would you be comfortable with that?
- May our associates tour your facilities?
- Which trade journals do you read? Which seminars and trade shows do you regularly attend? Would it be possible for us to attend these with you?
- If we could wave a magic wand over your business, what would you want to happen?

  What is the most important aspect of dealing with a CPA [or lawyer] for you?

- If price weren't an issue, what role would you want us to play in your business? (Adapted from Baker, 2001: 176–77)

My colleague Dan Morris has all prospective customers complete the questionnaire shown in Exhibit 9.1, usually via the firm's Web site. This is very effective for prequalifying customers, for gauging their seriousness about dealing with you, and for determining their needs, wants, desires, and value drivers. The introductory letter is an excellent way to communicate your firm's culture, value proposition, and policy on value pricing. Notice how the minimum price is stated, and is required to be paid up front: This is an excellent screening device to weed out those customers who are not serious about doing business with you, and who may be just looking for free advice or a quote to use against their current service provider [they use the term *service agreement* in lieu of FPA].

(Text continues on page 200)

EXHIBIT 9.1   Questionnaire

MORRIS + D'ANGELO
NOT JUST ANOTHER CPA FIRM

Service Contract Overview and
Prospective Customer Questionnaire

On behalf of the partners and employees of Morris + D'Angelo, we thank you for your consideration of engaging our services. We have learned through past experience that this interview process needs to work in both directions. In order to evaluate the level and types of services you require, we have designed the following simple questionnaire to aid our analysis and determination as to your needs, wants, and our mutual compatibility.

There are no correct or "right" answers to these questions. The straightforward fact is that due to the unique makeup of our firm and the goals we set to accomplish for our customers, not all prospects fit the profile that enable a win-win scenario. This questionnaire and your subsequent initial interview are two of our tools to better determine each prospect's qualifications to become customers of our firm.

Inasmuch as we are interviewing you as to your qualifications, we highly recommend that you interview us. Over the years, we have come to accept that although our firm's approach to our services is unique, we are not the best solution for all prospects. Long-term value is only maximized when the customers' wants, needs, personality, and financial condition synergistically connects with ours.

We do not price our services by the hour. We believe that each party determines true value. No two relationships are equivalent, and accordingly no two engagements will have the same price and terms. Accordingly, comparison between your needs and wants with those of your acquaintances generally does not produce valid information. And, in as much as your relationship is confidential between you and our firm, we cannot discuss the terms and conditions of your friends and acquaintances that may happen to have relationships with our firm.

Although no two engagements are the same, we do have an established policy relative to new relationships. We require a minimum of $2,000 as an up-front retainer to be applied to the financial agreement between our firm and our customers. In as much as we provide a complete service satisfaction guarantee, we will gladly refund your prepayment should you unilaterally determine that we have not provided the services agreed to in our service agreement.

Prospective Client Questionnaire

BACKGROUND—Personal Information

Full Name:	DOB:	
Birthplace:	SS#:	
Street Address:		
City:	State:	Zip Code:
Home Phone:	Facsimile:	
Work Phone:	Pager:	
Cellular Phone:	Email:	
Employer:		
Title:	Tenure:	

EXHIBIT 9.1   *(Continued)*

Important Fringe Benefits:	
How long have you lived in the Bay Area?	
Where were you raised?	
What College did you attend?	
Where:	Major(s):
Degrees Granted:	
Professional Affiliations:	
Volunteer Activities:	
Charities Supported:	
Preferred Hobbies:	

BACKGROUND—Spouse/Family Information

Spouse Full Name:	DOB:
Spouse Birthplace:	
Spouse Employer:	
Title:	Tenure:
Important Fringe Benefits:	
Child(ren) Full Name(s) / *please list below:*	Child's Age/DOB:

BACKGROUND—Finances

Primary Bank:	Time with Bank:

Type(s) of Account(s):

Current Financial Advisor(s) Name:	Type of Relationship:	Level of Satisfaction:

Current Fee Relationship(s) with Advisor(s):

Do you think the price(s) charged were fair?

If not, why not?

Have you informed your previous accountant/advisor that you are meeting with us?

Do you have an outstanding balance with your previous accountant/advisor?

Investment Activities?

What types of investments do you have/make?

How would you rate your level of risk with your investments?

Do you have an established Estate Plan?

Do you have a Trust?

Is your Will current?

Who is your Attorney?

SERVICE RELATED QUESTIONS

How did you learn of MORRIS + D'ANGELO?

Why did you initiate this contact?

Please list your most important service issues:

What are your expectations from a CPA/advisor?

EXHIBIT 9.1   *(Continued)*

Please state how you would define a "successful" relationship:	
What is your annual advisor budget?	
How often would you like to meet with your accountant/advisor annually?	
Do you expect your accountant/advisor to contact you unilaterally throughout the year?	
On a scale of 1 to 10, with 1 being absolutely risk adverse and 10 being push to the "black line," rate your risk comfort level relative to tax avoidance options:	
How quickly do you expect a "returned" telephone call?	
What is your expected turn around time for preparation of reports received by this office?	
How do you feel about filing for tax return extensions?	
Would you like to receive email-based tax and financial related information?	
Do you have Internet access?	How often do you access the Internet?
How do you feel about being contacted by a firm member other than a partner?	

As you can see, some of these questions are quite personal, and when Morris originally proposed this questionnaire to his partners, it was met with tremendous resistance. However, since it has been implemented, the partners now agree it has been an excellent device for prequalifying new customers and communicating mutual expectations. Furthermore, the customers who have completed it have commented positively that it is the first time a professional has asked them these types of questions. And one customer, who complained that the questions were too invasive and the firm had no business asking them, in the end, essentially self-identified as a poor fit for the firm, thereby saving time developing the relationship. (You can download—and modify to fit your firm's culture—this questionnaire by visiting the Morris + D'Angleo Web site at www.cpadudes.com).

The second step before setting a price is to ask questions to which the firm itself needs answered. We recommend you consider the following questions as a customer service team, and include at least one member of the firm who *does not* know the customer, and therefore has no emotional commitment to the relationship. It is necessary to have someone who is objective, to ensure the firm will not make unwarranted price concessions. Some firms have taken this a step further by establishing a pricing committee, where all FPAs, change orders and pricing decisions are approved internally before being communicated to the customer. Let us consider the questions the American Bar Association recommends you consider before establishing a price.

The American Bar Association's Model Rules of Professional Conduct outline attorneys responsibilities in dealing with customers. Specifically, Model Rule 1.5 states "A lawyer's fee shall be reasonable" (they have not progressed to using the word "price," yet). It sets forth the following factors to consider in determining a price:

1. The time and labor required, novelty and difficulty involved, and required skill needed to perform the services
2. The likelihood, if apparent to the client, that acceptance of the assignment will preclude other employment
3. The customary fee charged for similar services in the locality
4. The amount involved and results obtained
5. Time limits imposed by the client or circumstances
6. The nature and length of the professional relationship with the client
7. The experience, reputation, and ability of the lawyers performing the services
8. Whether the fee is fixed or contingent

In addition to the ABA's considerations, you should ask yourself the following:

Questions the Firm Should Ask Internally before Setting a Price

- Whom on the organizational chart am I dealing with?
- Who referred the customer to me?
- What is the nature of the relationship with the referral source?
- What is the time line on the decision to select a professional?
- What are the impending deadlines driving the decision to engage a professional?
- Who is paying for the service?
- Are there any competitors to our firm in the arena ? Who?
- Any price information from those competitors (bids, RFPs, etc.)?
- How profitable is the organization? How long has it been in business?
- Who was their prior professional and why are they changing?
- If a new business, who is the banker, the attorney, CPA, board members, and other professionals?
- How sophisticated is the customer with respect to our services?
- What is the price the customer would pay for the service internally?
- Does this customer add to the firm's intellectual capital, or are we simply utilizing existing skills?

- What risk is the firm exposed to with this customer?
- What is the potential profit (or loss) to the customer from our service(s)?
- Does this customer open up a new niche or market segment for the firm?
- Do we like this customer? Is he or she in a business in which we are interested?
- What price do we desire for this engagement? (Adapted from Baker, 2001: 173–177.)

Notice how these questions and considerations (ours and the ABA's) go far beyond just the time and labor involved. Basically, you are trying to determine the value to the customer by looking at an entire range of factors; the more you know, the better able you will be equipped to set a price commensurate with value. There is nothing wrong, per se, about estimating the amount of labor required, but this should be done before the engagement, not after. Also, it should not be the determining factor in setting a price, but one of many. Customers do not buy hours, thus they are superfluous in determining value.

The last question—What price do we desire for this engagement?—is particularly important. We suggest the firm establish three desired internal prices for each FPA or change order (or fixed price for those customers not on FPAs):

Reservation price. This is the walk-away price, below which the firm will not, for any reason, go. It could be based on an estimate of standard hourly rates, but should also factor in all of the other strategies, value drivers, and other factors we have discussed. This will provide the firm with a *normal* profit.

Hope-for price. This is a price that will generate a *supernormal* profit for the firm.

Pump-fist price. This is a price that will generate a *windfall* profit for the firm.

These prices are critical to establish internally before agreeing with the customer. As we discussed, there is no reason for the firm *not* to establish a price up front, and then determine if it can profitably invest in the internal costs to generate a profit the firm is comfortable with (similar to how Iacocca priced the Ford Mustang).

You will never become an effective negotiator unless you are willing to walk away from the deal. That is your penultimate bargaining position—the ultimate bargaining position is understanding and delivering your value—and it is how the best firms in the world avoid competing solely on price (and also why they turn down a large percentage of potential customers). The reservation price provides this point of demarcation. You should never go below this price in order to obtain *market share*. You cannot take market share to the bank, only profitability. If the customers are not willing to pay the reservation price, then ask them which services they would like you to remove from the bundle; or have them do more of the work themselves; or, if it is a marginal reduction they are seeking, change the payment terms and get your full price up front. No matter what, do not make a *unilateral* price concession without getting the customer to give something up in return. You do not want to reward that type of behavior. And do not add capacity (or consume too much existing capacity) for low-price customers. Sure, you can take on some marginal coach customers, but a firm must also get its share of business-class and first-class customers in order to be profitable. Further, you must reserve a portion of your fixed capacity for your best customers' immediate needs—they will be far less price-sensitive than new customers starting out at the bottom of the value curve.

The pump-fist price is the one at the top of the value curve. This would be the firm's best estimate as to the true price the customer is willing and able to pay if you had perfect information. Many professionals are hesitant about this price, but you should not be. You have to believe you are worth it in order to ever get it. And we are not suggesting that you will obtain this price a majority of the time (based on our experience in working with firms that utilize this method, you will receive it between 20 and 40 percent of the time). But there is one thing we know for sure: If you never ask for a pump-fist price, you will never get it. Hockey great Wayne Gretzky's comment is absolutely true: "You miss 100 percent of the shots you don't take."

Most of the time, your final price will end up at the hope-for level, which is a supernormal profit. Because you are bundling services, providing a price and service guarantee, offering fixed-payment terms and prices, you should be able to command premium prices over the competition. The goal is to compete on service and value, not price.

It is also appropriate in certain circumstances to ask customers what they believe the service is worth, and let them set the price. Often, you will be surprised to learn the customer selects a price well above your reservation price. It also makes collection much easier since it is very hard for customers to later dispute a price they set.

In those instances where the customer will not offer a price, then the ball is in your court. Quote the pump-fist price first, since it is much easier to start high and move down than it is to go in the opposite direction. Then, *be quiet*. If you say anything after that, you will be on your way to cutting price and you will have lost control of the negotiation (and will have gained nothing). Let the customer go through sticker shock, and a moment of silence, since that is very natural. Being silent at this point is difficult (humans do not like silence), but you have to refrain—it usually will not last longer than 30 to 60 seconds.

This may seem like a daunting task at first, but like all knowledge work, it is an iterative process. The more you do it, the more confidence you gain, and the better you get at it. Moreover, by having your team members involved in this process, you are cultivating an entrepreneurial mind-set among them and offering valuable (and positive) human capital on the process of pricing on purpose and for profitability.

PAUL Sometimes we need personal experiences to make concepts come alive, even more so emotionally, so that they become part of our belief system (you'll remember the point about belief change preceding behavior change). With that in mind let me share with you some experiences that may help that process.

At a client advisory board I was conducting in England, the subject turned to price. "I've got a real problem with the way this practice prices things," said one client. To explain it, let me ask you this question: Do they have tailors in Australia?"

"Well yes of course," I replied. (Maybe the client thought we had just kangaroos on street corners!)

With that the customer stood up and literally took the floor. "Well, imagine," he said, "that I go into my local tailor shop, I try on a suit, and the jacket is too long. So I go up to the person behind the counter and ask him how much it would cost to shorten the sleeves. The salesperson says, 'Well, that depends.' My response obviously is, 'Depends on what?

"Next the salesperson says, 'Well it depends on how long it takes. And if I do it it'll take longer than my boss. His rate for doing it is £5 an inch and mine is £4 per inch. Which would you like?'"

The customer was now warming to the task of telling the story. "Paul, tell me, how am I going to feel?" And before I could answer, he answered his own question with what the British would call "gusto." "I'm going to be pissed off, that's how I'm going to feel!" Then he got to the point: "Don't you see, that's exactly how it is dealing with this accounting firm? I don't care who does it, I don't care how long it takes, all I care about is getting the job done right."

Isn't that precisely how your customers feel? More to the point, isn't it how *you* feel? If it is, come with me to the podiatrist's office. (Before you say, "What does that have to do with pricing?" the answer is, "Plenty, stay tuned.")

Podiatrists are very, very useful if you spend a lot of time on stage doing a lot of purposeful pacing. You effectively walk miles in a day! And if you're 50 plus, your feet can start to develop very painful corns. Well, the one on my left foot was extremely painful. People were asking me if I'd broken an ankle, I was hobbling so much. So after months of agony (and travel) I arrived home and went to see my friendly neighborhood podiatrist, whose name is Chris.

"Ooh, that is a bad one," he observed. "But we'll soon have it off; it'll take about 45 minutes to really do a good job." As he got to work I inquired as to the fee. I was told somewhat sheepishly it was $50.

Now pause for a moment. What would your reaction be? Pretend for a moment that, like me, you spend most of your life telling professional accountants that their prices are way, way too low: your reaction would be precisely like mine. "Is that all?" I ask. "Chris, wait a minute. When I came in I could barely walk; in 45 minutes or so I'll be like brand new and you're only charging me $50. I insist you charge me more." (Okay, maybe I am weird!)

Chris was, to say the least, somewhat taken aback. He told me he had never heard anyone say that before. We discuss it as he works on my little (and getting ever littler!) left toe. I explain that most professionals have more trouble with their price structures than anything else, and how the customer (or buyer) almost always has *fewer* problems with the price than the seller. Price resistance is almost always in the mind of the seller *not* the buyer.

RON It seems that it is the professionals who actually *project* their own price resistance onto the customer.

PAUL Chris next told me no one had ever explained pricing to him before. I then learn that he has been in business for only a year and that he feels he has to start by charging low (but he also admitted that no one had ever said his prices were too high—a major clue there—and that he had often thought he should increase them).

"Do it now," I exclaim. So we agree to $70. But it's not over yet. We walk out—yes I can walk again—to the reception area, where the receptionist tells me it'll be $50. "Oh no it's not," I say, "it's $70—ask him (pointing to Chris)." He coughs nervously. "Yes, it's $70."

Picture now a totally confused receptionist wondering what the heck is going on. "No, no, no," she says, "you're wrong. It's $50." I encourage Chris to stick to his guns. Eventually, I give the receptionist two $50 bills and she gives me $30 change.

The point is, of course, that if I'd have let Chris off the hook and said to him, "Okay, you can charge me $50, but make sure you charge the next person $70," he would never have done it—it would never have happened. He would have found some reason to stay with the lower price. (Maybe I should have charged him for the advice! That would have ensured action on his part.) Therein lies the crucial point again: price resistance is almost always in the mind of the seller not the buyer.

A few days after the experience at the podiatrist, I spoke with Reginald, an accountant in public practice in England. We were discussing positioning and he was explaining to me that some of his clients (significantly, the ones he charges less) treat him with less respect than they do their window cleaner. Again you see the point.

But don't be misled. This is not about simply raising prices (although that is surely part of it). It is first and foremost about increasing the value we bring, and then charging accordingly. That said, I remain convinced that no profession so undervalues what it does than the accounting (and to a lesser extent, the legal) profession.

Chris helped me to walk better. Accountants and attorneys help their clients run their businesses more effectively. Since that experience, Chris has never looked back. He walks a little taller these days, I notice, and there's surely a message there, too.

RON To prove these strategies work, consider the following two e-mails I received from participants in a one-and-a-half day California CPA Education Foundation course I taught in late October 2000, in Napa Valley, California. Titled "Value Pricing Graduate Seminar," it was attended by 13 CPAs who had taken a value pricing course as a prerequisite, and who had begun to implement value pricing strategies in their firms.

> February 28, 2001
>
> Hi Ron,
>
> I've been too busy with my new program to write, but wanted to get a quick message off to you to thank you for your book (*Professional's Guide to Value Pricing*) and seminar. I read the book three times while on Christmas break, returned to the office to write my fixed-price agreement for all tax returns, fired all my pain-in-the-a-- customers, and raised my prices substantially (two to four times the prior tax preparation price). I've had an overwhelming response from my customers who love the new FPA and all the services they perceive they will be receiving. Many customers are not returning, but those who aren't seem to be the ones I can do

without anyway—all the whiners and criers who don't value my services. I have actually had three local CPAs call me to congratulate me on having the guts to do what I've done. I didn't have the time or the energy to sell any customers to another firm, but figured I was so exhausted at the prospect of another dreary tax season that I simply didn't care. The new customers that I have acquired have very high FPAs. Six new customers have replaced 26 old ones! I love this!

Anyway, my life has changed for the better. More money, more satisfaction, but most of all more time for my family and my life.

Diane Green

February 23, 2001

Hello Ron,

I would like to update you on my progress. At this point, I have secured two new FPAs and converted one existing customer with great success. As promised, the customers love having the opportunity to agree to a price up front.

After our class, I had to free up enough time to implement the new vision. As expected, I am meeting with a great deal of adversity from my partner who lives and dies by the billable hour. While I am still hoping he will see the light, I am moving forward whether he joins me or not. I feel that this experience may be useful to others who have the same implementation challenges.

Here is what I am doing. First, I did a Pareto analysis. The results were no surprise and it was a great wake-up call that gave me the mind-set to release 114 customers. If you remember, I inherited many low-level customers from my partner who died and I was struggling with choosing between immediate cash flow and servicing the types of customers I love. I chose the latter and we found a CPA who was just starting a practice and sold the customers to her for 70 percent of last year's revenues.

Then I put together a letter for all my tax customers. (My partner did not participate at first, saying his customers were "old school" and would not like the changes. This created some confusion among our team members, but was resolved with time and success of the program). [The letter] set forth some terms of our relationship along with pricing information that included a discount for waiving the tax season appointment. Then a team member who has great communication skills followed up with a phone call to poll the customers on their feelings about the new system and find out if they wanted an appointment. The success has been overwhelming and we have received benefits that I never dreamed of when I was anticipating the customer's reactions. Since I raised everyone's prices, it has given customers the opportunity to vent about the price up front. I won't have to spend time listening to complaints after I send out the invoice. Additionally, it front-loaded our cash flows since people are paying in advance or when they pick up their return—not after they get our invoice. We know who is coming back and who isn't (very few aren't).

After tax season, I will be pushing to convert more good customers to FPAs and I will be pursuing eliminating the billable hour [and timesheets] completely. I am going to need all the help I can get so if any of you have advice, I would appreciate it. I am hoping that if I come up with some great KPIs [Key Performance Indicators, discussed in Chapter 10], my partner will be more receptive.

I hope all is going well for the rest of you, and I look forward to more success stories after tax season.

Regards,

Leslie Chapman

Notice how partner buy–in can be a sensitive issue; and I have to be honest, some partnerships have broken up over this pricing issue. If you and your partner(s) have a different vision of value propositions, pricing policies, and other strategic issues, then implementing FPAs and change orders—not to mention getting rid of timesheets, the subject of Chapter 10—will only increase the tension. Sometimes, divorce is the only solution, which ultimately was the outcome for Leslie. Other times, one partner will implement these ideas, achieve success, and others will come onboard. Even the most recalcitrant professional will find it very difficult to deny successful results.

Here is a letter reporting on the success of implementing FPAs, which I received following a presentation on value pricing, given at a conference in Las Vegas in September 2000. The point is not to take any personal credit—Paul deserves just as much as I since he taught the Chicago Boot Camp in 1998—but to illustrate the salutary effects implementing FPAs can have, and to point out that most firms have adopted these ideas gradually, over time, not all at once.

April 6, 2001

Dear Ron:

As a CPA and economist, did you ever think you'd be getting fan mail? Well, I never thought I'd be writing it! But as a team member of a Lakewood, Colorado, CPA firm, I feel compelled to share with you the impact *Professional's Guide to Value Pricing* and your presentation at the September 2000 RAN [Results Accountants' Network] Conference have had on our firm. I'm proud of the success we've had adopting and implementing your pricing practices, and I know our partners are too modest to tell you about it themselves. So please allow me to brag a bit on behalf of our firm, and to keep your attention, I'll be bragging on you, too!

Let me start with a little background. Bradley, Allen & Associates has been in business since 1982. When the three partners (Tim Bradley, Mark Allen, and Tom Swart) attended the Results Accountants' Systems Chicago Boot Camp in 1998, all were in their early forties, well established in their careers, and firmly entrenched in the rate-times-hour billing mentality. It was at that conference they first heard your name and a bit about your book. A year went by, and after a partner from a Georgia firm, whom they'd met at Boot Camp, raved about your book, they decided that selected team members of our team should read it. So we bought five copies and gave ourselves a deadline to finish the book. Shortly afterward, Tim "stepped out on the ice" to negotiate his first FPA. In the first nine months of 2000, Tim and one service provider negotiated FPAs with nine clients, generating about $70,000 in revenue.

Then came the RAN Conference in Las Vegas—and your dynamic, passionate, and compelling presentation on value pricing! As an administrator with a knack for implementation, I was invited to attend the conference with the partners, and we all agreed your four-hour portion of the conference was worth the price of the two-day trip. We were psyched! We came back to the office with renewed enthusiasm, and for the first time, a conviction that value pricing was a philosophy we could truly embrace. I think we've always known that our many loyal clients appreciate our history with them and our knowledge of their businesses, and we also realize it's our relationship with them that matters most. But our epiphany came in realizing it was okay to be compensated for that value. After all, we had no billing code for "relationship!"

So we ordered a copy of your book for every member of the team, established a six-week program of reading and lively group discussions, and began to get everyone onboard with the philosophy, lingo, and techniques of value pricing. Even with all that enthusiasm and knowledge, the partners and service providers still didn't find the idea of actually "selling" or "talking price" very palatable. But as each of them had a victory and shared it with the team, confidence grew—and "success begot success."

I am very proud to report that between October 2000 and April 2001, our three partners and five service providers sold $918,000 in FPA services, in 56 contracts ranging from $2,000 to $84,000!

Of course, the real test of our success will be in how well we're able to service these clients and manage our costs. I'm confident we'll excel at that, too. The firm's partners are excellent managers, and I expect they will continue to see rate-times-hour as a valid way of evaluating how effective we've been at delivering our services. So although we've not yet abandoned "the Almighty Hour," we're using timesheets more as a management tool than a pricing tool.

Ron, you've had a profound affect on how Bradley, Allen is doing business in the new millennium. We thank you, and offer a standing invitation to visit us anytime you're in the Denver area. We'd love to show you some Colorado hospitality—and have you sign the 17 dog-eared copies of your book we now own!

Sincerely,

Patti Carpenter

This letter teaches how important it is to adopt these ideas incrementally, at a pace that is comfortable for the firm and its customers. There is no need to rush this process. Based on our experience, firms can get anywhere from 50 percent to 80 percent of their revenue under the aegis of FPAs in anywhere from six months to two years. Move at a pace you are comfortable with, but make sure you celebrate your successes along the way (and dissect any setbacks or failures).

THE TIP CLAUSE

RON *The New Yorker* once ran a cartoon of a coffee shop: in the window, a sign read: "Tipping is considered an insult"; on the counter, a box was labeled, "Deposit insults here."

I will always remember a story I heard at a seminar I conducted in 1997 for a Top 15 accounting firm. It left such an indelible impression in my mind because it illustrates so well the essential limitation of pricing by the hour, especially in situations where the firm is providing an extraordinary level of service and adding enormous value to a transaction. It became the genesis for the To Insure Performance, or TIP, clause.

Tim was the managing partner of this particular city's office, and his best, long-term customer (of 20 years) had come to him within the past quarter wanting to sell his $250 million closely held business. He told Tim (and I am paraphrasing here), "You've been my CPA for 20 years and I trust you with my life. It is time for me to sell my business and enjoy my golden years. Here is what I want you to do:

* Update our business valuation in order to maximize the sales price.
* Fly with me anywhere we have to go to meet with potential buyers.
* Be actively involved at every stage of the sales negotiation.
* Perform the due diligence, along with the attorneys, of the qualified buyers.
* Work with the attorneys on the sales contract to make sure my interests are protected.
* Perform tax planning and structure the deal in such a manner as to maximize my wealth retention."

Obviously, this was a very sophisticated customer, and Tim was not utilizing FPAs; but if he had been, chances are this engagement would not be included in it—this would require a change order. And, in fact, the customer has already laid out the scope of the engagement. It is true that Tim had no idea at the outset of this engagement how long it would take to close the deal, and how much firm capacity (his and his team members) it would require. But he did know more than an average salesman would know. He knew the customer's business was well niched, profitable, and growing. This would indicate a very high probability of success. He also knew this customer was an audit customer of the firm's and therefore he would not be able to charge a contingency price based upon a financial outcome (such as a percentage of the sales price or of any tax savings).

I asked Tim how he priced this engagement, and he proudly proclaimed that every hour charged to this project—no matter from what level in the firm—was charged out at his highest consulting rate of $400 per hour. That indicated that Tim knew right from the start there was more value on this project than he would ever be able to lie on a timesheet to capture. He further explained that he had updated the business valuation, negotiated with two buyers, and did all of the other tasks requested by the customer. As a result of Tim's work, the customer received (and saved in taxes) an additional $15 million, and acknowledged that Tim was directly responsible for this outcome. In Tim's own words, the customer was "elated."

Tim then told the group how he priced the engagement. He reviewed all of the hours from the work-in-progress time and billing system, believed it did not adequately reflect the value he provided, and marked it up an additional 25 percent over the $400 hourly rate. He then sent out an invoice for $38,000, which the customer promptly—and happily—paid. He believed that was value pricing. It was not—it was *value guessing*, since the customer had absolutely no input into the price, and only a customer can determine value.

When I asked Tim what he thought the customer would have paid if he had utilized a TIP clause (also referred to as the *retrospective price*, or *success price*), such as the following sample:

> In the event that we are able to satisfy your needs in a timely and professional manner, you have agreed to review the situation and decide whether, in the sole discretion of XYZ, some additional payment to ABC is appropriate in view of your overall satisfaction with the services rendered by ABC and/or the financial results achieved by XYZ for this transaction.

The wording here would have to be modified since this was an audit customer and it is therefore illegal to base the TIP on a financial outcome. To do so you would simply remove "and/or the financial results achieved by XYZ for this transaction." Therefore, the TIP is being based on the "overall satisfaction with the services rendered," not by any financial contingency, which is the origin of the acronym TIP—To Insure Performance. This TIP clause would be used in conjunction with the change order and discussed with the customer *before* any work began. If needed, you could put a minimum price on the change order (such as $10,000 to $30,000) to cover immediate firm capacity. But in this case, given the 20-year relationship with the customer, even a price *solely* determined by a TIP would have been acceptable, since the customer was not likely to take advantage of Tim after the services he rendered.

In answer to my question, Tim said his customer would most likely have paid him $500,000, a sum I believe to this day is below the real number—but at least better than the $38,000 he finally charged. Nevertheless, since Tim knows the customer better than I, let us take his number as correct.

I informed Tim he had made the Ultimate Accounting Entry (from Charlie Larson's book, *Innovative Billing and Collection Methods That Work,* 1995: 42):

	Debit	**Credit**
Experience	$462,000	
Cash		$462,000

Tim was at the top of the value curve, yet he dragged a bottom-of-the-curve pricing strategy up there with him—the hourly rate. This is why it is imperative to extinguish the rate-times-hours mentality from your firm. No one I have shared this story with believed Tim would have received less than $38,000 for his services on this engagement. In effect, Tim paid a *reverse risk premium*—he was assured he would not go below his hourly rate, but in return he gave up the added value the customer already believed he had provided. This is not a risk worth taking if you want to maximize your firm's profitability. Since Tim had a long relationship with this customer, it would have been acceptable for him to release his *price leverage* and let the customer determine the price after the engagement. However, it is imperative to have the TIP discussion and get authorization in writing, *before* you do the work. If you do not have a long-term relationship, then as an alternative you could place a higher minimum price in the change order, but still utilize the TIP clause if you have no reason to believe the customer would take advantage of you (and if you do have reason to believe that, why is he or she a customer in the first place?).

The deleterious effects of this run deeper than just being deprived the value from the work you provided on any one engagement. The problem lies at the very core of a firm's measurement system and points out how it does not offer the opportunity to learn from lost pricing opportunities, or pricing "mistakes."

The Wrong Mistakes

In his inimitable way, Yogi Berra explained this problem eloquently in his book *When You Come to a Fork in the Road, Take It!*:

> When we played the Pittsburgh Pirates in the 1960 World Series, it was hard to believe we lost. It was real strange. We crushed their pitching. We won three of the games, 16–3, 10–0, and 12–0. We were the more experienced and stronger team. But we lost in a wild and weird Game 7 when Bill Mazeroski hit that homer in the ninth inning over my head in left field. To this day, I thought the ball was going to hit the fence. Anyway, when a reporter asked me later how we could lose to the Pirates, I said, "We made too many wrong mistakes" (Berra, 2001: 75).
>
> In baseball, like everything, mistakes are physical or mental. In tennis, they say "forced and unforced errors." I like to say there's mistakes—and there's wrong mistakes. What I mean is that wrong mistakes are more serious, more avoidable, more costly. They're usually more mental than physical (Ibid: 74).

When it comes to pricing, the wisdom from Yogi is profound. Tim made the *wrong mistake*, and here is why: He will not learn anything from it because the firm's primary assessment is billable hours. When the partners review the realization report on this engagement, they will see 125 percent, which is excellent when you consider most firms realize less than 100 percent overall. Most likely, Tim will get nothing but accolades and praise from his fellow partners. No one will ask where the $462,000 is because the billable-hour metrics do not have a way to capture that type of information, which is precisely why pricing is an art not a science.

This is an excellent example of a wrong mistake because Tim (or the firm) will not learn anything from this lost pricing opportunity. The $462,000 simply vanishes into thin air (or, more precisely, it remains on the customer's income statement). No knowledge was gained by the firm on how to price the next similar engagement in accordance with value; it will simply perpetuate the same mistake, over and over.

That is not to say that with value pricing you will never make mistakes. You certainly will. The difference is they will be the *right mistakes*, because with value pricing you are forced to receive input from the customer as to your value, and have in place pricing strategies that will capture more of that value (like the TIP clause). If you engage in postmortem value assessments of each engagement and elicit feedback from your customers, you will learn from your mistakes and become better at pricing in the future. Value pricing is a skill similar to baseball, tennis, or golf: the more you do it, the better you get.

The billable-hour metrics of realization rates, cost accounting, Generally Accepted Accounting Principles (GAAP) financial statement reporting—even activity-based costing analysis—prevent professionals from pricing commensurate with value since pricing mistakes (or missed opportunities) do not show up in any of these reports. As such, the firm is denied the chance to acquire the proper value metrics and develop intellectual capital on pricing in order for it to become a core competency within the firm and among its professionals. All of the traditional metrics of a professional service firm focus on *internal* measurements, whereas value is always an *external* issue—in the hearts and minds of the customers. Innovative pricing strategies such as the TIP clause have allowed more and more professionals around the world to capture more of the value they provide, as the following stories illustrate.

PAUL This TIP story comes from New Zealand. We met Peter at a seminar in Auckland. He had always been a champion of the work we were doing and had written me an e-mail that he had received so much value and so many ideas from Ron's book.

At the seminar, Peter told about a customer (we'll call him Frank) of his accounting firm who was nearly eighty years old. For years Frank had been pursuing a special dream to own a farm, but had never been able to make it come true. Peter, by using some very creative thought processes and a lot of skill, had at long last helped Frank buy his farm.

Peter explained that, prior to reading Ron's book, he would have billed the client $5,000 on a normal rate-times-hour basis. But in his heart Peter realized that the customer had received much more value than that (indeed, he had experienced a transformation!) so Peter decided to charge $150,000, a full 30 times higher. (Unfortunately, Peter had already performed the work prior to reading Ron's book, and thus did not discuss a TIP with the customer in advance, which is not the way we recommend you negotiate the TIP; it must be done up front. Fortunately, in this case the outcome was still positive!).

Peter recalled the moment he told Frank about the invoice. He expected some reaction but not the one he got. Frank said, "Peter, it's not enough. It's really not enough." (You can imagine Peter's face at this point.) "I'm going to write you the check right now for the $150,000; and, Peter, I insist that you, your wife, and your son take that European holiday you've been wanting, but at my expense—if that's okay with you!"

So it was that some seven months later, Peter and his family took a detour on their European holiday to join me at my home in France for a few days.

Let's revisit a truth at this juncture: We, the sellers of services, nearly always have a lower perspective of the value than the buyer. And the most fundamental truth is this: Firms of the future do *not* bill hours-times-rate. If as you read this, you're still billing that way, make the commitment right now today to stop doing it. It's wrong. It's that simple.

I know what you'll try to do. You'll try to find all sorts of reasons why it's right. You'll say things like, "What if the client doesn't value what I do?" There's a simple answer to that: Either charge nothing for it or don't do work that people do not value; or make sure you make people value what you do by learning and using the strategies (like FPAs, for example) to effectively communicate the value you bring.

Again, clients do not buy hours, so don't you dare try to sell them!

RON Another TIP success comes from Gus Stearns, whom I met on September 25, 2000, at the RAN conference in Las Vegas. Gus tracked me down at the dinner party, walked me over to the bar, and over a glass of wine told me his amazing TIP story. This was not an audit customer and hence Gus had no independence issues. Here are the two e-mails I received from Gus explaining his success, the first one prior to our meeting in Las Vegas and the second one after:

> April 20, 2000
>
> Hello Ron,
>
> I hope the tax season finds you well. I was fortunate enough to be at the Atlanta conference [January 2000] when you spoke and picked up an autographed copy of your book, which I devoured on the plane trip back.
>
> The engagement that I refer to ($180,000 total price) had already started a month or two before, and I had used the old standard rate-time-hours routine and billed about $2,000 at a standard rate of $180/hour. After listening to you and reading the book, I was determined to reevaluate the price structure and simply went back to my customer and said, "Guys, this is what I am bringing to the table. It brings a lot of value which is etc., etc. I don't believe hourly rates based upon time is appropriate. I am unable to place a value on this. I need your help. You tell me what the value of all this is to you. You are the customer and only you can truly establish the value. I know I'll be happy with whatever you come up with." This is almost an exact quote.
>
> I left it at that two months ago. I was handed a check for the first installment of $50,000 on the way out at the end of the engagement. I guess this is what you call "outside-in pricing." I like it.
>
> Gus Stearns, CPA

It gets better, since this engagement was in two phases. Here is the follow-up e-mail from Gus explaining the final result after the job was done (which is the story he told me over an excellent glass of Cabernet Sauvignon). The outcome was the perfect gift for an author:

> Hello Ron,
>
> Basically the large engagement was for a previous client that I had hired a controller for. He took over the tax work, at my suggestion, as he was a CPA. The engagement was an exit and management succession strategy, which involved some fairly hefty income tax savings as well. The total time expended was about 100 hours, although a lot of the time was on unrelated things that I did not want to charge for due to the magnitude of the price (we quit using timesheets some time ago and have substituted "daily activity sheets" to make sure our clients get invoiced, based upon our perceived value of each engagement).
>
> I used a flip chart in the presentation, pointing out the value of what they were getting. At the end of the presentation, I asked how much they thought it was worth, and suggested $300,000, $500,000, a million? I wanted them to think in big numbers. The CEO was rather excited and said a million. Knowing that this would be difficult to obtain in one fell swoop I suggested $400,000 down and a retainer of $4,000 per month. They agreed but asked that I serve on the board of directors and attend quarterly meetings through 2008, when the note to the previous owners would be paid off. They were also kind enough to put me on salary so I could participate in their pension plan, which is a 25 percent direct contribution from the company. This all adds up to a little bit over $1 million.
>
> Never once was the word "time" used or referred to by myself or my client. They couldn't have cared less about time. In all of our engagements, I never used the word. By concentrating on value and encouraging the client to participate in the valuation of the engagement our prices have skyrocketed. You were absolutely on-target when you said that accountants are terrible at valuing our services (myself included).
>
> Keep up the wonderful work,
>
> Gus

We understand these types of engagements are not the rule in your firm, they are the exception. Nonetheless, they do arise, and when they do it is critical to recognize you are at the top of the value curve and to utilize innovative pricing strategies that will help capture that marginal value. This also demonstrates why pricing is the most potent lever you have in terms of increasing your firm's profitability, much more than cutting costs or increasing efficiency.

We include these stories not because we believe you will earn a $1 million TIP, but rather to illustrate how the hourly rate mentality has placed a self-imposed artificial ceiling over the heads of professionals. The hourly rate has actually negatively affected the level of self-esteem for professionals, making them feel as if the hourly rate is all they are worth. Never in his wildest dreams would Gus have placed a $1 million value on his work; but the customer did. Does he not deserve it? Don't you?

VALUE PRICING AND SELF-ESTEEM

Ron Frank Lloyd Wright, at the age of eighty-nine, testified in a trial he was "the greatest architect in the world." Afterward, his wife suggested modesty would have been more effective. Wright replied, "You forget, Olgivanna, that I was under oath."

When I first started to study and teach pricing, I never gave any thought to self-esteem, though I was always amazed when colleagues would challenge me on their ability to raise their prices. Or they said they would feel guilty about charging above their hourly rates. The epiphany for me was that this was not a strategic issue, but rather a low self-esteem issue. Then in the August 1996 *CPA Profitability Monthly* newsletter, Timothy J. Beauchemin wrote an article that resonated with me and explained the comments I was hearing from CPAs around the country. Timothy passed away in February 1997, but his seminal thinking on many topics endures to this day, as this passage from his article—"No More Begging for Work: Self-Esteem Is the Key to a Better Practice"—illustrates:

> I see too much of what I call "begging" in our industry—begging for work (especially by underpricing) and then begging to get paid. I have never really understood why this is, particularly when you consider the training, hard work, and risk that accountants go through. The only explanation I can see is that accountants tend to have rather low self-images, unfairly and unreasonably low, but low just the same (Beauchemin, 1996: 4).

Not only is pricing an art, it is also a game, one that is played between your ears. It requires negotiation, and since professionals are trained to be precise and accurate, they struggle with the ambiguity necessary to become an effective negotiator. Psychologist Nathaniel Branden has studied self-esteem extensively, and his books are must-reads to gain a deeper understanding of this much-ignored subject. His treatise on the subject is *The Six Pillars of Self-Esteem*, wherein he defines self-esteem as:

1. Confidence in our ability to think, confidence in our ability to cope with the basic challenges of life; and
2. Confidence in our right to be successful and happy, the feeling of being worthy, deserving, entitled to assert our needs and wants, achieve our values, and enjoy the fruits of our efforts (Branden, 1994: 4).

In his book *Self-Esteem at Work: How Confident People Make Powerful Companies,* Branden discusses the critical role self-esteem has in the success of enterprise:

> A simple example is the fact that analyses of business failure tell us that a common cause is executives' fear of making decisions. What is fear of making decisions but lack of confidence in one's mind and judgment? In other words, a problem of self-esteem.
>
> Yet another example pertains to competence at negotiating. A study discloses that whereas people with healthy self-esteem tend to be realistic in their demands, negotiators with poor self-esteem tend to ask for too much or too little (depending on other personality variables)—but in either case being less effective than they could be (Branden, 1998: xii).

There is virtually no aspect of business activity—from leading to managing to par-
ticipating in teams, and from dealing with customers to engaging in research and development to responding to new challenges and new ideas—that is not significantly
affected by the level of one's self-esteem (Ibid: xiii).

In today's competitive business environment, low self-esteem is a competitive disadvantage, while high self-esteem among your firm's professionals confers a competitive advantage. Yet how can professionals feel good about themselves, their work,
and their service to the customer and the greater community if they believe they are
commodities, and are constantly being beat up over their price or the lack of billable
hours they are charging? Consider this e-mail I received from Diane (who also wrote
the e-mail on FPAs) that illustrates the importance of self-esteem and the effect it can
have on a professional's life:

> September 28, 2002
>
> Dear Ron,
>
> Finally (and I may have told you this before) the biggest change in all of this has
> been to my self-esteem. About 10 years ago, not long after beginning my solo
> practice, my mother-in-law, who is an attorney, said to me, "Diane, just remem-
> ber, men are in business to make money and women are in business to take care
> of people. Get over it!" What she meant was that the female attitude of "I'll take
> care of you" will give you little satisfaction and make you no money. If you are
> going to be taken away from your family, you might as well make a hell of a lot
> of money and feel really good about it. But that is easier said than done. I fell
> into the trap of helping my clients and forgetting myself. Was I popular? Did my
> clients love me? Yes! But I didn't feel the same. Only when I took my practice
> seriously and began placing a value on my services with the FPA did I begin to
> feel successful. If you feel successful, you are successful and then the money fol-
> lows. When you reduce your value to an hourly rate it feels lousy, no matter how
> high the billing rate.
>
> Good luck, and keep up the good work! Keep in touch.
>
> Diane Green

You will never get paid more than you think you are worth. And if you do not think
you are worth more than your hourly rate, why would your customers? I have had
countless professionals tell me, in no uncertain terms, they could *never* double their
prices, and yet we know countless others who have, and not only do the customers not
leave, they appreciate the extra level of service and all the other salutary effects of
value pricing.

VALUE PRICING AND ETHICS

RON The issue of the ethics of value pricing always comes up as we teach it around
the world, and I welcome—even encourage—the discussion. It is a vitally important

issue, and one that needs to be discussed intelligently and understood before you will feel comfortable applying these strategies. (For those who want a deeper exploration, see my *Professional's Guide to Value Pricing, Fourth Edition*, especially Chapter 16: "Ethics, Hourly Billing, and Value Pricing.")

Cost-plus pricing gained acceptance, and to a large extent retains its luster, because it is perceived as a *fair* pricing method. This concept dates back to the medieval church's concept of *justum pretium*—"the right price." A business should only earn a reasonable profit on its internal costs. Of course, this begs the question of who gets to determine what is fair and just? The fact of the matter is there is a natural—and healthy—tension between buyer and seller, tempered by the competition in the marketplace.

Nothing in this chapter should be construed as a prescription to rip off your customers or charge extraordinarily high prices for your services. On the contrary, we are arguing that it is the *customer* who ultimately determines your value, and that is why we advocate the 100 percent money-back guarantee, and the price guarantee. Taking this a step further, I truly believe it is of questionable ethics and morality not to establish a price up front, with the full consent and agreement of the customer. The questionable practice of attorneys—and to a lesser extent, accountants—of padding their timesheets to inflate their prices testifies to the inherent conflict that exists between hourly billing and efficaciously servicing the customer.

We fervently believe that professionals are subject to the same laws of economics, customer psychology, and pricing emotions as all other business, and must therefore stop hiding behind the cloak and security of the billable hour, and price up front and accept the concomitant risk and uncertainty that entails. The notion that professionals are not subject to these same fundamentals of human behavior is the height of hubris, and an enormous amount of ethical challenges and conundrums would be solved if prices were established transparently and with the full consent of the customer.

The American Bar Association, and various state bar associations, have been debating the ethical quandaries of hourly billing for decades, and have come up with no definitive standards per se. However, recently there has been recognition that prices set between a willing seller and buyer are by their very definition *fair*, as the New York State Bar Association pointed out:

> Indeed, subject to the economic realities of the situation and an attorney's professional obligations, virtually any billing method that attorney and client can both agree upon and abide by will result, almost by definition, in a fair fee.

The free market demands fair dealings between buyer and seller, and any business violates this at its own peril. Beyond that, capitalist acts between consenting adults are allowed. Value pricing and ethics are not mutually exclusive; they coexist in the marketplace everywhere else—from airlines having different fares for different passengers and designer ice cream manufacturers charging a premium price to movie theater popcorn and hardcover books being priced at a premium. It is time for this form of pricing to be adopted with respect to professional services everywhere, and the firms of the future are leading the way.

AMERICAN BAR ASSOCIATION'S COMMISSION
ON BILLABLE HOURS REPORT

Historically, the legal profession was the first to utilize pricing by the hour. By the 1960s this practice was endemic in the profession, and was also learned by accountants. In the 1980s, the ABA established a task force to study the effects of the billable hour, as it was the subject of major criticism in certain segments of the profession. The Task Force on Alternative Billing Methods was established in 1987–1988 as part of the Law Practice Management Section of the ABA. Three books were published as a result of this task force, two edited by Richard C. Reed, and one authored by him, between 1989 and 1996.

The ABA, under its President Robert E. Hirshon, is once again studying the effects of the billable hour on the legal profession. In the first part of 2002, the ABA established the Commission on Billable Hours, and the commission issued its report in August, 2002. In an article by Hirshon entitled "Law and the Billable Hour: A Standard Developed in the 1960s May Be Damaging our Profession," he points out:

> Studies suggest an unease in our profession, especially among younger lawyers. The causes are varied but all seem to lie in the difference between working in a profession versus working a job. Mentoring, life-balance, workplace stimulation, and innovation are affected when the timesheet reigns. The billable hour is fundamentally about quantity over quality, repetition over creativity. Because a lawyer's time is not an elastic variable, increased billable hour requirements are squeezing out other aspects of what it means to be a lawyer. Although I have a specific interest in how this phenomenon has adversely affected our profession's ability to do pro bono work, the demoralizing consequences of billable hours extend much more broadly. Many believe that if we innovate our billing models, not only are the same revenues attainable, but also lawyering itself will become more enjoyable.
>
> Firms will have to think differently—not an easy proposition for traditionally conservative, risk-adverse institutions. But for the sake of profitability and the preservation of that wonderful law firm life (one I've spent 30 years enjoying), we must begin to look at value instead of cost when determining fair payment for services rendered. It will mean accepting some risk. It will mean that efficiency and process improvements will increase profits.
>
> Richard Reed, an expert on this issue, offers tips to law firm leaders who seek new ways: First, he says, gather your best people and think globally about how the practice is changing. Read everything you can about alternative billing methods, but more importantly, become a student of value analysis. Consider small practice areas to pilot new billing strategies. Have your finance people run mock-parallel billing strategies on current projects. Think about how your marketing efforts could be enhanced by innovative billing methods.

U.S. Supreme Court Justice Stephen G. Breyer served as an honorary member on the commission, and wrote the foreword to the commission's report, making these salient comments with respect to the deleterious effects of hourly billing on the legal profession, which go far beyond merely limiting the profitability of legal firms:

Roscoe Pound wrote that the legal profession is characterized by a "spirit of public service." That spirit explains why so many lawyers respond "pro bono" to the needs of those who cannot afford to pay for legal assistance, why they participate in the work of the many government and nongovernment committees engaged in law reform, and why they teach to others, both inside and outside the profession, the values that have made the rule of law possible in America. Yet over the past four decades it has become increasingly difficult for many lawyers to put this spirit into practice.

The villain of the piece is what some call the "treadmill"—the continuous push to increase billable hours. As one lawyer has put it, the profession's obsession with billable hours is like "drinking water from a fire hose," and the result is that many lawyers are starting to drown. How can a practitioner undertake pro bono work, engage in law reform efforts, even attend bar association meetings, if that lawyer also must produce 2,100 or more billable hours each year, say 65 or 70 hours in the office each week. The answer is that most cannot, and for this, both the profession and the community suffer.

The Commission on Billable Hours hopes to begin to combat the problem by examining the billable hour itself. Does that kind of charge unnecessarily aggravate the pressures that threaten to confine the lawyer to the office, insulating him or her from the community? Moreover, does the billable hour contribute to or undermine a practitioner's ultimate goal—to provide clients with the best legal services possible? And to the extent billable hours are counterproductive on either or both counts, how, when, and to what extent, might it be possible to change billing methods?

The committee's technical task, then, concerns not just a better or more efficient way to run a law firm. It concerns how to create a life within the firm that permits lawyers, particularly younger lawyers, to lead lives in which there is time for family, for career, and for the community. Doing so is difficult. Yet I believe it is a challenge that cannot be declined, lest we abandon the very values that led many of us to choose this honorable profession. I am pleased that this committee has begun, in a very practical way, to address this critically important problem (American Bar Association: 2001–2002: vii).

Once again, the CPA profession will be following the legal profession's lead, away from the billable hour to value pricing. We applaud the efforts of the ABA, its president, and the commission's report, and are proud to make our own contribution to the ultimate death of the billable hour. It is simply not an ethical or just method for pricing intellectual capital. It is an idea from the day before yesterday, and it is time for it to be discarded onto the ash heap of history.

SUMMARY AND CONCLUSIONS

In the June 3–16, 2002, issue of *Accounting Today*, Roger Russell authored an article entitled "Value-Pricing Not Yet Au Courant: Do CPAs Lack Self-Esteem?" wherein he proclaimed: "The jury is still out on CPA Ron Baker's crusade to bury the billable hour in favor of value-pricing." What was interesting about the article were the comments from prominent consultants to the CPA profession. West Chester, Pennsylvania, consultant Donald Scholl, and Eustis, Florida, consultant Allan Boress, had this to say on the value pricing movement: "To truly do value-pricing a firm has to change its whole philosophy of how it renders services to clients." The concept will make additional progress over the next five years, but whether it becomes the industry standard is doubtful, according to Scholl. "Most accountants are reticent to talk about fees with clients at all, and to get them to sit down with a client and figure out what the engagement is worth really pushes the envelope a long way."

"CPAs despise change," said Allan Boress. "The reason value-pricing won't work is because CPAs won't make any changes that they don't have to," he said.

To Mr. Scholl we would say: Every other business has to price its products and services up front, and that is hardly pushing the envelope. In fact, it pushes the envelope to price *after* the engagement is over. No doubt it is true firms will have to radically change their philosophy of pricing, but so what? So have thousands of other businesses—especially those in the intellectual capital field—that discovered cost-plus pricing is not an effective pricing method to capture value.

We have tremendous respect for Allan Boress, but we are also much more optimistic about our colleagues' willingness to change, because we have seen so many adopt value pricing with alacrity. We do not agree with the notion that CPAs hate change; we think they are uncertain about the *consequences* of change, and that is the reason we have provided so much detail in this chapter: to show how other professionals have adopted these ideas successfully. The profession has, after all, gone through tremendous change in its 100-plus year history.

We have encountered mind-numbing opposition to value pricing from leading consultants, both inside and outside the profession. We always thought consultants were supposed to be change agents for the better, if they knew the solutions they suggested worked and stood the test of time. Adam Smith, the Austrian school of economists, and the other thinkers cited in this chapter were certainly not management gurus proposing another fad of the month. Their theories have been around for hundreds of years and have stood well the test of time. We have come to believe that consultants are sometimes as myopic and subject to the same entrenched orthodoxies as the industries they purport to improve. With behavior like this, it is interesting to ponder whether consultants are necessary at all.

In any event, this resistance to value pricing from the consultants is certainly not unusual; which brings to mind the late economist Julian Simon's struggle with airlines. If you have ever been bribed off an oversold airplane—with a free flight voucher, upgrade, or airline money equivalent—you have Mr. Simon to thank. Until 1978, travelers were bumped off overbooked planes rather capriciously (the airlines preferred to bump old people and military personnel on the theory they would be least likely to complain) and this caused enormous amounts of customer complaints and ill-will. Sometimes an entire flight would be cancelled and rebooked at proper capacity, causing even greater outrage. Worse yet, the problem fed upon itself, because passengers began to expect to be bumped and so would book several flights under various names to ensure a seat on at least one; this caused the airlines to increase bookings even more in order to insure decent load factors. A flight attendant friend who worked for United Air Lines told Simon of this problem:

> The next day, when shaving, it occurred to me that there must be a better way; indeed,
> an auction market could solve the problem, by finding those people who least mind

waiting for the next flight. The practical details fell into place before the shave was complete.

In 1966 and 1967, I wrote to all the airlines suggesting the scheme. The responses ranged from polite brush-offs to denials that they overbooked to assertions that the scheme could not work to derision.

. . . I was unable to persuade any airline (or the Civil Aeronautics Board) to conduct an experiment for even one day on a single airline at a single airport at a single boarding gate—an experiment that I believed would be sufficient, even with the inevitable breakdowns in any new activity. (Simon, 2002: 289–94).

Good ideas may be neglected, but they seldom die. It is natural for humans to resist new ideas and methods of operating. Yet, how can anyone deny the benefits of discussing terms, scope, and pricing up front with the customer when this practice is so ubiquitous it seems self-evident? For consultants to not act as change agents in this area is either malpractice or an irrational repudiation of the truth that exists all around them.

Fortunately, some consultants are beginning to see the light. McKinsey & Co. conducted a study of 1,000 companies and found that a 1 percent increase in price, at a constant sales volume, produced an average of 7.4 percent increase in profitability (a similar study by Accenture found an 11 percent, or more, increase in profits from a 1 percent price increase). It went further, to conclude that pricing has a greater impact on profitability than either sales volume increases, cost reductions, or improved efficiency, areas that usually receive much more attention among management, especially professionals.

This is precisely why pricing has become one of the most critical functions within businesses of all sizes. Thomas T. Nagle and Reed K. Holden (authors of *The Strategy and Tactics of Pricing: A Guide to Profitable Decision Making*), have probably done more in the past 20 years to put pricing in the title—and on the organizational charts—of many businesspeople. Organizations such as the Professional Pricing Society, among others, offer educational conferences, events, newsletters, and studies on a wide range of pricing issues and industries.

Even with all of this attention being paid to price in recent decades, Reed Holden estimates that only 15 percent of companies use value-based strategies to price their products or services. While the penetration is poor, the opportunities are large, with some businesses reporting double profits by utilizing these strategies. We believe the 15 percent estimate is even lower among professional service firms, probably in the range of 5 percent to 10 percent. Yet the opportunity is just as large for professional service firms as it is in other industries.

Søren Kierkegaard wrote, "Purity of soul is to will one thing." We have dedicated ourselves to eradicating, once and for all, the Almighty Billable Hour from the professions. The professionals in the firms of the future will *price on purpose*, and will be richly rewarded with what their customers already believe they are worth. They also will not utilize timesheets, another manifestation of the Almighty Hour, to which we now turn.

10

MEASURE WHAT COUNTS:
EFFECTIVENESS OVER EFFICIENCY

Things that matter most
Must never be at the mercy of things that matter least.
The first sign we don't know what we are doing is an obsession with numbers.

—Johann Wolfgang von Goethe

In the sixteenth century, a new word appeared in English dictionaries: *pantometry*, which means counting everything. Ever since, humans have been obsessed with counting things, from themselves and sheep to the amount of tobacco imported to the number of McDonald's hamburgers served. Being able to count and measure is one of the traits separating humans from animals. Lord Kelvin's famous phrase—slightly misquoted—is inscribed in the stones of the Social Science Building at the University of Chicago: "When you cannot measure it, when you cannot express it in numbers, your knowledge is of a meagre and unsatisfactory kind. . . . It may be the beginning of knowledge, but you have scarcely in your thoughts advanced to the stage of science (quoted in McCloskey, 2000: 80).

RON Today, we have all heard the famous saying (often referred to as the McKinsey Maxim, named after the famed consulting firm), "What you can measure you can manage." This has become such a cliché in the business world that it is either specious or meaningless: specious because companies have counted and measured things ever since the Italian Fra Luca Pacioli brought double-entry bookkeeping to the world in 1494, and meaningless because it does not tell us what ought to be measured. Measurement for measurement's sake is senseless, as quality pioneer Philip Crosby understood when he uttered, "Building a better scale doesn't change your weight."

PAUL During the four-day Accountants' Boot Camp programs, within the first hour, we projected a slide that boldly proclaimed: "What you can measure you can manage." When it appeared, you saw the accountants' eyes light up; then we made the accountants feel even better by asking them, "Who do you know that is great, in fact specially trained, at measurement? You are." It was as if, all of a sudden, they saw their true worth and value. So measurement of almost anything became the norm, and yet another group of pantometrists was unleashed!

RON The problem for the pantometrists is the same one facing businesspeople today: What should be measured? Facts and figures do not provide a context nor reveal the truth; we still need our imaginations and creativity. Jeremy Bentham, the founder of social utilitarianism, and author of *Introduction to the Principles of Morals and Legislation*, published in 1789, is famous for his theory that humankind is governed by two sovereign masters, pain and pleasure. He thought this pleasure-pain nexus needed quantification—what he termed *felicific calculus*—and he took great pains to try and measure both, with *utils*, as if one could put a numerical value on joy and sorrow. Bentham thought the ultimate goal of society should be the *greatest happiness principle*— "the greatest happiness of the greatest number." No doubt his insights led to the cost-benefit analysis, which states that a project should only be undertaken if the benefits outweigh the costs. Yet the bigger problem for Bentham was that numbers alone did not provide the answer on how to achieve happiness for everyone.

When Robert Malthus predicted mass starvation in his 1798 book *Essay on Population*—because population would grow at a geometric pace while food production increased only arithmetically—all the figures he looked at did not provide the solution to the alleged problem. It turned out he was wrong, largely because he did nothing but analyze the numbers and did not take into account the immeasurable ingenuity of humans to solve an ever-increasing range of problems.

The ultimate manifestation of this mentality was Robert McNamara, President John F. Kennedy's Secretary of Defense from 1961 to 1968, thereafter president of The World Bank. McNamara was an accounting instructor at Harvard Business School before World War II, then served as a specialist in operations research projects with the U.S. government during the war. After the war, he was hired by Henry Ford II—along with the so-called Whiz Kids—to revitalize the sagging profits of the Ford Motor Company. He brought a mechanistic mind-set to the War in Vietnam, trying to micromanage it by the numbers. He apologized for this ill-conceived strategy in his 1995 autobiography.

Blindly relying on measurements can obscure important realities. The ultimate problem with numbers and measurements is what they *don't* tell us, and how they provide a false sense of security—and control—that we know everything that is going on. In fact, one could put forth the argument—running counter to the McKinsey Maxim—that the most important things in life cannot be measured. Despite Bentham's noble attempt, how do you measure happiness? How do you measure love, joy, respect, or trust? How do you measure the success of your marriage?

Consider the traditional measurement of per capita income. Assume there is a family of two, and the wife has just given birth to their first child. Per capital income has just fallen by one-third, and if that is the right measurement—or even an approximation—of happiness, then the birth of a child should be among the worst moments in your life. But how many parents would feel this way? You cannot *measure* happiness;

it has to be *experienced*. There is something seriously wrong with a measurement that quantifies per capita wealth going down when a child is born, and increasing when a sheep is born (since it raises the Gross Domestic Product).

Another example of how measuring income cannot only mislead but actually obscure reality is by looking at the per capita income of the town of Stanford (at the California University) and East Palo Alto, California. If you were never to visit these two places and merely relied on income and wealth statistics, you would emphatically conclude that East Palo Alto is wealthier than Stanford, since most of the residents of Stanford are students, hence have relatively low incomes. If we are going to count and measure, we should do so only with those things that are *truly* meaningful.

In an intellectual capital world, the costs that exist in the tangible items of software and silicon—or the paper and binding of this book—are a tiny fraction of the value they provide. This is precisely why the cost-plus pricing mentality takes upon less significance in an economy predominantly driven by intellectual and human capital. Human beings do not lend themselves to easy measurements. Perhaps we need a corollary to the McKinsey Maxim, what author David Boyle calls the *McKinsey Fallacy*: What is really important cannot be measured.

Yet this corollary to the McKinsey Maxim will no doubt be met with tremendous resistance. It goes against the very grain of the MBA mind-set—the modern-day pantometrists—who are taught that everything needs to be quantified and counted. The Russian novelist and social critic Alexander Solzhenitsyn once said, "It is a very dangerous thing to speak against the fashion of the times." But we are going to do it anyway, and let us begin by reviewing how the McKinsey Maxim became the conventional wisdom.

THE GOSPEL OF EFFICIENCY

Why is it that when I buy a pair of hands, I always get a human being as well?

—Henry Ford

RON In the first decades of the twentieth century, the passion for efficiency swept the country, and was likened to a "secular Great Awakening." The efficiency experts of the day had ideas that were implemented in businesses, factories, hospitals, schools, churches, homes, and every level of government. It led to the foundation of some of the oldest surviving policy research organizations, such as Brookings Institution, the Twentieth Century Fund, and the National Bureau of Economic Research. Humankind has always been preoccupied with finding better and more efficient—and less time-consuming—ways to achieve desired results ever since the invention of fire.

Despite present-day management gurus who claim to have discovered the concept of core competency, in reality this a very old principle, which Adam Smith explicated in his treatise, *An Inquiry into the Nature and Causes of the Wealth of Nations*:

One man draws out the wire, another straightens it, a third cuts it, a fourth points it, a fifth grinds it at the top for receiving the head; to make the head requires two or three distinct operations; to put it on is a peculiar business; to whiten it is another; it is even a trade by itself to put them into paper. . . . I have seen a small manufactory of this kind where ten men only were employed and where some of them performed two or three distinct operations. But though they were very poor, and therefore but indifferently accommodated with the necessary machinery, they could, when they exerted themselves, make among them about twelve pounds of pins a day. There are in a pound upwards of four thousand pins of a middling size. Those ten persons, therefore, could make among them upwards of forty-eight thousand pins in a day. . . . But if they had all wrought separately and independently . . . they certainly could not each of them make twenty . . . perhaps not one pin a day (quoted in Dougherty, 2002: 53).

Smith's famous pin factory example illustrates the importance of the *division and specialization of labor*, a central cause of the wealth of nations Smith so eloquently wrote about. Henry Ford had a similar epiphany when touring a Chicago meatpacking plant, where he saw animal carcasses hung on an overhead rail being moved from butcher to butcher. When Ford inquired how long they had been processing meat like this, the reply was something to the effect that, "This is how we have done it for years." Hence a tradition in one industry became a quantum revolution in another.

The most famous preacher of the Efficiency Gospel was Frederick Winslow Taylor, who observed endless ways to make laborers' work more rational, quantifiable, and scientific, writing about the "science of shoveling" and the "law of heavy laboring," topics that today would most likely make for lackluster book sales, but in Taylor's time ushered in a new era of management thinking. Taylor was born on March 20, 1856, into a prominent Quaker family in an upper-middle class suburb of Philadelphia. As a teenager he became obsessed with cricket, which, like baseball, is a game where the statistics and batting averages are more exciting than the game itself. Allegedly, he never smoked or drank alcohol, tea, or coffee. And when he attended dances, he drew up charts classifying all the girls in attendance as attractive or ugly, and precisely calculated his time so he spent one-half in conversation with each.

Taylor became an industrial engineer testing his time-and-motion theories on the factory floor among his coworkers at the Midvale Steel Company in Philadelphia. As David Boyle explains in his wonderful book, *The Sum of Our Discontent: Why Numbers Make Us Irrational*, Taylor's experiments went something like this:

First, you break down any job into its component parts—as far as it would go, to the basic movements.

Next, you time each of those parts with a stopwatch to find out just how quickly they can be achieved by the quickest and most efficient workers.

Next, you get rid of any parts of the job that aren't necessary.

Then you add in about 40 percent to the time for unavoidable delays and rest. This bit was what he used to call "rule of thumb" before the idea of scientific management required that there be no such thing. It was always one of the most controversial parts of the package . . .

Finally, you organize your pay system so that the most efficient people can earn considerably more money by meeting the optimum times, while the average have to struggle to keep up (Boyle, 2001: 93).

Taylor took all the romance out of work, and instead of a "noble skill" it was sub-divided into a series of simple motions, much as the pin workers Adam Smith observed. All of the other aspects of human beings—creativity, initiative, innovative-ness, and the like—were to be done somewhere else in the organization, usually the province of upper management, who did the "thinking" while the workers did the "doing." This did not foster an environment of trustworthiness in the factories where Taylor's ideas were implemented, but it did yield increased productivity, which also increased the wages of the common worker. It was Taylor, after all, who replaced the phrase "working harder" with "working smarter."

Taylor's ideas were not implemented without friction, however. He viewed both managers and workers as "dumb oxen," and trade union opposition was on the increase. In 1915, Congress passed legislation, which stayed on the books until 1949, that banned Taylor's beloved stopwatches from government factories. Interestingly, Taylor met a bricklayer, Frank Gilbreth, in 1907, who had done his own time-and-motion analysis on laying bricks and was able to increase his output from 1,000 to 2,700 per day. Apparently, Gilbreth was more obsessed with his stopwatch than was Taylor, as 2 of his 12 children later wrote in a portrait of him titled *Cheaper by the Dozen*, later made into a Hollywood movie with Clifton Webb as Gilbreth. If Taylor was idiosyncratic, Gilbreth was an even stranger duck, as Boyle humorously points out:

> Gilbreth was obsessed with measuring, breaking down every manual operation into what he called "therbligs" (Gilbreth spelled backward). He buttoned his vest from the bottom up because it took four seconds less than buttoning it from the top down. He cut 17 sec-onds off his shaving time by using two brushes. Using two shavers cut 44 seconds, but then he cut himself and had to spend another two minutes looking for a plaster. He took most of his children with him on business trips and around factories, armed with pens and pads, but their home in Montclair, New Jersey, sounded a bit like Taylor's factories:
>
> [According to one of Boyle's children] "Dad installed process and work charts in the bathrooms. Every child old enough to write—and Dad expected his offspring to start writing at a tender age—was required to initial the chart in the morning, after he had brushed his teeth, taken a bath, combed his hair, and made his bed. At night each child had to weigh himself, plot the figure on a graph, and initial the process charts again after he had done his homework, washed his hands and face, and brushed his teeth. Mother wanted to have a place on the chart for saying prayers, but Dad said as far as he was con-cerned, prayers were voluntary" (Ibid: 100).

Gilbreth went on to eventually repudiate the validity of time-and-motion studies as unethical and "absolutely worthless." Taylor, however, pressed on, writing all of his theories down throughout the years, finally circulating them privately in 1911 in *The Principles of Scientific Management* (published later by Harper & Brothers) Taylor's theories have been credited with tripling output during World War II, making Mus-solini's trains run on time in Italy, German precision engineering, Lenin's Five-Year Plans, consumerism, Hitler's gas chambers, and the death of communism, all thanks to a simple stopwatch. No doubt Taylor's theories contributed to most of these, some more than others.

Peter Drucker credits Taylor with coining the terms *management* and *consultant* (Taylor's calling card identified him as a "Consultant to Management," and he charged the princely sum of $35 a day for his standard two-hour lecture), and for being the world's very first "knowledge worker." In his lecture, Taylor said every worker must ask two questions:

> Every day, year in and year out, each man should ask himself over and over again, two questions. First, "What is the name of the man I am now working for?" And having answered this definitely then, "What does this man want me to do, right now?" Not, "What ought I to do in the interests of the company I am working for?" Not, "What are the duties of the position I am filling?" Not, "What did I agree to do when I came here?" Not, "What should I do for my own best interest?" but plainly and simply, "What does this man want me to do?" (quoted in Ibid: 94).

In the winter of 1914, Taylor caught pneumonia and every morning he was in the hospital he arose out of bed to wind his precious watch. One morning, March 21, 1915, a nurse saw him winding it uncharacteristically early, 4:30 A.M. When she returned half-hour later, Taylor was dead, the day after his fifty-ninth birthday. Many of the so-called efficiency experts met an early death—makes you wonder what, exactly, they were saving all that time *for*?

FREDERICK TAYLOR ENTERS THE PROFESSIONS

RON Taylor's search for the "one best way" to use labor and material effectively and control productivity (not so much to monitor financial costs) swept all levels of the world's economic and social institutions. In an 1891 brochure for the Electric Signal Clock Company, the time clock named the Autocrat was featured, touting these benefits:

> "Gives military precision, and teaches practicality, promptness, and precision wherever adopted. A school, office, or factory installing this system is not at the caprice of a forgetful bell ringer, nor anyone's watch, as the office clock is now the standard time for the plant" [providing management and supervisors a means to extend their disciplinary reach beyond their vision].
> The 1914 catalog of the International Time Recording Company [later to become IBM] suggested that time clocks would "save money, enforce discipline and add to the productive time." Also, the time recorded induces punctuality by impressing the value of time on each individual (Levine, 1997: 67–68).

The manifestation of Taylor's theories in the professional service firm was the timesheet. Along with the Du Pont Return on Investment (ROI) formula, as early as 1945 legal firms began using timesheets as a way to monitor the costs and desired net income from each project, as discussed in Chapter 9. Although the timesheet was originally adopted as a *cost accounting* procedure, it quickly transmogrified into a tool to measure the *productivity* of the professional, then, ultimately, for *pricing* the professional's services.

This chapter will put the timesheet on trial for its life. In professional firms today, the timesheet serves multiple purposes, at least according to its staunchest defenders.

First and foremost, it is a *pricing* tool, allowing the firm to track the labor on any one job and set a price accordingly. Of course, this is nothing but the manifestation of Marx's labor theory of value. Second, the timesheet is used to gauge the *productivity and efficiency* of team members and keep control over their workflow. Third, they are used for *cost accounting*—or to a lesser extent, activity-based costing—in order to determine the profitability of any customer or job.

We have serious doubts that the timesheet is the most effective tool for all of these purposes, and we have already broken the link between time and pricing. Next we want to challenge the other two defenses and offer an alternative measurement system—known as Key Performance Indicators (KPIs)—to replace the timesheet. Before we get there, though, let us take another important historical detour and explain how the economics profession was getting into the counting and measuring act.

ECONOMISTS POSIT THEORIES

RON As schools and businesses were installing time clocks and conducting time-and-motion studies, and professional service firms began utilizing timesheets, to assist in implementing Taylor's theories, around the world the economics profession was developing national income and product statistics accounting to measure the macro-economic economy. In the United States, Simon Kuznets (1901–1985), a Russian-born economist and Harvard professor, invented the Gross National Product (now commonly known as the Gross Domestic Product) in the early 1940s. In 1971, he won the Nobel Prize for his seminal statistical work on national income.

Once we began to measure the economic performance of a national economy, the next logical step was to begin to *forecast* the performance of the economy. In order to do this, economists had to develop a plethora of economic indicators to measure where the economy was heading, by looking at where it had been. There is no reason to discuss how these indicators came about, or even their validity. On the contrary, we will focus on the purpose they serve and how there are different indicators for different purposes.

Economic indicators provide a snapshot of the economy's health. Similar to how a doctor checks your vital signs, an economist might check the vital signs of the economy by looking at Gross Domestic Product (GDP), Consumer Price Index (CPI), or the unemployment rate. Unlike management accountants and auditors, who tend to focus on lagging indicators—such as a business's financial reports—economists developed not only *lagging indicators*, but also *leading* and *coincident indicators*. These terms refer to the timing of the turning points of the indexes relative to those of the business cycle:

- *Leading indicators* anticipate the direction in which the economy is headed.
- *Coincident indicators* provide information about the current status of the economy.
- *Lagging indicators* change months after a downturn or upturn in the economy.

Here are the different types of indicators, originally produced by the Department of Commerce and now by the privately run Conference Board, which the government and other organizations use to measure aggregate economic activity and to get a sense of where the economy has been and where it is heading:

Leading Indicators: Anticipate a Business Cycle

Average workweek (manufacturing)

Initial unemployment claims

New orders for consumer goods and materials

Vendor performance

Plant and equipment orders

New-building permits for private housing units

Change in business inventories

Sensitive material prices

Stock prices (S&P 500)

M1 and M2 money supply

Change in consumer debt

Coincident Indicators: Run in Sync with Business Cycle

Number of employees on nonagricultural payrolls

Industrial production

Personal income minus transfer payments

Manufacturing and trade sales volume

Civilian employment to population ratio

Gross Domestic Product

Lagging indicators: Follow Changes in Business Cycle

Average duration of unemployment

Manufacturing and trade inventories

Commercial loans

Ratio of consumer debt to personal income

Change in labor cost per unit of output, manufacturing

Short-term interest rates

This is not to claim that economists can predict the future; far from it. These indicators, some have suggested, failed to predict *any* of the last three American recessions. A tremendous amount of history supports the observation that no one can predict the future. (For a tremendous book on this subject, see *The Experts Speak: The Definitive Compendium of Authoritative Misinformation*, by Christopher Cerf and

Victor Navasky, from the Institute of Expertology, whose sole purpose is to collect predictions from prominent people and publish them for posterity. There's an old joke that asks: Why did God create economists? Answer: To make weather forecasters look good.) No doubt these indicators have expanded our knowledge of how an economy operates, and may even provide a clue as to where it is heading, but they still comprise a compendium of averages, and averages can be very misleading—on average, everyone in the United States has one testicle. Further, the debate over which indicators should be used is by no means settled theory. Keynesian economists focus on demand-side indicators, while monetarists focus on the money supply; and supply-siders concentrate on business investment, entrepreneurial growth, venture capital investments, and production.

What these indicators do teach us is how to develop a theory about where the economy is heading. Recall from Chapter 2 that a theory should be able to explain, predict, or prescribe certain outcomes or behaviors. The indicators noted here are just that: they are theories, testable in the real world to see how well they accomplish those three goals. If the theories are falsified, then they are revised and tested again. Taylor developed theories on efficiency that were tested in organizations the world over, and found to be valid. It is a much easier task to develop a set of indicators for a business than it is for an entire economy.

Yet when one examines the major indicators in the business world, and especially the ones focused on by accountants, they are financial indicators such as the balance sheet, income statement, and statement of cash flows. These are examples of *lagging* indicators, as they report on where the business has been. This may or may not be useful in determining where the business is headed. Real-time financial statements would rise to the level of *coincident* indicators, since they would track present performance. But what every business should develop is a set of *leading* indicators that would enable it to get a sense of what direction the business is heading.

ACCOUNTING IS NOT A THEORY

RON Developing leading indicators requires evolving a set of falsifiable theories the business can test to determine the relationship between those indicators and future financial performance. The accounting profession has simply not taken a lead in this area. The reason for this may be explained by a joke told by a graduate economics student:

> One day in microeconomics, the professor was writing up the typical "underlying assumptions" in preparation to explain a new model. I turned to my friend and asked, "What would Economics be without assumptions?" He thought for a moment, then replied, "Accounting."

Accounting is not a theory. Despite the fact that the CPA exam used to test for accounting theory, the principles of accounting are not a theory. They are simply a set of guidelines, rules, and procedures for measuring financial items such as assets, liabilities, revenues, and expenses, grounded by postulates such as relevance, reliability, and materiality. Is it any wonder the accounting profession has not taken the lead in movements such as the Balanced Scorecard, or social and environmental audits, which attempt to look at more indicators than merely historical financial performance metrics? Yet every management team should develop a set of leading indicators they can use to properly lead the business to profitability and excellence.

Try this thought experiment. You are the CEO of Continental Airlines: Which leading indicators would you want to look at on a daily—or even hourly or shorter—basis to determine whether Continental was fulfilling its mission of flying passengers around the world profitably. It is relatively easy to develop *lagging* indicators, such as profit, revenue per passenger mile, cost per passenger mile, repeat customer bookings, frequent-flyer miles earned, and so on. But those are lagging indicators, and all of the employees would not be able to influence those results on a day-to-day basis. How would the baggage handler's behavior change as a result of learning last month's load factor?

You could certainly develop *coincident* indicators, by tracking all of the lagging indicators mentioned earlier in real time; and no doubt the airlines do this internally to some extent. But that still does not necessarily help the flight crews, baggage handlers, or food service caterers fulfill the goals and objectives of the airline. What are needed are leading indicators that have some *predictive* power; in other words, they anticipate the financial results of Continental. In his book, *From Worst to First: Behind the Scenes of Continental's Remarkable Comeback*, Gordon Bethune details how he was able to turn around the failed airline (which had filed for Chapter 7 bankruptcy twice in the preceding decade) between February 1994 and 1997, turning it into one of the best and most profitable airlines in the sky. It is a remarkable story, and it illustrates the importance of utilizing leading KPIs to focus the entire organization on its purpose and mission. Bethune basically tracked, daily, three leading KPIs:

- On-time arrival
- Lost luggage
- Customer complaints

Continental ranked dead last in all of these indicators, which are also measured by the Department of Transportation. Bethune analyzed the problems—and there were many—and discovered the culture of the airline was focused on driving down cost per available seat mile (the standard measure of cost in the airline industry). It cut costs at every opportunity, by packing the planes with more seats, reducing the food and drink portions, paying its people poorly, and so forth. It believed its mission was to cut costs; but as Bethune constantly pointed out, "We aren't in business to save money, we are in business to put out a good product. . . . You can make a pizza so cheap nobody wants to eat it. And you can make an airline so cheap nobody wants to fly it" (Bethune, 1998: 123, 50). There is an enormous difference between controlling costs and being cheap. A business must make investments that deliver value to the customer.

This goes back to Peter Drucker's marketing concept and the sole purpose of a business: to create wealth for its customers, not simply to be efficient. What makes the three indicators just listed leading is they measure success the same way the customer does. And that is critical, because ultimately the success of any business is a result of loyal customers who return. In other words, profit is a lagging indicator of what is in the hearts and minds of your customers. A leading indicator, by definition, should measure success the same way the customer does. None of the three indicators would show up on a financial statement, but as the airlines have learned over the years—by testing the theory—they have a predictive correlation with profits. Any indicator that can be had from a financial statement is most likely a lagging—or at best coincident—indicator, since most leading indicators are nonfinancial in nature. The other important point about the three indicators is that *every* employee of Continental can influence the outcome of each of them, from the baggage handlers and flight crews to the gate agents and reservation operators. It is worth quoting Bethune at length on this vital point:

> Before I came to work at Continental, the company wanted to be a successful airline. But it measured only one thing: cost. That made Continental an airline that ran on low cost, paid its employees poorly, and delivered a really, really crappy product. That was not what our customers wanted (Ibid: 233).
>
> Don't forget, Continental got what it seemed to want at the time: By saying that cost was the thing that defined its success, Continental's management got everybody to focus on cost. That turned out to be the wrong thing to focus on, though, and they just couldn't get that through their heads. It was what they focused on, it was what they measured, and they simply believed that somehow it would lead to success. That's why, even before the organization almost gave up the ghost, even when it was still trying as hard as it could, Continental just couldn't find the key to success—because the key didn't reside in cost, and cost was the main thing Continental focused on (Ibid: 233).
>
> When we're looking for goals for an entire company, we make sure our employees know what we're going for: to get the planes on time, not to aim for a certain return on investment. Goals such as certain equity or debt ratios or interest percentages work fine for the accountants, just as striving to repair a specific number of engines or reduce the number of seconds before the phone gets answered are goals set for particular departments. But when it concerns the whole company, we need a companywide goal—something that employees can immediately identify (Ibid: 208).
>
> At the risk of oversimplifying, this is basically the key to running a successful business. You have to decide what constitutes success. If it's a fishing contest, are we trying to catch the heaviest fish or the longest fish? If it's a baseball game, what makes an out and what scores a run? If it's an airline, what are the indications that it is doing well? You have to explain to the people who work with you what those are, and the people have to buy into that. You have to measure that, and let them know how you're going to measure it. And you have to reward them if they succeed. That's it (Ibid: 232).
>
> Your employees are very smart. They pay close attention. What you're measuring and rewarding, they're going to do. So even if you define success right but you still measure and reward the wrong thing, your employees are going to figure out what you're measuring and give you that. If we had said that our goal was to be a great airline that gets its planes to their destinations on time and treats its customers right, but we also said that we were going to measure that by checking attendance very closely and making sure that people followed the rules of the employee manual [which Bethune burned in the park-

ing lot upon becoming CEO] to the letter, we would have had the best goal in the world, but we would have ended up with very prompt employees who kept their noses in their manuals. And, probably, we would have had a pretty lousy airline (Ibid: 234).

This is one of the most common problems in businesses. Businesses fail because they want the right things but measure the wrong things—or they measure the right things in the wrong way, so they get the wrong results. Remember? Define success the way your customers define it (Ibid: 233).

Obviously the KPIs for the airline industry will evolve over time, since they deal with customer expectations, which are dynamic and not static. Since these KPIs are an actual theory, they must constantly be tested and falsified, and new ones developed to reflect changing market conditions. These KPIs are not only critical for internal management, but are also becoming information that outside investors and other third parties are interested in to assess the health and direction of the business. Employee and customer satisfaction information, sales and marketing success measurements, brand value, percentage of revenue derived from new products offered, number of patents received, and a host of other measurements that one cannot find on the company's financial statements are beginning to be demanded by third parties.

To make the task even more challenging, no two businesses will use the exact same KPIs, although certain standards can be established for an industry, such as the "Triple Crown" criteria discussed for the airlines. Dell Computer, for instance, has developed a customer "dashboard" that measures three critical success factors for its business: order fulfillment, product performance, and service support. These critical success factors are sometimes referred to as a dashboard because they serve the same purpose the dashboard in an automobile does: They inform the driver of the key measurements that he or she wants to constantly monitor and are essential to keep the car moving forward—fuel capacity, speed, RPMs, temperature, oil pressure, and so forth.

Lexus considers the lifetime ownership costs to be an essential KPI for the customer, and it works diligently to drive down the lifetime costs of owning a Lexus. This is accomplished by using high-quality parts in the design and the development of the Certified Preowned Auto Program that enables dealers to recondition used cars and offer a manufacturer's warranty for up to 100,000 miles, thereby increasing the resale value of a Lexus, which lowers the lifetime cost of ownership. Lexus's parent company, Toyota, also uses this lifetime ownership cost as a KPI.

Before we proceed, keep in mind that for a KPI to be a leading indicator, it must define success the same way the customer does.

IT'S 12:41 A.M.: DO YOU KNOW WHERE YOUR PACKAGE—AND CPA—ARE?

RON It is September 9, 2002, and two CPAs depart at noon from two different Bay Area airports; they converge on Memphis, Tennessee, International Airport by 10:00 P.M. that evening. Precisely at 10:30 P.M., they are met by Karl, the manager of Quality & Process Improvement, at FedEx. As they drive around the Memphis terminal and approach the 400-acre FedEx facility, they are taken aback by its enormous size. They enter the facility at 11:15 P.M., are met and greeted warmly by various FedEx representatives, given guest name badges, and ushered through metal detectors—this is, after all, an airport—and into the central hub of FedEx.

That night, approximately 174 aircraft from points around the world will land in Memphis, as 9,000 FedEx team members unload, sort, and reload between 1.2 and 1.5 million packages. All of this activity will take place between 10:30 P.M. and 4:45 A.M., in an amazing display of coordination, efficiency, timeliness, and effectiveness. More than 400 miles of conveyors will be used to sort the packages, as they pass through laser scanners that capture a wealth of information, such as the destination address that guides each package from the Primary Sort to the Secondary Sort area. There are video terminals everywhere showing the countdown and projected times various flights must be loaded to make the demanding on-time delivery goals (talk about leading indicators). The CPAs are shown the central control room where all of the estimated times are counted and tracked and all the problems are handled.

Throughout the early A.M. the planes are loaded and the pilots await word from the Control Center. In 90-second bursts, each plane takes off for its respective destination, its packages to be unloaded and placed onto a fleet of 50,000 delivery vehicles throughout the world and hand-carried to their destinations. Approximately one-half of the total volume of FedEx passes through the Memphis hub, with the remaining 50 percent processed in mini-hubs throughout the country.

It is the FedEx value statement of People-Service-Profits put in motion every night. As the CPAs are shuttled around to the various tour points, they drive past the airplanes and one of them notices a first name painted underneath the pilot's window of each aircraft. He asks if that is the pilot's name and is told, no, it is the name chosen from a lottery drawing in which all FedEx team members are eligible to participate. Each time a plane is painted, a new name is drawn and the plane is dedicated to that person—usually a child of a FedEx team member. The CPAs wonder how it must feel for a ten-year-old to have his or her name on a FedEx airplane!

Most of the 9,000 team members are part-time, and have jobs elsewhere. However, FedEx provides them with full-time-equivalent benefits—such as health insurance, 401(k) and a defined benefit pension plan (for example, the CPAs' tour guide works during the day for a not-for-profit, and said FedEx was his "retirement").

It is truly an amazing sight, and FedEx has come along way from its first day of operations on March 12, 1973, when it had only six packages to deliver—four of which were from salespeople testing the system, and only two from paying customers. Not bad for Fred Smith, a guy who got a "C" on his term paper that contained the idea for FedEx.

For many years, FedEx operated under the 95 percent rule, which was a curve that showed to improve on-time delivery beyond 95 percent would be cost-prohibitive and would require a price not acceptable to the majority of its customers. Conversely, to drop below 95 percent on-time delivery would also be unacceptable to the customer, so 95 percent was thought to be the optimal operating level, both in profitability and customer service. As Michael Basch explains in his book *Customer Culture: How FedEx and Other Great Companies Put the Customer First Every Day*:

Fred Smith has a way of standing back from the business and challenging the basic tenets of the business. One day he challenged the "95 percent rule" —a sacred cow since the very early days.

"If we handle a million packages a day and we mess up 5 percent, that means we mess up 50,000 packages a day," he reasoned. "And since one person ships to another, that means we've disappointed 100,000 people each day. It doesn't take a rocket scientist to figure out that before long you've disappointed everyone in America who ships or receives packages."

Then he created what he called a Hierarchy of Horrors. Of the 5 percent disappointments, what is the worst thing you can do to the customer? What is the next worst thing, and so on? He and his senior management team identified eight major horrors (Basch, 2002: 162).

The so-called Hierarchy of Horrors was the genesis for the FedEx Service Quality Index (SQI), which is a system of weighted KPIs that measure the functions of critical importance to the customer. The SQI measures the following functions, each weighted according to the degree of customer aggravation caused by a failure to perform. The number of "average daily failure points" is multiplied by that component's assigned weight to calculate the SQI:

Item	Weight
Right-day late-service failures	1
Wrong-day late-service failures	5
Traces	1
Complaints reopened by customers	5
Missing points of delivery	1
Invoice adjustments requested	1
Missed pickups	10
Damaged packages	10
Lost packages	10
Overgoods	5
Abandoned calls	1
International SQI indicator	1 (Albrecht and Zemke, 2002: 94)

Since being placed in service in 1987, the SQI has enabled FedEx to increase its on-time delivery performance from 95 percent to 99.7 percent without adding significant marginal costs. FedEx credits team member commitment for achieving this outstanding result, similar to Bethune's turnaround of Continental Airlines.

The most critical technology that enables FedEx, and its customers, to track every single package anywhere in the system is its sophisticated package-tracking system, now known as COSMOS®, for the FedEx Customer-Oriented Service and Management Operating System. COSMOS monitors the movement of all shipments within the FedEx network—more than 3 million each business day. Customers can tap into COSMOS via the Internet to verify a shipment's status—and they do so millions of times each month.

When Fred Smith implemented the tracking system, many asked why he would invest such large sums of money in a technology that would not speed up delivery by one second. But that was not the point. By providing FedEx customers real-time access to their package information, he was creating an *excuseless culture* inside FedEx, by designing a system that held all team members accountable to the success factors important to the customer.

We have always used FedEx as an example of Key Performance Indicators that should be used in professional service firms, and have discussed the implications of what we had learned from FedEx for the firm of the future.

KPIs FOR THE FIRM OF THE FUTURE

RON When developing theories, one has to make sure they are testable based upon observed reality, and that they make sense in explaining the actual behavior.

> A scientist has two large jars before him, one containing many fleas, the other empty. He gently removes a flea from the flea jar, places it on the table before the empty jar, steps back, and commands, "Jump," whereupon the flea jumps into the empty jar. Method-ically he gently removes each flea, places it on the table, says "Jump," and the flea jumps into the originally empty jar.
>
> When he has transferred all the fleas in this way, he removes one from the now full jar, carefully pulls off its back legs, and places it on the table before the original jar. He commands, "Jump," but the flea does not move. He takes another flea from the jar, care-fully pulls off its back legs, and places it on the table. Again he commands "Jump," but the flea does not move. Methodically he goes through this same procedure with the remaining fleas, and gets the same results. The scientist beamingly records in his note-book: "A flea when its back legs are pulled off, cannot hear" (Paulos, 2000: 129–30).

British philosopher Alfred North Whitehead defined the *fallacy of misplaced concreteness*—the mistake of confusing the manifestation of something with the thing itself. Every doctor knows a fever is not a disease, merely a manifestation of one, and it is important to diagnose and treat the disease, not just the fever. A golfer does not have a scratch handicap, he or she swings the clubs, and if he or she does so with enough skill, a scratch handicap will be the result.

It is the same with profit—it is a lagging indicator of customer behavior. The point of the Continental Airlines and FedEx examples is important and goes to the heart of what a professional service firm should measure. Who would suggest customers of professional service firms define success by how many hours are logged on a timesheet? Is this the right metric to track? What, exactly, does it measure? And why do firms everywhere devote such an enormous amount of time completing, tracking, and printing out reports based upon billable hours? We would suggest there is an enor-mous gap between what firm leaders want their team members to do—charge hours—and what the customer wants them to do.

Let us be clear: Timesheets are a *lagging* indicator. They in no way measure the success of a professional in the same manner a customer does. It would be as if the air-lines tracked the amount of time the planes spent in the air instead of whether they arrived on time. Before we can measure, we must first understand. Since it is impor-tant to recall how customers define the success—and failure—of their professionals, let us reexamine why we lose customers. We discussed this in Chapter 9, but will review here in order to look at these factors from a different perspective, one of KPI development.

According to the Aquila and Koltin article, the top seven reasons why people leave their accountant were:

1. **My accountant just doesn't treat me right."** [Two-thirds of the responses].

2. CPAs ignore clients.

3. CPAs fail to cooperate.

4. CPAs let partner contact lapse.

5. CPAs do not keep clients informed.

6. CPAs assume clients are technicians.

7. CPAs use clients as a training ground [for new team members]. (Aquila and Koltin, 1992: 67–70)

Now recall the Rockefeller Corporation study on why customers defect:

1% The customer dies.
3% The customer moves away.
5% The customer has a friend [who provides the service].
9% The customer is lost to a competitor.
14% The customer is dissatisfied with [some aspect] of the service.
68% **The customer believes you don't care about them.**

And why people select accountants:

- Interpersonal skills
- Aggressiveness
- Interest in the customer
- Ability to explain procedures in terms the customer can understand
- Willingness to give advice
- Perceived honesty (Winston, 1995: 170)

David Maister, in *The Trusted Advisor*, offers the most commonly expressed customer suggestions regarding what they want from their professional relationship:

1. Make an impact on our business, don't just be visible.

2. Do more things "on spec" (i.e., invest your time on preliminary work in new areas).

3. Spend more time helping us think, and helping us develop strategies.

4. Lead our thinking. Tell us what our business is going to look like 5 or 10 years from now.

5. *Jump* on any new pieces of information we have, so you can stay up-to-date on what's going on in our business. Use our data to give us an extra level of analysis. Ask for it, don't wait for us to give it to you.

6. Schedule some off-site meetings together. Join us for brainstorming sessions about our business.

7. Make an extra effort to understand how our business works: sit in on our meetings.

8. Help us see how we compare to others, both within and outside our industry.

9. Tell me why our competitors are doing what they're doing.

10. Discuss with us other things we should be doing; we welcome any and all ideas! (Maister, et. al., 2000: 180).

If a professional service firm wanted to develop leading KPIs, shouldn't it study these lists—both the professions' "hierarchy of horrors," to borrow Fred Smith's phrase, and those services customers desire—to determine how it can create KPIs that would either discourage—or encourage—the behavior described in them? This requires modeling a theory of factors important to measure and reward, no small task for the professions. And in our experience with thousands of firms around the world, very few have taken the time to do this, let alone think about it.

Fortunately, we have been able to conduct hundreds of workshops on this very issue, and have had professionals from all categories brainstorm to come up with some KPIs for a professional service firm. We won't share all of them with you, for two reasons: one, some are much better than others; more important, we have found that presenting too many KPIs is overwhelming to the average firm, leaving members with analysis paralysis, which means they stick to their timesheets. We believe the following KPIs are a superior alternative to timesheets, and as of this writing there are dozens of firms we know that have trashed their timesheets and replaced them with KPIs from among the following.

It is important to note there is ample evidence that between 3 to 10 KPIs are enough for *any* business to have predictive power of the key value drivers for customers. We provided enough here so you can at least begin to think in this direction and perhaps develop even better ones for your particular firm. They are broken down between firmwide and individual team member KPIs:

Firmwide KPIs: Velocity

Turnaround time

Completed jobs/uncompleted jobs (ratio)

Firmwide KPIs: Financial

Revenue per person

Labor as a percentage of gross revenue

Innovation sales

Net income percentage

Profit per partner

Firmwide KPIs: Pricing

Percentage of FPAs rejected

Average difference between initial and final price

Percentage of reservation, hope-for and pump-fist price realizations

Firmwide KPIs: Customer

Customer loyalty

Share of customer wallet

Value gap

Percentage of revenue from "A," "B," "C," "D," and "F" customers

Customer churn

Forced churn

Team Member KPIs

Marginal contribution to firm revenue

Customer feedback

Effective listening skills

Effective communication skills

Risk taking, innovation, and creativity

Knowledge elicitation

Effective knowledge producer/consumer

Ability to deal with change

Continuous learning

Effective delegator

Mentoring and coaching skills

Personal development

Personal marketing plan

Professional pride

Number of customer contacts per week

Please keep in mind we are emphatically *not* suggesting you adopt all 31 KPIs shown here. *Do not boil the ocean.* If you try to measure too many KPIs, you end up knowing nothing, and you will have replaced the timesheet method with something even more burdensome, as Jeffrey Pfeffer, the Thomas D. Dee Professor of Organizational Behavior at Stanford Graduate School of Business, recently said in an interview for *Fast Company*:

There's an old saying in business: What gets measured is what gets done. What's happening today is the flip side of that. Measurement has become a tyranny that makes sure that nothing gets done.

I've developed what I like to call the Otis Redding Theory of Measurement, which is named for his song "(Sittin' on) the Dock of the Bay." In that song, Redding sings, "I can't do what 10 people tell me to do, so I guess I'll remain the same." That line sounds as if it could be about companies' misconceptions about measurement.

Companies have managed to convince themselves that, since what gets measured is what gets done, the more they measure, the more stuff will get done. Last summer, I met a woman who works for a large oil company, and she told me that the company has 105 measures for which she is responsible. So I asked her, "How many of those 105 measures do you pay attention to?" Her answer? "None." Because in the end, she's measuring so many things that she doesn't pay attention to any of them—105 equals zero (Pfeffer, 2000).

Selecting the Right KPIs for Your Firm

Excellence is an art won by training and habituation.
We are what we repeatedly do.

—Aristotle

There ain't no rules around here! We're trying to accomplish something!

—Thomas Edison

When choosing your firm's KPIs, do not overintellectualize the process. Selecting KPIs is not merely a matter of left-brain analysis; your firm's right-brain is important, too. You are testing a theory, which will greatly influence what you are measuring and observing. You are looking for KPIs that will measure and reward results over activities, output over input, performance over methodology, responsibilities over procedures, and effectiveness over efficiency. Timesheets measure efforts. But no customer buys efforts, they buy results, so we must align our metrics with the desired behavior. The old joke among physicians applies here, where the surgeon is admiring his competence, "The operation was a complete success! Although the patient died, we kept him in perfect electrolyte balance throughout!"

Let us examine each of the firmwide and team member KPIs listed, and explain their logic, the results they are trying to measure, and the behavior they are trying to encourage.

Turnaround Time. Michael Dell likes to refer to the time lag between a customer placing an order and the company assembling and shipping the finished product as *velocity*. We believe professional service firms should also be diligent about tracking when each project comes in, establishing a desired completion date and measuring the percentage of on-time delivery. This prevents procrastination, missed deadlines, and projects lingering in the firm while the customer is kept in the dark.

Borrowing Fred Smith's philosophy of creating an *excuseless culture*, imagine installing 360-degree webcams everywhere in your firm. Also imagine your customers could log on to your secure Web site, type in their name and password, and the appropriate web camera would find their file and give them a real-time picture of it, probably laying on a partner's floor or credenza awaiting review. Would this change the way work moved through your firm? Would this hold the firm accountable for results, not merely efforts? FedEx and UPS do exactly this, and in fact some of the larger law firms utilize intranets that provide their customers with real-time access to the work being performed on their behalf. Even some daycare facilities have installed webcams so parents can watch their child(ren) over the Internet while at work. This one metric would go a long way to solving most of the reasons customers defect (not kept informed, customers feel ignored, and so on).

The turnaround KPI also implements Peter Drucker's recipe for avoiding the pitfalls of procrastination, by implementing the alliterative triad of steps:

> Definition, delegation, and deadline. The executive needed to define the problem or the task, delegate accountability to a specific person, along with responsibility for the specific thing to be accomplished, and establish a firm deadline for completion. The definition ensured a sense of purpose, the delegation identified who was going to do the actual work, and the deadline substituted action for inertia (quoted in Flaherty, 1999: 328).

It is an interesting question whether the firm should communicate a deadline to the customer. We have encountered firms that do, and they swear by this policy and say it has improved customer service and communication dramatically. Obviously, the date has to be extended in some circumstances if the customer has not provided all of the information, but it is hard to argue with the results these firms have had by informing the customers of the date they can expect their work to be completed.

If that makes you too nervous, a good interim step is to simply set an *internal* deadline, and hold the team members accountable for their percentage of on-time completions (better yet, have the team decide on the deadline). Turnaround time can be tracked at the firmwide level, as well as the team member level. If a particular team member is missing deadlines, it is a good indication he or she has been given too much work, does not have adequate training to do what has been assigned, is unclear on the assignment responsibilities, or is simply not up to the job. Whichever it is, the turnaround time provides a leading indicator to firm executives to intervene and correct any problems. The timesheet does not provide this advantage, because once it has been discovered the problems are history.

If we had to commit to only *one* KPI for a firm, we would select turnaround time. It will bring to light—quickly—a lot of the reasons customers become dissatisfied with their professionals. Every firm that has replaced timesheets with KPIs has implemented the turnaround time KPI, as we strongly suggest.

Completed Jobs/Uncompleted Jobs (Ratio).   This KPI has been used by tax firms that handle a volume of work within the busy season. Each team member knows how many returns he or she is responsible for, and the ratio of completion is tracked to project capacity into the future. Although not a substitute for the turnaround time KPI, this KPI is being utilized in some firms that have replaced their timesheets.

Revenue Per Person.   This is a financial KPI, and is simply gross firm revenue divided by the number of full-time equivalent team members in the firm (either professionals or the whole team, depending on what type of statistics you are comparing against). This result is then benchmarked against other firms to see how the firm compares to the competition. Although this is a lagging indicator, it can be used to formulate specific growth and revenue goals for the firm's future. (Hint: Any KPI that can be obtained from a financial statement is usually a *lagging*—or if the information is timely enough, *coincident*—indicator.)

The natural tendency to divide the revenue per person one more time by the number of each person's billable hours is superfluous. What, exactly, does that say about the firm? Do most firms do it simply because everyone else does? Is not revenue per person just as adequate a comparison? Why break this number down further, especially since no customer buys hours?

Labor as a Percentage of Gross Revenue.   Although another lagging indicator, this is a useful metric for benchmarking against the competition. Not only the raw percentage, but also the percentage change is important. Why is it increasing or decreasing? Do we need to expand or reduce our capacity?

Innovation Sales.   This metric measures revenue from services introduced in recent years, and measures the firm's innovation in offering additional services to its customers. It is an essential measurement to determine the lifetime value of the firm to the customer, as we discussed in Chapter 8. For example, Hewlett-Packard wants 50 percent of its revenue from products that did not exist two years ago. Intel achieves100 percent of its revenues from products developed within the last three years. 3M targets 30 percent from products that did not exist four years ago.

Firms spend an enormous amount of resources measuring billable hours and realization rates, but we have found very few that measure innovation sales and make that figure a key component of its strategic vision. If the firm's executives determine a KPI is important, then it takes on an aura of a leading indicator, or perhaps a value indicator, since we are what we measure. We are not claiming firms are anti-innovation; it is more a matter of not being pro-innovation, by not having measurements and reward systems in place to encourage this behavior. Innovation is essential to creating new wealth, and as Gary Hamel asks: "What does it matter to an investor if a company is earning its cost of capital if its rivals are capturing the lion's share of new wealth in an industry?" (Hamel, 2000: 285).

Net Income Percentage and Profit Per Partner.   Another set of lagging indicators, but useful benchmarks to compare to the competition. Again, we are not just interested in the absolute percentage and profit, but also the change. Why is it increasing or decreasing? Is the firm making adequate investments in its intellectual capital for the future, or is it consuming all of its seed corn in partner draws and wages?

Percentage of FPAs Rejected.   To change the firm's culture to one that prices on purpose, we offer three KPIs that can be used to measure your rate of success—and failure—in implementing the new pricing paradigm. The percentage of FPAs rejected is a way to track the firm's success rate in getting customers to enter into a long-term relationship with the firm. Do not fall into the trap of believing the optimal percentage to be 100 percent; that is a sign you are taking on the wrong type of customer or not pricing your work in accordance with value.

Average Difference between Initial and Final Price.   Another metric to determine pricing for value and the firm's capability to understand, communicate, convince, and capture the value the firm is delivering to the customer. If this gap is too large, it could be a sign the firm is not doing an adequate job qualifying the customer or determining exactly what the customer needs. It could also signal the firm is not getting enough customer involvement into the design and terms of the FPA.

Percentage of Reservation, Hope-for, and Pump-Fist Price Realizations.   This is another leading indicator that the firm is capturing the value from its offerings. Too high a percentage of pump-fist price realizations could signal it is being set too low. This is why postmortem pricing analysis is so important, for the firm to make pricing a core competency among its professionals. We believe pump-fist realization should be between 20 and 40 percent of the time, while hope-for realization should be 50 percent, and reservation 10 to 30 percent.

Customer Loyalty.   Frederick Reichheld, in his work with Bain & Company, estimates that fewer than 20 percent of corporate leaders rigorously track customer retention. For professional service firms, which derive anywhere from 80 to 95 percent of their revenue from existing customers, this is a big mistake. Also, when you consider it costs an average of 4 to 11 times more to acquire a customer than to retain one, this metric must become part of the firm's value system.

Share of Customer Wallet.   This changes the firm's focus from *market* share and revenue growth to *better* growth by increasing the percentage the firm derives from each customer's budget for professional services. To increase this share over time, the firm must explain up front to all customers that share of wallet is an important part of their long-term relationship. Unless you have a strategic reason for doing so, the firm should not allow its customers to distribute their work among many firms. You should make it part of the expectation with each customer that you want the lion's share of the work, over the long run. This ensures a deeper relationship, increased loyalty, premium prices, higher switching costs, and greater profitability.

Value Gap.   This measurement attempts to display the gap between how much we could be yielding from our customers and how much we actually are. It is an excellent way to reward cross-selling additional services, increase the lifetime value of the firm to the customers, and gain a larger percentage of the customer's wallet. What actions can your firm take to close the value gap?

Percentage of Revenue from "A," "B," "C," "D," and "F" Customers.   This measures how your firm's fixed capacity is allocated between first-class, business-class, full-fare coach, coach, and bereavement fare passengers. You should be getting your share of "A" and "B" customers, otherwise you are misallocating your capacity to customers who do not value your total offering.

Customer Churn. This is another customer loyalty and defection metric. You simply divide the number of customers lost by the number of customers gained. You can also use lost-customer revenue divided by new-customer revenue. If you are in the process of firing customers, this rate will obviously increase, which is fine. You want to make sure, however, that you are churning the "C," "D," and "F" customers, as opposed to the "A" and "B" customers.

Forced Churn. As was discussed in Chapter 8, this is an excellent method to adopt if you want to abandon your low-end customers gradually. Depending on the number of "C," "D," and "F" customers you have, the forced churn would dictate you fire somewhere between one and four old customers for every new one you acquire. It is an excellent method to upgrade the customers in your airplane.

> NOTE: Below we analyze individual team member KPIs. Obviously some of the firmwide KPIs, such as turnaround time and completed versus uncompleted jobs and the pricing KPIs, can be tracked on an individual basis. We are attempting to develop measurements that will shape team member behaviors in ways the customers value. If we are what we measure, it is time we measured what we want to be. You will notice that some of these KPIs are "fuzzy," "subjective," and are considered "soft measures" by some of the critics who prefer "hard" and "objective" measures (even if they measure things that are not important to the customer, such as billable hours). It is as if they would rather be totally correct about the *wrong* question than approximately wrong about the *right* question. We take the position that it is better to be vaguely right about a soft measure than precisely wrong about a hard measure. We have attempted to develop team member KPIs that supplant bureaucratic rules and billable hour quotas for measurements the customer deems important, since they are the ultimate arbiter of success. These types of KPIs do what no supervisor or team leader can: they guide performance from an externally controlled standard and instill a sense of pride in helping others, which is one the main reasons people enter the professions to begin with.

Marginal Contribution to Firm Revenue. This is not taking the team members' book of business, or worse, hours multiplied by rate; instead it measures the *marginal* contribution they make to the firm's revenue. How many new customers have they acquired? Have they cross-sold any of the firm's services to existing customers? Have they negotiated any FPAs or change orders? What price—reservation, hope-for, or pump-fist—did they realize?

Firms claim they want team members to develop an entrepreneurial mind-set, but rarely do they measure and reward such behavior, preferring instead to hold junior team members to stringent billable hour quotas. But no one develops marketing and rainmaking skills simply by putting in time. This development requires resources, education, and a firm that holds people accountable for their share of the firm's growth. Not everyone is cut out to be a rainmaker, but every team member can spot change orders or cross-sell additional services to existing customers. These forms of incremental revenue should be part of every team member's performance evaluations.

Customer Feedback.   What are the customer's saying—good and bad—about the team member? Would you trade some efficiency for a team member who was absolutely loved by your customers? How does the firm solicit feedback from its customers on team member performance? Does the firm reward team members for delivering outstanding customer service or for going above and beyond the call of duty for a customer? Are these stories shared with the rest of the firm so they can become part of its culture, as they are at Nordstrom, Southwest, FedEx, and Disney?

Effective Listening and Communication Skills.   If reading and writing go together, so too do speaking and listening. Yet is anyone really ever taught to listen? It is well known that speaking and listening are harder to teach than reading and writing, and if we lament the low level of reading and writing being taught in the schools, just think how much less developed speaking and listening skills must be. Unlike reading and writing, which are solitary undertakings, listening and speaking always involve human interactions.

Aristotle's book, *Rhetoric*, explained the art of persuasion by using the three Greek words: *ethos*, *pathos*, and *logos*. Ethos signifies a person's character, the sense that you can be trusted and know what you are talking about. Pathos is arousing the passions of the listeners, getting their emotions running in the direction you are trying to take them. It is the motivating factor. Logos is the intellectual reasons—and note the Greeks put it last. Think of the old saying, "People do not care how much you know until they know how much you care." Reasons and arguments can be used to reinforce your position, but it is the passion that will move the listeners in the right direction.

But how do you measure listening and communication skills? It is truly a soft measure, but is it not a critical skill for the development of a true professional? I observed a panel discussion at the AICPA's Group of 100 meeting of individuals in corporations and government agencies who hire CPAs. The number-one capability they look for—and it influences their decision to hire one firm over another, before price or quality—is communication skills. Firms need to invest in the education necessary to make their team members exceptional in these skills.

Risk Taking, Innovation, and Creativity.   Another soft measure, but critical skills for any professional. How often do team members take risks or innovate new ways of doing things for customers or the firm? Do they engage in creative thinking in approaching their work? Most firms say they want their people to "think out of the box," but when you look at what they measure and reward there is an enormous gap between what they say and what they do. But this story from PricewaterhouseCoopers offers some hope:

> To goose its innovative ability, professional services firm PricewaterhouseCoopers (PwC) did something that has elements of each—it made the business case personal. Says George Bailey, one of PwC's managing partners: "We'd give speeches about how important innovation is—evolve or die' and all that—but there's a difference between talking about it and convincing people about it. People were still measured on billable hours." To change that equation and to reward, celebrate, and encourage innovation, the

company sponsored a contest. With the world's largest roster of employees who earn more than $100,000 a year, it wasn't likely they would get people's attention with mouse pads or gift certificates for dinner at the Olive Garden. Instead, in July 1999 the firm announced a prize of $100,000 to be given to each of 150 innovators, who could be individuals or teams. Like the prospect of being hanged in a fortnight, a hundred grand concentrates the mind, even the consulting mind, wonderfully. Yet for a firm the size of PwC, $15 million's not too much to pay for even one great idea, and it's chicken feed if it produces a flock of them. Which, of course, it did: By the 1999 deadline, PwC had 700 applications from several hundred individuals and teams. Among them (and among the winners) was FPML, Financial Products Markup Language, a way to stick electronic name tags on financial derivative products (using the XML software protocol), devised by PwC with J.P. Morgan; FPML makes it possible for financial institutions to trade derivatives and other instruments over the Net and has become the industry's e-commerce standard. Another was a process for restructuring worthless real estate assets held by Japanese banks; a third was a certification for lumber products (inspired by "Dolphin Safe Tuna" labels) that marks them as having been harvested according to standards of sustainable forest management. Would these have happened without the contest? Maybe—but not all. The contest sent an electrifying message to the company about the importance of innovation, which (helped by the fact that the contest is being repeated) increased the amount of innovation the firm does and the prestige of the people who do it. Furthermore, by publicizing ideas, the contest speeded their adoption and diffusion. "No one's even asking if we got our money's worth," says Bailey. "We got it many times over" (quoted in Stewart, 2001: 185–186).

PwC's efforts are to be applauded, but it leads one to wonder if it takes a contest for professionals to be innovative. Wouldn't it be better if innovation and creativity were not viewed as separate from the rest of the business, but rather an integral part of it? Shouldn't firms work to make innovation ordinary?

This is precisely why 3M implemented the "15 percent rule," which encourages technical people to spend up to 15 percent of their time on projects of their own choosing and initiative. We are met with *staring ovations* when we suggest professional service firms adopt a similar policy. But who can deny 3M is one of the most successful companies in terms of profitability and innovation? As Ikujiro Nonaka says in *The Knowledge-Creating Company: How Japanese Companies Create the Dynamics of Innovation*, "Allow employees time to pursue harebrained schemes or just sit around chatting, and you may come up with a market-changing idea; force them to account for every minute of their day, and you will be stuck with routine products."

Knowledge Elicitation. Ross Dawson in his book *Developing Knowledge-Based Client Relationships: The Future of Professional Services*, describes knowledge elicitation as "the process of assisting others to generate their own knowledge." Note that this encompasses more than simply learning new things; it involves educating others so they generate their own knowledge. One of the most effective techniques for knowledge workers to learn any subject—especially at a very deep level—is to teach it. As they say, to teach is to learn twice. How often do team members facilitate a lunch and learn from an article or book they've read or CPE seminar they've attended? How good are they at educating their customers?

Effective Knowledge Producer and Consumer.   This is designed to measure how well team members draw from—and contribute to—the firm's intellectual capital. Are they simply consumers of IC, or do they also produce IC? How many After-Action Reviews have they written up? How many times were those AARs accessed by other members of the firm? How well do they convert their *tacit* knowledge into *explicit* knowledge the firm can reuse and make part of its structural capital? Do they look for the most effective way to leverage knowledge, or do they merely reinvent the wheel? This type of evaluation will help ensure the firm is leveraging what really counts—its IC—and developing more of it.

Ability to Deal with Change.   How well do team members adapt to discontinuity, ambiguity, and tumultuous change? How do they assist others—colleagues and customers alike—in dealing with change? Sure, this is another soft skill, but a critical one in developing the type of temperament required to become a successful professional.

Continuous Learning.   What do team members know this year they did not know last year that makes them more valuable to the firm and its customers? This is more than simply logging time in CPE courses; it would actually measure what they learned. Are they constantly enhancing their skills to become a more effective professional? How many books have they read this year? More important, what did they learn from the books they read? Does the firm adequately invest in its members' education in order to fulfill this mission? Most do not, and the majority of team members are starved for additional education, and will gravitate to those firms that offer it.

Effective Delegator.   David Maister and Patrick McKenna say that, "Estimates given to us by our clients of the amount [of work they do] that could be done by someone more junior range up to 50 percent or more of each senior person's time" (McKenna and Maister, 2002: 17). If true—and we suspect it is, although we know of no empirical study that confirms it—this is an astonishing statistic. This supports the claim I have made for years, and several times in this book, that in too many professional service firms what is really taking place is the equivalent of surgeons piercing ears. Think of the additional leverage if your firm's senior team members were able and willing to delegate up to 50 percent of their work. Not only would it provide needed skills for junior team members, it would make available more capacity to service first-class and business-class customers with top-of-the-value-curve projects. If the firm's executives were to become better at delegation, it would increase profitability many times more than an increase in efficiency could ever provide. Does your firm encourage senior team members to become effective delegators, as opposed to hoarding work to meet billable hour quotas? It is worth thinking about.

Mentoring and Coaching Skills.   How well does the firm develop team members who can coach and mentor those less experienced? Are adequate resources being invested in this area? We have seen our share of mentoring programs fail, and are not convinced of their worthiness. Perhaps the reason is that a mentor cannot be thrust upon someone; rather, it is a voluntary relationship that develops over time. But this does not preclude it from happening within the firm; and coaching is also important. We are of the opinion that professionals cannot be managed—recall our contention that that word is obsolete. They can, though, be coached, motivated, directed, focused, and inspired. Even Tiger Woods is coached, and the best players are not necessarily the best coaches.

Personal Development. What inspires team members? Why did they enter the profession in the first place? What is their preferred vision of the future? How is the firm helping—or hindering—their professional development? These are all vital areas if you intend to maintain your human capital investors, who are, remember, ultimately volunteers.

Personal Marketing Plan. In many progressive firms all team members—at all levels—develop a marketing plan. This may include measuring the number of customer meetings and lunches, joining professional organizations, giving speeches or seminars, writing articles, or setting and meeting revenue goals for cross-selling and new customers. If your firm has a marketing director, this is the perfect person to assist each team member with his or her own marketing plan, and then hold each one accountable for it.

Professional Pride. We agree with Jon Katzenbach, coauthor of *The Wisdom of Teams*:

> Pride is a more effective motivator of a professional's talent than money. And you can motivate that talent with pride in more than just belonging. There is pride in the specific work product that you deliver to clients, pride in the kinds of clients that you serve, pride in the expertise that you can apply, pride in the values of your firm (quoted in Ibid: 148).

If you thought some of these other KPIs were hard to measure, how would you measure pride? Yet it is obvious to us that pride in one's work, customers, colleagues, and values are critical in order to operate with passion and commitment.

Number of Customer Contacts per Week. Since two-thirds of customers defect from professional firms because of perceived indifference, why not encourage all of the firm's team members to meet regularly with the customers they serve? This is not to say the first-year team members should lunch with the CEO of your customer, but they could develop a relationship with someone at an equivalent level inside the customer's firm. This keeps the firm visible and in front of the customer; leads to more services and a higher wallet share; develops the communication and listening skills of the team; and increases customer loyalty.

KPI Summary

The firms that have gotten rid of their timesheets and replaced them with some (usually between three and eight) of the KPIs listed here have also implemented this change in a very rational manner. That is, they involved the team members in the change. Although it is widely believed that people do not like change, we believe there is a difference between change *imposed* and change *adopted*. As Michael Basch reminds us: "People don't mind change. They mind being changed."

Let the team members decide for which KPIs they want to be held accountable. These are smart, bright, motivated, and professional people who want to do an outstanding job not only for the customers and the firm, but also for themselves. They know what the key drivers of success are. The debate about organizational control is not whether it is needed—it certainly is—but about how it is best achieved. Imposing controls such as billable hours, which do not have a palpable relationship with customer success, might cause obedience and the minimum level of effort to obtain the standards, but it will not drive firm excellence. Of course, you will encounter resistance from those who charge the most hours—the tailless dog praises taillessness according to the historian Collingwood—and who feel threatened by KPIs that measure actual output and results. But so what? This is precisely the historically hysterical mind-set we are trying to change.

All of the firms who have let the team decide on the KPIs discovered, usually to their pleasant surprise, that the team chose KPIs that were tougher on themselves than the partners would have been. People who select their own goals are usually more demanding of themselves than when those goals are selected for them.

Robert B. Cialdini, the Regents Professor of Psychology at Arizona State University, labels this the "Principle of Consistency." In his article titled "Harnessing the Science of Persuasion," in the *Harvard Business Review*, he explained this principle:

> People align with their clear commitments. Make their commitments active, public, and voluntary. My own research has demonstrated that most people, once they take a stand or go on record in favor of a position, prefer to stick to it. . . . Israeli researchers writing in 1983 in the *Personality and Social Psychology Bulletin* recounted how they asked half the residents of a large apartment complex to sign a petition favoring the establishment of a recreation center for the handicapped. The cause was good and the request was small, so almost everyone who was asked agreed to sign. Two weeks later, on National Collection Day for the Handicapped, all residents of the complex were approached at home and asked to give to the cause. A little more than half of those who were not asked to sign the petition made a contribution. But an astounding 92 percent of those who did sign donated money. The residents of the apartment complex felt obligated to live up to their commitments because those commitments were active, public, and voluntary.
>
> More than 300 years ago, Samuel Butler wrote a couplet that explains succinctly why commitments must be voluntary to be lasting and effective: "He that complies against his will/Is of his own position still" (Cialdini, 2001: 76–77).

Social controls are far more effective than financial controls for influencing your team members' behavior. This explains why most professional firms that have trashed timesheets tend to hold frequent meetings—both on marketing and work-in-process—in which everyone is held accountable for the selected KPIs. If you know your peers are holding you responsible and answerable for your activities, you are more likely to act in a manner consistent with the wishes of the group.

Jim Casey, founder of UPS in 1907, said in 1947: "A man's worth to an organization can be measured by the amount of supervision he requires." Isn't it time professional service firms recognize they are dealing with knowledge workers, not Taylor's factory workers? Knowledge work is not subject to the same rhythms and cadences of an assembly line; it is an iterative process of the mind, and the traditional time-and-motion studies are out of place in the modern firm. It is time for the firms of the future to remove the Sword of Damocles—the timesheet—hanging over the head of their professionals, and unleash them from a theory that is no longer applicable to the intellectual capital economy of the modern office. To borrow a phrase from the last lines in Karl Marx's *The Communist Manifesto*: "Professionals of the world unite! You have nothing to lose but your timesheets."

REFUTING THE EFFICIENCY DEFENSE FOR TIMESHEETS

Was Einstein "on budget" for his research? Who knows? Or cares?
—Tom Peters, Professional Service Firm 50

RON Professionals are the ultimate knowledge workers, and knowledge is not defined so much by *quantity* as it is by *quality*. As explained in Chapter 9, it is also not defined by its *costs*. It is defined by its *results*. It may be possible in a widget factory to work harder, but in a knowledge factory, working smarter is the only option. Frederick Taylor started with the assumption that there was "one best way" to achieve productivity, and it is not determined by the physical—or even mental—characteristics of the job. But in knowledge work, the traditional tools of measurement need to be replaced by *judgment*, and there is a difference between a measurement and a judgment: a measurement requires only a stick; a judgment requires knowledge.

Frederick Taylor did not attempt to measure the productivity and efficiency of knowledge workers because there were not very many in his day. He did not focus attention on how to train the workers to do the job better next time, because he developed systems and procedures that removed the need for them to use their imagination. He substituted rules for thinking. It took approximately a half-century before companies began to learn this made their organizations complacent and stupid—not the traits you want in an auto factory, let alone among professionals. Knowledge work can only be designed *by* the knowledge worker, not *for* them. In a factory, the worker *serves* the system; in a knowledge environment, the system should *serve* the worker.

Productivity measurements on knowledge work are in their infancy; we do not have a modern-day Frederick Taylor who has done pioneering research in the field—except, perhaps, for Peter Drucker (and two other thinkers we will introduce later). Here is what Drucker has to say about knowledge-worker productivity in his book *Management Challenges for the 21st Century*:

> Work on the productivity of the knowledge worker has barely begun. In terms of actual work on knowledge worker productivity we are, in the year 2000, roughly where we were in the year 1900, a century ago, in terms of the productivity of the manual worker. But we

already know infinitely more about the productivity of the knowledge worker than we did then about that of the manual worker. We even know a good many of the answers. But we also know the challenges to which we do not yet know the answers, and on which we need to go to work. *Six* major factors determine knowledge-worker productivity:

1. Knowledge worker productivity demands that we ask the question: *"What is the task?"*
2. It demands that we impose the responsibility for their productivity on the individual knowledge workers themselves. Knowledge workers *have* to manage themselves. They have to have *autonomy*.
3. Continuing innovation has to be part of the work, the task, and the responsibility of knowledge workers.
4. Knowledge work requires continuous learning on the part of the knowledge worker, but equally continuous teaching on the part of the knowledge worker.
5. Productivity of the knowledge worker is not—at least not primarily—a matter of the *quantity* of output. *Quality* is at least as important.
6. Finally, knowledge-worker productivity requires that the knowledge worker is both seen and treated as an "asset" [we would say volunteer] rather than a "cost." It requires that knowledge workers *want* to work for the organization in preference to all other opportunities (Drucker, 1999: 142).

Drucker believes the main focus of the knowledge worker must be on the task to be done—with all other distractions eliminated as much as possible—and this is defined by the worker him- or herself. Whenever we meet with firms, we ask the following questions of the team members, and learn a great deal about the organization (these are adapted from Peter Drucker and other sources):

- What is your task?
- What should it be?
- What should you be expected to contribute?
- How fair are those expectations?
- What hampers you in doing your task and should be eliminated?
- How could *you* make the greatest *contribution* with your strengths, your way of performing, your values, to what needs to be done?
- What *results* have to be achieved to make a difference?
- What hinders you in doing your task and should be eliminated?
- What progress are you making in your career?
- How is the firm helping you to achieve your professional goals and aspirations?
- What does the firm do right and what should it continue doing?
- What are the firm's weaknesses and what should it stop doing?
- What critical things should the firm start doing?

These are excellent questions for firm leaders to ask the team members periodically. Between the KPIs listed and these questions, the firm will be able to focus its resources and attention on external opportunities, rather than on internal bureaucratic procedures, rules, and systems that probably do not add much value to the customer experience.

So many firm leaders we meet actually seem frightened at the thought of removing timesheets; they feel as if they are relinquishing total control over their team. Worse, they believe our suggestion to get rid of the timesheet is tantamount to giving the team members total freedom, and will create anarchy in the firm. But we are not suggesting freedom for people "to do their own thing"; that is not freedom, it is *license*. With KPIs, you *are* holding people accountable for the *results* they achieve, hardly a prescription for anarchy and chaos. We truly believe when firm leaders feel they need to tightly control a knowledge worker, they have made a hiring mistake. Peter Drucker has offered a practical suggestion for holding people accountable for their contribution, which he called *the management letter*:

> This [setting objectives] is so important that some of the most effective managers I know go one step further. They have each of their subordinates write a "manager's letter" twice a year. In this letter to his superior, each manager first defines the objectives of his superior's job and of his own job as he sees them. He then sets down the performance standards that he believes are being applied to him. Next, he lists the things he must do himself to attain these goals—and the things within his own unit he considers the major obstacles. He lists the things his superior and the company do that help him and the things that hamper him. Finally, he outlines what he proposes to do during the next year to reach his goals. If his superior accepts this statement, the "manager's letter" becomes the charter under which the manager operates (quoted in Flaherty, 1999: 93).

Implementing KPIs and the management letter suggested by Drucker requires leadership, not management. It has often been observed that most firm leaders could not lead a trail of ants to a picnic lunch. That may or may not be true—we have seen evidence that support each conclusion. But there is no doubting the fact that the antiquated measurement system of the timesheet is destroying the morale of the professions and hindering effectiveness and customer service. And since it is not even an effective method for measuring the results of knowledge workers, why do the professions insist on clinging to it, despite all of the evidence to the contrary there is a superior alternative?

A business does not exist to be efficient; it exists to create wealth for its customers. The traditional focus on efficiency in an intellectual-capital-based economy is misplaced. This is not to say that productivity is not important, rather that it should not be the talisman for guiding the firm to its core purpose: the creation of wealth.

Efficiency can be taken to ludicrous extremes. For instance, I doubt any efficiency expert would have suggested to the Nordstrom brothers to place pianos and hire piano players in their department stores. What could this possibly add to efficiency? Yet, how *effective* is it in providing a competitive differentiation that Nordstrom can leverage to create a more valuable experience for its team members and customers?

If efficiency were the ultimate purpose of an organization, than perhaps Walt Disney should have made *Snow White and the* Three *Dwarfs*—think of the cost savings from removing nearly 60 percent of the dwarfs!

Knowledge companies understand this dynamic. Disney and Microsoft know there is a vast difference between being efficient and being *persuasive*. Gordon Bethune saw first-hand the pernicious effects of focusing on nothing but costs when he took over the helm at Continental Airlines; and even Ben & Jerry's understood that a business simply could not operate at—nor price for—100 percent efficiency. The new companies that have created so much wealth in the past decades, from Yahoo! and Intel to Starbucks and Microsoft, did not get where they are by focusing on efficiency. They focused on creating wealth for their customers. Why, then, do professional firms worship on the altar of efficiency?

It is time to replace efficiency with *effectiveness*, and begin to measure what counts, rather than counting for the sake of counting. The timesheet has no place in the firm of the future because it is not an accurate measurement of the *results* and *wealth* knowledge workers create for their customers.

Again, the three major defenses of the timesheet are:

- Pricing tool
- Productivity and efficiency measurement tool
- Cost accounting (or ABC) tool

We have refuted the first two of these defenses, and now will focus on the third.

REFUTING THE COST ACCOUNTING DEFENSE FOR TIMESHEETS

RON The cost accounting defense of timesheets is perhaps the strongest of the three major defenses put forth, but it is not impervious from prosecution. As the opening salvo from the prosecution against this particular defense, recall from Chapter 9 how the *standard hourly rate* in professional service firms is calculated:

$$\text{Hourly Rate} = \frac{\text{Overhead} + \text{Desired Net Income}}{\text{Expected Billable Hours}}$$

The first fact to note is that this is not cost accounting, it is *profit forecasting*. There is no cost accounting that allocates desired profit—or a return on investment—among its costs. That is an opportunity cost concept; and while economists may use that theory, cost accountants do not. Once you remove the desired net income from the equation, it becomes apparent in the first order that the hourly rate would drop by one-third to one-half, or perhaps even more, depending on the net income percentage of the firm. Given this reduction, it becomes apparent in the second order that it is very difficult to actually *lose* money in a professional service firm on any customer, or project. Hence, the more relevant question firms need to be asking is: "Did we *optimize* the profit from this customer?" not "Did we make money on this customer"—chances are extremely high you did. The equation—or cost accounting in particular—cannot answer the more relevant question.

This is not to say losses do not happen, but that they are more the result of pricing errors and scope creep than they are of too much overhead being allocated to the job. After all, the price drives the cost, and if the firm loses money on any one customer, it probably priced—or forecast its internal costs—incorrectly. Despite the argument, most firms are not using timesheets for cost accounting purposes; they use them to price. And since pricing mistakes and lost opportunities do not show up on cost accounting or realization reports, the firm gains no new knowledge for how to price better in the future. Firms can increase profitability much more with better pricing than with accurate cost accounting.

Furthermore, the overhead in a professional service firm is *fixed*, at least in the short and medium term. In the long term, all costs are discretionary, because you can always close your doors. In fact, professional firms have a higher percentage of fixed costs than do the airlines, yet look how many times the airlines change their prices— approximately 12 million times per day—to capture the value of each seat, not because their costs are changing that many times. Once you hire a professional at a fixed salary, it does not much matter whether he or she is submitting bids on eBay (the peak time hours for submitting bids come between noon and 6:00 P.M., supposedly when most Americans are hard at work), making copies, or doing high-level estate work: the salary is fixed. A firm only hires an additional worker in the first place when it can reasonably project that the additional revenue from that person will exceed his or her cost. Why then is it necessary to break up that fixed cost among one customer, or one job for one customer?

We simply do not believe that professionals do not know who their profitable versus unprofitable customers are. In our seminars we always ask, "Can you rank your customers by profitability, without looking at any financial data?" The answer is always yes, as it should be. There is a high correlation between the customers you enjoy and their profitability; it is not a perfect correlation but then we would suggest you should not work for people you do not enjoy, even if they are profitable.

Interestingly, this same question is asked with respect to team members: "Do you know which of your team members are stars and which are not, without looking at timesheets?" The answer is always yes. If that is the case, what light is being shed on the situation by timesheets?

Engage in this thought experiment: It is day one of your fiscal, or calendar, year. For the next year your firm is going to have exactly the same customers, for whom you will do the same work, at the same price as last year, and with the same cost structure as last year. If you adopted fixed-price agreements—there would be no change orders since you are not going to be selling additional work—for all of those customers, set them up on payment terms, would you need timesheets in order to know you are profitable? The answer is no.

Expand the experiment. Assume that for every new customer, or every change order on an existing customer, you price utilizing the philosophy of Chapter 9, that is, pricing on purpose and for profitability. You enhance your firm's value proposition, you offer payment terms and reduce the need to send out invoices, offer a service and price guarantee, bundle your services, and so forth: Is there any doubt in your mind you will be able to price at a higher level of profitability than the billable hour? Your income statement will show your profitability. Yes, it is a lagging indicator, but so are timesheets.

If a consultant can enter the firm from the outside, run the Pareto Analysis, figure out how your airplane seats are configured (the ratio of first-class, business-class, full-fare coach, coach, and leisure seats), ask Peter Drucker's questions among the team members, analyze your firm's financial statements and compare them to competitors based on benchmark data, and compute a few of the KPIs listed, is there any doubt in your mind the consultant would be able to get an accurate picture of your firm? If that can be done from the *outside*, why can't the same thing be done from the *inside* by the firm's leaders? Timesheets, like financial statements, are *lagging* indicators of financial performance. We prefer to assess the firm's financial statements in total, rather than dissecting its hourly rate realizations, which provide no information on how to improve profitability.

When you reward people for billable hours, you get billable hours, even if those hours logged on the timesheet are outright lies or are worthless in terms of creating results for the customer. You also create an incentive measurement that will verify C. Northcote Parkison's Law: "Work expands to fill the time available." Any of the team member KPIs outlined in this chapter would do a superior job in determining the worth of an associate as compared to simply looking at billable hours.

Andrew Carnegie's favorite sayings was, "Watch the costs and the profits will take care of themselves." In the firm of the future, we would replace that maxim with: "Watch your price, and the profits will take care of themselves."

Now, obviously, there is a lot more to it than price, but price is how the firm *captures* the results of its value proposition, and since you are what you charge, we do not want to add complexity to the maxim.

This debate between cost accounting and profitability is not over. Much work is being done in this area. In 1987, H. Thomas Johnson and Robert S. Kaplan published *Relevance Lost: The Rise and Fall of Management Accounting,* which was named in 1997 one of the 14 most influential management books to appear in the first 75 years of *Harvard Business Review's* history. The book is credited with launching the activity-based costing (ABC) revolution. Yet these two thinkers have gone down very different paths as of late: Kaplan is doing pioneering work in the field of the Balanced Scorecard, and Johnson has moved on to what he calls "Management by Means." In fact, they are now feuding with each other, and have not spoken in years.

Because this book deals not only with the future of the firm, but also the future of the professions, we thought it would be useful to highlight the disagreements between these two seminal thinkers in the accounting and management field, and then provide some concluding remarks on where we stand in their debate. We do this because, as just noted, this debate is not over, and will continue to influence management thinking for decades to come. Exhibit 10.1 is an article by Art Kleiner, titled "What Are the Measures That Matter?" Reproduced here in its entirety, it first appeared in the first quarter of 2002, in *strategy + business*, published by Booz Allen Hamilton, Inc.

We have drawn inspiration from both Kaplan and Johnson. Many of the KPIs were inspired by Kaplan's Balanced Scorecard approach of determining nonfinancial indicators that drive profitability. As the Balance Scorecard is implemented throughout companies of all sizes, more empirical research will have to be conducted to test its true effects. That being said, there is no doubt any business should be able to come up with KPIs—or critical success factors—that have the qualities of being a leading indicator and can help shape the company's strategy and vision.

(Text continues on page 262)

EXHIBIT 10.1   What are the Measures That Matter?

By Art Kleiner

**A 10-year debate between two feuding gurus sheds
some light on a vexing business question.**

Like all leading characters in a good feud story, Bob Kaplan and Tom Johnson have become living symbols of something much larger than themselves. Once they were research partners and coauthors and shared their success. But they have not spoken in years, and each has publicly staked his professional reputation on the other one being wrong.

Their quarrel, which has lasted more than 10 years, is at heart a fundamental disagreement about the source of business success. Does it accrue to those who drive their businesses with numerical targets and performance measures, as Professor Kaplan asserts? Or to those who believe, as Professor Johnson argues, that management through measurement is fundamentally dangerous?

The debate, of course, is not just about business measurement. It's about control. In most companies, top management relies on measurements—not just bottom-line targets, but other numerical goals from "fast-cycle" targets to desired "customer satisfaction" survey results—to signal its priorities. Is that, or is that not, a healthy way to run a company?

To Professor Kaplan, it's not just healthy, but essential to profitability. Robert S. Kaplan, the Marvin Bower Professor of Leadership Development at Harvard Business School, is the most visible figure behind Activity-Based Costing (also known as ABC) and the Balanced Scorecard (which also is part of the title of the 1996 bestseller *The Balanced Scorecard: Translating Strategy into Action*, published by Harvard Business School Press, that Professor Kaplan coauthored with consultant David P. Norton). Although ABC and the Balanced Scorecard are derived from accounting methods, Professor Kaplan sees both as full-scale cultural changes for management in general. They break down the implicit cultural barriers between finance and accounting, on the one hand, and operations-oriented management, on the other, all for the sake of developing strategies that encompass both.

Activity-Based Costing, for instance, incorporates into corporate financial calculations the kinds of hidden costs that have traditionally been evident only on the shop floor: errors in a production process as it snowballs out of control, wasted effort in cumbersome part-ordering processes, or time spent traveling from one building to another. Taking advantage of computers to gather this information from assembly-line measurements and employee surveys, ABC divides these costs among particular projects, processes, and products. This means, for instance, if the least profitable 10 percent of products are cut using the ABC method, the cut will be more accurate—increasing profitability more—than it would have been under traditional cost accounting.

Opposing Views

If ABC helps financial controllers see what operations people see, then the other Kaplan method, the Balanced Scorecard, moves in the other direction. It helps managers incorporate into their strategies the insights of accountants—the best accountants, the ones who know how to draw forth from a mass of numerical data those few statistics and results that genuinely matter.

The Scorecard, one version of which was originally developed at Analog Devices Inc. (a semiconductor company based in the Boston area), is a sort of update of the Management by Objectives (MBO) system that Peter Drucker helped pioneer in the 1960s. Under MBO, managers were asked to set financial targets and hold themselves account-

EXHIBIT 10.1 *(Continued)*

able for them. The Balanced Scorecard expanded this to include not just financial targets, but also business process improvement goals, customer satisfaction goals, and "learning and growth" objectives (e.g., "What have you done, this quarter, to improve the capabilities of people in your department?"). The "balance" in the Scorecard is the way it trains managers to consider all four criteria, and evaluates them on all four—thus making it less likely (for instance) that they will release products that meet bottom-line cost targets but that no one wants to buy.

"ABC represents the supply curve from Microeconomics 101," says Professor Kaplan. "It tells you what things cost, but not what they're worth. The Balanced Scorecard is like a multidimensional demand curve. It tells you what's creating value." Together, he says, the two systems "make the concepts of economics operational for complex organizations."

That's where his opponent in the feud draws the line. To H. Thomas Johnson, the Retzlaff Professor of Quality Management at Portland State University in Oregon, the adaptation of microeconomics to management decision making has been a kind of original sin dating back at least to the 1950s. As he explains in his recent book (written with Swedish consultant Anders Bröms), *Profit Beyond Measure: Extraordinary Results through Attention to Work and People* (Simon & Schuster Inc., Free Press, 2000), economics-dominated business schools mistakenly teach young MBAs to make decisions entirely from quantitative information, rather than from explicit, detailed knowledge of how a company conducts work. "In time, this teaching contributed to the modern obsession in business with 'looking good' by the numbers," writes Professor Johnson, "no matter what damage [it] does to the underlying system of relationships that sustain any human organization."

Professor Johnson doesn't like to think of himself as a fervent or proselytizing person, but he comes across as one. Writing about the use of numbers to set priorities and control operations, he uses words like "crippling" and "lethal." He blames the troubles that mainstream companies get into—for example, the current predicaments of the U.S.'s big three automakers—on the misuse of measurement. He says if companies would focus on the "means" (for instance, designing a production system that makes errors visible and correctable the moment they occur), they wouldn't have to worry about enforcing targets and goals. Error counts would naturally get lower. The "ends" would take care of themselves.

Even to some of Professor Johnson's friends, this sounds like a utopian dream sometimes, and he would have an awfully hard time making his case if it weren't for the fact that one major multinational corporation is successfully running all its factories this way. That corporation is quite possibly the most admired and envied manufacturing organization in the world: the Toyota Motor Corporation.

Dying by the Numbers

Unquestionably, Professor Kaplan is the more successful of the two feuders, at least if you judge by the number of companies adopting his ideas. The Exxon Mobil Corporation's attractive new retail strategy emerged from a Balanced Scorecard exercise; Fannie Mae, Brown & Root, Cigna, and the city of Charlotte, N.C., are all featured in Professor Kaplan and Mr. Norton's new book, *The Strategy-Focused Organization: How Balanced Scorecard Companies Thrive in the New Business Environment* (Harvard Business School Press, 2000). Dozens of companies use ABC, and the apparent value of "stretch targets" and other kinds of performance measures has never been higher.

What, then, does Tom Johnson see that Bob Kaplan does not? Or, more to the point: Which is more likely to succeed? Toyota? Or just about every other well-known manufacturer today?

To get a satisfying answer to that question, you have to look back to 1983, when Professor Kaplan was dean of the Graduate School of Industrial Administration at Carnegie-Mellon University in Pittsburgh. A Westinghouse Electric Company executive named Thomas J. Murrin (now a dean at Duquesne University's business school) pointed Professor Kaplan to a controversial article in the *Harvard Business Review* published several years earlier. Called "Managing Our Way to Economic Decline," by the Harvard Business School's William J. Abernathy and Robert H. Hayes, the article was the first of a series of broadsides against the tenets of financially oriented management. American companies that lived by the numbers, said the article, were dying by the numbers; they were shutting down profitable product lines because they looked costly on paper, and were making themselves unnecessarily vulnerable to competition from Japan.

Professor Kaplan was a financial guy himself, but he found the argument convincing. When he was asked to speak about this at a major accounting conference, he looked for a business historian to help him trace the roots of the problem. A mutual friend recommended Professor Johnson, who had studied with Harvard's most eminent management historian, Alfred Chandler. Professors Kaplan and Johnson recognized their symbiotic interests and went on to collaborate on a book for Harvard Business School Press, published in 1987 under the title *Relevance Lost: The Rise and Fall of Management Accounting*.

Relevance Lost has gone through nine printings since then, enough to make it a business-book classic. I vividly remember my first encounter with it, as a fledgling management historian, looking desperately to understand the influence of financial methods on corporate decision making. Reading *Relevance Lost*, I felt like I had cracked the code. The historical chapters (written mostly by Professor Johnson) showed how management accounting wasn't just a *feature* of the newly emerging large corporations of the 19th century; it probably made them possible. Andrew Carnegie's watchword, for instance, was "Watch the costs, and the profits will take care of themselves." Cost analysis gave the Carnegies of American business (and their successors, like General Motors' Alfred Sloan and General Electric's Ralph Cordiner) the power to create huge, multifaceted, and yet coherent and consistent enterprises that continually outbudgeted and outmaneuvered their competitors.

But cost accounting per se was no longer enough (argued Professors Kaplan and Johnson) amid global competition, demanding consumers, and cutthroat pressures of the 1970s and later. Indeed, like many remedies that are overused, cost accounting had become poisonously destructive to its hosts. The authors asked rhetorically why it had taken so long for the toxicity of calculations like return on investment to become apparent. They explained it by writing that managers had compensated, below the visible surface, with human judgment. But when short-term pressures increased, and managers spent less and less time in each position, human judgment was diminished. The net effect was to make managers more dependent on the numbers.

To Professor Kaplan fell the task of writing most of the material about current management practice, including two chapters describing potential solutions—since accountants had created this mess, how could they help clean it up? He had recently begun to work with Robin Cooper, a Harvard faculty member whose research focused on innovative cost-management practices, and who was writing a case study of Schrader Bellows, a North Carolina hydraulics components company. The company had connected its MRP data bank (a standard "Manufacturing Resource Planning" computer system for production scheduling, sold by IBM in those days) so as to provide information directly into the assignment of overhead costs to products. The term Activity-Based Costing was not mentioned directly in *Relevance Lost*, but the prototype ABC practices featured in the book soon became its primary deliverable, and thus the center of both authors' speaking engagements.

EXHIBIT 10.1   *(Continued)*

"We didn't argue," recalls Professor Johnson. "It was obviously going to be a wave to ride. So we rode it."

Battle Lines Are Drawn

Then it was Professor Johnson's turn to be approached by a manufacturing guy. As Professor Johnson recalls, Richard Schoenberger, an industrial engineering professor from the University of Nebraska, pulled him aside after a talk to say, "This is really good stuff. You've told the accountants what we industrial engineers have been trying to tell them for decades. But you don't go far enough. Activity-Based Costing talks about tracing the overhead costs to elements of work. But if you could organize the work differently, the overhead costs wouldn't be there in the first place. And without those overhead costs, why would you need any cost accounting at all?"

That set Professor Johnson off on his own quest. He began to study Japanese and American quality methods, system dynamics, and management ideas rooted in the "new sciences" of quantum physics and evolutionary biology. (For disclosure's sake, I should add that this path led him to become a contributor to a book I edited, *The Dance of Change: The Challenges to Sustaining Momentum in Learning Organizations*, with Peter Senge and others.) By September 1992, Professor Johnson had changed his views enough to publish an article in *Management Accounting* called "It's Time to Stop Overselling Activity-Based Concepts." The result of systems like ABC, he wrote, was "unstable processes, unhappy customers, and loss of jobs." Professor Kaplan responded only two months later in the same journal, in the form of a Socratic dialogue. "Some supporters," he wrote, obviously meaning Professor Johnson, "have developed a mystical faith in the ability of [quality improvement] to solve virtually all managerial and organizational problems."

The battle lines were drawn. The two stopped speaking, and in their next books— *Relevance Regained: From Top-Down Control to Bottom-Up Empowerment* (Simon & Schuster Inc., Free Press, 1992) by Professor Johnson, and *Cost and Effect: Using Integrated Cost Systems to Drive Profitability and Performance* (Harvard Business School Press, 1997) by Professor Kaplan and Professor Cooper—they each devoted a chapter to excoriating the ideas of the other.

Soon thereafter, Professor Johnson was invited to study the Toyota system first-hand, particularly in its new plant in Georgetown, Ky. In *Profit Beyond Measure*, he describes his findings in detail. The plant produces about 500,000 cars per year, employing about 7,500 people to do so. Unlike most automakers, Toyota doesn't ask its dealers to guess what the most popular packages of options and styles will be and produce its wares accordingly. Instead, it assembles each car to match an individual customer's specification in real time.

Although Toyota makes some use of quantitative indicators of performance—such as first-pass throughput rates, defect rates, and team leader on-line work rates—they have little to do with operational decision making. Procedures on the shop floor are defined largely by team members and team leaders; everything around them is designed to improve the alertness, interest, and well-being of people working there. The plants are remarkably clean and quiet (as such observers as the auto-industry analyst Maryann Keller have noted). People on the line switch stations every two hours to avoid stress and boredom. A Toyota ergonomics engineer once told Professor Johnson that "coming off a shift should feel like finishing a tough but energizing workout."

Each station is essentially the supplier of the next station in line (its "internal customer"), providing the components the next station needs at exactly the appropriate moments. This, in turn, means people at each station must be aware of the flow of product through the entire plant. They achieve this awareness because the pace of the assembly line is not set to meet a target based on cost or other financial considerations. It ebbs and flows with the pace of customer demand. (Toyota people call this rhythm "*takt* time," after a German word for musical meter that the company borrowed during the 1930s.) Machines and workers almost effortlessly retune themselves with every new product variation. People are attuned to notice inefficiencies—the kinds that might show up weeks later as a number on an Activity-Based Costing spreadsheet—and deal with them immediately.

Cords near every station can be pulled when something "feels" wrong. When a cord is pulled, it does not cause the whole line to shut down (as it probably would in a typical plant, with supervisors fretting about the thousands of dollars lost during the downtime). Instead, support staff members rush to investigate; a part of the line then may halt while activity goes on around it.

Plants like Toyota's save money in part by giving up the enormous overhead of accounting and control systems. They replace them with trust that, given the appropriate training and technological designs, people will manage production more effectively than numbers ever could. "The problem with managing by data," Professor Johnson says, "is that it creates a mind-set that leads people to pay less attention to the day-to-day particulars of work."

Professor Johnson has been criticized for being vague and unconvincing. But the deeper reason for the criticism (like that of W. Edwards Deming before him, who referred to goal setting as "management by fear" and called it "pointless") is that measurements and rankings seem like the natural way to drive people to improve. Most managers intuitively believe that they can get better results only by setting goals and targets, especially the sophisticated "process drivers" of the Balanced Scorecard and similar methods. If managers, following those targets, cut costs in mechanistic or ineffective ways, then they aren't disciplined enough. "A cost is not a natural thing to measure, like revenues," said Professor Kaplan in an interview recently. "It's a construct; you have to create it." Without such constructs, he argues, even businesses that emphasize quality can fail financially.

The Amoeba vs. the Crystal

For someone like me, who writes about management without having to be accountable for results, it's very tempting to side with Professor Johnson and Toyota. But then I think of what David E. Meador said. He is the chief financial officer of DTE Energy Co., and a former financial officer at Chrysler, where he was in charge of implementing an ABC practice. "Some people hear Tom talk and they say, 'This sounds like taking the company off the deep end. It's a real distraction from near-term results.' And I know that frustrates him, because it's not his intent. But listen, if I don't drive some near-term results, I'm not going to be in a job. Keep the company competitive and keep me in a job, and *then* I can go work on some enhancements and refinements."

In other words, to move your company in the direction of Toyota, you have to give up most of your current practices *and* your ingrained, habitual belief that things will get done only if they are relentlessly controlled and monitored. Toyota has been refining its manufacturing system for more than 60 years, building on its early experience as a loom manufacturer. By contrast, a viable ABC/Balanced Scorecard system can be created in a year or two.

We know that the benefits of the Johnson approach will be slow to surface, and initial resistance will be great. And we know that the Kaplan approach will catch on quickly, and benefits will surface quickly. But we *don't* know the long-term dangers of the Kaplan methods. What if the constant use of "process drivers," measurements, and stretch goals cripple organizations in the long run, by wearing down their people until

EXHIBIT 10.1 *(Continued)*

they leave or their skills atrophy? This is exactly what Harvard professors Abernathy and Hayes noticed, in the article that started both Professor Johnson and Professor Kaplan on this long intellectual quest.

If Professor Johnson is right, then many of the organizations that embrace ABC and the Balanced Scorecard will exhibit the same kind of decline eventually. Indeed, some early aficionados of ABC now express disillusionment about its results. Robin Cooper recently said, "No one is negating its superior capabilities. Yet, look across all the firms that tried it, and a large number failed to take advantage of the insights it provided."

To my knowledge, no one has yet conducted the kind of long-term in-depth analysis of various companies' successes and failures that might help us truly judge which professor is correct. In the meantime, you can be reasonably confident that—other factors being equal—Professor Kaplan's methods will leave you ahead of the game, able to outperform all competitors in the short run, at least. Except, of course, for those very few companies like Toyota that follow a completely different path to management success. Inevitably, they acquire the reputation of inimitable anomalies, as different from conventional business as an amoeba is from a crystal. The crystal feels like a far surer bet, but only the amoeba is poised to evolve.

What Are the Measures That Matter? by Art Kleiner, from **strategy+business** Issue 26, 1st Quarter 2002, from **strategy+business**, the quarterly management magazine of Booz Allen Hamilton. *www.strategy-business.com* & *http://www.well.com/user/art*

Nevertheless, it is hard to refute Johnson's work. His book, *Profit Beyond Measure: Extraordinary Results through Attention to Work and People*, is a seminal work, although not yet fully developed. And while I have severe misgivings about some of his environmental rants in the book, when he profiles Toyota and Scania— now owned by Volvo—as two manufacturers that do not have a standard cost accounting system, he is on firm ground. It is hard to argue with results, and Toyota is one of the most respected companies in the world, and has produced one of the highest-quality products at the lowest cost in the industry for years. It has an unbroken record of profits, with zero layoffs, since 1960 (a record unparalleled in the industry); is a fierce innovator; and ranks top in any measure of productivity you care to analyze. Its market value is close to the combined value of the Big 3 automakers in almost every year except 1998. In 1997, it exceeded the market value of the Big 3.

As Glenn Uminger, a financial controller since 1988 at Toyota Motor Manufacturing-Kentucky (TMM-K)—which Johnson studies in depth in his book—says: "TMM-K has never had a standard cost system to track operating costs, and we probably never will." So how do they do it? How can a manufacturing company run without a standard cost accounting system? The answer lies in the subjective theory of value we explained in Chapter 9, and how Lee Iacocca priced the Ford Mustang. Toyota understands that price drives costs, not the other way around. Here is how Johnson explains it in his book, *Profit Beyond Measure*:

None of these comments is meant to imply that Toyota does not have accounting and production planning information systems. Of course it does. Toyota has a comprehensive array of information systems, accounting and otherwise, with which to *plan*, in advance of operations, and to *report* results of operations after the fact. But information from such systems is *not allowed to influence operational decisions* (Johnson and Broms, 2000: 106).

Toyota management discharges its responsibility for costs not by taking arbitrary steps to manipulate operations, but largely in the vehicle planning stage. During the design stage, long before the first penny has been committed to making a vehicle, Toyota has always placed enormous importance on setting and achieving cost targets. To do so, over the years Toyota has developed a famous technique for target costing. Simply stated, target cost is the maximum cost the company can afford to incur to produce and sell a vehicle and still earn a required profit at the price customers are expected to pay (Ibid: 109).

Professional service firms certainly operate on higher gross profit margins than Toyota does, so if Toyota can engage in target pricing, what is the professional firm's excuse? Johnson goes on to explain his theory that Toyota operates under "management by means" rather than "management by results." It is an interesting viewpoint because it views the organization as a living system, based upon interdependent relationships, and those are nearly impossible to quantify. He notes Dr. Edward Deming's observation that over 97 percent of the events that affect a company's results are not measurable, while less than 3 percent of what influences final results can be measured. He states:

> Managers who adopt the new thinking offered here will accept as second nature the idea that what decides an organization's long-term profitability is the way it organizes its work, not how well its members achieve financial targets. This chapter compares the long-term records of Toyota and the American "Big Three" automakers to demonstrate the truth of this proposition. It posits Toyota's principles as an example of new management thinking called "management by means." Management by means is the antithesis of "managing by results," practices identified . . . with Toyota's American competitors. Those who manage by results focus on bottom-line target and consider that achieving financial goals justifies inherently destructive practices. Those who manage by means consider that a desirable end will emerge naturally as a consequence of nurturing the activities of all employees and suppliers in a humane manner. Managing by means requires a profound change in thinking that is a bold alternative to conventional management thinking and practice (Ibid: 12).

> Management accounting simply takes accounting revenue, cost, and profitability information, which is appropriate for measuring the overall financial results of a business, and inappropriately attempts to trace it to the particular activities and products of the business that gave rise to those results. Assigning such quantitative measures to parts of a mechanistic system makes sense. However, the parts of a natural living system cannot be so treated. Accounting measures are unable to penetrate the organic, multifaceted union between customer and company that ultimately is the source of a company's financial results. This union is the reason any company exists (Ibid: 145).

> Because cost and profit are not objects, but are properties that emerge from relationships, quantitative measures can only describe them, they cannot explain them. Quantitative measures, unlike art, music, or the stories and myths that humans fashion with words, cannot convey understanding of the multidimensional patterns that shape the relationships from which results, such as cost and profit, emerge in a living system (Ibid: 188).

If Carnegie said, "Watch the costs and the profits will take care of themselves," Johnson is saying: "Nurture the means. The results will take care of themselves." Kaplan would say, "Measure the result and the means will take care of themselves." We say, "Watch your price, and the profits will take care of themselves." The truth, most likely, lies somewhere in between, which is why we have borrowed ideas from both of these thinkers. Though, we suspect, Johnson is closer to the truth than Kaplan, as even Peter Drucker might agree:

> I do not believe that one can manage a business by reports. I am a figures man, and a quantifier, and one of those people to whom figures talk. I also know that reports are abstractions, and that they can only tell us what we have determined to ask. They are high-level abstractions. That is all right if we have the understanding, the meaning, and the perception. One must spend a great deal of time outside, where the results are. Inside a business one only has costs. One looks at markets, at customers, at society, and at knowledge, all of which are outside the business, to see what is really happening. That reports will never tell you (quoted in Flaherty, 1999: 86).

The world needs a new Frederick Taylor—and excepting Peter Drucker, who is in a class all his own—Kaplan and Johnson are certainly serious contenders. Let the feud continue.

IS THERE ONE BEST ECONOMIC DENOMINATOR TO TRACK?

RON In his book, *Good to Great: Why Some Companies Make the Leap . . . and Others Don't*, Jim Collins asks an absorbing question worth pondering for the firm of the future:

> [W]e did notice one particularly provocative form of economic insight that every good-to-great company attained, the notion of a single "economic denominator." Think about it in terms of the following question: *If you could pick one and only one ratio—profit per x (or, in the social sector, cash flow per x)—to systematically increase over time, what x would have the greatest and most sustainable impact on your economic engine?* We learned that this single question leads to profound insight into the inner workings of an organization's economics.
>
> Walgreens switched its focus from profit per store to *profit per customer visit.* Convenient locations are expensive, but by increasing profit per customer visit, Walgreens was able to increase convenience (nine stores in a mile!) *and* simultaneously increase profitability across its entire system.
>
> Gillette: profit per customer. Key insight: Shift from profit per division to profit per customer reflected the economic power of repeatable purchases (e.g., razor cartridges) times high profit per purchase (e.g., Mach3, not disposable razors) (Collins, 2001: 104–106).

PAUL Larry Selden of Columbia University's business school teamed with *Fortune's* editorial director Geoffrey Colvin to write a fascinating article in the September 30, 2002 edition of *Fortune Magazine*. It was headed, "Will this customer sink your stock? Here's the newest way to grab competitive advantage: Figure out how profitable your customers are." The opening of the article hits a huge nail on the head:

Who are your unprofitable customers? We recently asked that question of top executives at one of America's biggest retailers. They responded defiantly that they had *no* unprofitable customers.

Now understand that this company was in trouble—it wasn't earning enough to cover its cost of capital. Wall Street analysts were beating it up and its stocks were performing worse than most of its competitors. Yet its leaders insisted that through some dark financial voodoo that millions of profitable customers somehow added up to an unprofitable company.

The truth—which shocked them—was that some of their customers were deeply unprofitable. Simply doing business with certain customers was reducing the firm's profits and shareholder value. Other customers were fabulously profitable—but the effect of bad-news buyers was overwhelming them.

This company was actually spending money to bring in customers who were reducing the value of the firm (Selden and Colvin: 2002).

The article goes on to point out the value of the profit-per-customer metric to businesses ranging from retailers to banks. It is as eye-opening as Ron's comment: "Bad customers drive out good ones," which I refer to as Baker's Law. And don't overlook this point: Even if you hold on to those bad customers because you are scared to fire them, they are effectively driving *you* out!

RON So what would be the one metric for the firm of the future? We do not know. Perhaps profit *per unit of intellectual capital*, but we do not yet have the tools and methodologies to measure this (though models do exist that attempt to). We lean toward the *value gap* KPI explained earlier; that is, the gap between what you could potentially provide to a customer over his or her lifetime versus what you actually are providing (measured in revenue). Closing this one gap would increase customer loyalty, reduce customer churn, allow for premium pricing, and maintain the firm's position on the top of the value curve.

Or, perhaps, Charles Handy is right. In a lecture to the Royal Society of Arts in London in 1996, he described "the fallacy of the single criterion":

Trying to find one number that is the sum of everything is misguided. There is never any one number that will actually explain success in life and we are foolish ever to think that it might be there. Money certainly isn't it. Businesses know very well that profit is not the only measure. Sensible organizations now have about 18 different numbers they look at. Nevertheless, the myth pervades our society that if you are profitable you are successful. Or if you're in the public sector, then efficiency is what matters. But efficiency is not quite the same as effectiveness. You can have a very efficient hospital if you don't take in very sick people or people who are not going to get better, like the old ones. So you push them outside. You're efficient but you're not terribly effective. Looking for the one number has corrupted our society (quoted in Boyle, 2001: 192).

Handy is right in one respect when it comes to professional service firms: the one criterion is not the *realization per hour*. That metric tells us nothing about how well the firm is pricing, how much money it is leaving on the table, or anything about the external wealth it is creating for its customers, and has indeed corrupted the professions.

SUMMARY AND CONCLUSIONS

Science progresses funeral by funeral.

—Max Planck, physicist

Peter Drucker recommends that for a business to be truly innovative, it must not only do *new* things, it must stop doing *old* things. It is not possible to create tomorrow unless one first gets rid of yesterday. Maintaining yesterday is always difficult and time-consuming, and wastes resources on nonresults. The human body has an automatic mechanism to discharge waste, but the corporate body does not—that requires leadership. It requires every policy, procedure, service, and activity to be put on trial for its life, every two to three years, by asking the following questions: "If we didn't do this already, would we go into it the way we are now? And if the answer is no, then the question is, What would we do?" (Drucker, 2002: 71).

Knowing what you now know about the deleterious effects of pricing by the hour, and using timesheets as a lagging indicator of firm performance, is it not time to abandon these procedures and activities? We are always asked what it takes to implement these ideas, and must reply by disagreeing—strongly—with Max Planck's remedy from the opening quote. We do not think a profession would progress by shooting its oldest members. It is too simple to say people do not like to change—people love change if it brings hope of a better future.

It requires leadership and a vision. It requires knowing you are doing the right things, not just doing things right. It requires focusing the firm on the external results it creates for the customer and simultaneously building the type of firm people are proud to be a part of and contribute to. It requires a sense of dignity and high self-esteem that you are worth every penny you charge, and you will only work with those customers whom you like and respect, and who reciprocate those feelings. It requires an attitude of experimentation, not simply doing things because that is the way it has always been done. It requires less measurement and more trust.

We offer these theories in the spirit of a scientific hypotheses, and realize they will be subject to criticism, misunderstanding, rejection, exploration of alternatives, and, after a while, clarification, grudging acceptance, and finally incorporation as part of the conventional wisdom. Then we hope they will be supplanted by even better theories. We only hope to live long enough to see this process unfold.

11

THE TIMELESS PRACTICE

I set as the goal the maximum capacity that people have—I settle for no less.
I make myself a relentless architect of the possibilities of human beings.

—Benjamin Zander, Conductor, Boston Philharmonic Orchestra

Three or four years ago, at Results Accountants' Systems (RAS), we used a model to illustrate the elements that drive profit in a service firm (the *profit drivers*). The model was intended to convey a ladder effect:

Customer loyalty drives profitability and growth.

Customer delight drives customer loyalty.

Value drives customer delight.

Productivity drives value.

Commitment and systems drive productivity.

Team happiness drives commitment.

Internal quality drives team happiness.

Leadership drives internal quality.

Vision drives leadership.

Paradigm drives vision.

PAUL It's important to start by saying that we talked about this model before we developed the new Practice Equation, and today, we would replace *productivity* with *effectiveness*. Nevertheless, as you look at the ladder, observe that many firms trying to make a difference (perhaps with some new training program) start by working on the top five "rungs" of the ladder. And, no doubt, doing that will have some positive effects. But the firm of the future understands that those top five rungs can be (and often are) only temporary fixes.

What we need are fixes that have strength and durability. When you think of it this way, you realize that working on the bottom five rungs is the key to sustainable performance, so let's talk briefly about each of them.

PARADIGM DRIVES VISION

PAUL You could wryly observe that any program launched since 1980, and worth its salt, had to have the word "paradigm" in it. It became one of those "in" words used throughout the eighties and nineties. Here it serves its purpose well since we're using it to convey the sense that how you look at the world, the frame of reference you use, is critical to the way you expound your vision.

Classically, if you see the world as a place full of people waiting to take advantage of you, as a place of scarcity, you'll expound your vision in a very nonexpansive way. Conversely, if you see the world as full of opportunities for you to make a difference, as a place of abundance, you'll expound a vision that's full of positives and possibilities.

VISION DRIVES LEADERSHIP

PAUL There are many definitions we could give you for vision and the need for it, but we suspect you know them well enough. So we'll just define it in the simplest of terms: Vision is where you see yourself tomorrow or at some slightly more distant point in the future. It is therefore a crucial component of your culture. Without it, you have no idea where you're going, hence no idea when you "arrive" ("arrive" is not used in the classical sense). Here's an example.

In 1994, I ventured for the first time into an English firm, Lathams, in the small town of Chorley. Lathams was already regarded as a leading-edge firm. It was winning quality work from the then Big 5 and second-tier firms. At the time, we would have described it as meeting many of the criteria of a firm of the future.

Keith Seeley had started the firm some 14 years earlier. At the time of my visit, the firm occupied an impressive nine-story building that really stood out in the small town; the building could be seen for miles. On the first day, Keith took me just five doors down the street to where he had first established the practice in a cute, small terrace house. He observed there were three other houses on the street where accountants had started practices at almost the same time. These others still were operating in their original locations.

I asked Keith to what he attributed the somewhat remarkable difference in growth. As he led me back into his nine-story building, he pointed to words on the plaque hanging above the reception desk. It read: "Our vision is to help our clients and ourselves achieve more than we both thought possible and to have fun doing it." After I'd read it, he added, "I've always believed that. And it's important to understand that the purpose of our vision is to set ourselves a target that we constantly aim for but never actually hit because we keep moving the target."

You may look at Keith's vision statement and ask, understandably, "What target?" because no target is specified. But on closer inspection, you'll see that there is. We'll return to it in a moment.

But first consider this somewhat more formal expression of a working vision:

> In 10 years from now we will be known as the preeminent accounting firm in our region. We will have at least 70 percent of our revenues being generated from business consulting services. Our revenue target will be set at $10 million—a required growth rate of 27 percent per year.
>
> Our customers and team members will be loyal advocates of the firm. The firm will proactively pursue the objective of maximizing its clients' wealth. The firm will be an enjoyable place to work for both partners and team members.
>
> Profit per partner will be among the highest in the industry for firms of equivalent size, and team members will benefit from premium compensation levels.
>
> The firm will hire only the best people available and will ensure that they have the best training, experiential opportunities, and excellent long-term career opportunities. People will eagerly seek employment at the firm.

At least that statement has some revenue targets, as well as some required growth rates; plus there's that nice line about "70 percent of our revenue coming from business consulting." The problem I see with it is the one thing that doesn't get quite enough emphasis. More on that later, too.

For now, the point is, vision is where you want to be tomorrow.

LEADERSHIP DRIVES INTERNAL QUALITY

PAUL We've already made the obvious point that leadership matters. But now we want to suggest an idea that may give you a different perspective on what leadership actually is. To do that, we'll first look at leadership in the specific role of driving internal quality, for which there is no better example than the story Tom Connellan tells in his book, *Inside the Magic Kingdom.*

Greatly condensed, the story features eight people from different industries and professions who are attending a program at Disney University on service and leadership. On the second night, the group strolls the streets of Walt Disney World's Magic Kingdom to observe the Electric Light Parade and to take notes on what they observe. The group arrives early to get a good view. (If you've ever been to Disney World, you know that the crowds are 15 to 20 deep and that they stretch for half a mile at least.) Standing behind a rope barrier they observe across the road a man bending down to pick up litter. Assuming that he is a member of what Disney calls "the custodial crew," they yell across the street, "How many people are there on the custodial crew?" The man looks up, and through the noise yells back what sounds to some in the group like "four to five thousand." Others are sure the man said "45 thousand." They make their notes accordingly.

The next day the group is up early to attend a special team meeting, at which Disney CEO Michael Eisner will be presenting. The group is positioned at the back of the room with their notepads. As Eisner walks in, everyone rises and gives him a standing ovation (imagine a standing ovation before you open your mouth!). As Eisner begins speaking to the group, some recognize Eisner as the man who had bent down the night before to pick up the trash. When Eisner finishes his talk, he asks if there are any questions. One of the group asks him, "Was it you we saw across the street last night picking up litter? If so, we're the ones who asked how many people are on the custodial crew." "Yes," Eisner said, "it was me. And I hope you got the right answer—45,000. In other words, *everyone* in the park is on the custodial crew—including me!"

What a great demonstration of leadership that is. All too often we see leaders who preach but do not practice. We hear leaders tell their customers about customer care, but then refer to customers in pejorative terms behind the scenes to get a laugh. If there's one thing that leadership must be it is *consistent*.

And please don't misunderstand: the story about Eisner is not intended to suggest that effective leadership necessarily requires a charismatic figure or someone in the limelight. Far from it, as Joseph L. Badaracco explains in his book, *Leading Quietly*:

> Every profession and walk of life has its great figure, leaders, and heroes. Think of the men and women who create or transform major companies, the political leaders who reshape society, the firefighters who risk their lives to save others. We exalt these individuals as role models and celebrate their achievements. They represent, we feel, the true model of leadership.
>
> But do they really? I ask this because over the course of a career spent studying management and leadership I have observed that the most effective leaders are rarely public heroes. These men and women aren't high-profile champions of causes and don't want to be. They don't spearhead ethical campaigns. They move patiently, carefully, and incrementally. They do what is right—for their organizations, for the people around them and for themselves—inconspicuously and without casualties.
>
> I have come to call these people *quiet leaders* because their modesty and restraint are in large measure responsible for their impressive achievements (Badaracco, 2000: i).

Translation: You can be one, too!

INTERNAL QUALITY DRIVES TEAM HAPPINESS

PAUL The traditional way of thinking about internal quality and its relationship to happiness is to implement systems that make it easier for people to do things, and to implement them once without reworks: that will lead to team happiness (a crucial goal as you'll discover in a moment). Certainly, systems traditionally have helped enormously. But when you study many (most?) companies, you discover that there are systems for every conceivable activity except the most important: the way human beings communicate with each other. This lack of a crucial system results in stress, not happiness. Fortunately, this can be rectified. To show how, consider the

Australian dentist, Dr. Paddi Lund. His fascinating story has many read-between-the-lines points that I'll point out as we go along. The implications are positively remarkable.

I first met Paddi at a seminar, where he identified himself as a dentist during the opening session. And because I had some problems with my teeth at the time, I made a point of seeking him out during lunch. As I was talking to him, I decided to come straight to the point and ask him if he could fix them (since I felt he was looking at them anyway). I remember his response as he looked even closer: "This is bulk dentistry," he said with a big smile. (It turned out he was right, by the way.) During my many visits with him, I came to regard him not just as a dentist but as a genius, not just as a dental practitioner, but much more importantly, for his astute observations on business.

Over time we became very close friends. I learned that just a few years before we met, Paddi had been working in a very different environment from the one you see today, which is very, very special. Starting with the name—Dental Happiness—it is apparent immediately that this is no ordinary dental practice. On arrival, clients push a discreetly located bell, and upon entering are welcomed by a preassigned care nurse. Then they are handed a menu—not of dental services, but an actual list of food and drink (at a dentist's office!). There is no reception desk. It has been replaced by a small counter that looks very much like one at a Starbucks, complete with a huge four-handled cappuccino machine (the coffee smell effectively replaces the typical off-putting dental smell). To the left are chairs and tables arranged to look like a cute, old English restaurant where you might "take tea." On every table is a framed copy of what is called "Our Courtesy System." It describes in a simple but effective bulleted list, how everyone, including the customers, are expected to communicate in the environment. (Details on this in a moment because communication is a central part of creating the kind of culture to take pride in.)

If you are already one of Paddi's customers, your care nurse ushers you to your special client lounge—with your picture or name on the door. Inside are comfortable round chairs, a coffee table, some great books, and a phone. Your care nurse takes your order for food and drink. Shortly thereafter, there's a knock on the door (*your* door, remember!), and of course you say, "Come in." (This is no small point: they're doing every little thing they can to make you feel totally in control of what's happening.) Then your coffee, tea, and/or your snack are beautifully served to you.

If you are a first-timer, upon being escorted to a client lounge, and after taking your snack order, the care nurse leaves you with a copy of the courtesy system to study, plus a questionnaire and a pen. Upon returning, your care nurse goes through both the courtesy system and the questionnaire with you. The questionnaire itself is not so much about the problems you're experiencing with your teeth, but the *outcomes* you want, the *expectations* you have. (Hopefully, by this time, you're beginning to see some major parallels to your firm.)

After perhaps 30 minutes, your care nurse tells you that Dr. Lund is really looking forward to meeting you. "I'll go get Dr. Lund for you, if that's okay with you." (Note in particular the words "if that's okay with you?" as they are words that you must use to let customers feel they're in control of the situation.) The nurse may even suggest you visit the restroom. And if you do, you'll see something else surprising: above the sink is an array of wonderful perfumes and colognes; and above them, a notice that reads, "Please feel free to use the toiletries; they're for you."

Back in your lounge, you await the appearance of Dr. Lund. Again there's a knock on the door. When you say "come in," Paddi moves across to you so that you can remain seated. He leans down to shake your hand and says, "Hello, I'm Paddi Lund; it's great to see you. May I sit down?" This is all so natural that you're not aware this is being done to make you feel important and in control. By this time, Paddi, of course, has reviewed your questionnaire with your care nurse, so he's already aware of the outcomes you want. He then explains that he's going to take a detailed look at your mouth, after which the two of you will come back to your lounge to review what needs to be done and to let you know ahead of time what your investment will be to get the outcomes you want. In effect, he gives you an FPA! (How Paddi actually practices dentistry is beyond the scope of this discussion, but suffice it to say that, it too, is very, very special, featuring precisely the same level of attention to detail and care.)

When your session with Paddi is over, you pay immediately (he has no bad debts; in fact, he has a negative accounts receivable). Then you sit back down in your lounge to have a coffee, tea, or beer with Paddi. You leave with two referral cards and six fantastic cakes, referred to as Dental Buns. (In an interesting case of intellectual capital leverage, Paddi now markets his recipes for the cakes.) The referral cards (in the shape of an apple) read as follows:

> If we ask, (we don't ask everyone) we would like you to try to refer at least one person whom you feel would like the things we offer. In this way we can continue to have a flow of new people, and be here for you when you need us next time.

Paddi operates this way for a very simple reason: he has no listing of any kind in any telephone directory. When Paddi decided to create a referrals-only business, he was serious.

Now that you know how Paddi runs his business today, let me explain how he used to operate. Paddi was literally wracked with stress to the extent that he began to suffer from Obsessive Compulsive Disorder (OCD). Ultimately, he was so tormented he came very close to committing suicide. Fortunately he stopped to ponder what was happening to him, and why. He realized that he was picking up stress from his clients, who most likely were responding to his own stressful behaviors. His team, too, were stressed, to the point that resignations were occurring—of long-term people. So he began to think about how he could build a dental practice that was totally different. The answer came from something one of his dissatisfied team members said to him. And it was so simple. The team member said, "You don't treat me like you care. You never say please and thank you."

So began a journey for Paddi, a journey to create what he refers to as the "happiness-centered business." In the context of this chapter, think of it as the happiness-centered *vision*. Why shouldn't happiness be part of what we envisage for tomorrow or the day after? In fact, why shouldn't we put happiness at the *top* of our list? (Now perhaps you understand my point about Keith Seeley's vision emphasizing fun.)

Paddi went to work creating a business with happiness at its core. He realized that people experienced pain while at the dentist in part because they *expected* pain, so he changed anything and everything that conveyed or contributed to the "you're about to experience pain" environment. He sawed his front desk in two and carted it away. In its place came the coffee machine and the Starbucks (or cute English café) design. He transformed the experience, right down to replacing those hi-tech (and scary) dental chairs that patients cling to for dear life at the sound of the drill; in their place are couches. (In the midst of this transformation, his former team members began to return.)

But mind you, at Paddi's, only those people who fit Paddi's customer profile have the privilege of experiencing his happiness-centered business. Remember the point made in Chapter 8 about customer selection, and Baker's Law about bad customers driving out good ones? Paddi had precisely that insight, though perhaps he would rephrase Baker's Law this way: Bad customers give me stress; good ones bring me happiness." So Paddi ran the classic "A," "B," "C," "D" profiles on his customers. He realized, simply, that he didn't like some of them; and, perhaps even more to the point, they didn't really like him! So in essence he packaged up the "Ds" and transferred them (gracefully) to another local dentist (who, by the way, was happy to have them).

Bear in mind that Paddi did all this only to lower his stress level. There was no other motive. The results: fewer work hours and lower stress levels, both for him and his team. More surprising to him was that his income went up (Baker's Law in action!). He figured there must be a relationship there.

Next, he realized that his "C" customers had effectively become "Ds," so he passed them on to the local dentist, who couldn't believe Paddi's generosity. And guess what? Even fewer hours at work, far less stress (equals more happiness), and still greater profit. (Again, it's important to point out that, for Paddi, the profit increase was an unexpected by-product.) Now Paddi knew for sure there was a relationship there. By default, then, the "Bs" had become the "Ds". Paddi found another dentist to pass them to, when the first dentist couldn't handle more new clients.

The quantifiable results are these: Dr. Paddi Lund now works 22 hours a week, yet earns between three and four times more than the average dentist in Australia. The messages should be clear by now.

But there's one more important point: Paddi recognized that second only to himself, his team members were the most important aspects of his business (certainly more important than customers). So he set about refining the culture even further. He and his team instituted the Courtesy System, based on measuring their stress and what caused it.

It is all so disarmingly simple that you may be inclined to dismiss these revelations. But that is the real beauty of it! To clarify, let's break the process Paddi went through into four steps:

1. Lift the spirit of the organization. The two key standards are:
   - Speak politely: say please and thank you.
   - Greet and say goodbye to everyone using their name and a touch.

2. Challenge deep-seated personal behaviors.

- Talk about people as if they were present—use their names.
- If you have a problem with someone, talk only with him or her.

3. Discover anew powerful business tools.

- Apologize and make restitution if someone is upset by your actions.
- Blame a system not a person.

4. Celebrate and reinvent the personal approach at work.

- Tell the truth.
- Use positive conversation.

Consider the first item under step 1 for a moment—saying please and thank you. Are you thinking it's far too soft, that as a business leader you ought to be able to get things you want without going through that; that it's a waste of time; that you might relinquish your power? In response, I suggest you consider these gems from a manual Paddi uses to educate others to become happiness-centered businesses.

> Often we are more polite to strangers than to those who most directly affect our happiness.
> Politeness is the oil of the wheels of society. It is even more important between married people than strangers.
> Whenever we interact with another member of the team, we treat him or her at least as well as we would our best customer.

These comments make Paddi seem more of a philosopher than a dentist, don't they? Now consider these comments from team members about Paddi's greeting and goodbye standards:

> A warm and positive greeting makes me feel welcome and respected. I am more likely to enjoy my day and work efficiently and effectively. I will be more productive on a day like this.
> At the end of a long day, a genuine farewell thanks me for my efforts and puts me in a positive frame of mind to enjoy my evening. It fills me with positive energy to pass on to my family and friends. It helps me to look forward to the days ahead.

I could go on but no doubt you get the point. Often, we all see examples of the exact opposite, where barriers are erected in place of a great culture and to people performing at their best. Perhaps you could use the paragraph below as a wall chart to continually express the point: "It's not my job to motivate the team—they bring extraordinary motivation. It's my job not to *de*motivate them. It's not the things you do to or for people—it's the impediments you *take away*, leaving space for people to do tremendous things."

Think about that in relation to timesheets. To repeat from Chapter 10 what Ikujiro Nonaka and Hirotaka Takeuchi wrote so eloquently in *The Knowledge-Creating Company: How Japanese Companies Create the Dynamics of Innovation*:

Allow people time to pursue harebrained schemes or just sit around chatting, and you may come up with a market-changing idea; force them to account for every minute of their day, and you will be stuck with routine products (Nonaka and Takeuchi, 1995).

Put more bluntly, if you're still hanging on to timesheets, you're missing huge opportunities to build a better culture. It's that simple.

RECASTING THE ROLES

PAUL To become a firm of the future takes more than recognizing new value systems. Building a new culture and implementing a new vision requires a complete rethinking (and recasting) of traditional roles.

In the traditional professional practice, you have the partners (most likely those with the highest hourly rate) and then their subordinates, those who in one way or another keep the work flowing. The partner is revered as all-seeing, all-knowing, and (regrettably) all-doing. It's different in the firm of the future. In such a firm, the owner might put it like this: "To create our financial success we're hiring good people, energizing them, and turning them loose!" Note well the last six words. Each partner's role is principally to "orchestrate" superb performance from the team. The partners do not *do* the work. The practice operates as a business, as opposed to a practice. Indeed, one key to recognizing a firm of the future is when the managing partner's chargeable time drops from the traditional 1,400 (or in an extreme case, 2,500) hours to zero.

The metaphor of orchestrating leads me back to Benjamin Zander, quoted at the beginning of this chapter. In a documentary produced to explore his role, Zander is seen in front of the orchestra conducting. Then he turns to the camera with the orchestra still playing and says, "Observe that the orchestra is playing what Neil Diamond used to refer to as a 'beautiful noise.' But most importantly observe that I am not playing a single instrument!" The parallel to the typical professional firm is clear: The managing partner(s) categorically are *not* conducting. They're attempting to play the first violin, the second violin, the cello, the woodwind, the drums, even the triangle! Not only is this noise (as opposed to music), it is demonstrably not a profitable way to operate.

"But," you protest, "I can't trust my people to do the work as well as I can." Read again this gem from Zander:

I set as the goal the maximum capacity that people have—I settle for no less. I make myself a relentless architect of the possibilities of human beings.

Therein lies a major key (no pun intended) to building a firm of the future. And that key links to profitability, too. For example, in highly successful firms around the world there is an *inverse* relationship between the chargeable hours at a senior partner level and the profitability of the firm. Orchestrating then (or at least conducting) seems to be important. And that links perfectly with having a vision and a culture of turning the practice into a business. But when you look at many professional practices, you see not businesses in the strict sense; you see instead partners each with his or her own clients; essentially, all they share are expenses. In contrast, when you look at successful businesses, you see defined outcomes for each key unit. Put another way, the business does not depend on the partner.

Michael Gerber hit the nail right on the head when he observed in his book *The E-Myth Revisited* that the purpose of creating a business is to sell it. Yet so many of us (you *and* your clients) create businesses that depend on us. Stop and ask this question: If you were buying a business, would you pay more or less for a business that depended on the current owner, as opposed to a business that had structure and depended instead on systems? The answer is pretty clear isn't it?

Perhaps you're thinking at this point, "That's all very logical. But my clients want *me*!" Well, actually, your clients don't want you; believe it or not, they would much prefer to be dealing with your well-trained team members. Your clients (as well as your team) want you to conduct the practice like Zander conducts his orchestra. And it's time you did. It's time you created a culture that serves you. As Christina Kirk pointed out in an article she wrote for the *Australian Financial Review BOSS Magazine*:

> A growing body of increasingly sophisticated research in the public domain emphasizes the importance of culture on corporate performance. John Kotter, of the Harvard Business School, conducted the landmark study of cultures of leading U.S. organizations for the period 1978 to 1989. He found that high-performing organizations with cultures focused on the interests of their key stakeholders—customers, staff, shareholders—had an average 900 percent increase in stock price over a 12-year period as against 74 percent for organizations lacking a similar focus (Kirk: 2000).

Those are staggering numbers. But they refer to more than 20 years ago. Kirk goes on to effectively verify the point that John Kotter was making, by concluding her article with these words:

> Culture is more critical to high performance than ever. The real issue is to move from rhetoric to reality; to stop talking about the importance of people and to demonstrate that we really believe this by our actions (Ibid).

We can only add "hallelujah." Of course, whenever we talk about culture and an inspiring vision, people ask "So what's yours? If you were running a professional practice, what would your vision be?" Rather than answer that (after all, it's *your* vision that's important here), let me share with you a recurring dream I have. I see the world as you might see it on a large, flat map. On it are all the countries spread out. And then, suddenly, from every country, tiny little lights start to glow, to beckon. These lights represent, for me, the firms of the future. They are, in every sense, centers of excellence, centers of communities that do the right things extraordinarily well, to the extent that team members and customers are drawn to those lights. They are centers that influence the communities they serve in profound and positive ways. And, yes, they're happiness-centered businesses, too, which choose to deal only with other happiness-centered businesses. And thanks to the amazing power of the Web, they're effectively connected, sharing their stories and their expertise (and maybe even their customers and their team members). Their lights grow ever brighter.

WOULD YOU WANT YOUR SON OR
DAUGHTER TO WORK THERE?

Our future is too important to be left to the statisticians and logicians.
They can predict based only on a straight-line continuation of the
past and present, a pretty sorry prospect. Valuable as such planning is, we
need to stop being so logical. The future should be left to the dreamers.

—Stanley Marcus, *Stanley Marcus from A to Z: Viewpoints Volume II*

RON After I had read Paul's words here, I had a fortuitous phone conversation with Dr. Sheila Kessler, a remarkable woman. She is a consultant for more than 100 of the Fortune 500 companies, a former California Baldrige Quality Award examiner for the California Council on Service and Quality (CCQS), and author of nine books; and she has worked and consulted in 54 countries. Every time I have the good fortune to speak with her, my intellectual capital rises immeasurably.

During our conversation Sheila asked the question: "How many companies do you truly admire?" This goes far beyond merely doing business with them, but more relates to whether I would want a son or daughter to work for them. It is an excellent question, and for all of her experience—with literally hundreds of companies around the world—she said there are perhaps 20 that would make her list. *Only 20?*

As I thought about it, I could not name more than 20 myself; and although Sheila's and my list differ on the companies we truly respect and admire, is it not a sad commentary that we cannot name more?

This is a very reflective question, because it caused me to think deeply about the business education most of us have received at universities, continuing education courses, seminars, and conferences, and especially from the books we read. It seems as if, at various times and places, different companies are held up as models to emulate for different purposes—Disney, Nordstrom and Ritz-Carlton for customer service; Southwest for managing customer's expectations and competing on low price; 3M for innovation; and so on—and we are guilty of this as well in this book. But reflecting on my education, I would have to say I have learned more from business autobiographies and biographies than from all of the business books I have read *combined* (with the exception of those by Peter Drucker).

The history of business is the history of dreamers and entrepreneurs, those rare individuals who cast aside the security of a paycheck, mortgage everything they have, and chase a dream that ends up creating our futures. The great economist Joseph Schumpeter referred to this process as the "perennial gale of creative destruction." The factories and technologies of tomorrow—that may be nothing more than a glimmer in the eyes of a garage tinkerer—will at some point rise up and supplant the old order, disrupting the status quo and making a mockery of static income distribution tables. It is the sophomore dropout who starts a software company and creates the world's standard operating system—Microsoft's Bill Gates. It is the perseverant student who charges against the odds despite receiving a "C" on his term paper and launches a company that, most likely, every reader of this book has used, or uses, on a regular basis—Fred Smith's FedEx. Yet most visionary companies are not built upon a single idea, despite the conventional wisdom.

The tempo of business is not one of stability and order, but rather of disequilibrium and instability. Stability exists only in the graveyards. Ralph Waldo Emerson once wrote, "An institution is the lengthened shadow of one man." Mike Vance, former dean of Disney University, tells this story of Walt Disney's final hours in 1966 in his book, *Think Out of the Box*:

> At Disney studios in Burbank, California, Mike could gaze out of his office window, across Buena Vista Street, to St. Joseph's Hospital where Walt Disney died. The morning he died, Mike was talking on the telephone when he saw the flag being lowered over at the hospital around 8:20 A.M. His death was preceded by an amazing incident that reportedly took place the night before in Walt's hospital room.
>
> A journalist, knowing Walt was seriously ill, persisted in getting an interview with Walt and was frustrated on numerous occasions by the hospital staff. When he finally managed to get into the room, Walt couldn't sit up in bed or talk above a whisper. Walt instructed the reporter to lie down on the bed, next to him, so he could whisper in the reporter's ear. For the next 30 minutes, Walt and the journalist lay side by side as Walt referred to an imaginary map of Walt Disney World on the ceiling above the bed.
>
> Walt pointed out where he planned to place various attractions and buildings. He talked about transportation, hotels, restaurants, and many other parts of his vision for a property that wouldn't open to the public for another six years.
>
> We told this reporter's moving experience, relayed through a nurse, to each one of our organizational development (OD) groups . . . the story of how a man who lay dying in the hospital whispered in the reporter's ear for 30 minutes describing his vision for the future and the role he would play in it for generations to come.
>
> This is the way to live—believing so much in your vision that even when you're dying, you whisper it into another person's ear (Vance and Deacon, 1995: 30).

Soon after the completion of Walt Disney World, someone said, "Isn't it too bad Walt Disney didn't live to see this?" Vance replied, "He did see it—that's why it's here."

We do not mean to imply that it is only entrepreneurs, or men and women of incredible foresight and tenacity, who should be held up for emulation and education. I will admit a personal bias for entrepreneurs, and consider them to be more interesting to study than the CEO of an established company, such as Jack Welch. But you can learn from both. This is also not to imply that an organization is the result of only one person—for it certainly is not. The amount of social and human capital that is required to build a Microsoft, FedEx, and Disney—not to mention have them outlive their founders' lives—is staggering. Most of the day-to-day business in our worldwide economy is carried out in the more prosaic fashion of the local barber, and with the skilled precision of the oncologist.

It is also too simplistic to say that all any firm of the future needs is an excellent vision statement, or the right type of culture, or adequate leadership. No doubt these are all important, but they are not enough to ensure a timeless practice, those flickering lights on the map Paul mentioned.

Consider this list of corporate values from a 2000 Annual Report: Communication: "Respect, Integrity, Excellence." These were the values of Enron; and while they are the same words found in many value statements, were they meaningful? Did the company live up to them? Did they set a shining example for the rest of the business community to emulate?

Core values are critical, do not misunderstand. But the true test of whether the leaders of an organization actually mean what they say is when those core values are upheld in good—and bad—times, even at tremendous cost to the company. Roy Disney was once asked the secret to his and his brother's incredible success with their company:

> It's no secret. We've always tried to manage by our values because, when you know what your values are, decision making is easier.
>
> You've got to have your values in synch with your goals; then people are self-motivated. They don't require a shot in the arm or motivational hype, although it doesn't hurt to perk things up once in a while.
>
> Most people have ability. You've got to encourage them by setting lofty standards and then help them master their skills. This is why we put so much emphasis on training and education (Ibid: 180).

CORE IDEOLOGY = CORE VALUES + PURPOSE

RON In the introduction to the paperback edition of their book, *Built to Last: Successful Habits of Visionary Companies*, James Collins and Jerry Porras explain what it takes to build a visionary company:

> The only truly reliable source of stability is a strong inner core and the willingness to change and adapt everything except that core. People cannot reliably predict where they are going and how their lives will unfold, especially in today's unpredictable world. Those who built the visionary companies wisely understood that it is better to understand who you are than where you are going—for where you are going will almost certainly change. It is a lesson as relevant to our individual lives as to aspiring visionary companies (Collins and Porras, 1997: xx).

A visionary company does not necessarily start out with a highly innovative or successful first product. Collins and Porras point out that of the 18 visionary companies they profile, only three—Johnson & Johnson, General Electric, and Ford—began with a so-called great idea. The others did not, but instead saw creating a visionary organization as their ultimate purpose, what the authors distinguish between "clock building" rather than merely "telling time." The essential ingredient of building a visionary company is to develop and articulate a core ideology, which Collins and Porras define as follows:

Core Ideology = Core Values + Purpose

Core Values: The organization's essential and enduring tenets—a small set of general guiding principles; not to be confused with specific cultural or operating practices; not to be compromised for financial gain or short-term expediency. Purpose: The organization's fundamental reasons for existence beyond just making money—a perpetual guiding star on the horizon; not to be confused with specific goals or business strategies (Ibid: 73).

Consider the core values and purpose of Johnson & Johnson, in a statement titled "Our Credo," a copy of which is carved in stone at the company's New Brunswick, New Jersey, headquarters. Founder R.W. Johnson wrote this credo in 1943 and it has often been cited as precedent for tactical decisions made since then, especially during the Tylenol crisis the company faced in 1982:

Our Credo

We believe that our first responsibility is to the doctors, nurses, hospitals, mothers, and all others who use our products. Our products must always be of the highest quality. We must constantly strive to reduce the cost of these products. Our orders must be promptly and accurately filled. Our dealers must make a fair profit.

Our second responsibility is to those who work with us—the men and women in our plants and offices. They must have a sense of security in their jobs. Wages must be fair and adequate, management just, hours reasonable, and working conditions clean and orderly. Employees should have an organized system for suggestions and complaints. Supervisors and department heads must be qualified and fair-minded. There must be opportunity for advancement for those qualified, and each person must be considered an individual standing on his [or her] own dignity and merit.

Our third responsibility is to our management. Our executives must be persons of talent, education, experience, and ability. They must be persons of common sense and full understanding.

Our fourth responsibility is to the communities in which we live. We must be a good citizen—support good works and charity, and bear our fair share of taxes. We must maintain in good order the property we are privileged to use.

We must participate in promotion of civic improvement, health, education, and good government, and acquaint the community with our activities.

Our fifth and last responsibility is to our stockholders. Business must make a sound profit. Reserves must be created, research must be carried on, adventurous programs developed, and mistakes paid for. Adverse times must be provided for, adequate taxes paid, new machines purchased, new plants built, new products launched, and new sales plans developed. We must experiment with new ideas. When these things have been done the stockholder should receive a fair return. We are determined with the help of God's grace to fulfill these obligations to the best of our ability.

Is this a company you would want your son and daughter to work for? The company will tolerate mistakes but not "sins," defined as a breach of the core ideology. The difference between a visionary company such as Johnson & Johnson and Enron is putting these values in action, and remaining faithful to them, even at the expense of profits.

It is a rare company that survives the ages that puts greed and profits ahead of creating wealth for its customers. Money simply is not enough of an inspiration to partake in work that serves a larger purpose, as a visit to any local charity or Salvation Army office should teach us. No one has pictures of money hanging on their walls, but rather those things we care most deeply about—family, friends, trophies, and memories that acknowledge the achievements in our lives for what we contributed, not what we earned.

Some of the more prominent companies' core purposes are:

Fannie Mae: To strengthen the social fabric by continually democratizing home ownership.

Hewlett-Packard: To make technical contributions for the advancement and welfare of humanity.

Mary Kay: To give unlimited opportunity to women.

McKinsey: To help leading corporations and governments be more successful.

Nike: To experience the emotion of competition, winning, and crushing competitors.

Sony: To experience the joy of advancing and applying technology for the benefit of the public.

Wal-Mart: To give ordinary folk the chance to buy the same things as rich people.

Walt Disney: To make people happy.

Charles Schwab: We are the guardians of our customers' financial dreams.

Even the pope understands the importance of creating wealth and generating a profit for the owners of the business. In his 1991 encyclical *Centesimus Annus* ("The Hundredth Year"), Pope John Paul II approves of profit (quite a change from the prior viewpoint of the Catholic Church) but also admonishes that profit is not to be considered the sole indicator of the success of the business—capitalism is not a system merely of *things*, but about the human spirit as well:

> The church acknowledges the legitimate role of profit as an indication that a business is functioning well. When a firm makes a profit, this means that productive factors have been properly employed and corresponding human needs have been duly satisfied. It is possible for the financial accounts to be in order, and yet for the people—who are the firm's most valuable asset—to be humiliated and their dignity offended. This is morally inadmissible [and] will eventually have negative repercussions on the firm's economic efficiency. The purpose of a business firm is not simply to make a profit, but is to be found in its very existence as a community of persons who in various ways are endeavoring to satisfy their basic needs and who form a particular group at the service of the whole of society. Profit is a regulator of the life of a business, but it is not the only one; other human and moral factors must also be considered, which in the long term are at least equally important for the life of the business.

One thing that separates humans from animals is that humans know they have a past and a future, and they are willing to invest to improve the future, even though they know as mortals they will not be around to enjoy the fruits of those investments. Animals are not wealthy or poor; they are either well fed or hungry. History remembers the *builders* and *creators* of wealth, never *consumers*. In a sense, there is a free lunch, since each generation is living off the accumulated intellectual capital of its ancestors. Walt Disney was certainly a builder who created and shaped the future by building a visionary company:

> You reach a point where you don't work for money. . . . When I make a profit, I don't squander it or hide it away; I immediately plow it back into a fresh project. I have little respect for money as such; I regard it merely as a medium for financing new ideas. I neither wish nor intend to amass a personal fortune. Money—or, rather the lack of it to carry out my ideas—may worry me, but it does not excite me. Ideas excite me.
>
> I could never convince the financiers that Disneyland was feasible, because dreams offer too little collateral.

LEADERSHIP

Consensus is the negation of leadership.

—Margaret Thatcher

RON We certainly do not subscribe to the "leadership is everything" school of thought. Not every company can have a Walt Disney or a Jack Welch in the position of leadership. Ascribing all successful and unsuccessful characteristics of a business to leadership is an abdication to further our understanding of how wealth is generated and successful companies are built.

What we do know from working with professional service firms around the world is that most of them are overmanaged and underled. In far too many firms, the managing partner is among the largest revenue producer, if not the largest. We believe one of the reasons for this phenomenon is the old Practice Equation, which is more of a *management* model than a *leadership* model. You have to control and leverage people, make sure they work enough hours at the proper realization rate, and follow the rules. It is not a model that instills trust. It is a model that leads to commanding people, rather than inspiring them.

In 1990, the American Bar Association Young Lawyers Division conducted an extensive study of lawyer dissatisfaction by interviewing more than 3,000 lawyers under the age of 36, or those with fewer than three years experience, and they cited the following three major causes for job dissatisfaction:

- Lack of time for self, family, and friends, owing to billable hours requirements.
- Poor communication and isolation within the firm.
- Lack of training and mentoring within the firm (cited in Tupman, 2001: 97).

This lack of leadership is a sad commentary on the state of professional service firms, and yet surveys of accounting and consulting firms report essentially the same findings. Fred Smith sums up this situation nicely in the article, "Breakthrough Leadership," in the *Harvard Business Review*:

When someone joins an organization, they have five questions: What do you expect from me? What's in it for me? Where do I go if I have a problem? How am I doing? And is what I'm doing important? You always have to answer those five questions, but you have to adapt your leadership style to the situation at hand.

Managing partners should understand that their only customer is *the firm*. All of the talk about the end of hierarchy and flat organizations sounds nice, but the fact is, in any institution, there has to be a final authority, someone who is responsible—and held accountable—for making decisions. This is never truer than in times of crisis. Consensus is not leadership. A law from ancient Rome said the slave with three masters was a free man. Human nature being what it is, it is perilous to put people into a conflict of loyalties by having more than one person to whom they are accountable.

One of the major problems with the traditional partnership structure in the majority of professional service firms is that no one person is accountable, as in a corporate setting. The partners make every decision on consensus, hence the most trivial matters are dealt with at the partnership level, at the expense of the most important matters. We have been regaled with countless stories of partnership meetings at which the most important matters discussed were the color of the carpets to be changed or the model photocopier to be purchased. This does not even rise to the level of surgeons piercing ears, but interior decorating.

Probably the most important job a leader has is to trust people, provide them the necessary resources to do their jobs adequately, instill a sense of passion and pride in the firm, and then get out of the way and let their people do extraordinary things. Leadership is not about *personality;* it is about *performance*. Leaders should spend their time working *on* the firm, not *in* it. They have to build an organization that is not necessarily the biggest, rather flexible, versatile, and adaptable to a changing world.

Of course, the ultimate test of any leadership role is succession. Flaherty quotes Peter Drucker:

> "[T]he interaction between an institution and its outside environment [is] a flux between past and present. . . . [S]uccession [is] a bridge linking these two time spans. Because the institution must be capable of perpetuating itself, it has to be able to survive the tenure of one person's rule."
>
> Drucker took pains to point out that succession might appear to be a metaphysical abstraction in the short run, but in the long run its impact was anything but intangible. Although the question of succession did not lend itself to immediate measurability, measurable results would appear, for better or for worse, many years later. On one occasion he ridiculed the supposedly indispensable executives who would not resign, remarking, "The only way to get rid of incompetent management at the very top is a heart attack." Then he added, "But it usually strikes the wrong person. It is not reliable" (Flaherty, 1999: 274).

Charles de Gaulle used to say, "The graveyards are full of indispensable men." Yet most professional firm partners do not pay enough attention to succession, and this was the reason why the consolidators in the CPA profession—American Express, H&R Block, among others—were able to purchase CPA firms; the employees did not want to.

Leadership also affects culture, and culture affects how people behave—*especially when they are not being watched*. But like leadership, this is also not the answer to everything. All companies have a culture. So what? What might be a better explanation than culture among leading companies—like Nordstrom, Ritz-Carlton, Disney, Apple Computer, and others—is cultism, or cultlike. I use an Apple Computer, and have since 1984. As they say, if you cut a Macintosh fanatic, they bleed in the six colors of the Apple logo. In its halcyon days, Apple certainly had a cultlike culture, and it attracted a certain kind of person, one bent on changing the world by bringing the power of the computer to every desktop. Nordstrom has a strong customer service culture, but also a very demanding performance system (your performance is your appraisal), and those who do not perform are quickly weeded out of the system.

Yet the concept of culture cannot be measured; it has to be experienced. There is no single best culture, but it is important to be aware of your firm's cultural signals and what they say about your values and purpose. It is difficult enough to earn the loyalty of knowledge workers—since they are not so much loyal to any one organization as they are to their profession—without the added burden of not fostering a culture and developing leaders who inspire professionals to serve your customers.

WHAT ABOUT STRATEGIC PLANNING?

Life is what happens while you're making other plans.

—John Lennon

RON The firm of the future will be controlled more and more by strategy than by ownership. There will still be partners, or owners, naturally, but also joint ventures, minority stakes, networks, associations, and other forms of alliances. Strategic business planning fell out of favor in the 1980s and 1990s because it was not delivering on its promises. We are referring to the long-term planning, the 5- to 50-year elaborate planning models that are more reminiscent of the former Soviet Union's five-year plans than a market economy dominated by creative destruction, dynamism, and constant change. Preparation for the future is an art, not a science, and strategic planning became nothing more than mathematical models and detailed business plans that did not have much relationship to reality. This is why Jack Welch shut down General Electric's 200-strong planning department in 1983.

For as far as strategic planning has fallen from grace—especially after Henry Mintzberg's *The Rise and Fall of Strategic Planning* utterly drove a nail in its coffin—it is rather surprising how many firms still believe they must have a "strategic plan." Worse, consultants to the profession perpetuate this idea and facilitate expensive strategic planning sessions, whose results are mediocre at best, and positively detrimental at worst. The problem is nobody can predict the future, and strategic plans most likely become mere exercises in extrapolating the status quo rather than trying to create change. Rarely do these strategic plans *abandon* yesterday, but simply carry it into the future.

What happened to the 5- or 10-year strategic plan of Arthur Andersen? Or those of its competitors and alliance partners affected by its rapid demise? This is not to say an organization should not have goals, or even a broad strategy, rather that the plan should not be a substitute for adapting to change. Further, these strategies should be rather short-term, one to two years, not elaborate projections for a decade or more into the future.

SUMMARY AND CONCLUSIONS

What is your firm's core ideology? How will you a build a visionary practice where people voluntarily decide to contribute their human capital? How will you create a timeless practice that junior members will want to purchase at some point in their careers? Will you a build a practice at which you would be proud to have your son or daughter work?

What is the vision of the timeless practice? That is for you to decide. Our vision would include being able, in perhaps 10 or 20 years' time, to name more than just two handfuls of firms we admire and at which we would be proud to have our sons and daughters work. The legal and accounting professions are noble callings, and we worry about the deteriorating morale in each, and challenge today's leaders to create a more passionate tomorrow. May we be wise enough to abandon those practices that are eroding the morale of the professions and making them less attractive to new human capital.

Let us stop ineptly pursuing yesterday's tomorrow and instead let us create tomorrow's tomorrow. The founding framers of America began their new country with a clear vision of the future, *Novus Ordo Seclorum* ("A new order of the ages"), as is printed on the back of each dollar bill. We offer the vision of a timeless practice—one where your sons and daughters would gladly work and eventually purchase—a new way of thinking and operating, emphasizing customer value and a sense of service to others first. A world in which these virtues are practiced as much as they are preached. A reality whose time is here.

12

SOME WORDS ON THE FUTURE

History doesn't repeat itself—but it rhymes.

—Attributed to Mark Twain

PAUL Ron and I often debate books and authors—along the lines of "this guy is on track, this one doesn't make sense." One we argue about is Tom Peters. But Peters is right on point when he talks about destruction. He would prefer the role of the CEO to be that of a CDO, the chief *destruction* officer, because he sees the role as one of essentially destroying the status quo since, as he puts it, "If you don't, your competitor will."

Other authors make the same point. Michael Hammer said in *Reengineering the Corporation*, "Don't fiddle with what we've got but throw it away." Nicholas Negroponte wrote, "Incrementalism is innovation's worst enemy." And Lew Platt, a former CEO of Hewlett-Packard used to say that "whatever made you successful in the past won't in the future."

When you look at the accounting profession right now, surely these words ring truer than at any time in the past. Yet the vested forces—in particular, the industry bodies—don't act that way. They are always tinkering at the edges. Of course, one could argue they do so because their members are always tinkering at the edges, too. As a former president of the Institute of Chartered Accountants in England and Wales said to me as recently as 1999, "How can I lead this organization to greatness when I am still receiving letters from members typed on old-fashioned typewriters?"

RON *Non sibi sed allis*, Latin for "not for ourselves but for others" is one of the core values of any profession. Twentieth-century scholarship on the professions conveys two shifts, both beginning in the 1950s and culminating in the 1970s and 1980s: a *normative* shift from approbation to criticism and a *theoretical* shift from functional-

287

ist to structuralist analyses of professions. A profession is defined by three characteristics: expertise, association, and service. The shift from approbation to criticism has often been harsh and has often been manifested in more severe regulations or restrictions; at other times, it has been expressed as biting wit, in the form of accountant and attorney jokes told the world over. No one has done a better job at poking fun at (chartered) accountants than Monty Python, as this sketch from its television series demonstrates (first aired on November 30, 1969):

(Cut to a small board meeting. An accountant stands up and reads . . .):

Accountant (Michael Palin): Lady chairman, sir, shareholders, ladies and gentlemen. I have great pleasure in announcing that owing to a cutback on surplus expenditure of twelve million Canadian dollars, plus a refund of seven and a half million Deutschmarks from the Swiss branch, and in addition adding the debenture preference stock of the three and three quarter million to the director's reserve currency account of seven and a half million, plus an upward expenditure margin of eleven and a half thousand lire, due to a rise in capital investment of ten million pounds, this firm last year made a complete profit of a shilling.

Chairman (Graham Chapman): A shilling Wilkins?

Accountant: Er, roughly, yes sir.

Chairman: Wilkins, I am the chairman of a multimillion pound corporation and you are a very new chartered accountant. Isn't it possible there may have been some mistake?

Accountant: Well that's very kind of you sir, but I don't think I'm ready to be chairman yet.

Board Member (John Cleese): Wilkins, Wilkins. This shilling, is it net or gross?

Accountant: It's British sir.

Chairman: Yes, has tax been paid on it?

Accountant: Yes, this is after tax. Owing to the rigorous bite of the income tax, five pence of a further sixpence was swallowed up in tax.

Board Member: Five pence of a *further* sixpence?

Accountant: *(eagerly)* Yes sir.

Chairman: Five pence of a further *sixpence*?

Accountant: That's right sir.

Chairman: Then where is the other penny?

Accountant: . . . Er.

Board Member: That makes you a penny short Wilkins. Where is it?

Accountant: . . . Er.

Chairman: Wilkins?

Accountant: *(in tears)* I embezzled it sir.

Chairman: What, all of it?

Accountant: Yes all of it.

Board Member: You naughty person.

Accountant: It's my first. Please be gentle with me.
Chairman: I'm afraid it's my unpleasant duty to inform you that you're fired.
Accountant: *(crying)* Oh . . . *(he leaves)*
Chairman: Yes, there's no place for sentiment in big business. (Monty Python, 1989: 82–83).

We show this sketch in our courses and it always produces uproarious laughter from the audience. Yet despite the stereotypes that exist of the professions—accountants as bean counters and lawyers as scriveners—both are noble callings. The purpose of this chapter is not to pick on the professions, but to speak to some of the issues confronting them in the coming decades.

I am a CPA, and claim no special expertise in the area of the law or the legal profession, hence I will restrict my comments to those issues confronting the legal profession that I do know something about—specifically, multidisciplinary practices, hourly billing reform, and alternative pricing models. As for the CPA profession, I know more and will discuss the current state of the financial statement audit, a new financial reporting model, accounting reform in the wake of Enron and other scandals, the accounting education curriculum, and attracting students to the profession.

The purpose of these discussions is not to claim any prescience, and not to encourage you think *like* me, rather, to have you think *with* me about these important issues facing our profession. The last chapter on the profession has yet to be written. There is always room for more words.

IS THE AUDIT AN EDSEL?

RON CFO.com reported on April 11, 2002, that NFO WorldGroup, a provider of research-based marketing information and counsel, conducted a survey in April 2002 of companies that purchase outside accounting services. Using its own index—where a score of 100 is the equivalent to an A—auditors received a score of 61—a D—compared to other general business-to-business service providers that received an 80—a B. Only 55 percent ranked the overall performance of the auditor as excellent or very good, compared with 70 to 75 percent in other service categories.

Further, only 55 percent said they definitely or probably would recommend their auditors to business colleagues, compared with between 75 and 80 percent for other categories. Auditors scored very well in terms of trust, personal ethics, integrity, and maintaining a position of independence; but as the study concluded:

> "These weak scores should be a clear warning bell that the accounting profession has serious, fundamental client-relationship problems that are different from the issues dominating the headlines about Andersen and Enron," says Shubhra Ramchandani, stakeholder management practice leader for North America at NFO. The problem isn't integrity—it is value. Most clients rate their outside accountants' business ethics very highly, but what they question is the performance and value of the services they receive (Taub, 2002).

Most accountants take the easy way out and claim the audit is a commodity, a specious notion we laid to rest, hopefully, in Chapter 9. Yes, it is true the audit is a requirement most companies have to comply with; but it is important to remember that audits were performed for the vast majority of public companies listed on the stock exchange long before the Securities and Exchange Commission made them mandatory. The audit is actually an insurance product, designed to mitigate the principal-agent problem; that is, principals (owners) hire managers (agents) to run their business, and one way to watch over them and hold them accountable is to conduct an independent audit. This is why the market placed a value on audits long before the government made them mandatory for public companies.

That being said, the accounting profession has held the view since the 1980s that the audit is nothing more than a commodity, and they priced it as a loss leader in the hopes of acquiring the more lucrative tax and consulting work. It is the one government-sanctioned franchise—meaning, to be blunt, a monopoly—and the accountants have been giving it away. Worse, they have not priced it based on actuarial risk models but rather on an arbitrary—and often heavily discounted—hourly rate, falling prey to the labor theory of value. Perhaps no price was adequate enough for Andersen to audit Enron, and in twenty-twenty hindsight I conjecture the partners wished they would have followed Baker's Law, since in this case one bad customer drove away *all* the good ones.

On June 5, 2002, in his first public appearance since resigning from Arthur Andersen in March, Joseph F. Berardino spoke at the Commonwealth Club in Palo Alto, California, on how the Enron scandal will change the accounting profession forever. Here are his more provocative points (as published in *The Washington Post*):

> The process of giving investors financial information to make decisions is broken. And all the change in the world won't fix it if we continue to place the entire burden on the accounting profession.
>
> [He spoke of fundamental flaws in financial reporting] Like the tax code, we've made accounting a game of rules, loopholes, and legalisms.
>
> Performance indicators also need to be more clearly defined, and investors need to see more balanced information on business risks.
>
> [He proposed] auditors move toward a grading system for the quality of financial statements: report cards with commentary. If the results do not make sense, the auditor should object and state the reason.
>
> The profession must change its pricing structure, adding that he was "amazed" at the low auditing fees former Andersen clients have negotiated with their new auditors (Wong, 2002: E04).

I want to deal with the latter comment here first. I find it sad that a man like Berardino can rise to the pinnacle of a once-venerable accounting firm and not realize the *pricing model* is broken until the firm's demise. I know of no better damnation of the old Practice Equation and the billable hour than this epiphany from Berardino. At times, I remain deeply pessimistic about our profession's ability to learn anything new and not simply repeat the same mistakes over and over. If Enron and Arthur

Andersen taught us one thing, it is that the audit is emphatically not a commodity. No commodity—not even lettuce, bottled water, or coffee—could wreak so much havoc in the financial markets and affect so many investors' lives.

It is time the profession comprehended the value of the audit and understood it as an insurance product, one that needs to be priced actuarially. If this requires that we hire actuaries, then so be it, but at least we can learn a fundamental axiom from them for all future audit engagements: *There are no bad risks, just bad rates.*

The accounting scandals of 2001 and 2002—Enron topping the news coverage initially, but there were others—certainly rocked the accountant's world, or at least the 15 percent of CPAs engaged in auditing in the United States. But I have a different perspective on these scandals than the conventional wisdom, and this is where I depart from my colleagues and join ranks with the economists.

I believe the accounting scandals are not so much about fraud, malfeasance, or other crimes, but rather illustrate the increasing *irrelevance* of the traditional accounting reporting model. If we are serious about accounting reform, we are going to have to face some unpleasant truths. The present accounting model is over 500 years old and it is in bad shape. In an intellectual capital economy, it may be possible to track revenue and expenditures, but it is difficult to know how expenditures relate to results created outside of an organization.

The traditional Generally Accepted Accounting Principle (GAAP) financial statements are based upon a liquidation value of the business, essentially historical cost assets less liabilities. The income statement was set up to account for the most important cost in an industrial society: cost of goods sold. But in an IC economy, cost of goods sold—*cost of revenue*—is less meaningful, with Microsoft averaging 14 percent of sales, Coca-Cola roughly 30 percent, and Revlon 34 percent. Even though intellectual capital is the main driver of wealth, you will look in vain to find them in the traditional GAAP statements—the balance sheet, income statement, and statement of cash flows. Increasingly, these statements are being referred to as the "three blind mice."

Coca-Cola's brand name alone is estimated to be worth $72.5 billion, according to Interbrand, a London firm that calculates the value of brand names by comparing the premium priced earnings of branded products with what could be earned by a generic equivalent (you can find more information at www.interbrand.com). Some critics, such as Thomas Stewart, have asserted:

> Most important, the case against conventional accounting has become—it seems to most observers—open and shut: It's incontrovertibly true that present financial and management accounting does not give investors, directors, the public, or management the information they need to make informed decisions. It is time, once and for all, to drive a stake through the heart of traditional accounting, which is draining the life from business (Stewart, 2001: xiv).

I am not prepared to go as far as Stewart, but I am sympathetic to his arguments. Accountants have to admit—and even start educating the public—that the audit is a *lagging* indicator, albeit a necessary and valuable one; but it is not the be-all and end-all of investors' and other users' needs. It is no longer enough for the auditors to come in after the battle and bayonet the wounded. They need to start positing *leading* indicators for their customers, and attest to these as well. Unfortunately, the profession has simply not taken a leading role in this area, allowing consulting firms and even nongovernmental organizations (NGOs) to enter the field and capture a good portion of this work.

The longer you have been in business, the less likely it is that you understand the needs and wants of your customers. T.J. Rodgers, president and CEO of Cypress Semiconductor Corporation, has become an outspoken critic of GAAP, attacking its arbitrary rules on stock options and the ban on pooling accounting in 2001. He gave a speech entitled "When Accountants Attack Profits: The GAAP Accounting Exodus," to the Stanford Director's College on June 3, 2002, where he offered a cogent indictment of GAAP rules and procedures that did not reflect reality. Here is some of what he had to say:

> One would think that in this current environment, my company, Cypress Semiconductor, would be reporting exclusively with the "seal of approval" of the Generally Accepted Accounting Principles (GAAP). But we do not. We publish two sets of financial numbers: one in the GAAP standard and the other in the "pro forma" standard, which we have turned to as the basis of our communication to our investors over the last few years.
>
> Why would we issue two sets of financial numbers, when a simple, single report would have served better in the current environment? Simply stated, the GAAP accounting rules, as mandated by the Financial Accounting Standards Board (FASB), no longer conform to reality. Our GAAP-based report misrepresents the finances of our company to our investors, necessitating the second, pro forma report.
>
> What company would risk deviating from GAAP accounting standards in the post-Enron era? The answer: Intel, Advanced Micro Devices, Conesant, Fairchild, LSI Logic, Motorola, STMicroelectronics, Texas Instruments, Cypress, and many others. Indeed, a PricewaterhouseCoopers survey found that 74 percent of semiconductor companies issue pro forma earnings statements. . . . [T]he GAAP exodus is happening in other high-technology industries, as well.
>
> Finally, if we can't get GAAP accounting to work right—and that's my guess—we will need to create a framework of standards behind pro forma accounting to give it a real "seal of approval." Perhaps Mr. Schuetze [former chief accountant of the SEC] would accept the job of chairing the pro forma Accounting Standards Board (PASB). Our FASB/government monopoly surely needs a competitor with common sense (Rodgers, 2002: 1, 9).

To corroborate Rodger's claims, SmartStockInvestor.com, an online analyst, reported that in the first three quarters of 2001, the 100 companies making up the NASDAQ—such as Microsoft, Intel, Cisco Systems, Oracle, and Dell—reported pro forma earnings of $19.1 billion; but under GAAP, this turned into a loss of $82.3 billion.

It is simply too easy to dismiss Rodgers as a disgruntled member of an industry with a special interest to promote. *He is a customer of auditors.* His concluding remark regarding the establishment of a competitor to FASB should not be ostracized too quickly. There are many similar ideas in the field of regulation, school reform, and other areas of the economy, where economists want to introduce competition in order to improve the efficiency and effectiveness of regulatory bodies (we will explore one of the more fascinating ideas later in the chapter).

The accounting profession is a mature industry, and, as pointed out previously, it has not had a single new innovation since 1978, when it offered financial statement compilations and reviews to its customers. There are three possible roads the profession can travel. On the first, it can do nothing, which is usually the road traveled most by stagnating industries. Thinking that the past will somehow equal the future, the leaders simply see no reason to change. No doubt the profession would survive in some shape, since a lot of its work is governmentally mandated, but it will relinquish its status as the premier financial profession if it chooses this path.

On the second road, outsiders could replace the profession, the "perennial gale of creative destruction" Joseph Schumpeter wrote about. In some instances, this is already taking place with respect to Key Performance Indicators, social audits, brand valuation, and intellectual capital measurements, among others, being performed by consulting firms and NGOs. This is unfortunate since the accounting profession should be out in the forefront in these areas, but it has simply rested on its past successes.

Finally, on the third road, the profession could innovate and become its own creative destroyers. None of these options is very pleasant, and they will cause disruption of the status quo, but can there be any doubt the current offering of auditors is the Edsel of our time? Is it not incumbent on the profession to shape its own destiny, rather than being relegated to part-time governmental bureaucrats destined to comply with the ever-increasing tax code and growing GAAP rules promulgated by a body that, at the whim of politicians, could be nationalized? Don't we owe it to ourselves to create a better future for the next generations of CPAs by leaving them a legacy that is relevant to the realities of the marketplace? It is not the automobile that is being rejected, but instead the make and model. Let us begin by looking at how the present financial model could be reformed.

FINANCIAL MODEL REFORM

RON The nineteenth-century German writer and scientist Johann Wolfgang von Goethe described double-entry bookkeeping "as one of the most beautiful discoveries of the human spirit," because it signifies the basic truth that every economic event has two opposite and equal sides: the debit and the credit. Although this is true from an accounting identity point of view—assets less liabilities equals capital—it reveals far less about how wealth is created in an IC economy. The two sides to any transaction are a willing seller and buyer, and they are anything but equal, as Adam Smith taught us over two centuries ago. Their accounts may balance when they buy and sell from each other, but the wealth they create in the process is not equal.

As of March 2001, the Standard and Poors (S&P) 500 companies (among the largest 500 companies in the United States) reported one dollar of book value for every six dollars of market value. In other words, only one-sixth of the value of a company could be found on its balance sheet.

Noted accounting professor Baruch Lev, the Philip Bardes Professor of Accounting and Finance with the Stern School of Business at New York University, has written extensively on the deficiencies in the present GAAP financial statement model. He believes information on intangible assets—those assets that are not on the balance sheet but are the cause of the wealth of most companies, compromising their IC—can be voluntarily disclosed by companies in other venues besides the financial statements, such as meetings, conference calls, or research reports by analysts.

He further points out that financial statements convey much more than merely historical cost numbers, by arguing that almost every significant account on the balance sheet requires subjective estimates about the future, such as accounts receivable reserves, depreciation estimates, obligations for pensions, and so on. He still thinks the current accounting system needs to be changed but that it will require regulatory intervention (*see* Lev, 2001: 18–19, 81, 122).

I do not find Lev's arguments compelling. There are major shortcomings in the present financial model; how else to explain the inability of the balance sheet to capture only a fraction of the value of a company, or the pro forma earnings reported as a supplement by so many companies? His notion that further governmental regulation is required in order to reform is also dubious. We already have an enormous amount of regulation and oversight of the accounting profession and the rules and standards it promulgates; why would anyone think that piling on more will solve the fundamental problem, rather than just dealing with a few symptoms? As with any regulated industry, innovation is usually stifled, and the consumer's best interest are not at heart, an issue we discuss later.

The proposals put forward by Robert G. Eccles, Robert H. Herz, E. Mary Keegan, and David M.H. Phillips in *The ValueReporting Revolution: Moving beyond the Earnings Game*, are much more compelling than those of Lev. An optimistic note was rung in the reform movement when Robert Herz recently accepted the job of chairman of FASB. Herz believes principles, not rote rules, should play a larger role in the standards-setting process.

The authors describe their book as an "opening shot across the bow" of the accounting profession. I would describe it as a shot into the *hull* of the profession. This book is required reading for any CPA who is interested in the future of the financial reporting model, and it deserves much more attention than I can give it here. In short, the authors lay out a plan for "taking back the high ground," which is worth quoting in full:

> What can accounting firms do to serve their clients, shareholders, and other stakeholders as completely as possible? What should they do to get back to their former role of urging clients to do the right thing, rather than just the required thing?
>
> They can and should work with their clients to:
>
> - Identify all the key components and value drivers [KPIs].
> - Become experts on the business processes and related controls surrounding the measurement of value drivers and financial and operating risks.

- Specify the relationship among value drivers (the "business model").
- Develop methodologies for measuring value drivers.
- Participate in or even organize the industry consortia that will turn the methodologies into industry standards.
- Encourage their clients to report information on the measures in as timely and detailed a fashion as possible.

Accounting firms cannot do this if their role is limited to simply performing statutory audits. Instead, they must have a much broader advisor role that involves developing business models, creating measurement methodologies, and applying these methodologies in processes, many of which require a high level of IT skills. In a real-time world with many performance measures, the distinction between monitoring and controlling and between auditing and advising largely disappear (Eccles, et. al., 2001: 266).

Accounting firms certainly seem to have an opportunity to take back the moral high ground. But will they seize it? That depends on two things. First, they must have the will. Accounting firms should reestablish the role they played many years ago when they led rather than followed their clients in establishing measures and reporting practices. Second, the will must be matched with capability. The accounting firms must have people who have the skills to do it (Ibid: 267–268).

Of course this would require the accounting profession to enter the arena of positing theories, constantly testing them against reality, and then revising them, in a never-ending iterative process. In total, the profession does not possess much IC in this arena, but it is going to have to import it if it wants to stay on top of the financial reporting value curve.

There are, however, some encouraging signs the profession is beginning to seize the opportunities before it. The authors—and I concur—believe these reforms can be accomplished without further government intervention. But much more needs to be done. The profession has already lost ground to other organizations, and unless it reasserts itself as the dominant financial specialist, it will be relegated to performing statutory audits and filling out tax returns. One indication of the ground lost is the recent legislative reforms passed by Congress, which we will now address.

SUBSTITUTING GOVERNMENT FAILURE FOR MARKET FAILURE

The difference is that a private firm that makes a serious blunder may go out of business. A government agency is likely to get a bigger budget.

—Milton and Rose Friedman, *Free to Choose: A Personal Statement*

RON The recent spate of accounting scandals has led some to say it is time to replace economics with accounting as "the dismal science." If the business corporation fails to meet its moral responsibilities, then the odds for the rest of society are not good. Business is the main creator of jobs and wealth; no other institution even comes close. Corporate behavior can be backed up by law, but as we have seen, the law often arrives after the damage has been done. John Stuart Mill and all of the moral philosophers of the Enlightenment understood that economics was merely a branch of ethics, the whole system being based on trust, honesty, and clarity. In the daily life of any businessperson, trust is more real than money, for when it is missing, money becomes worthless.

Auditors will start to test more for fraud and to develop hypotheses to predict the probability of fraud. Work has already progressed in this field, and advances will continue. Yet most of the underlying causes of the so-called scandals were buried in the hype of accounting reform and political posturing. Keep in mind that the free market has worked fairly well in these scandals. By detecting—albeit late—that these companies were cooking the books, they were driven into bankruptcy; and some of the managers will no doubt face criminal prosecution and other sanctions as well. It is hard to conceive that humans could ever devise a system where no company would ever commit fraud or where investors would not be at risk.

Take the example of companies concocting subsidiaries to conceal self-dealing and massive debt—known as *special-purpose entities*. The tax code bears a lion's share of the responsibility for this Byzantine maze of special-purpose entities. Yet how many times was that issue even mentioned? Or the fact that the 1993 tax bill limited salary deductions to $1 million, which encouraged the use of stock options, which are now being blamed as part of the problem (but are actually quite insignificant in a $9 trillion economy)?

Not many commentators mentioned the double taxation of dividends. The United States is one of the few countries in the world whose tax system punishes dividends, by taxing them twice. If it were not for this double taxation, more companies would pay out dividends. While management can fudge the books, it is really hard to fudge a dividend check, since it is real cash, not an accounting entry. Throughout most of the stock market's history, companies distributed approximately one-half of their annual profits in dividends to shareholders; in 2000, a year of record profits, one-fourth of the S&P companies paid no dividends at all, the highest proportion in history.

The old canard about the conflict of interest caused by accounting firms offering both auditing and consulting was also dusted off and made part of the national debate. Despite the fact there is no evidence to support the claim that auditor independence is impaired by also providing consulting, the government has now interfered with the workings of the free market by disallowing certain consulting activities. Taken to its logical extreme, the fact that auditors are paid by the corporations they audit creates a conflict of interest and makes the argument for all audits to be conducted by a government (or quasi-governmental) agency. If it is really the case that no consulting would improve audits, the free market would automatically pay more for audits conducted by firms that did not consult with their customers. The fact this premium has not been reflected in the price of audits—or that users of financial statements have insisted on it—casts doubts as to the validity of the initial premise.

Then there are the further regulations initiated by the SEC. Arthur Andersen was duly punished for its misdeeds—right or wrong—but the SEC will emerge with a bigger budget. Alan Reynolds, senior fellow at the Cato Institute focuses on the SEC's built-in bias for failure:

The SEC is focused on keeping politicians happy and getting rave reviews in the head-lines. These incentives normally lead to maximizing paperwork and minimizing contro-versy. Smart bureaucrats "blow the whistle" last, never first. The risk of blowing the whistle too early is a lost job if you're wrong. The reward for taking that risk will be identical to the salary for never rocking boats. So the SEC normally waits until the patient is long dead before conducting an expensive autopsy.

Regulatory agencies also have institutional incentives to fail. The bigger the failure, the more the agency will be rewarded with more authority and a bigger budget. This is happening now with the SEC.

Still the SEC's cluelessness about Enron has been sufficiently embarrassing that the agency has been trying to look hyperactive, launching highly publicized investigations of Xerox, Qwest, PNC Financial Services, Hewlett-Packard, and Waste Management, to name a few. Although the SEC is charged with protecting stockholders, the market responds to the SEC's public displays of affection as rape rather than seduction (Reynolds, 2002).

I find it baffling that the profession is not enlisting economists into the debate regarding the effectiveness of the SEC itself. Many economists have studied this agency, and have concluded, on balance, there is no demonstrable evidence it helps the average shareholder; and some have found a net harm to shareholders.

The Security Act of 1933 established the Securities and Exchange Commission, which consists of five members appointed every five years by the president of the United States. Its first chairman was Joseph P. Kennedy. In the United States, it costs approximately $500,000 to take a company public, since a company has to gain approval of all 50 states, and that can take up to a year. As a result, many new U.S. companies go to Canada, where registration and listing are much faster and cheaper (usually less than $100,000).

Nobel Prize-winning economist George Stigler (along with Claire Friedland) stud-ied the effects of government regulation extensively. With respect to the SEC, here is what they concluded, as told by Jim Powell in *The Triumph of Liberty: A 2000-Year History, Told through the Lives of Freedom's Greatest Champions*:

The SEC has had its greatest impact on new stock issues, since investors have the least amount of information about these; there's abundant information about seasoned issues. Stigler proposed a simple test: "How did investors fare before and after the SEC was given control over the registration of new issues? We take all the new issues of indus-trial stocks with a value exceeding $2.5 million in 1923–1927, and exceeding $5 million in 1949–1955, and measure the value of these issues (compared to their offering price) in five subsequent years. It is obviously improper to credit or blame the SEC for the absolute differences between the two periods in investors' fortunes, but if we measure stock prices relative to the market average, we shall have eliminated most of the effects of general market conditions." He concluded that "investors in common stocks in the 1950s did little better than in the 1920s, indeed clearly no better if they held the securi-ties only one or two years. In fact the differences between the averages in the two peri-ods are not statistically significant in any year. . . . These studies suggest that the SEC registration requirements had no important effect on the quality of new securities sold to the public. . . . Grave doubts exist whether if account is taken of costs of regulation, the SEC has saved the purchasers of new issues one dollar."

Stigler maintained that investors benefit far more from efficient capital markets than from SEC regulations. A serious drag on capital markets, he observed, was SEC-sanctioned collusion among Wall Street firms to fix brokerage commissions.

After these articles appeared, an increasing number of economists tested the effects of regulations, and their findings were more radical than those of Stigler and Friedland: that the effects of regulation were the opposite of what policymakers had intended. In response, Stigler wrote "The Theory of Economic Regulation," an enormously influential article that appeared in the Spring 1971 issue of *Bell Journal of Economics and Management Science*. He expressed an insight that catapulted him into the major leagues of economic thinkers: "As a rule, regulation is acquired by the industry and is designed and operated primarily for its benefit." He explained that the actual purpose of regulations is to provide special privileges for the powerful interest groups that want to restrict competition and raise prices, so regulations hurt the public (Powell, 2000: 374–375).

One of the most innovative proposals to reform securities regulations comes from economist Roberta Romano, as put forth in *Entrepreneurial Economics: Bright Ideas from the Dismal Science*. She proposes that corporations be able to "opt out" of SEC regulation in favor of the state regulation it chooses. This would prevent the costly and burdensome necessity of registering in all of the states the securities would be sold. Also, it would force the 50 states to compete for the best regulatory model. Investors would then be able to determine how much value to place on each state's regulatory apparatus; those states that offered more value would attract more new issues. In effect, the 50 states would compete against one another for new issues, as they do for corporate charters. This is an enormously innovative regulatory reform, forcing competition onto the regulators rather than blindly accepting they are prescient and always create the desired results they intend.

To the extent possible, government regulations should be subject to the same results-based test as the products and services of the free market. Erecting barriers to competition and imposing excessive regulations is not the path to wealth creation, and there is plenty of empirical evidence to support this contention. One need only study the abject failure of centrally planned economies to create the dynamism and private property institutions so essential in generating wealth.

MULTIDISCIPLINARY PRACTICES

RON The recent accounting scandals, as well the American Bar Association's opposition, has taken the issue of multidisciplinary practices (MDP) off the radar screen. MDPs are nothing new; they originated after the end of World War II in Germany, where lawyers may practice in partnership with tax accountants. Since then, MDPs have become common in other European countries, as well as in Hong Kong and

Singapore, and Australia, Canada, and a number of Latin American and African countries. Moreover, the Big 4 accounting firms have been actively seeking law firms in Japan, Korea, Southeast Asia, and India.

Professor Mary C. Daly, in *Multidisciplinary Practice: Staying Competitive and Adapting to Change*, explains the legal profession's opposition to MDPs:

> The prohibition against MDPs is rooted in the perception that it prevents a layperson from exercising undue influence over the independence of a lawyer in the representation of a client in an attempt to subordinate the protection of clients to the pursuit of profit. The ABA Commission on Evaluation of Professional Standards (the Kutak Commission) originally proposed relaxing these prohibitions. But the House of Delegates rejected its proposal. These were among the objections raised:
>
> 1. The Commission proposal would permit Sears, Montgomery Ward, H&R Block, or the Big Eight accounting firms to open law offices in competition with traditional law firms.
> 2. Nonlawyer ownership of law firms would interfere with the lawyer's professional independence.
> 3. Nonlawyer ownership would destroy the lawyer's ability to be a professional regardless of the economic cost.
> 4. The proposed change would have a fundamental but unknown effect on the legal profession (quoted in Munneke, 2001: 52–53).

These objections indicate the mind-set of protected guild, not that of professionals operating in a free, dynamic, and competitive marketplace. For starters, the protection of customers and the pursuit of profits are not at odds; in fact, one could make the claim they are a perfect alignment of interests. Moreover, these objections are specious on their face:

- *Objection 1*: Why is competition objected to? We know consumers benefit tremendously from competition, and any action that restricts competition by government fiat—known as *rent seeking* among economists—is a net harm to the very consumers the legal profession purports to protect.

- *Objection 2*: Also dubious, since nonlawyer owners could be subject to various rules of independence.

- *Objection 3*: Pure hyperbole, as there should be no correlation to ownership rules and conducting oneself as a professional, subjected to a code of ethics and principles.

- *Objection 4*: Perhaps the most humorous, being summed up as: "We don't know the effects, but we are going to oppose it anyway." Is not any new business idea or model an experiment? And as long as no laws are violated, private individuals should be able to test their ideas in the free marketplace.

Imagine the argument being made against FedEx because it would open up the U.S. Postal Service to competition, and its effects would be unknown. This is simply ludicrous and not a worthy argument coming from professionals who supposedly act in the public interest.

One could not fill a phone booth with economists who would subscribe to the arguments against MDPs put forth by the critics. MDPs should be allowed, and leave the free market—meaning consumers acting voluntarily and in complete sovereignty—to decide their ultimate fate. If they turn out to be not competitively viable, then the status quo has absolutely nothing to worry about. And if they are successful, it is very hard to argue that customers are not acting in their own best interest, let alone do not know what those interests are.

SUMMARY AND CONCLUSIONS

When the technology sector imploded in March 2000, applications for the Law School Admissions Test rose 18.6 percent over June 2000, and law school applications rose 5.6 percent, the highest jump since 1995. The crisis in accounting, however, remains, as these facts from professors W. Steve Albrecht and Robert J. Sack point out in a 2000 monograph, *Accounting Education: Charting the Course through a Perilous Future*:

- The percentage of college students majoring in accounting dropped to 2 percent in 2000 from 4 percent in 1990.

- The percentage of high school students who intend to major in accounting fell to 1 percent in 2000 from 2 percent in 1990.

- More than 80 percent of faculty members surveyed said there were fewer qualified accounting students than five years ago.

- Accounting department heads reported that information systems graduates commanded the highest starting salaries among business-related graduates.

- Faculty members and practitioners agreed paying higher starting salaries was the most important step corporations and accounting firms could take to attract better students into the accounting profession.

- Most accounting educators and practicing accountants would not major in accounting if they began their education again (Albrecht and Sack, 2000).

While the number-one major among college students is *undecided*, the decline in accounting enrollment does not bode well for the future of the profession. There has been a slight uptake in enrollment after all of the accounting scandals made headline news—the so-called Al Capone effect, first noted when applications to the Internal Revenue Service increased after Capone's tax evasion conviction. Why is it that a high school student who takes an accounting course is actually *less likely* to major in accounting once he or she matriculates in college? Perhaps more CPAs need to teach accounting at the high school level, to give students a true picture of what they actually do.

That may not help either, considering such a large percentage of CPAs would not enter accounting if they had to do it all over again, or given the number of parents who actively *discourage* their children from becoming CPAs. These are significant *leading* indicators on the future of the profession. We can debate whether the accounting education curriculum requires a major revision in order to teach the broad range of skills required by today's CPAs, and we can even repeal the 150-hour requirement, but those will be Band-Aids on a broken leg if we do not instill a passion in young people about the profession.

Fortunately, steps are being taken by the American Institute of CPAs and the state societies to make young students more aware of the profession and to offer them a host of resources they can access to learn precisely what CPAs do and the many career options the designation offers. But more needs to be done, and we hope by increasing the quality of life among the professionals who work in the firms of the future—through the implementation of the ideas contained in this book—we can work together to reignite the passion among our colleagues that made them choose to become CPAs in the first place.

13

EPILOGUE

Wanderer, there is no path. You lay a path in walking.

—A. Machado, Spanish poet

PAUL I've just reread Malcolm Gladwell's brilliant little book *The Tipping Point: How Little Things Can Make a Big Difference*. It's so masterful in describing change and how "epidemics"—be they a huge uptake in people buying Hush Puppies or the rise of teenage smoking—occur. Many paragraphs stand out, but one may be appropriate here among our final thoughts.

Gladwell talks about the *diffusion* model, an academic approach to looking at how innovation moves through a population. He quotes a study on a new hybrid corn seed introduced to farmers in Iowa. The new seed was superior in every respect to that which had been used for decades, yet adoption was slow. Of the 259 farmers in the study, only a handful had planted the new seed. Two years later, 16 more had begun planting it. Twenty-one more followed suit one year later; in subsequent years, the numbers of adoptees were: 36, 61, 46, 36, 14, and 3; after nine years, only 2 had not made the switch.

We suspect that the same adoption cycle might be happening with our new Practice Equation. Change does, after all, take time. And though our equation is not a new seed, it does comprise the seeds of new ideas and, most important, new questions to ask of yourself, your colleagues, and your team. That may well be what it takes for our new seed to spread: questions, questions that lead you to better answers, hence a better business and, most important, an even better life.

RON Imagine you had to give a commencement address to a graduating class of students who were about to enter your chosen profession. What would you say to them?

What would be the main message you would want them to walk away with and remember for the rest of their lives? If you have ever had the privilege of being asked, you know this is a daunting challenge. How can you possibly sum up the main lessons you have learned in your years on this planet in a 30-minute speech?

I feel exactly the same way about writing the conclusion to this book, except I am speaking to my colleagues and brethren who have also learned their own lessons from the years spent in the professions. I have one other advantage: more time than 30 minutes.

Many would say the purpose of life is to find happiness. Happiness is not a frivolous nor selfish concern, but a serious subject and a noble goal. It is also a uniquely human aim. But how does one define, or measure, happiness? Nobel Prize-winning economist Paul Samuelson tried to do just that in his ubiquitous and famous economics textbooks, where he presented the following equation:

$$\text{Happiness} = \text{consumption} \div \text{desire}$$

At first glance, this appears to be crassly materialistic, but it does not have to be viewed that way. It can also describe Buddha-like levels of serenity—reduce your desire to zero and happiness becomes infinite. It has often been observed that if you define your happiness by your level of success, you can never achieve enough success to make you happy. When one works simply to make money, the work is rarely joyful or meaningful, which is why so many people volunteer at not-for-profit organizations where they feel they are making a significant contribution. The acid test to determine if you love what you do is to ask yourself: Would you continue to work if you won the lottery?

The Chinese philosopher Lin Yutang made this keen observation in his book *The Importance of Living*:

> From my own observation of life . . . the great humbugs of life are three: Fame, Wealth and Power. There is a convenient American word which again combines these three humbugs into the One Great Humbug: Success. But many wise men know that the desire for success, fame, and wealth are euphemistic names for the fears of failure, poverty, and obscurity, and that these fears dominate our lives (Yutang, 1965: 102).

The relationship between the humbugs Yutang mentions and happiness is indeed tenuous. Witness Hollywood actors who achieve all three and burn out at relatively young ages, or seem to live in misery. The Federal Reserve Board reports more than 250,000 American households have a net worth exceeding $10 million; 500,000 have a net worth in excess of $5 million; and a million are worth $3.7 million or more; and those with $1 million in net worth has soared above 5 million. During the dot-com boom, the term *sudden-wealth syndrome* entered the lexicon to describe the many people who now had the mansions and cars of their dreams, but were still not happy. We seem to have become richer and less happy. Michael Novak says, "The aftertaste of affluence is boredom."

Perhaps this is why Andrew Carnegie wrote, "The man who dies rich dies disgraced," arguing the rich should give away their money before they died. Carnegie worked diligently to follow his own advice, spending the last 17 years of his life giving away his vast fortune, some $332 million (Rockefeller, by comparison, gave away

$175 million). Despite his Herculean efforts, he could not give away his money fast enough, for by the time he gave away approximately $180 million, his fortune had grown—through the magic of compound interest—to a sum nearly as large as where he started, which is why he transferred what remained to the largest philanthropic trust ever before known, the Carnegie Corporation. All told, he had given away 90 percent of his fortune, 80 percent going to support the human mind in universities, libraries, institutes, schools, grants and pensions for college teachers, and so forth. Not too bad for someone born quite poor in the town of Dumferline, Scotland, in 1835, and whose family immigrated to Pittsburgh, Pennsylvania. Why does there seem to be no correlation—indeed, in some instances, an inverse relationship—between wealth and happiness?

Being the richest person in the cemetery is pointless. Happiness is not discovered in the same way Columbus discovered America. Happiness is the consequence of *peace of mind*, or tranquility of being, a point Adam Smith made in his first book, *The Theory of Moral Sentiments* published in 1759. If you have ever doubted that true wisdom is timeless, consider the following "Parable of the Poor Man's Son," from Smith:

> A poor man's son, whom heaven in its anger visited with ambition, begins to look around himself and admire the condition of the rich. He finds the cottage of his father too small for his accommodation, and fancies he should be lodged more at ease in a palace. He is displeased with being obliged to walk a-foot, but sees his superiors carried about in carriages, and imagines that in one of these he could travel with greater convenience. He judges that a numerous retinue of servants would save him from a great deal of trouble. He thinks if he had attained these conveniences he would sit contentedly in the tranquillity of his situation. He is enchanted with the distant idea of this felicity.
>
> To obtain these conveniences, he submits in the first year, nay in the first month of his application, to more fatigue of body and more uneasiness of mind than he could have suffered through the whole of his life from the want of them! He slaves to distinguish himself in some laborious profession which he hates, forces himself to be obsequious to people he despises, and, by so doing, finally acquires all the material riches he so long sought. But by now he's in the last dregs of life, his body wasted with toil and diseases, his mind galled and ruffled by the memory of a thousand injuries and disappointments, and he begins at last to realize that wealth and fame are mere trinkets of frivolous utility, no more adapted for procuring ease of body or tranquillity of mind than the tweezer-cases [small boxes of tiny tools, carried in Smith's day by men of leisure] of the lover of toys (quoted in Wight, 2002: 91).

As usual, Smith makes a very compelling argument. How would this affect your commencement address? Oscar Wilde wrote, "No man is rich enough to buy back his past." All in all, if I were restricted to four key topics in a commencement speech, they would be: *vocation*, *intellectual capital*, *adventure*, and *legacy*.

WHAT IS CALLING YOU?

RON Most of us have had career goals, since that is how you pass the Bar or CPA exam. A vocation, on the other hand, is something quite different, and is usually not discovered until later in life, after many paths have been followed. Vocation originates in the Latin *vocare*, meaning to *call*. It literally calls you to contribute your talent, energy, passion, enthusiasm, and desire to work you love and believe in.

Each individual's calling is unique, and requires talent. It is measured by the renewed energy it gives us, even when it involves drudgery. There is no greater joy than watching someone engage in their true calling with their entire mind, body, and soul.

CONTINUOUSLY DEVELOP YOUR INTELLECTUAL CAPITAL

RON One of the central themes of this book is that, as a knowledge worker, your intellectual capital is what enables you to create wealth for others, and in turn for yourself. Like any other form of capital, however, IC is subject to obsolescence and must be constantly renewed. The best professionals are constant students, willing to look at the world in absolute wonder and think about why things are the way they are. Continuing professional education will be one of the major growth industries in the coming decades, since IC is constantly being developed, making it nearly impossible to keep up with in your area of specialty.

Remember, though, that your IC is more than your human and structural capital. It also consists of your social capital, the relationships that will have a profound impact on the rest of your life. If you think the Pareto Principle is true in a business setting, think about it in terms of your personal life. Meeting someone and falling in love takes relatively little time but will have a major impact on your future. Or meeting a colleague or mentor—as I met Paul for the first time in 1996—who will take you in a totally new direction. You are whom you associate with. I do not feel the need to tell you things you already know; suffice it to say, do not pollute your social capital with people who have a zero-sum mentality and believe you can win only if someone else loses. Develop relationships with a mentor and with individuals you truly admire and respect, whether they are colleagues, authors, or just friends in whom you can confide. And become a mentor to a younger person and guide him or her with your accumulated wisdom.

ADVENTURE

RON Profit comes from taking risks, and here I mean profit not just in the business sense but the personal as well. We live in a world of *dynamic disequilibrium*, where the only stability is in the graveyard. The best companies compete against themselves, as do the most talented athletes. Not content to let the past stand in the way of the future, we all engage in a never-ending cycle of creative destruction. Change is our middle name, and we will continue to embrace and accept it as the progress it represents. We tear down the old order every day, whether in business, science, literature, art, architecture, cinema, politics, and the law.

George Gilder, author, economist, and eclectic thinker wrote of the ultimate conflict in *Wealth and Poverty*:

In every economy, as Jane Jacobs has said, there is one crucial and definitive conflict. This is not the split between capitalists and workers, technocrats and humanists, government and business, liberals and conservatives, or rich and poor. All these divisions are partial and distorted reflections of the deeper conflict: the struggle between past and future, between the existing configuration of industries and the industries that will someday replace them. It is a conflict between established factories, technologies, formations of capital, and the ventures that may soon make them worthless—ventures that today may not even exist; that today may flicker only as ideas, or tiny companies, or obscure research projects, or fierce but penniless ambitions; that today are unidentifiable and incalculable from above, but which, in time, in a progressing economy, must rise up if growth is to occur (Gilder, 1981: 235).

Buying—and even reading—a book about change is easier than actually implementing change. If you think of the future as a threat, you will never innovate. In order to try something new, you must stop doing something old. Ultimately, the power of the ideas in this book rests in their implementation. Those who are most complacent and comfortable with the present—or worse, a nostalgic past—are likely to remain trapped inside it forever. It is the uncomfortable and dissatisfied ones who take the risks and ultimately create our future.

LEAVING A LEGACY

RON In *The 7 Habits of Highly Effective People*, Stephen Covey lays out the second habit: "Begin with the End in Mind." He has you imagine being at your own funeral. What would you want people to say about you?

When I read what Paul said he wanted on his tombstone—"He made a difference to the profession"—I was amazed. It was precisely what I had been saying about Paul even before I met him. It was based on the transformations I had observed taking place among my colleagues who had attended the Accountants' Boot Camp.

If you study business history, you quickly discover successful cultures have been the result of original thinking. And it is precisely those cultures where original thinking is stimulated and encouraged that leave behind the richest legacies. Think of Walt Disney and the impact he still has on the company he founded, embodied in the continuously asked question: "What would Walt do?" Ben Franklin's epitaph, which he wrote, reads:

> B. Franklin, Printer; like the Cover of an old Book, Its Contents torn out, And stript of its lettering and Gilding, Lies here, Food for Worms. But the Work shall not be wholly lost, For it will, as he believ'd, appear once more, In a new & more perfect Edition, Corrected and amended By the Author.

What do you want your legacy to be? Part of our legacy will be this book, which in Voltaire's words has provided us "the great consolation in life [of saying] what one thinks." You have read our beliefs, values, and convictions (from the Latin word *convictum*, "that which is proven or demonstrated"). We have attempted to demonstrate the superiority of the new Practice Equation over the old one. It challenges the wisdom of the ages because truth is not defined simply by seniority.

We have offered you a testable hypothesis, one that is subject to the falsification principle described by Karl Popper, which is how all scientific knowledge progresses. As authors we would desire nothing more than having our theories and ideas accepted as part of the conventional wisdom—not to mention practices—of the professions. We have stated what we believe is the truth, and we are now ready to accept the consequences, hoping that what is false will be exposed and that what is true will be admitted.

Clare Boothe Luce used to say, "The only difference between an optimist and a pessimist, is that a pessimist is usually better informed." When it comes to the professions, we certainly hope she was wrong. But the road not yet traveled is long, and it seems the professions, to paraphrase Winston Churchill's exhortation of America, will do the right thing—once they have exhausted the alternatives.

Despite this, we remain optimistic. Milton Friedman's tells a wonderful story that may illustrate what we need:

> A young nun was out driving a car down a superhighway and ran out of gas. She remembered that a mile back there had been a gas station. She got out of her car, hiked up her habit, and walked back. When she got to the station she found that there was only one young man in attendance there. He said he'd love to help her but couldn't leave the gas station because he was the only one there. He said he would try to find a container in which he could give her some gas. He hunted around the gas station and couldn't find a decent container. The only thing he could find was a little baby's potty that had been left there. So he filled the baby potty with gasoline and gave it to the nun. She took the baby potty and walked the mile down the road to her car. She got to her car and opened the gas tank and started to pour it in. Just at that moment, a great big Cadillac came barreling down the road at 80 miles an hour. The driver was looking out and couldn't believe what he was seeing. So he jammed on his brakes, stopped, backed up, opened the window, and looked out and said, "Sister, I only wish I had your faith!" (quoted in Poole and Postrel, 1993: 10).

If we reinvigorate and revitalize the professions, and begin to understand and leverage the intellectual capital it creates, there is no limit to what we can achieve, as long as we do not lose faith in ourselves.

REFERENCES

Albrecht, Karl. 1992. *The Only Thing That Matters: Bringing the Power of the Customer into the Center of Your Business*. New York: HarperBusiness.

————. 1994. *The Northbound Train: Finding the Purpose, Setting the Direction, Shaping the Destiny of Your Organization*. New York: American Management Association.

Albrecht, W. Steve, and Robert J. Sack. 2000. *Accounting Education: Charting the Course through a Perilous Future*. Available at www.aaahq.org/pubs/AESv16/toc.htm.

Albrecht, Karl, and Ron Zemke. 2002. *Service America in the New Economy*. New York: McGraw-Hill.

American Bar Association. 2002. "ABA Commission on Billable Hours Report, 2001–2002." Available at: www.abanet.org/careercounsel/billable.html.

Aquila, August J., and Allan D. Koltin. 1992. "How to Lose Clients without Really Trying." *Journal of Accountancy* (May).

Badaracco, Joseph L. 2000. *Leading Quietly*. Boston: Harvard Business School Press.

Baker, Ronald J. 2001. *Professional's Guide to Value Pricing, Third Edition*. New York: Aspen Law & Business.

Basch, Michael D. 2002. *Customer Culture: How FedEx and Other Great Companies Put the Customer First Every Day*. Upper Saddle River, NJ: Prentice Hall.

Beatty, Jack. 1998. *The World According to Peter Drucker*. New York: The Free Press.

Beauchemin, Timothy J. 1996. "No More Begging for Work: Self-Esteem Is the Key to a Better Practice." *CPA Profitability Monthly* 8 (August). (Note: This newsletter was *published as Partner-to-Partner*, by Aspen Law & Business, New York.)

Becker, Gary S. 1983. *Human Capital: A Theoretical and Empirical Analysis, with Special Reference to Education, Second Edition, Midway Reprint*. Chicago: The University of Chicago Press.

————. *Accounting for Tastes*. 1996. Cambridge, MA: Harvard University Press.

Beckwith, Harry. 2000. *The Invisible Touch: The Four Keys to Modern Marketing*. New York: Warner Books.

Berra, Yogi, with Dave Kaplan. 2001. *When You Come to a Fork in the Road, Take It!: Inspiration and Wisdom from One of Baseball's Greatest Heroes*. New York: Hyperion.

Bernstein, Peter L. 1996. *Against the Gods: The Remarkable Story of Risk*. New York: John Wiley & Sons, Inc.

Bethune, Gordon. 1998. *From Worst to First: Behind the Scenes of Continental's Remarkable Comeback*. New York: John Wiley & Sons, Inc.

Boulding, Kenneth. April 16, 2001. http://netec.wustl.edu/JokEc.html. (Finnish Web site with economists' jokes.)

Boyle, David. 2001. *The Sum of Our Discontent: Why Numbers Make Us Irrational*. New York: Texere.

Branden, Nathaniel. 1994. *The Six Pillars of Self-Esteem*. New York: Bantam.

———. *Self-Esteem at Work: How Confident People Make Powerful Companies*. 1998. San Francisco: Jossey-Bass Publishers.

Buchholz, Todd G. 1990. *New Ideas from Dead Economists: An Introduction to Modern Economic Thought*. New York: Plume.

Buckley, Reid. 1999. *Strictly Speaking: Reid Buckley's Indispensable Handbook on Public Speaking*. New York: McGraw-Hill.

Buckley, William F., Jr. 2000. *Let Us Talk of Many Things: The Collected Speeches*. Roseville, CA: Forum.

Calder, Lendol. 1999. *Financing the American Dream: A Cultural History of Consumer Credit*. Princeton, NJ: Princeton University Press.

Canabou, Christine. 2002. "Gone, But Not Forgotten." *Fast Company* (May): 28–30.

Carlzon, Jan. 1987. *Moments of Truth: New Strategies for Today's Customer-Driven Economy*. New York: Harper & Row, Publishers, Inc.

Cavanaugh, Francis X. 1996. *The Truth about the National Debt: Five Myths and One Reality*. Boston: Harvard Business School Press.

Cerf, Christopher, and Victor Navasky. 1998. *The Experts Speak: The Definitive Compendium of Authoritative Misinformation*. New York: Villard.

Cialdini, Robert B. 1993. *Influence: The New Psychology of Modern Persuasion*. New York: Quill.

———. 2001. "Harnessing the Science of Persuasion. *Harvard Business Review* (October): 72–79.

Coase, Ronald H. 1994. *Essays on Economics and Economists*. Chicago: The University of Chicago Press.

Collins, James C. 2001. *Good to Great: Why Some Companies Make the Leap . . . and Others Don't*. New York: HarperBusiness.

Collins, James C., and Jerry I. Porras. 1997. *Built to Last: Successful Habits of Visionary Companies*. New York: HarperBusiness.

Connellan, Tom. 1997. *Inside the Magic Kingdom*. Austin, TX: Bard Press.

Conquest, Robert. 2000. *Reflections on a Ravaged Century*. New York: W.W. Norton & Company.

Conway, Susan, and Char Sligar. 2002. *Unlocking Knowledge Assets: Knowledge Management Solutions from Microsoft*. Redmond, WA: Microsoft Press.

Covey, Stephen R. 1989. *The 7 Habits of Highly Effective People: Powerful Lessons in Personal Change*. New York: Fireside.

Crawford, Fred, and Ryan Mathews. 2001. *The Myth of Excellence: Why Great Companies Never Try to Be the Best at Everything*. New York: Crown Publishing.

Cross, Robert G. 1997. *Revenue Management: Hard-Core Tactics for Market Domination*. New York: Broadway Books.

Dauten, Dale. 1999. *The Gifted Boss: How to Find, Create, and Keep Great Employees.* New York: William Morrow and Company, Inc.

Davenport, Thomas O. 1999. *Human Capital: What It Is and Why People Invest It.* San Francisco: Jossey-Bass Publishers.

Dawson, Ross. 2000. *Developing Knowledge-Based Client Relationships: The Future of Professional Services.* Boston: Butterworth Heinemann.

Disney Institute. 2001. *Be Our Guest: Perfecting the Art of Customer Service.* New York: Disney Editions.

Dougherty, Peter J. 2002. *Who's Afraid of Adam Smith?: How the Market Got Its Soul.* Hoboken, NJ: John Wiley & Sons, Inc.

Drucker, Peter F. 1993. *The Effective Executive.* New York: HarperBusiness.

———. *Adventurers of a Bystander.* 1994. New Brunswick, NJ: Transaction Publishers.

———. *Management Challenges for the 21st Century.* 1999. New York: HarperBusiness.

———. 2002. *Managing in the Next Society.* New York: St. Martin's Press.

Eccles, Robert G., Robert H. Herz, E. Mary Keegan, and David M.H. Phillips. 2001. *The ValueReporting Revolution: Moving beyond the Earnings Game.* New York: John Wiley & Sons, Inc.

Flaherty, John E. 1999. *Shaping the Managerial Mind: How the World's Foremost Management Thinker Crafted the Essentials of Business Success.* San Francisco: Jossey-Bass Publishers.

Fletcher, Tony, and Neil Russell-Jones. 1997. *Value Pricing: How to Maximize Profits through Effective Pricing Policies.* London: Kogan Page Limited.

Fog, Bjarke. 1994. *Pricing in Theory and Practice.* Copenhagen: Handelshojskolens Forlag.

Frank, Robert H. 1999. *Luxury Fever: Why Money Fails to Satisfy in an Era of Excess.* New York: The Free Press.

———. 2000. *Microeconomics and Behavior, Fourth Edition* (International Edition). New York: Irwin McGraw-Hill.

Freiberg, Kevin, and Jackie Freiberg. 1996. *Nuts! Southwest Airline's Crazy Recipe for Business and Personal Success.* Austin, TX: Bard Press.

Freidheim, Cyrus. 1998. *The Trillion-Dollar Enterprise: How the Alliance Revolution Will Transform Global Business.* New York: Perseus Books.

Friedman, David D. 1990. *Price Theory: An Intermediate Text, Second Edition.* Cincinnati: South-Western Publishing Co.

———. 2000. *Law's Order: What Economics Has to Do with Law and Why It Matters.* Princeton, NJ: Princeton University Press.

Friedman, Milton. and Rose Friedman. 1980. *Free to Choose: A Personal Statement.* New York: Harcourt Brace.

Fukuyama, Francis. 1995. *Trust: The Social Virtues and the Creation of Prosperity.* New York: The Free Press.

Gerber, Michael E. 1995. *The E-Myth Revisited: Why Most Small Businesses Don't Work and What to Do About It.* New York: Harperbusiness.

Gilder, George. 1981. *Wealth and Poverty.* New York: Basic Books, Inc.

Gladwell, Malcolm. 2000. *The Tipping Point: How Little Things Can Make a Big Difference.* Boston: Little, Brown and Company.

Goodman, John. June 1999. "Basic Facts on Customer Complaint Behavior and the Impact of Service on the Bottom Line." www.e-satisfy.com.

Hamel, Gary. 2000. *Leading the Revolution.* Boston: Harvard Business School Press.

Hart, Christopher W. 1998. *Extraordinary Guarantees: Achieving Breakthrough Gains in Quality and Customer Satisfaction.* Brookline, MA: Spire Group, Ltd.

Hart, Christopher, W.L., and Christopher E. Bogan. 1992. *The Baldridge: What It Is, How It's Won, How to Use It to Improve Quality in Your Company.* New York: McGraw-Hill.

Hemp, Paul. 2002. "My Week as a Room-Service Waiter at the Ritz." *Harvard Business Review* (June): 50–62.

Hornsby, Jr. William E. 2000. *Marketing and Legal Ethics: The Boundaries of Promoting Legal Services, Third Edition.* Chicago: American Bar Association.

Johnson, H. Thomas, and Robert S. Kaplan. 1991. *Relevance Lost: The Rise and Fall of Management Accounting.* Boston: Harvard Business School Press.

Johnson, H. Thomas, and Anders Broms. 2000. *Profit beyond Measure: Extraordinary Results through Attention to Work and People.* New York: The Free Press.

Johnson, Paul. 1997. *A History of the American People.* New York: HarperCollins Publishers, Inc.

Kanter, Rosabeth Moss. 2001. *Evolve! Succeeding in the Digital Culture of Tomorrow.* Boston: Harvard Business School Press.

Kessler, Sheila. 1996. *Measuring and Managing Customer Satisfaction: Going for the Gold.* Milwaukee: ASQC Quality Press.

Kimball, Bruce A. 1995. *The "True Professional Ideal" in America: A History.* Lanham, MD: Rowman & Littlefield Publishers, Inc.

Kirk, Christina. 2000. Australian Financial Review BOSS Magazine.

Koch, Richard. 2001. *The Natural Laws of Business: How to Harness the Power of Evolution, Physics, and Economics to Achieve Business Success.* New York: Doubleday.

Krass, Peter, ed. 1999. *The Book of Entrepreneurs' Wisdom: Classic Writings by Legendary Entrepreneurs.* New York: John Wiley & Sons, Inc.

Landsburg, Steven E. 2002. *Price Theory and Applications, Fifth Edition.* Cincinnati: South-Western.

Lanning, Michael J. 1998. *Delivering Profitable Value: A Revolutionary Framework to Accelerate Growth, Generate Wealth, and Rediscover the Heart of Business.* Cambridge, MA: Perseus Books.

Larson, Charles B., and Joseph W. Larson. 1994. *Innovative Billing and Collection Methods That Work.* Burr Ridge, IL: Irwin Professional Publishing.

Lawler, Edward E, III. 2000. *Rewarding Excellence: Pay Strategies for the New Economy.* San Francisco: Jossey-Bass Publishers.

LeBoeuf, Ph.D., Michael. 2000. *How to Win Customers and Keep Them for Life: Revised and Updated for the Digital Age.* New York: Berkley Books.

Ledeen, Michael A. 1999. *Machiavelli on Modern Leadership: Why Machiavelli's Iron Rules Are as Timely and Important Today as Five Centuries Ago.* New York: St. Martin's Press.

Leonhardt, David. May 14, 2002. "Big League Baseball Tips Its Hat to Adam Smith." *International Herald Tribune*.

Lev, Baruch. 2001. *Intangibles: Management, Measurement, and Reporting*. Washington, DC: Brookings Institution Press.

Levine, Robert A. 1997. *A Geography of Time: The Temporal Misadventures of a Social Psychologist, or How Every Culture Keeps Time Just a Little Bit Differently*. New York: Basic Books.

McCloskey, Deirdre N. 2000. *Economical Writing, Second Edition*. Prospect Heights, IL: Waveland Press, Inc.

————2000. *How to Be Human—Though an Economist*. Ann Arbor: The University of Michigan Press.

McGrath, Rita Gunther, and Ian MacMillan. 2000. *The Entrepreneurial Mindset: Strategies for Continuously Creating Opportunity in an Age of Uncertainty*. Boston: Harvard Business School Press.

McKenna, Patrick J., and David H. Maister. *First Among Equals: How to Manage a Group of Professionals*. New York: The Free Press, 2002.

Maister, David H. 1997. *True Professionalism: The Courage to Care About Your People, Your Clients, and Your Career*. New York: The Free Press.

Maister, David, Charles H. Green, and Robert M. Galford. 2000. *The Trusted Advisor*. New York: The Free Press.

Maital, Shlomo. 1994. *Executive Economics: Ten Essential Tools for Managers*. New York: The Free Press.

Marcus, Stanley. 1995. *The Viewpoints of Stanley Marcus: A Ten-Year Perspective*. Denton, TX: University of North Texas Press.

————. 2000. *Stanley Marcus from A to Z, Viewpoints Volume II*. Denton, TX: University of North Texas Press.

Marx, Karl. 1995. *Value, Price, and Profit*. New York: International Publishers (paperback edition).

Mintzberg, Henry. 1994. *The Rise and Fall of Strategic Planning*. New York: The Free Press,

Monty Python, Graham Chapman, John Cleese, Terry Gilliam, Eric Idle, Terry Jones, and Michael Palin. 1989. *The Complete Monty Python's Flying Circus: All the Words, Volume I*. New York: Pantheon Books.

Morris, Edmund. 1999. *Dutch: A Memoir of Ronald Reagan*. New York: Random House.

Morse, Jennifer Roback. 2001. *Love and Economics: Why the Laissez-Faire Family Doesn't Work*. Dallas: Spence Publishing Company.

Munneke, Gary A., and Ann L. MacNaughton, eds. 2001. *Multidisciplinary Practice: Staying Competitive and Adapting to Change*. Chicago: American Bar Association.

Murray, Charles. 1984. *Losing Ground: American Social Policy 1950–1980*. New York: Basic Books, Inc.

Nagle, Thomas T., and Reed K. Holden. 2002. *The Strategy and Tactics of Pricing: A Guide to Profitable Decision Making, Third Edition*. Upper Saddle River, NJ: Prentice Hall.

Nonaka, Ikujiro, and Hirotaka Takeuchi. 1995. *The Knowledge-Creating Company: How Japanese Companies Create the Dynamics of Innovation*. New York: Oxford University Press.

O'Rourke, P.J. 1998. *Eat the Rich: A Treatise on Economics*. New York: Atlantic Monthly Press.

————. 2001. *The CEO of the Sofa*. New York: Atlantic Monthly Press.

O'Shea, James, and Charles Madigan. 1998. *Dangerous Company: Management Consultants and the Businesses They Save and Ruin*. New York: Penguin Books.

Paulos, John Allen. 2000. *I Think, Therefore I Laugh: The Flip Side of Philosophy*. New York: Columbia University Press.

Payne, Ric. 2002. "Where Is the Accounting Profession Heading?" Part I and Part II. www.consultingaccountant.com.

Peters, Tom. 1994. *The Tom Peters Seminar: Crazy Times Call for Crazy Organizations*. New York: Vintage Books.

————. 1998. *The Circle of Innovation: You Can't Shrink Your Way To Greatness*. New York: Random House.

Pfeffer, Jeffrey. Interview, June 2000, *Fast Company* (www.fastcompany.com/online/35/pfeffer.html).

Pine, B. Joseph, II, and James H. Gilmore. 1999. *The Experience Economy: Work Is Theatre and Every Business a Stage*. Boston: Harvard Business School Press.

Poole, Jr., Robert W., and Virginia I. Postrel. 1993. *Free Minds and Free Markets: Twenty-Five Years of Reason*. San Francisco: Pacific Research Institute for Public Policy.

Postrel, Virginia. 1998. *The Future and Its Enemies: The Growing Conflict Over Creativity, Enterprise, and Progress*. New York: The Free Press.

Powell, Jim, 2000. *The Triumph of Liberty: A 2,000-Year History, Told through the Lives of Freedom's Greatest Champions*. New York: The Free Press.

Prusak, Laurence, and Don Cohen. June 2001. "How to Invest in Social Capital." *Harvard Business Review:* 86–93.

Reichheld, Frederick F. 2001. *Loyalty Rules! How Today's Leaders Build Lasting Relationships*. Boston: Harvard Business School Press.

Reichheld, Frederick F., and Thomas Teal. 1996. *The Loyalty Effect: The Hidden Force Behind Growth, Profits, and Lasting Value*. Boston: Harvard Business School Press.

Reynolds, Alan. 2002. "Where's the Stock Market?" *The American Spectator* (May/June): 14.

Rodgers, T.J. "When Accountants Attack Profits: The GAAP Accounting Exodus." Transcribed, edited speech given to the Stanford Director's College, June 3, 2002, available at www.cypress.com/pub/gaapaccounting.pdf.

Rosenbluth, Hal F. 1992. *The Customer Comes Second and Other Secrets*. New York: William Morrow.

Ross, William G., 1996. *The Honest Hour: The Ethics of Time-Based Billing by Attorneys*. Durham, NC: Carolina Academic Press.

Russell, Roger. 2002. "Value-pricing not yet au courant: Do CPAs lack self-esteem?" *Accounting Today,* vol. 16 no. 10 (June 3–16): 3–4.

Satinover, Jeffrey. 2001. *The Quantum Brain: The Search for Freedom and the Next Generation of Man*. New York: John Wiley & Sons, Inc.

Schmitt, Bernd H. 1999. *Experiential Marketing: How to Get Customers to Sense, Feel, Think, Act, and Relate to Your Company and Brands*. New York: The Free Press.

Selden, Larry, and Geoffrey Colvin. September 15, 2002. "Will this customer sink your stock? Here's the newest way to grab competitive advantage: Figure out how profitable your customers really are." *Fortune Magazine*.

Sertoglu, Cem, and Anne Berkowitch. 2002. "Cultivating Ex-Employees." *Harvard Business Review* (June): 20–21.

Sewell, Carl. 1990. *Customers for Life: How to Turn That One-Time Buyer into a Lifetime Customer*. New York: Pocket Books.

Simon, Julian L. 2002. *A Life Against the Grain: The Autobiography of an Unconventional Economist*. New Brunswick, NJ: Transaction Publishers.

Skousen, Mark. 2000. *Economic Logic*. Washington, DC: Capital Press.

———. 2001. *The Making of Modern Economics: The Lives and Ideas of the Great Thinkers*. Armonk, NY: M.E. Sharpe, Inc.

Smith, Adam. 2000. *The Theory of Moral Sentiments*. New York: Prometheus Books (paperback edition).

Smith, Adam. 1786. *An Inquiry into the Nature and Causes of the Wealth of Nations* (Original published 1776). London: Strahan and Cadell.

Sowell, Thomas. 1980. *Knowledge and Decisions*. New York: Basic Books, Inc.

———. 1994. *Race and Culture: A World View*. New York: Basic Books, Inc.

———. 2000. *Basic Economics: A Citizen's Guide to the Economy*. New York: Basic Books, Inc.

Stewart, Thomas A. 1997. *Intellectual Capital: The New Wealth of Organizations*. New York: Currency.

———. 2001. *The Wealth of Knowledge: Intellectual Capital and the Twenty-First Century Organization*. New York: Currency.

Stieber, John A. 1998. *Profit Is Not a Four-letter Word*. New York: Amacom.

Sullivan, Gordon R., and Michael V. Harper. 1996. *Hope Is Not a Method: What Business Leaders Can Learn from America's Army*. New York: Broadway Books.

Tabarrok, Alexander, ed., 2002. *Entrepreneurial Economics: Bright Ideas from the Dismal Science*. New York: Oxford University Press.

Taub, Stephen. 2002. "Survey: Corporates Give Auditors a Near-Failing Grade." *CFO.com*. (April 11): www.cfo.com.

Tupman, Simon. 2001. *Why Lawyers Should Eat Bananas: Inspirational Ideas for Lawyers Wanting More Out of Life*. Byron Bay, Australia: Simon Tupman Presentations Pty Ltd.

Vance, Mike, and Diane Deacon. 1995. *Think Out of the Box*. Franklin Lakes, NJ: Career Press.

Vanderbilt Arthur T., II. 1999. *The Making of a Bestseller: From Author to Reader*. Jefferson, NC: McFarland & Company, Inc., Publishers.

Veblen, Thorstein. 1994. *The Theory of the Leisure Class*. New York: Penguin. [1899 original]

Verrier, Richard. May 15, 2002. "Disney develops big-screen versions of 3 classic attractions." *Orlando Sentinel*, A1, A6.

Vishwanath, Vijay. and David Harding. 2000. "The Starbucks Effect." *Harvard Business Review*, (March–April): 17.

Watson, Robert A., and Ben Brown. 2001. *"The Most Effective Organization in the U.S.": Leadership Secrets of the Salvation Army*. New York: Crown Business.

Waugh, Troy A. 2001. *Power Up Your Profits: 31 Days to Better Selling*. Novato, CA: Select Press.

Weiss, Alan. 1994. *How to Maximize Fees in Professional Service Firms*. East Greenwich, RI: Las Brisas Research Press.

Wetherbe, James C. 1996. *The World On Time: The 11 Management Principles That Made FedEx an Overnight Sensation*. Santa Monica, CA: Knowledge Exchange.

Whyte, David. 2001. *Crossing the Unknown Sea: Work as a Pilgrimage of Identity*. New York: Riverhead Books.

Wight, Jonathan B. 2002. *Saving Adam Smith: A Tale of Wealth, Transformation, and Virtue*. Upper Saddle River, NJ: Prentice Hall PTR.

Williams, Roy H. 1998. *The Wizard of Ads: Turning Words into Magic and Dreamers into Millionaires*. Austin, TX: Bard Press.

————. 1999. *Secret Formulas of the Wizard of Ads*. Austin, TX: Bard Press.

————. 2001. *Magical Worlds of the Wizard of Ads: Tools and Techniques for Profitable Persuasion*. Austin, TX: Bard Press.

Winninger, Thomas J. 2000. *Full Price: Competing on Value in the New Economy*. Chicago: Dearborn Trade.

Winston, William J., ed. 1995. *Marketing for CPAs, Accountants, and Tax Professionals*. New York: The Haworth Press.

Wong, May. 2002. Berardino Calls for Change: Ex-Andersen CEO: System Is 'Broken.'" *The Washington Post* (June 5): E04.

Wright, Bruce R. 1997. *The Wright Exit Strategy—Wealth: How to Create It, Keep It, and Use It*. Simi Valley, CA: The Wright Company.

Younkins, Edward W. 2001. *Three in One: Essays on Democratic Capitalism, 1976–2000, Michael Novak*. New York: Rowman & Littlefield Publishers, Inc.

Yutang, Lin. 1965. *The Importance of Living*. New York: William Morrow.

INDEX

317

loyalty, 60, 138–139
brand, 137–138
from complaint handling, 143
earning, 68–69, 135, 157, 284
factors in, 64
increasing, 139–142
price and, 174–175, 179
rewarding, 142
tracking, 244
Luce, Clare Boothe, 308
Lund, Paddi, 271–273
luxuries, 115

M
Machlup, Fritz, 2
Mackay, Harvey, 99
Madigan, Charles, 109
Maister, David, 23, 149, 153, 238, 248
Maital, Shlomo, 114
Malthus, Robert, 224
management, 282
basis of, 258–259, 263–264
of knowledge workers, 71, 251
manager's letter, 253
of professionals, 47, 48, 249
scientific, 42
skills, 104
Management by Objectives (MBO) system, 257–258
Management of Accounting Practice (MAP) movement, 172
Marcus, Stanley, 33, 121, 122
marginalist revolution, 165
market forces, 95
market share, 16–17, 22, 138, 160, 202
market value, 293
marketing. *See also* advertising; promotion
for differentiation, 179
four Ps of, 25, 55, 159, 160, 169, 173–175
in hiring, 55
issues, 172–173
outward-looking, 168

personal plan, 249
pricing and. *See* pricing
marketing concept, 31
marketing strategy, 179
marketplace, realities of, 35, 39
markets, access to, 104
Marriott, 119, 143
Martin, Judith, 84
Marx, Karl, 14, 160, 161–163
Mary Kay Cosmetics, 97
Maslow, Abraham, 77
Matthews, Ryan, 54
McDonald's, 102
McKenna, Patrick, 248
McKinsey Global Institute, 109–110
McKinsey Maxim, 223, 224, 225
McNamara, Robert, 224
MDPs. *See* multidisciplinary practices
measurement, 223
conventional, 120
of customer satisfaction, 68–69, 139
economic denominators, 264
economic performance, 229
effect of, 241
of effectiveness, 27, 122
of efficiency, 27, 229
of firm learning, 47
importance of, 257–262
of income, 224–225
KPIs. *See* key performance indicators
of knowledge conversion, 48
lagging indicators. *See* lagging indicators
leading indicators. *See* leading indicators
need for, 26, 42
of productivity. *See* productivity
profit per customer, 264–265
reliance on, 224
soft, 245, 246

of success, 138, 233
in TQM, 136
traditional pricing metrics, 212
of value, 159
what to measure, 26, 90, 223–225, 237, 254
Menger, Carl, 165, 167
mentoring, 248–249
Mercedes-Benz, 125
meritocracy, 60, 76–77
metaphor, 150
Microsoft, 41–42, 84
Miksis, Steve, 29–30
Mill, John Stuart, 296
Milliken & Company, 137
mind-set. *See* belief
mission, 60–61, 79
mistakes, 33, 211–212
models, 277
moment of truth (MOT) method, 128–130, 140
moral responsibilities, 295
morale, 148
erosion of, 5, 13, 24
poor performers' effect on, 77, 78
of profession, 253, 285
Morita, Akio, 170
Morris, Dan, 16, 79, 110, 155
customer questionnaire, 196–200
MOT. *See* moment of truth method
Motorola, Inc., 137
movies, 81–82
multidisciplinary practices (MDPs), 101, 103–104, 289, 298–300
Murray, Charles, 34

N
Nagle, Thomas T., 156, 166, 173, 180, 221
names, power of, 65
National Car Rental Systems, 174
Negroponte, Nicholas, 287
net income percentage, 243
networks, 99, 112
alumni, 106